UIRY

E

112. lled Drugs

in the Community

*Presented to Parliament by the
Secretary of State for the Home Department and
the Secretary of State for Health
by Command of Her Majesty
July 2004*

Cm 6249   £26.00

WILTSHIRE
COUNTY COUNCIL
EDUCATION
& LIBRARIES

The Rt. Hon. David Blunkett MP
Secretary of State for Home Affairs
Queen Anne's Gate
London
SW1H 9AT

The Rt. Hon. John Reid MP
Secretary of State for Health
Richmond House
79 Whitehall
London
SW1A 2NS

15th June 2004

Dear Secretaries of State,

Shipman Inquiry - Fourth Report.

I have pleasure in submitting my Fourth Report, which deals with the regulation of controlled drugs in the community. In my First Report, I explained how, over a very long period, Shipman had acquired large amounts of diamorphine which he had used to kill his patients. In the penultimate Stage of the Inquiry, I set out to discover why the existing systems of regulation had failed to prevent or detect these acquisitions. The Inquiry's Terms of Reference also required me to recommend what steps, if any, should be taken to protect patients in future.

I have to report that there is no easy way to prevent a doctor who is determined to obtain illicit supplies of a controlled drug from doing so. Nor is there any foolproof way of detecting, after the event, that a doctor has diverted controlled drugs to his or her own use. However, there is much that could be done to improve the present position. I have made a number of recommendations, which I am confident would, if implemented, make it far more difficult for a dishonest doctor to obtain drugs illicitly and would greatly improve the prospects of detection after the event. Perhaps the most important single recommendation is for the creation of a controlled drugs inspectorate, to replace the fragmented provisions for inspection and monitoring that exist at the present time.

There has been virtually no revision of the legislation relating to controlled drugs for over thirty years. Some of the existing provisions are sound in principle but others are out of date or have become over complicated. In particular, many of the existing rules prevent the proper and sensible use of computer technology. It is time for revision. The Home Office Drugs Branch is aware of the need for change but there has been little movement to date, possibly owing to a lack of resources. At present, the impetus for change is coming from the Department of Health, through the development of information technology systems. These changes are primarily designed to improve health care and may not take sufficient account of the need for security in dealing with controlled drugs. In my view, the two Departments should join in the revision of the legislation, so that the new framework can allow for the use of computer technology with an eye to improved regulation as well as improved patient care.

Yours sincerely,

Janet Smith

Janet Smith

The Shipman Inquiry, Gateway House, Piccadilly South, Manchester M60 7LP
Tel: 0161 237 2435/6 Fax: 0161 237 2094 E-mail: theshipmaninquiry@shipman.gsi.gov.uk
www.the-shipman-inquiry.org.uk

Independent public inquiry into the issues arising from the case of Harold Shipman

FOREWORD

In the First Report of the Shipman Inquiry, I described how, over a period of more than 20 years, Shipman acquired large quantities of diamorphine which he used to kill over 200 patients. It was clear that the arrangements that had been in force during that time for the regulation of controlled drugs had not been adequate either to prevent those acquisitions or to detect them once they had occurred. The Inquiry's Terms of Reference required me to examine the actions of those involved in the operation of these arrangements and to recommend changes that would lead to the better protection of patients in future.

The focus of investigation was to find out how the systems of regulation worked in practice and to see how and why Shipman had been able to escape detection for so long. My main objective was to devise systems that would deter or detect the activities of any other dishonest healthcare professional who might seek to obtain controlled drugs for his/her own improper purposes or to allow supplies of controlled drugs to be diverted to the illicit drugs market. To these ends, I have made a number of recommendations to strengthen the statutory requirements and to improve the systems of inspection and monitoring. Other recommendations range more widely and seek to promote the safety and welfare of patients for whom controlled drugs are prescribed. I have, at all times, recognised that there are other important public interest objectives to be borne in mind besides the prevention and detection of misconduct. The primary function of the healthcare system is to provide care to patients. Doctors who wish to prescribe controlled drugs for the genuine needs of patients must not be unduly hindered from doing so. Pharmacists must not be over-burdened with administrative requirements when dispensing controlled drugs. District nurses visiting patients should not have to spend more time on administrative tasks than is necessary. Plainly, it is important to prevent the abuse of controlled drugs but measures taken to achieve that end should not adversely affect the provision of health care. The balancing of these different objectives must, in the end, be a matter for Parliament but I hope that this Report will provide a basis for a full and well-informed discussion of the issues.

Before making my recommendations, I considered a great deal of evidence, and have received the views of a large number of people. I am grateful to the many witnesses who provided statements and to those who attended to give oral evidence. The distribution to interested bodies, and the publication on the Inquiry's website, of the Discussion Paper 'The Use and Monitoring of Controlled Drugs in the Community' produced many valuable contributions. The Inquiry held seminars on three days in January 2004 and I would like to thank all those who participated for bringing such a constructive approach to the discussion of the issues. I particularly wish to express my gratitude to Dr Brian Taylor, Deputy Registrar, College of Physicians and Surgeons of British Columbia, and to Dr Michael Mawhinney, Misuse of Drugs Inspector, Department of Health, Social Services and Public Safety, Northern Ireland, who gave presentations explaining aspects of the systems in operation in those provinces.

I also wish to thank the Inquiry team for their generous support during this Stage of the Inquiry. Their dedication to the analysis of the wide range of material assembled has made the production of this Report possible. I must particularly mention Christopher Melton QC, Senior Counsel to the Inquiry, who conducted all the hearings and acted as moderator at the seminars. He was assisted by Anthony Mazzag and Martin Beckett. I particularly appreciated their work in checking the factual accuracy of the draft Report. I am, as ever, grateful to Dr Aneez Esmail for advice on myriad medical issues. The administrative team, led by Henry Palin, has provided faultless support during a period of intense activity.

In the Foreword to my Third Report, I expressed the hope that some good might come from the tragic events which gave rise to the need for this Inquiry. In presenting my Fourth Report, I express my further hope that the work of the Inquiry will lead to changes in the regulation of controlled drugs that will enhance both the safety of patients who may in the future need to use controlled drugs and that of the wider public.

CONTENTS

SUMMARY

Introduction

1. From my First Report, in which I found that, over a period of more than 20 years, Shipman had secretly obtained very large quantities of diamorphine and had used it to kill many of his patients, it was apparent that the regulatory framework governing the use of controlled drugs had not operated as it should. The purpose of regulation is to ensure accountability for the use of controlled drugs so as to avoid their diversion to improper use and to detect such diversion if it occurs. The Inquiry's Terms of Reference required me to enquire into the performance of the functions of those statutory bodies, authorities, other organisations and individuals with responsibility for monitoring the use of controlled drugs and to recommend what steps, if any, should be taken to protect patients in the future. The Inquiry's investigations into the reasons why Shipman's illicit acquisition of controlled drugs had not been detected for so long required an examination of the systems and rules relating to the prescribing, dispensing and keeping of controlled drugs. Also, the Inquiry considered the arrangements by which the use of controlled drugs in the community is monitored and the operation of the systems is inspected.

2. I was told that the scale of the problem of diversion of controlled drugs is unknown but that, quite apart from Shipman's activities, it is extensive enough to warrant attention. I found that the present systems of regulation and monitoring require improvement and modernisation. Because I did not wish to confine myself to making recommendations designed purely to 'catch another Shipman', I was also drawn into consideration of a number of issues, not directly related to Shipman, but concerned with the security of controlled drugs and with the safety and wellbeing of patients using such drugs.

The Legislative Framework

3. For more than 80 years, there has been legislation regulating the prescribing, possession and supply of certain medicinal drugs that are known to be addictive and to have a potential for abuse. The Home Office is the Government Department responsible for the legislation governing controlled drugs, which were formerly known as 'dangerous drugs'. The current legislative framework is the Misuse of Drugs Act 1971 (MDA 1971) and regulations made thereunder. The Regulations currently in force are the Misuse of Drugs Regulations (MDR) 2001, the Misuse of Drugs (Supply to Addicts) Regulations 1997 and the Misuse of Drugs (Safe Custody) Regulations 1973. The principles of regulation have not changed since 1973 when the MDA 1971 and the first set of Regulations made under it came into force. The basic principle is that it is unlawful to possess a controlled drug or to deal with one in any way without authority. Authority is provided by the issue of a licence by the Home Office or is conferred on certain classes of person by statute. For present purposes, the important classes of person who possess such authority are medical practitioners, pharmacists and patients. Medical practitioners, acting as such, are authorised to possess, prescribe, supply and administer any controlled drug for the treatment of organic disease. They may also prescribe some controlled drugs, such as methadone, for the treatment of addiction, although only specially authorised doctors are

allowed to prescribe diamorphine, cocaine and dipipanone for the treatment of addiction. Medical practitioners who keep a stock of certain types of controlled drug must keep them in a lockable receptacle and maintain a controlled drugs register (CDR), which is a chronological record of all purchases and supplies of the drugs in question. Pharmacists are authorised to deal with controlled drugs in the course of business, subject to compliance with the Regulations. These impose a duty to maintain a CDR and to keep some types of controlled drugs in a locked safe, cabinet or room. Patients are authorised to possess controlled drugs prescribed for them but cannot lawfully supply them to anyone who is not authorised to possess them.

4.   All controlled drugs are listed in one of five Schedules to the MDR 2001, according to their therapeutic usefulness, their potential for abuse and the perceived need for control. Drugs within Schedule 1 have little or no therapeutic value, are addictive and have a high potential for abuse; they are the most strictly controlled and can be lawfully dealt with only under a Home Office licence. Schedule 2 contains opiate drugs such as diamorphine, morphine, methadone and pethidine, as well as stimulants such as amphetamines. These drugs have real therapeutic value but are highly addictive. Their use is quite strictly controlled. There are special prescription requirements, and Regulations relating to record keeping, safe storage and destruction apply. Schedule 3 comprises barbiturates and some benzodiazepines, such as temazepam. They are less rigorously controlled than drugs in Schedule 2. Schedule 4 Part 1 contains most of the benzodiazepines, such as diazepam and nitrazepam; Part 2 contains the anabolic and androgenic steroids which have a potential for abuse by athletes. These drugs are only lightly regulated. Schedule 5 includes preparations containing controlled drugs such as codeine or morphine, used in such low strength that they present little or no risk of abuse and can be sold over the counter.

5.   Responsibility for inspecting and monitoring the operation of the controlled drugs regime in the community is divided between the Home Office, the police and primary care trusts (PCTs), the NHS bodies responsible for the provision of primary care. The Home Office Drugs Inspectorate (HODI) has overall responsibility for the regulatory system but undertakes routine inspections only of the premises and operations of those persons or organisations that have been licensed by the Home Office to deal with controlled drugs, such as private hospitals and drug treatment clinics. Police chemist inspection officers (CIOs) have a statutory power (but no statutory duty) to inspect the controlled drugs stocks and CDRs at pharmacies. Pharmacies are also inspected by inspectors of the Royal Pharmaceutical Society of Great Britain (RPSGB) but there is no requirement that these inspections should focus on the arrangements for controlled drugs and, in fact, they do not. The medical advisers of PCTs have the power (but no duty) to inspect the controlled drugs arrangements and CDRs at general practitioners' (GPs') surgeries and at the premises of GPs who also dispense medicines, as well as prescribing them.

6.   Monitoring of the use of controlled drugs is carried out by PCTs, using prescribing data provided by the Prescription Pricing Authority (PPA), a special health authority whose primary duty is to pay pharmacists and dispensing doctors for the drugs, medicines and appliances they dispense under the NHS. However, the PPA also collects prescribing information on its database and processes it for monitoring purposes. This facility was

developed during the 1980s and 1990s and has gradually become more sophisticated, accurate and easy to use. However, the PPA does not collect information about drugs that are prescribed privately or purchased by doctors on requisition.

Pethidine and Diamorphine

7. The Inquiry has focussed mainly on diamorphine, the controlled drug used by Shipman to kill his patients, and pethidine, the controlled drug to which Shipman was addicted in the 1970s. Both drugs have a therapeutic use in the relief of pain. Both give rise to a sense of euphoria and are addictive. Both act as a respiratory depressant. Diamorphine, in particular, is dangerous for that reason. In overdose, respiration is slowed and eventually stops. The lack of oxygen to the brain leads to cardiac arrest and death. This was the means by which Shipman killed at least 214 patients.

8. In the 1970s, pethidine was widely used by GPs and midwives for the relief of pain in childbirth. Today, its use in general practice is limited, as more effective short-term analgesics are available. Diamorphine is widely used for the relief of severe pain in cases of terminal cancer. Since the early 1990s and the introduction into community medicine of the use of the syringe driver (a device which administers a continuous supply of a drug to the patient), the use of diamorphine has increased. The syringe driver allows greatly improved pain control, and more terminally ill patients can now be treated at home. Often, quite large quantities of the drug are required, as patients become habituated to it. Daily dosages of 1000mg or sometimes even substantially more can be needed. Some GPs also use small quantities of diamorphine for the relief of acute pain during a heart attack or following trauma. In such circumstances, the usual dosage is up to 5mg, although 10mg might be required. Many GPs keep a personal supply of 5mg ampoules for emergency use. Diamorphine is supplied in ampoules containing 5mg, 10mg, 30mg, 100mg and 500mg. The very large ampoules are only rarely used.

Shipman's Use of Pethidine in the 1970s

9. In March 1974, Shipman entered practice as a GP in Todmorden, West Yorkshire. Within a short time, he began obtaining large quantities of pethidine from Boots the Chemists (Boots) by presenting requisitions or signed orders for the drug. He told the pharmacist that the drugs were required for use in the practice. He also began to issue NHS prescriptions for pethidine in the name of an elderly patient who lived on the outskirts of Todmorden. Shipman presented these prescriptions and collected the drugs, saying that he would deliver them to the patient. In fact he kept the pethidine, or most of it, for himself. In early 1975, inspectors from the Northern Regional Office of the HODI, examining the records of a wholesale supplier, noticed unusually large deliveries of pethidine to Boots, Todmorden. The Boots CDR showed to whom it was being supplied. In July 1975, two HODI inspectors and an officer of the West Yorkshire Police (WYP) interviewed Shipman and inspected the practice's controlled drugs stock and CDR. There was no pethidine in stock. It was found that Shipman had entered the amounts of pethidine obtained into the CDR but had made no entries in the 'drugs supplied' pages and had not, therefore, accounted for the removal of the drug from stock. Shipman claimed that he did not know

that this was required. The HODI inspectors advised Shipman as to his duties and resolved to keep watch on his activities. Shipman continued to obtain pethidine on requisition and by collecting supplies dispensed against prescriptions issued by him in the names of patients. After a short while, his partners were informed; Shipman admitted that he had been using the pethidine himself. It emerged that, since the visit of the HODI inspectors in July, he had not made any entries at all in the practice CDR.

10.   Shipman left the practice and, shortly afterwards, was admitted to a private hospital for treatment for addiction. While there, he was interviewed by a HODI inspector and the police. He admitted obtaining pethidine on requisition and by the improper use of prescriptions. He said that the patients for whom he had prescribed pethidine had received small amounts of the drug but that he had kept most of it himself. In fact, during a period of about 18 months, he had used over 83,000mg of pethidine. There is no evidence that Shipman used pethidine to kill patients, and I think it highly improbable that he did. In the First Report, I found that, while working in Todmorden, Shipman had killed one patient, probably using a strong opiate such as morphine or diamorphine. I was suspicious that he might have caused the deaths of six others.

11.   At the end of 1975, Shipman left hospital and early the following year found employment with the Durham Area Health Authority (AHA) in the field of child development. In February 1976, he pleaded guilty at the Halifax Magistrates' Court to eight offences of unlawful possession of pethidine, obtaining pethidine by deception, and forgery. He asked to have 74 similar offences taken into consideration. He relied on two psychiatric reports from doctors who had treated him. These said that he had undergone treatment for addiction to pethidine and had responded well. He was fined and ordered to pay compensation and costs.

12.   Shipman's convictions were notified to the General Medical Council (GMC), the doctors' regulatory body, so that it could consider disciplinary proceedings. The procedure at that time was for the circumstances to be considered by the Penal Cases Committee, which would decide whether the case warranted referral to the Disciplinary Committee on a charge of serious professional misconduct. If Shipman were to be found guilty of such misconduct, the GMC had the power to erase him from the register of medical practitioners or to suspend him for a period of up to a year. It had no power to impose conditions on his registration. The GMC obtained information about Shipman from the HODI and the WYP. Shipman's solicitors supplied copies of the two psychiatric reports prepared for the Magistrates' Court and an up to date report describing his recent progress. This expressed the view that it would be **'catastrophic'** if Shipman were not allowed to continue in practice. A letter from the Area Medical Officer of the Durham AHA reported that Shipman was doing well in his new post. On 28th April 1976, the Penal Cases Committee of the GMC decided not to refer his case to the Disciplinary Committee but concluded it with a warning to him against any repetition of his conduct. So far as the GMC was concerned, Shipman was free to practise medicine unrestricted. I shall consider the appropriateness of the GMC's decision in the Fifth Report.

13.   Under section 12 of the MDA 1971, the Home Secretary had (and, in theory, still has) the power to make a direction restricting the right of any doctor convicted of offences under

the Act to possess, prescribe, supply or administer any controlled drug. Until 1976, this power was regularly used in cases such as Shipman's. Before deciding whether to invite the Home Secretary to make a direction, Home Office officials would consult with the GMC and with the Department of Health and Social Security (DHSS). They did so in Shipman's case. It is not clear whether the DHSS responded; if it did, its response has been lost. The GMC responded by telling the Home Office that Shipman's case had been concluded.

14.   At about this time, it appears that there had been a change in policy within the Home Office as to the type of circumstances in which a direction under section 12 might be made. Previously, directions had been made in cases, such as Shipman's, where the doctor was addicted to a drug and had committed offences in the course of obtaining supplies for self-administration. For reasons that are now obscure, in about May or June 1976, it was decided that the Home Secretary would be invited to make a direction only where a doctor's offences involved supplying a controlled drug to someone else or allowing it to be so supplied. Shipman may have been the first doctor to benefit from this new policy. On 1st July 1976, Home Office officials decided not to invite the Home Secretary to consider making a decision in Shipman's case. His file was closed and he was free to practise medicine without restriction or supervision. I have concluded that no criticism should attach to the Home Office officials for this decision, which was made in accordance with the policy of the day. That policy did, however, leave a *lacuna* in the power of the authorities to protect patients from a drug-abusing doctor.

Shipman's Methods of Obtaining Diamorphine while Working in Hyde

15.   In about July 1977, Shipman applied for a vacancy at one of the GP practices which operated from Donneybrook House, Hyde. At interview, he explained that he had had a problem with pethidine and had been convicted of controlled drugs offences. I have found that he probably understated the seriousness of his convictions. He said that, in future, he did not intend to keep a personal stock of controlled drugs for emergency use; non-controlled alternatives were available. After making enquiries of the Home Office and the GMC, the Donneybrook doctors were satisfied that Shipman was free to practise without restriction and offered him the position.

16.   During the period of more than 14 years for which Shipman practised at Donneybrook House, he killed 71 patients, each time using an overdose of diamorphine. The deaths of 30 more patients give rise to suspicion. None of the other doctors in the practice had any reason to suspect him of misusing diamorphine. To all appearances, he kept to his word and did not maintain a stock of controlled drugs for emergency use.

17.   Very few pharmacy records from this period survive and I am unable to say with certainty how Shipman obtained his supplies of diamorphine. However, I think it highly likely that he used the same methods as he was to use later, during the 1990s, a period for which records are available that allow a clear picture of his activities to emerge. In short, I think it likely that he stole diamorphine prescribed for cancer patients, by prescribing more than was needed for their treatment. He would take either the whole or part of a consignment for himself instead of delivering it to the patient and would remove and keep any supplies left over after the patient's death.

18. These methods of obtaining diamorphine would not have been likely to arouse suspicion. The prescriptions would have been properly made out. The amounts would have been recorded in the CDR of the pharmacy at which they were dispensed. They would not have appeared excessive for the needs of a patient suffering from terminal cancer. The fact that Shipman had collected the drugs from the pharmacy, ostensibly to save the patient or his/her relative the trouble of so doing, would have been attributed by the pharmacy staff to his caring nature. In any event, the fact that he collected the drugs would not have been recorded in the CDR. There was no requirement that this should be done. Accordingly, the visiting CIO would have been unaware of Shipman's practice of collecting drugs unless informed of it by the pharmacist. The appearance of Shipman's name as the prescriber of diamorphine for patients would have appeared to the CIO to be entirely normal. Nor would Shipman's removal of drugs left over after the patient's death have given rise to suspicion. Since 1985, the MDR have permitted a doctor or pharmacist to destroy unwanted or returned controlled drugs without any formality, i.e. without having the destruction witnessed or recorded. So, it would have appeared entirely acceptable for Shipman to take the drugs, saying that he would dispose of them.

19. In January 1992, Shipman left the Donneybrook practice and set up as a single-handed practitioner. In the August, he moved to new premises at 21 Market Street, Hyde. Immediately adjacent to his surgery, at number 23, was a pharmacy, which was used by many of Shipman's patients. In September 1991, it had changed hands and a new pharmacist manager, Mrs Ghislaine Brant, had been appointed. A new CDR had been opened; it survives and provides a clear picture of Shipman's diamorphine prescribing practice between October 1991 and July 1998. Between March 1992 and August 1993, Shipman obtained a total of sixteen 30mg ampoules of diamorphine on prescriptions issued in the names of patients who did not need the drug; indeed, in at least six cases, the patient was already dead at the time the prescription was written. I shall describe in greater detail at paragraphs 22–30 the events surrounding the dispensing of a sequence of 14 of these ampoules between February and August 1993.

20. From November 1993 onwards, Shipman obtained diamorphine supplies by prescribing in the names of patients who were suffering from cancer. Some of them were in actual need of the drug for pain relief; for them, Shipman would prescribe more than was necessary and would collect the drugs and keep the whole or part of the consignment for himself. He would also take drugs left over after the patient had died, on the pretext of disposing of them, but would keep them for himself. Sometimes, he would prescribe diamorphine in the name of a patient who, although suffering from cancer, was not in pain and had no need of the drug. He would collect the supply from the pharmacy and keep it for himself. These dishonest methods of obtaining the drug were not likely to arouse suspicion, for the reasons I outlined above. There was nothing unusual for the visiting CIO to notice.

21. Between 1992 and 1998, Shipman obtained more than 24,000mg diamorphine illicitly. During that time, he killed 143 patients and I am suspicious about a further nine deaths. Yet no concerns were aroused about his use of controlled drugs and, had it not been that, in 1998, he came under suspicion for forging the will of Mrs Kathleen Grundy and of killing her, his activities would, I believe, have continued undetected.

Shipman's Abnormal Prescribing of Diamorphine in 1993

22.   Between February and August 1993, Shipman obtained for himself 14 single 30mg diamorphine ampoules by prescribing them in the names of 13 different patients. The question arose as to whether this pattern of prescribing was so abnormal that it should have aroused the concern of the pharmacist who dispensed them, Mrs Brant, and/or that of Detective Constable (DC) Patrick Kelly, the CIO for Hyde at the time.

23.   Examination of a diamorphine CDR will usually show that the drug has been prescribed by a doctor for a single patient over a period of days or weeks; the amounts prescribed on each occasion will usually be increasingly large, often culminating in supplies of as much as ten 100mg ampoules. The supplies come to a sudden end with the death of the patient. Such groups of entries will be interspersed with entries recording supplies to practices or individual doctors 'for practice use' in emergencies. Such supplies will usually be of a box of five 5mg ampoules. There will also be entries relating to prescriptions issued by other doctors. A single 30mg ampoule is a very unusual amount of diamorphine to prescribe. It is far too much to administer to a patient who is suffering from the acute pain of a heart attack and too little to prescribe for a patient who has chronic pain caused by cancer. It is, as one witness observed, 'neither one thing nor the other'. As a single dose, given to a 'morphine-naïve' patient, it would be fatal. In fact, Shipman was using these ampoules to kill his patients. The appearance of the diamorphine CDR of the pharmacy at 23 Market Street was most unusual. On one page, there appeared 12 consecutive entries, made between February and May 1993, each recording the supply of a single 30mg ampoule, each prescribed by Shipman, each in the name of a different patient. On four days – two of them within the same week – Shipman had prescribed two single ampoules for different patients on the same day. All but one entry had been made by Mrs Brant. Copies of the relevant pages appear at Appendix A to this Report.

24.   Mrs Brant told the Inquiry that Shipman had collected these 30mg diamorphine ampoules himself. At the time, she had not thought there was anything strange or suspicious about the prescriptions. She believed that, on the first occasion, he had prescribed a smaller ampoule, claiming it was required for the treatment of a patient suffering acute pain from a heart attack. She had had no small ampoules in stock and had supplied him with 30mg. Thereafter, he had prescribed 30mg ampoules. I rejected her evidence on this issue. I found that Shipman had prescribed 30mg ampoules from the start.

25.   Exactly what explanations Shipman offered when presenting these prescriptions I cannot say. Whatever they were, Mrs Brant accepted them. She held him in very high regard. She should have been aware that this pattern of prescribing was most unusual and she should have been concerned that Shipman always collected the drugs himself. She was not concerned because, she said, she trusted him completely and because the amount of drugs collected was not so large as to give rise to the suspicion that Shipman might be addicted to diamorphine, a sign that she knew it was her duty to look out for.

26.   Mrs Brant accepted that, in general, it was her duty, before dispensing a drug, to satisfy herself, so far as she could, that the drug and the dosage prescribed were appropriate for the patient. She had plainly not applied her mind to those issues in respect of the patients for whom Shipman had prescribed 30mg diamorphine although she had had the

opportunity to speak to Shipman on each occasion. However, she claimed that where, as here, she was supplying the drug directly to a doctor, it was reasonable for her to rely on the doctor's expertise. She said that she believed that, if 30mg was too much to give the patient, Shipman would use part of the ampoule and throw away the rest. I do not accept the distinction she drew; a pharmacist is under to a duty to ensure, so far as possible, that the doctor does not prescribe an excessive quantity of a controlled drug. The fact that the doctor is present when the drug is dispensed does not affect that duty.

27.   Mrs Brant also suggested that it was possible that, in prescribing single 30mg ampoules, Shipman was, on each occasion, 'replenishing' his own stock of diamorphine which he had used in an emergency shortly beforehand. Such a practice would be improper but it appears that some doctors do 'replenish' (it is less cumbersome than following the correct procedures) and that some pharmacists turn a blind eye. It is possible that Shipman said or implied that that was what he was doing. If he did, Mrs Brant should have realised that emergencies had suddenly begun to occur with unusual frequency in Shipman's practice.

28.   In my view, Mrs Brant should have realised that this course of prescribing was abnormal and should have at least discussed it with Mr Peter Rothman, the owner and superintendent of the pharmacy, or with the CIO or with an inspector from the RPSGB. She did not appreciate the unusual nature of these prescriptions because she had lost her professional objectivity when dealing with Shipman. My criticism of her is mitigated because I have no doubt that Shipman had deliberately set out to win her confidence and to deceive her.

29.   When DC Kelly of the Greater Manchester Police (GMP) visited the pharmacy at 23 Market Street in July 1993, he examined and signed the diamorphine register. He did not notice anything unusual about the page of consecutive entries for single 30mg ampoules, all prescribed by the same doctor. He did not know that Shipman had collected the ampoules as well as prescribing them. That is not recorded in the CDR and Mrs Brant did not tell him. At the time, DC Kelly was very inexperienced. He had been appointed as a CIO only three months before. His training had been inadequate. It comprised a few weeks' apprenticeship with a CIO who worked only part-time in that role. When he began to work on his own, DC Kelly had little knowledge of the characteristics of controlled drugs and would not have known that a 30mg single ampoule of diamorphine was a very unusual amount to prescribe. Even so, by the time he examined this CDR, DC Kelly had seen at least 150 CDRs and, in my judgement, he should have recognised that the consecutive entries in this one were very unusual. He had no supervisor with knowledge of the CIO's role but he could have asked the advice of his colleague, DC Robert Peers, who had trained him. He could have asked for Mrs Brant's views. Had he done so, however, it is likely that she would have reassured him that Shipman was a very well respected doctor and that there was no cause for concern. My criticism of DC Kelly is mitigated by his inexperience, by the inadequacy of his training as a CIO and by the lack of supervision from a more senior GMP officer. Although the GMP was responsible for the inadequacy of DC Kelly's training and supervision, I recognise that it provided a better CIO service than many other police forces. Moreover, in 1993, no training course was available for CIOs, as it is now.

30. I have found that if Mrs Brant or DC Kelly had been concerned about these entries and had reported them to an appropriate authority, it is likely that the HODI would have investigated Shipman. The inspectors would have known of his previous convictions in relation to pethidine and this would have raised their level of suspicion about him. What the outcome of such an investigation would have been is uncertain but my considered view is that it is unlikely that the true nature of Shipman's activities would have been uncovered. However, I think it likely that the investigation itself would have had a salutary effect on Shipman, who would probably have ceased killing for a time. In that way, at least some lives would have been saved.

Other Types of Misconduct Connected with Controlled Drugs

31. The Inquiry learned that the misuse of drugs by doctors, nurses and pharmacists is not uncommon. The ready availability of such drugs appears to create an increased risk of dependence or addiction. Doctors addicted to a controlled drug tend to obtain their supplies in ways similar to those used by Shipman. Some doctors, not addicted themselves, supplement their income by selling controlled drugs or by selling prescriptions to addicts. Such activities are plainly unlawful but they are not easy to detect. Often the prescriptions are issued privately (i.e. not on the NHS) and, as I explained earlier, are not subject to the same monitoring processes as are NHS prescriptions. Some doctors, while not prescribing illegally, prescribe controlled drugs in an irresponsible and unethical way. For example, they might prescribe large quantities, turning a blind eye to the possibility that the patient might be an addict and might be selling part of his/her supply to purchase other drugs. Others might provide prescriptions to 'patients' whom they hardly know, without making any attempt to contact the patients' usual medical advisers. Drug addicts will often seek to obtain supplies from more than one doctor, a practice known as 'double scripting'. Doctors who are not alert to that possibility and are not willing to query such requests act irresponsibly. The Inquiry has also become aware that some doctors prescribe controlled drugs for themselves and for their friends and members of their families. Such prescribing is not unlawful, although the GMC regards it as poor practice. The scale of any of these problems is not known. Since the existing systems of monitoring are inadequate (and, in the case of private prescriptions, virtually non-existent), there is at present no means of knowing.

Systemic Shortcomings

Inspection and Monitoring

32. At paragraph 5 above, I described how the inspection of the arrangements made and records kept by the various people and businesses that handle controlled drugs and the monitoring of the use of controlled drugs are carried out by a variety of different bodies. The HODI is responsible for the investigation of certain breaches of the MDA 1971 or the MDR 2001. It undertakes routine inspections of the premises and records of producers and wholesalers of controlled drugs and other persons licensed to deal with such drugs. It has not the resources to undertake routine inspections of pharmacies or GPs' surgeries. The evidence received by the Inquiry suggested that the HODI carries out its duties effectively.

33. The routine inspection of pharmacies is carried out by police CIOs. The duties of a CIO are to inspect the CDR and the safe custody arrangements for the stock of controlled drugs. While inspecting the CDR and through discussion with the pharmacist, the CIO is expected to keep a lookout for signs of unlawful or irresponsible prescribing by doctors in the area. He or she must also witness the destruction of 'out of date' or contaminated stock. All these duties, except the detection of unlawful or irresponsible prescribing, are well within the capabilities of any trained police officer. However, the detection of unlawful or irresponsible prescribing requires a considerable depth of pharmaceutical knowledge. Some CIOs develop this knowledge but many do not.

34. In some police areas, there are no CIOs. Some chief constables do not consider that CIO work is a proper use of police resources. In some areas, there is a CIO, but s/he is expected to carry out other duties and has insufficient time for pharmacy inspections. Until recently, training for CIOs comprised a short apprenticeship to an experienced CIO. Inevitably, its quality was variable. A training course has now been established and standards should rise. However, coverage and standards remain patchy. Even where a dedicated CIO is in post, the position is less than ideal because the CIO does not have ready access to pharmaceutical expertise. In my view, some aspects of pharmacy inspection can be satisfactorily performed only by a qualified pharmacist.

35. Very few GPs have had their CDRs or surgery arrangements inspected during the last ten years or so. Many GPs do not understand the Regulations or know how to comply with their duties under them. It is likely that, in many practices, the safe custody and record keeping requirements are not observed. PCT medical advisers, who have the power to undertake such inspections and to witness the destruction of out of date or contaminated stock, have many other duties and little time to devote to controlled drugs. CIOs have no power to enter or inspect the premises of GPs. A particular concern is that many doctors in rural areas dispense medicines, including controlled drugs, from their surgery premises; yet CIOs have no power to inspect the arrangements made and records kept in their dispensaries. The lack of any regular visit by a medical adviser or a CIO means that many GPs rarely have an opportunity to have the destruction of old stocks of drugs properly witnessed.

36. Prescribing information collected and analysed by the PPA is monitored by PCTs. It is now possible to examine the prescribing practice of any doctor in respect of any drug, although the data is not as accurate as it might be because doctors use each other's prescription pads. There should be some improvement in this regard in the future, when all doctors will be provided with their own personal prescription pad, at least for NHS prescribing. PCT officers and advisers can and do analyse the usage of controlled drugs, although they have many other issues to consider, not least the cost of the prescriptions issued by a particular practice or doctor. The main weakness in the present system of monitoring the usage of controlled drugs is that it does not include private prescribing or the purchase of supplies for practice use.

37. In short, the inspection and monitoring of controlled drugs is fragmented and unsatisfactory. In my view, the ideal solution would be the creation of a controlled drugs inspectorate, on the lines of the one operated in Northern Ireland. It should be organised on a regional basis and should be staffed by a multidisciplinary team, comprising some

pharmacists, a few doctors and some investigators with law enforcement experience. This team could be responsible for the inspection of all premises on which controlled drugs are kept (save perhaps those that are inspected by the HODI) and could also monitor the use of controlled drugs.

38.   In order that private prescribing can be monitored, it should be brought within the ambit of the PPA. For this to be achieved, it would be necessary for all private prescriptions for controlled drugs to be written on a special form, similar (although not identical) to the form currently used for NHS prescriptions. The prescribing information could then be scanned into the PPA database and analysed together with NHS prescribing information.

Post-Dispensing Regulation

39.   I indicated earlier that the Regulations impose various safe custody and record keeping requirements in relation to controlled drugs. These duties are imposed on pharmacists and doctors who have controlled drugs in their possession. However, once a controlled drug has been dispensed and handed over to the patient or the patient's representative, no further attempt at regulation is attempted. Rather surprisingly, a patient who sends a representative to collect a controlled drug on his/her behalf is not expected to provide written authority to show to the pharmacist, and the pharmacist is not expected to ask the representative to identify him/herself. A requirement that the identity of any person collecting controlled drugs from a pharmacy should be recorded in the CDR might well have deterred Shipman from collecting controlled drugs, ostensibly on behalf of patients, as often as he did. It would also have made it easier to detect his activities if he had persisted in such a practice. It is uncommon for a doctor to collect controlled drugs for a patient and Shipman's name would have stood out. Certainly, in 1993, the fact that, within a short period, he had collected 14 single 30mg ampoules of diamorphine on behalf of 13 different patients should have been striking to any CIO, even one as inexperienced as DC Kelly.

40.   Once the controlled drugs have left the pharmacy, the Regulations do not impose a duty on anyone to make a record of their use or of their destruction. In other words, there is no audit trail. Controlled drugs could be sold, given away or left lying around at the patient's home and no one in authority would have any means of knowing. It is impracticable to impose on patients the duty to keep records relating to the controlled drugs in their possession. However, some Schedule 2 controlled drugs used in the community have to be administered by healthcare professionals, usually district nurses, who are expected to maintain a proper record of their use and destruction.

41.   I have said that, nowadays, diamorphine is usually administered by means of a syringe driver. Usually, the patient is terminally ill and in need of nursing care. A district nurse attends daily and recharges the syringe driver according to the GP's instructions. Nurses enter the arrival of all supplies of diamorphine and the administration of each daily dose onto a patient drug record card (PDRC). They do so as a matter of good professional practice, not because the law requires it. If any supplies are left over after the patient's death, it is common practice for the district nurses to destroy the drugs in the presence of a colleague (or sometimes a relative or neighbour of the deceased patient) and record the

destruction on the PDRC. This system provides a measure of control. However, the system is not entirely satisfactory. A dishonest nurse could destroy some of the leftover drugs and steal the rest. He or she could then ask a relative of the deceased to witness the destruction by signing the PDRC. The relative would be unlikely to count the number of ampoules actually destroyed. The nurse's deceit would not readily be detected. Similarly, a doctor visiting the patient's home shortly after the death could take all the remaining drugs with him/her and write on the PDRC that s/he had taken the drugs for disposal. Shipman used such a ploy on several occasions. On the face of it, his actions appeared lawful.

42.   If the keeping of a PDRC for injectable Schedule 2 drugs were mandatory, and if the destruction of all such drugs had to be witnessed by a second healthcare professional or other authorised person and recorded on the PDRC, I believe that an additional useful safeguard would be provided. I also consider that the provision whereby all unwanted or 'returned' Schedule 2 controlled drugs can be destroyed without formality should be changed. A similar degree of formality should be required for 'returns' as is currently required for the destruction of out of date or contaminated stock.

Conclusion

43.   The measures I have suggested above could not be guaranteed to prevent a dishonest doctor or healthcare professional from obtaining an illicit supply of a controlled drug. However, they would make it more difficult for him/her to do so and would also make it more likely that such an activity, if repeated, would be detected. The increase in the likelihood of detection would, I believe, have a powerful deterrent effect.

44.   In paragraph 2, I said that I have considered a number of issues that are not directly intended to 'catch another Shipman' but are concerned more generally with issues of security and patient safety. I do not propose to include any discussion of those issues in this Summary. However, I have made a number of recommendations relating to these issues and these are included in the following section of this Report, together with the references at which a full discussion of the issues will be found.

45.   The implementation of some of my recommendations would require primary legislation and some would also require the reallocation of, and possibly an increase in, existing resources. For example, the formation of a controlled drugs inspectorate would probably require both. However, I regard such an inspectorate as essential because, at present, the inspection and monitoring arrangements are fragmented and unsatisfactory.

46.   One of the threads running through my recommendations is the need to apply the same degree of regulation and control to the use of controlled drugs in the private sector as is applied within the NHS. My recommendations include the use of a special form for the prescribing of controlled drugs in the private sector as well as under the NHS. The controlled drugs inspectorate could be responsible for the issue of the pads containing these special forms and would be able to ensure that they were supplied only to doctors who had a clinical need to prescribe controlled drugs.

47.   Finally, there is, in my view, a need for modernisation and rationalisation of the system of regulating controlled drugs. There has been virtually no revision of the legislation relating

to controlled drugs since the early 1970s. The requirements relating to controlled drug prescriptions and record keeping are out of date. The Schedules to the MDR have been amended in a piecemeal fashion and are now almost incomprehensible. I hope that they will be looked at afresh and that a simplified and principled structure will be developed. A new framework must make provision for the use of computer technology. Above all, any new legislation must be based upon the dual objectives of improving the regulation and monitoring of controlled drugs as well as enhancing patient safety and care.

RECOMMENDATIONS

This summary contains only a brief statement of each of my recommendations. To understand the reasoning behind each recommendation, the reader must refer to the Chapter(s) in which the evidence relating to it is described and the section(s) of Chapter Fourteen in which the issues are discussed. The relevant references accompany each recommendation.

Inspection Arrangements

1. A controlled drugs inspectorate should be created, comprising small multidisciplinary inspection teams, operating regionally but co-ordinated nationally. Each team would include pharmacists, doctors, inspectors and investigators, at least some of whom would have a law enforcement background. The inspectorate would be responsible for inspecting the arrangements in pharmacies, dispensaries and surgeries, as to both the safe keeping of stocks of controlled drugs and the maintenance of controlled drugs registers (CDRs) and other records. It could be responsible for the supervised destruction of controlled drugs. The inspectorate would also be responsible for the monitoring of the prescribing of controlled drugs by means of examination of prescribing analysis and cost (PACT) data, which would include information derived from NHS and private prescriptions and requisitions. It might be responsible for the issue of special controlled drug prescription pads. If thought appropriate it might also assume many of the inspecting and other functions currently performed by Home Office drugs inspectors. Inspectors and investigators would require access to background information about a doctor or pharmacist under scrutiny. There must be the facility to investigate expertly any irregularities or unusual features discovered as the result of such inspection and monitoring.
   (Chapter Five, Chapter Nine, paragraphs 14.182–14.205 and paragraphs 14.256–14.257)

Prescribing Rights of Medical Practitioners

2. A medical practitioner should be entitled to prescribe or administer controlled drugs only if s/he needs to do so for the purposes of the 'actual clinical practice' in which s/he is engaged. For the vast majority of doctors, the existence or otherwise of such a need will be obvious. A practitioner who wishes to prescribe controlled drugs may, where the need is not obvious, have to justify such need when applying for the issue of a special controlled drug prescription pad.   (Chapter Four and paragraphs 14.8–14.17)

3. It should be a criminal offence for a doctor to prescribe a controlled drug for him/herself, or to self-administer a controlled drug from his/her own or practice stock save in circumstances of emergency, which circumstances should be covered by an appropriately worded statutory defence. The doctor should be required to declare the position on the prescription.   (Chapter Four and paragraphs 14.18–14.32)

4. When a general practitioner (GP) has members of his/her immediate family on his/her list (which should happen only vary rarely), s/he should inform his/her local primary care trust (PCT) of the position. It should be unacceptable for a doctor to prescribe a controlled drug for an immediate family member who is not on his/her list, save in circumstances of

emergency. In all cases where a doctor prescribes a controlled drug for a member of his/her immediate family, the doctor should be required to declare on the prescription his/her relationship to the patient and, if it is the case, that s/he is prescribing in an emergency. (Chapter Four and paragraphs 14.18–14.32)

5.   The General Medical Council (GMC) should make plain that it will be regarded as professional misconduct for a doctor to prescribe controlled drugs for anyone with whom s/he does not have a genuine professional relationship.
(Chapter Four and paragraphs 14.18–14.32)

6.   A medical practitioner convicted or cautioned in connection with a controlled drugs offence should be under a professional duty to report the conviction or caution to the GMC, which should immediately consider what, if any, interim action should be taken and should report the facts and its own action to the practitioner's employer or PCT.
(Chapter Four and paragraphs 14.37–14.46)

7.   The Government should commission an independent review and audit of the way in which the GMC and PCTs are using their powers to restrict the rights of medical practitioners involved in controlled drugs offences to prescribe and administer controlled drugs. Only if satisfied that these powers are being properly exercised for the protection of the public should the Government allow the provisions of section 12 of the Misuse of Drugs Act 1971 to remain in abeyance or to be repealed.
(Chapter Four and paragraphs 14.37–14.46)

8.   Whenever a restriction is placed on a doctor's prescribing powers, this information must promptly be made available (preferably by electronic means) to those who need to know it, especially pharmacists who require access to such information at all times.
(Chapter Four and paragraphs 14.37–14.46)

Prescriptions

9.   A special printed form should be introduced for use when prescribing a controlled drug, whether within the NHS or on a private basis. Pads of such forms should be supplied only to doctors who need to prescribe such drugs in the course of their clinical practice. For the time being, these forms should be completed by hand, to the extent required by the Misuse of Drugs Regulations 2001 (MDR 2001). However, prescribers should be encouraged, where practicable, to print the prescribing information on the prescription form using a computer and to copy the information by hand. The existing handwriting requirements should not be repealed until Government is satisfied, by the conduct of pilot schemes, that the arrangements for computer generation and/or transmission of controlled drug prescriptions are sufficiently secure.
(Chapter Six and paragraphs 14.56–14.79)

10.   The special form should be in such format as will enable the Prescription Pricing Authority (PPA) to scan the prescribing information into its database so as to permit subsequent analysis and monitoring. (Chapter Six and paragraphs 14.56–14.79)

11.   The special form should show the GMC registration number of the medical practitioner to whom the pad of forms has been issued. No other practitioner should be permitted to use

it. The form should require the prescriber to indicate whether the prescription has been issued under the NHS or privately. Each prescription would have its own unique identification number.

(Chapter Six, paragraphs 14.69–14.79 and paragraphs 14.83–14.92)

12.   The special form should provide the prescriber with a space in which to record a brief description of the condition for which the controlled drug has been prescribed. Prescribers should be expected, as a matter of good practice, to ask patients to consent to the provision of this information.

(Chapter Seven, Chapter Thirteen and paragraphs 14.109–14.118)

13.   Consideration should be given to requiring that the patient's NHS number or some other patient-specific identifier should be included on the special form.

(Chapter Four, Chapter Thirteen, paragraph 14.36 and paragraph 14.76)

14.   The amount of a controlled drug that can be dispensed on a single prescription should be limited to a supply sufficient to last 28 days. This restriction would not apply to drugs in Schedule 5 to the MDR 2001.   (Chapter Four and paragraphs 14.93–14.99)

15.   The duration of validity of a prescription for controlled drugs should be limited to 28 days. This restriction would not apply to drugs in Schedule 5 to the MDR 2001.

(Chapter Six and paragraphs 14.100–14.102)

16.   When computer generated prescriptions are in general use for controlled drugs and when the electronic transmission of prescriptions is introduced, the software should be so designed as to ensure that both the time of issue of a prescription and the time at which it is dispensed are recorded.   (Chapter Seven and paragraphs 14.80–14.82)

Safe Custody and Record Keeping for General Practitioners

17.   The purchase of all stocks of controlled drugs for practice use should follow a procedure that is capable of being monitored. The same form which I have recommended for use when prescribing controlled drugs should also be used when ordering controlled drugs on requisition. The forms should be sent to the PPA for entry into its database so that all purchases of controlled drugs by any doctor can be monitored.

(Chapter Five, paragraph 14.127 and paragraph 14.133)

18.   GPs who keep a stock of Schedule 2 controlled drugs should be required (as now) to keep a CDR and to observe existing safe custody requirements. They should be permitted to keep the CDR in electronic form. The CDR should provide for the keeping of a running stock balance for each drug stocked. Each GP who is either a principal in or employed by a practice that keeps controlled drugs for practice use should be under a legal obligation to comply with the terms of a standard operating procedure (SOP) devised or approved either by the PCT with which the practice contracts or, if and when a controlled drugs inspectorate is set up, by that body. The SOP should specify, among other things, the frequency with which the stock must be checked. Adherence to such SOPs should be mandatory and should be subject to regular inspection. Any doctor working as a locum should be under an obligation either to comply with the practice SOP or to make his/her

personal arrangements to provide Schedule 2 drugs and to accept responsibility for keeping the necessary CDR. I suggest that the Healthcare Commission (or, if it comes into being, the controlled drugs inspectorate) should be responsible for approving SOPs for GPs in private practice and for ensuring compliance. Advice as to compliance and best practice should be issued nationally and should also be available from PCT officers in the course of the annual clinical governance visit or review.

(Chapter Six and paragraphs 14.119–14.133)

19.   When the new arrangements for the provision of out of hours services come into effect, PCTs should establish protocols governing responsibility for the provision of Schedule 2 drugs and for the keeping of any CDR. I recommend the use of an appropriate SOP.

(Chapter Six and paragraphs 14.128–14.133)

Controlled Drugs in the Pharmacy

20.   There should be some relaxation of the strict requirement that a pharmacist is not permitted to dispense a controlled drug prescription unless there is full compliance with every technical requirement of the MDR 2001. Where the defect is only technical and the pharmacist is confident that the intention of the prescriber is clear, and is willing to accept professional responsibility for dispensing the prescription in the form in which it is presented, s/he should have the discretion to amend the prescription, to correct the technical defect and to dispense the drugs.

(Chapter Seven and paragraphs 14.103–14.108)

21.   In the case of a controlled drug supply that must be recorded in the pharmacy CDR, a pharmacist should be required to ask the name and address of the person collecting the drugs, unless that information is already known to him/her. If the pharmacist does not know the person, s/he should also ask the person collecting the drugs to produce some form of personal identification. The name and address and a note of the form of identification provided should be recorded in the CDR, unless the collector is personally known to the pharmacist, in which case s/he should record that fact. If no identification is provided, the pharmacist should have discretion to supply or withhold the drugs and, if the drug is supplied, should record the fact that no identification was provided.

(Chapter Seven and paragraphs 14.139–14.149)

22.   Any healthcare professional, acting in his/her professional capacity, presenting a prescription or requisition for a controlled drug, the supply of which must be recorded in the pharmacy CDR, should, if not known to the pharmacist, be required to provide identification, preferably his/her professional registration card. The relevant information should be recorded in the CDR.   (Chapter Seven and paragraphs 14.139–14.149)

23.   Any person collecting controlled drugs in Schedules 3 and 4 from the pharmacy should be required to write and sign his/her name on the back of the prescription form.

(Chapter Seven and paragraphs 14.139–14.149)

24.   Pharmacies should be permitted to keep their CDRs in electronic form.

(Chapter Seven and paragraphs 14.150–14.154)

25. The keeping of a running balance in pharmacy CDRs should henceforth be regarded as good practice. The Home Office should make its view on this clear to pharmacists, and the Royal Pharmaceutical Society of Great Britain (RPSGB) should publicise the new position. When electronic CDRs have come into general use, the keeping of such a balance should be made obligatory. (Chapter Seven and paragraphs 14.161–14.171)

26. The name and professional registration number of the prescriber should be entered in the CDR, as should the name of the pharmacist responsible for supplying controlled drugs to a patient or his/her representative.

(Chapter Seven and paragraphs 14.172–14.178)

27. The current requirement that a pharmacy CDR be kept for two years should be amended and the period should be extended to seven or, possibly, ten years. When electronic records are used, it should be possible (and it may be desirable) for CDRs to be kept even longer. (Chapter Seven and paragraphs 14.179–14.181)

28. The RPSGB should provide guidance to its members as to the information and advice to be given to patients and their representatives when receiving a supply of a controlled drug. This should usually comprise an accurate description of the controlled drug prescribed and advice about the need to keep the drug safe because of the risk of diversion. Patients and their representatives should be advised to return unused drugs to the pharmacy. This information and advice should be given both orally and in writing. (Chapter Seven, paragraphs 14.209–14.218 and paragraphs 14.245–14.253)

Controlled Drugs in the Community

29. Pharmacists should be required to prepare a statutory patient drug record card (PDRC) to accompany every supply of injectable Schedule 2 drugs leaving the pharmacy. This should record the form and amount of the drug prescribed, the form and amount of the drug dispensed and the dosage instructions as they appear on the prescription.

(Chapter Eight and paragraphs 14.219–14.234)

30. The healthcare professionals who administer such Schedule 2 injectable drugs should be obliged to enter every administration and new supply of such a drug on a master PDRC and should keep a running balance of the remaining stock. The destruction of any unused Schedule 2 injectable drugs should be recorded on the PDRC, wherever it takes place. After the death of the patient or when the time has come when injectable drugs are no longer required by him/her, the completed PDRC should be sent to the PCT to which the patient's GP is contracted. The PDRCs should be examined for anomalies and then married up with the patient's GP records. The controlled drugs inspectorate (if and when there is one) might carry out an occasional audit of PDRCs.

(Chapter Eight and paragraphs 14.219–14.234)

31. Consideration should be given to changing the law so that all controlled drugs would become the property of the Crown on the death of the patient for whom they were prescribed. (Chapter Eight and paragraphs 14.241–14.244)

32. There should be increased formality attaching to the destruction of injectable Schedule 2 controlled drugs dispensed for administration in the community. Their destruction and

their removal from the home of the patient should be properly recorded and witnessed. The classes of person lawfully entitled to undertake or witness destruction should include doctors, pharmacists, nurses, suitably trained law enforcement officers or PCT officers, and inspectors of any new controlled drugs inspectorate.

(Chapter Eight and paragraphs 14.250–14.254)

33.   It should be the responsibility of PCTs to ensure that suitable arrangements are in place for the disposal of controlled drugs.   (Chapter Eight and paragraphs 14.239–14.253)

CHAPTER ONE

Introduction

Terms of Reference

1.1 In my First Report, I found that, over a period of more than 20 years, Shipman had secretly obtained very large quantities of diamorphine and had used it to kill many of his patients. It was apparent that the regulatory framework governing the use of controlled drugs had not operated as it should. The purpose of regulation is to ensure accountability for the use of controlled drugs so as to avoid their diversion to improper use and to detect such diversion if it occurs.

1.2 By its Terms of Reference, the Inquiry was required:

> **'... by reference to the case of Harold Shipman to enquire into the performance of the functions of those statutory bodies, authorities, other organisations and individuals with responsibility for monitoring ... the use of controlled drugs; and**
>
> **... following those enquiries, to recommend what steps, if any, should be taken to protect patients in the future, and to report its findings to the Secretary of State for the Home Department and to the Secretary of State for Health'.**

1.3 I decided that it must have been the intention of Parliament that I should interpret the word **'monitoring'** widely so as to encompass an examination of the whole system of control, regulation and inspection by which the use of controlled drugs is governed. Only by looking at the system as a whole would it be possible for me to determine how patients could best be protected. I received evidence about the systems in operation in England, Scotland, Wales and Northern Ireland but my recommendations are confined to the system in England.

Controlled Drugs

1.4 Regulations controlling the prescribing, possession and supply of certain medicinal drugs have been in existence for more than 80 years. Before 1971, such drugs were described in the legislation as 'dangerous drugs'. They are now properly and usually called 'controlled drugs'. Controlled drugs (with one or two exceptions) have legitimate therapeutic applications but they also have a potential for abuse and dependence and carry a concomitant risk of diversion into the hands of persons other than those for whom they are prescribed. The controls imposed are designed to prevent the drugs from being misused; they cover such matters as the form of prescriptions, record keeping and storage. They are intended to prevent and detect the unlawful acquisition and diversion of controlled drugs (the kind of conduct of which Shipman was found guilty in Todmorden) but are not aimed at preventing or detecting the use of controlled drugs deliberately to kill.

1.5 Since 1973, all controlled drugs have been listed in one of the Schedules to the Misuse of Drugs Regulations (MDR) 1973–2001. The drugs attracting the highest level of control are those that appear in Schedule 1 to the MDR 2001. They have no approved medicinal use. They include hallucinogenic drugs such as lysergide (LSD). The next highest level of control applies to drugs in Schedule 2 to the Regulations. Over 100 drugs are listed in this Schedule, which includes the major opiates such as diamorphine (commonly known as heroin), morphine and pethidine, as well as the major stimulants such as amphetamines. These have therapeutic properties but a very significant propensity for abuse and dependence. Schedule 3 includes most of the barbiturate drugs and a few minor stimulants. Barbiturates have sedative properties and physical and psychological dependence can result. Schedule 4 is divided into two parts. Part 1 comprises mainly the benzodiazepines. These drugs are widely prescribed for the relief of anxiety and insomnia. They are known to be addictive if taken over a long period. Part 2 comprises mainly the anabolic and androgenic steroids, which are liable to abuse, in particular by sportsmen and sportswomen. Schedule 5 includes certain preparations that contain a drug with a potential for abuse (usually a Schedule 2 drug) but in such form or strength that the risk of abuse is very small. For example, codeine is listed in Schedule 2 but tablets containing 15mg codeine phosphate fall within Schedule 5.

Pethidine and Diamorphine

1.6　　The Inquiry's main focus has been on pethidine and diamorphine, the two drugs that Shipman obtained and used illicitly. Both drugs have a therapeutic use in the alleviation of pain. Both (but more particularly diamorphine) act as a respiratory depressant. Both are addictive. They give rise to a sense of euphoria and are, therefore, sometimes taken for non-therapeutic reasons.

1.7　　In 1976, Shipman was convicted of criminal offences involving the diversion of pethidine for the purpose of self-administration. Those offences were committed during his brief period in general practice in Todmorden, West Yorkshire. While working there, Shipman killed at least one patient by the injection of an opioid (probably morphine or diamorphine), and it is possible that he killed several more in the same way. While working in Hyde, Greater Manchester, between 1977 and 1998, he killed at least 214 patients, by injecting them with lethal doses of diamorphine. Death was due to the respiratory depressant effect of the drug. When an overdose is given, respiration is slowed and eventually stops. The absence of oxygen supply to the brain leads to cardiac arrest and death.

1.8　　Despite the regulatory controls in place, Shipman's diversion of diamorphine went undetected for more than 20 years. When it eventually came to light, this was not because his unlawful acquisition of the drug had been detected (it had not) but because he had come under suspicion of murdering, and forging the will of, Mrs Kathleen Grundy. Although Shipman used diamorphine to kill patients, the same methods of obtaining the drug could have been used by persons wanting the drug for self-administration or to sell to others. Many of the problems identified in connection with pethidine and diamorphine also occur in relation to other controlled drugs. Where appropriate, therefore, the Inquiry has looked at the wider picture.

The Use of Pethidine in General Practice

1.9　　Pethidine is a short-acting analgesic. In the 1960s and 1970s, it was widely used in general practice, in particular for the relief of pain in childbirth and the symptoms of pain caused by renal stones. The usual dosage would be 50mg, administered intramuscularly. Nowadays, it has been superseded by other, more effective, modern analgesics, although it is still used occasionally in obstetric care and for the relief of severe short-term non-malignant pain.

The Use of Diamorphine in General Practice

1.10 Over the last 25 years or more, the most common use of diamorphine in general practice has been for the treatment of severe pain in cases of terminal cancer, when other treatment, such as oral morphine, is insufficient or when administration by mouth is difficult. If the terminal illness is prolonged, the amounts of diamorphine necessary for the relief of pain may become very large because the patient becomes habituated to the drug and the dosage has to be increased in order to achieve adequate pain relief.

1.11 Until the early 1990s, a general practitioner (GP) or a district nurse would administer the diamorphine by means of periodic injection. This did not always achieve adequate pain control, however, and repeated injection at the same site was prone to cause local soreness. Since the early 1990s (in Tameside, the change came in 1993), diamorphine has usually been administered to terminally ill patients by means of a syringe driver, a battery-operated device that administers a continuous flow of the drug to the patient and provides far better pain control than periodic injections. Whichever method is used, the GP will have to prescribe quite large quantities of diamorphine and supplies will have to be kept at the patient's home. It is now quite common for patients on a syringe driver to be on a daily dosage of 100mg diamorphine, and dosages of more than 2000mg a day are not unknown. One of Shipman's patients was in need of a daily dose of 2400mg by the time of his death. In such cases, diamorphine is prescribed in ampoules of 30mg, 100mg or even 500mg, although the use of the largest ampoules is relatively rare.

1.12 GPs also use diamorphine for the relief of acute pain, for example, the pain experienced during a heart attack or following serious traumatic injury. Much smaller doses are then required because the patient is not habituated to the drug. Usually, about 5mg will be sufficient and quite often less. Many GPs carry a few ampoules of diamorphine in their medical bags to meet such contingencies. The preferred sizes are 5mg or 10mg ampoules.

1.13 The respiratory depressant effect of diamorphine renders it dangerous in overdose and this effect is heightened if the patient is not in pain. For a patient who is not in pain and who is not habituated to diamorphine, an intravenous injection (by which the drug enters the nervous system very rapidly) of 20mg would be dangerous and possibly fatal. In a frail or elderly patient, it would almost certainly be fatal. I have formed the view that Shipman usually used about 30mg diamorphine to kill a patient.

Shipman's Use of Pethidine and Diamorphine

1.14 Shipman obtained his supplies of pethidine and diamorphine from community pharmacies. It was plainly necessary for the Inquiry to establish in as much detail as possible how Shipman had obtained the controlled drugs used to feed his own habit and to kill his patients. Only then would it be possible to discover how he had exploited the loopholes in the system of regulation and control so as to avoid detection. I described Shipman's illicit methods of obtaining controlled drugs in some detail in the First Report. I will summarise them below and will refer to them again, where appropriate, later in this Report.

Todmorden

1.15   Very shortly after Shipman commenced practice at the Abraham Ormerod Medical Centre in Todmorden in March 1974, he began ordering large amounts of pethidine from the pharmacy of the local branch of Boots the Chemists (Boots). He presented 'requisitions' or 'signed orders' (terms which I shall use interchangeably), representing to the pharmacist that the supplies were for use in the practice. A requisition is simply a written request by a doctor for the supply of a specified quantity of a specified drug. The document need not be in the doctor's own handwriting although it has to carry the doctor's name, address and profession and must be signed by him/her. The purchase of a controlled drug in this way is a private transaction and the doctor or practice pays the ordinary commercial price of the drugs, although, if the drugs are later administered in the course of NHS treatment, the doctor can seek reimbursement of the cost of the drugs and an administration fee. If administered privately, the patient will pay the cost.

1.16   While obtaining pethidine on requisition, Shipman was also obtaining it by writing NHS prescriptions for the drug in the names of patients who did not need it. He would present a prescription at the pharmacy, saying that he was about to visit a patient and that he would deliver the drug in order to save the patient or carer the trouble of collecting it. He did this most often in the name of one particular elderly patient, who lived some way from Todmorden town centre, thereby adding verisimilitude to his story. In fact, Shipman kept the pethidine for himself. As a variant of this method, he also prescribed pethidine for patients who did have a need for the drug. In those cases, he would prescribe more than was necessary for the patient and would deliver only part of the whole amount, keeping the remainder for his own purposes.

1.17   Whether a pharmacist dispenses the controlled drug on a requisition or on a prescription, s/he must make an entry in a special book called the controlled drugs register (CDR). The CDR must be kept for at least two years after the date of the last entry in the book. A requisition must also be kept for at least two years. Prescription forms need be kept only if they are private (i.e. not NHS) prescriptions. Details of private prescriptions must also be entered into a private prescriptions book, unless those details have already been recorded in the CDR. NHS prescriptions are sent to the Prescription Pricing Authority for processing and payment. The CDR, requisitions, private prescriptions and the private prescriptions book should be inspected periodically by a specially designated police officer known as a chemist inspection officer (CIO). If the CIO detects any sign of unlawful conduct, s/he may call in an inspector from the Home Office Drugs Inspectorate (HODI) to assist in the investigation. Except when they receive such a request for assistance, Home Office inspectors usually concentrate on the licensing and inspection of businesses engaged in the manufacture or wholesale supply of controlled drugs.

1.18   In January 1975, a routine HODI inspection of records held by a pharmaceutical wholesaler in the North of England revealed that unusually large supplies of pethidine ampoules were being delivered to the pharmacy at the Todmorden branch of Boots. The CDR held at the pharmacy showed that large quantities were being both requisitioned and prescribed by Shipman. In July 1975, two inspectors from the HODI and an officer from the West Yorkshire Police (WYP) interviewed Shipman and examined the controlled drugs stocks and the CDR held at his practice premises. They found that there was no pethidine in stock and that the CDR was not being kept properly. Shipman had entered the practice's acquisitions of pethidine but not the amounts of the drug supplied or administered to patients from the practice stock. It was suspected that Shipman might be appropriating the pethidine but it was decided to take no action other than to warn him and other members of the practice of their duty to keep proper records in the CDR. Meanwhile, the police and the HODI arranged to keep a watch on Shipman's dealings with controlled drugs. Shipman continued to act as before and, only two months later, these activities came to light. Shipman's partners were told and he was dismissed from the practice. He admitted that he had been abusing pethidine. A consultant psychiatrist arranged for his admission to a private hospital for treatment and rehabilitation.

1.19   The HODI and the WYP were notified and Shipman's acquisition and prescribing of pethidine were investigated by reference to the entries in his name in the CDR. Shipman's improper use of NHS prescriptions was confirmed when the HODI inspectors and the WYP officer asked him about each prescription for pethidine. He told them that some patients had received small quantities of the drug and that others had received none. Shipman had kept most of it for himself.

1.20   The system of inspection (of the wholesaler's records followed by examination of the Boots CDR) had worked essentially as it should; it had drawn attention to the large quantities of controlled drugs that Shipman was requisitioning and prescribing. Once that abnormality had been noticed, both his requisitioning and his prescribing for individual patients came under suspicion. However, it is important to recognise that it is unlikely that Shipman's diversion of pethidine by improper prescribing alone would have been detected through the routine inspection of the wholesaler's records and pharmacy CDR. The volumes prescribed might have been explicable as supplies to terminally ill patients and the CDR would not have revealed that Shipman himself had been collecting the drugs. If he had not used requisitions as well, he might not have been detected.

1.21   Shipman was charged with eight offences of unlawful possession of pethidine, obtaining pethidine by deception, and forgery. In February 1976, he pleaded guilty and was fined and ordered to pay compensation and costs. A total of 74 similar offences were taken into consideration. His conviction was referred to the Home Office in London and to the General Medical Council (GMC). The Home Secretary had the power to restrict Shipman's right to possess, prescribe, supply or administer controlled drugs following his conviction but, as the result of a very recent change in Home Office policy, the case was not put before him for consideration of the exercise of that power. The GMC had the power to erase Shipman's name from the medical register (or to suspend its entry there) but decided only to issue a warning as to his future conduct. By early 1976, Shipman had found work in County Durham, in a position in which he had no need to prescribe or administer any controlled drug and, so far as is known, he did not obtain any drug illicitly during that employment.

Hyde

1.22 In 1977, Shipman went to work as a GP at the Donneybrook practice in Hyde. When interviewed for the post, he told his partners about his previous abuse of pethidine and assured them that he did not intend to keep a personal stock of controlled drugs in future. He would not, therefore, need to keep a CDR. He was, however, free to prescribe controlled drugs for patients without keeping any record, other than making an entry in the patients' medical records. As is now well known, in 1978, Shipman did begin to obtain diamorphine illicitly and used it to kill patients. During the period of almost 15 years when Shipman worked at the Donneybrook practice, he killed 71 patients. After 1992, when he began working as a single-handed practitioner at 21 Market Street, Hyde, he killed 143 patients. I have concluded that he used an overdose of diamorphine in every case. There is no evidence that he self-administered any controlled drugs during this period.

Shipman's Methods of Obtaining Diamorphine in the Late 1970s and the 1980s

1.23 It has not been possible for the Inquiry to find out exactly how Shipman obtained his supplies of diamorphine during the late 1970s and the 1980s, as the relevant pharmacy records and prescription forms from that period have long since been destroyed. As I explained in the First Report, I think it most likely that he first obtained such supplies from cancer patients, after whose deaths there was a surplus. I think it highly unlikely that he reverted to the use of requisitions. He had been detected when doing that in 1975. From the evidence of the methods he used during the 1990s, I have inferred that, during the late 1970s and the 1980s, he used a variety of methods, essentially by over-prescribing for the needs of his cancer patients and retaining any supplies that were left over after the death. As I shall shortly describe, the fact that he had obtained diamorphine by those methods would not have been easily detected.

Shipman's Methods of Obtaining Diamorphine after 1990

1.24 Most of the controlled (and other) drugs prescribed by Shipman were dispensed from the pharmacy at 23 Market Street, next door to Shipman's surgery. From 1995, this was known as the Norwest Co-op Pharmacy. It had previously been known as Battersby's. The pharmacy CDR dating from 1991 was available to the Inquiry. Examination of this CDR has allowed the discovery of several of the methods Shipman had used to obtain diamorphine during the 1990s.

1.25 Shipman would sometimes prescribe diamorphine for a patient with cancer at a time when the patient had not yet developed a need for the drug; he would collect the drug from the pharmacy and keep it all for himself. Sometimes, for a cancer patient who had a genuine need of the drug and was receiving it regularly, he would prescribe more than was necessary, collect it from the pharmacy and keep part, or even the whole, of the consignment for himself. After a cancer patient had died, he would, if he had the chance, take any unused drugs for himself, although he would tell whoever was present that he was doing so for the purpose of destroying them. On at least one occasion in the 1990s, he prescribed a large quantity of diamorphine for a patient who died on the same day; he collected the drugs and kept them for himself.

1.26   None of these methods of obtaining was likely to lead to detection. The patients were genuinely suffering from cancer. The prescriptions were all properly made out. Each dispensing would be recorded in the pharmacy CDR and the record would look entirely normal. The quantity of the drug prescribed might be large but this would be quite plausible in the case of a patient in the last stages of terminal illness. The pharmacist would have no way of knowing that, as was sometimes the case, a patient for whom Shipman collected drugs had died shortly before the drugs were dispensed. Nobody would realise that Shipman had kept all or part of a consignment. A patient or relative who received a package of drugs would not know that Shipman had removed some. Shipman could easily remove the outer packaging and the label on which the quantity might be written. No formal records have to be kept once the drugs leave the pharmacy. Nobody would realise that Shipman did not in fact destroy the leftover drugs he took; he was not under any duty to make a record of the drugs he took for destruction.

The Method of Obtaining Diamorphine Adopted by Shipman in 1993

1.27   For a period of about seven months in 1993, Shipman adopted a method of prescribing that was not related to cancer patients. I suspect that he was not, at that time, treating any patients who were suffering from cancer and, being in need of supplies of diamorphine, he adopted a different method of obtaining the drug. This entailed a course of conduct that might have led to his detection.

1.28   Between February and August 1993, Shipman wrote 14 prescriptions for a single 30mg ampoule of diamorphine. The prescriptions were in the names of 13 different patients, none of whom needed the drug. Indeed, some of them were already dead at the time he wrote the prescriptions. It is now known that he used each of those 30mg ampoules to kill a patient.

1.29   The dispensing of each of these 30mg ampoules was duly recorded in the CDR of the pharmacy at 23 Market Street. As it happens, between February and May 1993, the only entries on the 'drugs supplied' page of the CDR related to 12 prescriptions issued by Shipman. The record, which usually contained a variety of doctors' names and recorded the dispensing of differing quantities of various sizes of ampoules of diamorphine, had a most unusual appearance. Moreover, 30mg ampoules are usually dispensed as part of a consignment for the treatment of cancer pain. To prescribe a single 30mg ampoule is most unusual. That amount is not enough for the treatment of chronic pain; the patient will need more ampoules for use on subsequent days. On the other hand, 30mg is far too much for a single treatment for acute pain in an opioid-naïve patient. It follows that the appearance of the CDR was very unusual indeed. A copy of the relevant 'drugs supplied' pages appears at Appendix A. I shall have to consider whether the pharmacist who dispensed all but one of these single ampoules should have regarded this sequence as sufficiently unusual to require it to be drawn to the attention of the Greater Manchester Police CIO. I must also consider whether the CIO himself should have noticed the unusual sequence of prescribing during an inspection and should have initiated an investigation of Shipman's prescribing practice. In the event, the sequence was not recognised as unusual and was not investigated. I shall describe the events of 1993 in greater detail in Chapter Eleven. Later in the year, Shipman gave up prescribing single ampoules; by November, he had access to supplies of diamorphine from a cancer patient. From that time on, he was never short of a source of supply from a cancer patient and, save for one fleeting moment, was never again in danger of being detected on account of his dealings with controlled drugs.

An Incident in 1998

1.30   The fleeting moment occurred in July 1998. Many of Shipman's cancer patients were cared for at home by district nurses. If a patient had been provided with a syringe driver, a district nurse would come in each morning to refill the syringe with a new supply of diamorphine, according to the dosage ordered by Shipman. Although they are not required by law to do so, district nurses keep a record of the supplies of medication received and administered, as well as a stock balance. Sometimes, Shipman would make an entry in the nurses' record. On one occasion after he had visited and had made an entry in the record, the stock balance did not tally with the stock. In fact, he had stolen five 10mg ampoules of diamorphine. The district nurse asked Shipman about the missing stock and he gave an account, which she eventually accepted. She did not report him. I shall discuss this episode in more detail in Chapter Eight. This incident has focussed attention on the value of the district nurses' records and has caused me to examine the feasibility of requiring records to be kept in respect of at least some types of controlled drug after they leave the pharmacy. It occurred only days before Shipman came under suspicion and after he had killed his last victim.

The Inquiry's Approach

1.31   The primary task in Stage Three of the Inquiry has been to investigate the ways in which the systems of control, regulation and inspection governing the use of controlled drugs failed to prevent or deter Shipman from obtaining controlled drugs unlawfully or to detect him when he did so. I have examined the systems in force during the whole period of Shipman's practice as a GP. They remain largely unchanged at the present time. In this Report, I suggest ways in which the loopholes Shipman exploited could be closed.

1.32   It has been said by some that, since Shipman could have used other, non-controlled drugs or substances (such as insulin or potassium) to kill his patients, it is inappropriate for the Inquiry to focus exclusively on controlled drugs. The Inquiry has done so primarily because it was required to do so by its Terms of Reference. The Terms of Reference are wide enough for me not to wish to extend them to other drugs without good reason. The fact that I have not considered in this Report how patients should best be protected from healthcare professionals who seek to harm them by the use of other drugs or substances does not mean to say that there should not be controls in place relating to such drugs. However, such controls are not a matter for this Stage of the Inquiry.

1.33   Nor is it a matter for this Inquiry to consider whether society is right to seek to control the use of addictive drugs and to treat their unauthorised possession or sale as a criminal offence. There are those who believe that the taking of controlled drugs should be decriminalised and that such a measure would reduce many of the undesirable effects of illicit trafficking. I shall say nothing about those issues. The Inquiry has sought only to find ways of improving the systems that are designed to achieve the objectives of the current legislation.

The Scope and Extent of Diversion

1.34   Diversion of controlled drugs occurs in many ways. It was inevitable that, when looking into the shortcomings of the system that Shipman exploited, I should learn about other abuses related to controlled drugs of which he was not guilty, so far as is known. For example, I have heard evidence that some doctors sell controlled drugs or prescriptions for them. Some prescribe controlled drugs on private prescription for patients whom they scarcely know, turning a blind eye to the fact that the patient is a drug addict who is selling part of his/her supplies in order to finance his/her next prescription. So far as I know, Shipman did not do those things. I have also come across inappropriate prescribing. For example, I have heard about doctors who prescribe controlled drugs for themselves or their families. Such prescribing is not unlawful if done in good faith for proper therapeutic reasons but it can be a cover for the illicit prescribing of a drug for the feeding of an addiction. Shipman did not do that either, so far as is known. However, such practices pose a risk to patient safety and are contrary to the public interest. It seems to me that it would be wrong if I were to decline to consider ways of reducing or detecting those practices just because they happen to fall outside the ambit of Shipman's criminality.

1.35   The Department of Health (DoH), the Home Office and many others who gave evidence to the Inquiry accept that the true extent of diversion of controlled drugs is not known. Dr Jim Smith, Chief Pharmaceutical Officer for England at the DoH, told the Inquiry that the development of palliative care over the last 30 years has resulted in a vast increase in the quantities of controlled drugs being supplied to cancer patients. He said that this increase had brought with it problems of diversion that could not be ignored. A report entitled 'Audit of Controlled Drugs Prescribing in England for the Financial Year 2002/03' published by the Prescribing Support Unit (PSU) of the DoH in October 2003 (the PSU Report) records that the number of Schedule 2 and Schedule 3 controlled drugs prescribed is increasing at an annual rate of 8%. No fewer than 2.7 million prescriptions for Schedule 2 and Schedule 3 controlled drugs were issued during 2002/03. As the volume of controlled drugs dispensed increases, so must the size of the problem of diversion. According to an internal Home Office memorandum from 1997, '... **the number of individual transactions of controlled drugs in Great Britain is in the order of 200,000 every day, with an opportunity for diversion in every one of them**'.

1.36   One of the HODI inspectors told the Inquiry that more than 50% of the benzodiazepine drugs that found their way onto 'the street' had been dispensed on prescription. Mrs Kay Roberts, Lead Pharmacist for the Royal College of General Practitioners National Drug Misuse Training Programme and pharmacist member of the Advisory Council on the Misuse of Drugs, confirmed that a 'street market' exists for these drugs, which are, as I have said, widely prescribed. Several other witnesses said much the same thing.

1.37   Mrs Roberts also spoke of anecdotal evidence of children selling methylphenidate hydrochloride (Ritalin), which had been prescribed (apparently lawfully) for their treatment. Her evidence about the problem was supported by that of Detective Constable Neville Hanley, the CIO for the WYP. The PSU Report describes a rapid increase in the amount of Ritalin prescribed, with nearly 17 million tablets dispensed in 2002/03.

1.38   Several witnesses told me that there is little actual evidence of diversion of diamorphine onto 'the street'. While I accept that there may be little actual evidence of it, it does not necessarily follow that no such diversion is taking place. First, Shipman diverted diamorphine for over 20 years without detection. Although he was using it to kill, he could equally well have been selling it to dealers or addicts. I also heard about other doctors whose diversion of diamorphine continued for several years before it was detected. Some doctors who divert the drug will never be detected. Second, police efforts are understandably focussed on the large volumes of heroin that are unlawfully imported, rather than on the more moderate quantities of pharmaceutical diamorphine that might emanate from an individual community pharmacy. Dr Smith said that, although he had 'no feel whatsoever' for the scale of diversion by professionals, he had heard anecdotes about it and accepted that it was probably significant. In his view, it must be taken seriously.

1.39   The PSU Report dealt only with the prescribing of controlled drugs within the NHS and not with private prescribing. The authors acknowledged that this was an important limitation, as a significant proportion of private prescribing is for controlled drugs. This is a cause for concern because private prescribing is not monitored to the same extent as NHS prescribing. As a result, the scale of private prescribing of controlled drugs is unknown.

1.40   Although, therefore, the scale of the problem of diversion of controlled drugs is not known, there is a recognised risk that any healthcare professional with access to controlled drugs (and this must include pharmacists and nurses), might divert such drugs to improper use. If the public interest requires that the risk of such diversion should be reduced so far as is possible, consistent with the needs of patients, the current regime must be strengthened. It appears to me that, where controlled drugs are concerned, it is unwise to rely on a system that depends wholly on trusting those professionals who have access to them. Everyone's actions should be subject to some degree of supervision, control and audit. I recognise that it may well be impossible to prevent a doctor or other healthcare professional from obtaining illicit supplies of controlled drugs if s/he is determined to do so. However, the system could be a great deal more effective than it is at present. In my view, much could be done to deter such misconduct and to improve the chances of detection if it occurs.

Patient Safety in General

1.41   My examination of the systems of regulating controlled drugs has also led, sometimes unintentionally, to a discussion of issues and problems of wider application. For example, I heard evidence about the frequency with which doctors make prescribing errors, which can have serious or even fatal effects, especially when a controlled drug is involved. This evidence led to a discussion about the need for a pharmacist to check very carefully the appropriateness and dosage of a controlled drug prescription. It was suggested that pharmacists should have access to patients' medical records so as to be aware of the condition for which the drug had been prescribed. Such a measure would permit the pharmacist to make a more satisfactory check and would contribute to patient safety. The pharmacists' point was that this would be a sensible measure not only in relation to controlled drugs but also with many medicines that are available only on prescription. Thus, at times in this Report, I find myself expressing a view on issues that are not directly related to Shipman and are not even limited to the regulation of controlled drugs. However, I have not strayed into these wider issues unless led there by evidence relating to the regulation of controlled drugs. There is nothing in this Report that is not linked to the final section of my Terms of Reference, which requires me to make recommendations for the safety of patients in future.

Striking the Balance

1.42   In this country, medical practitioners are given an almost unfettered freedom to prescribe any medicinal drug for the treatment of organic disease. They are free to prescribe or administer very powerful drugs such as diamorphine, which (as I have said) are readily susceptible to misuse and which can easily have fatal consequences if used carelessly or in bad faith. All doctors are also entitled to prescribe some types of controlled drugs for the purpose of treating drug dependence. Although the range of drugs is more limited, it includes the prescription of such drugs as methadone, which can also be dangerous. Many Western countries do not allow the use of such drugs as diamorphine even for the treatment of organic disease. They consider that the risks of abuse outweigh the advantage to patients and that other, less dangerous, drugs can adequately meet patients' therapeutic needs. At an early stage of the Inquiry, I was persuaded that such drugs as diamorphine are of very great benefit to patients, provided that they are properly used. I therefore decided that any recommendations I would make would not seek to limit the availability of controlled drugs for legitimate patient needs but would focus on ensuring that they were safely and lawfully used. At times, during the evidence and in discussion, it was urged that some ideas or proposals for change would be unacceptable because they might interfere with patients' access to drugs. I cannot accept that there must be no regulation that might affect the ease with which a patient has access to a controlled drug. In my view, the proper balance must be struck between the degree of regulation necessary to control abuse and the right of patients to have access to the drugs they need.

1.43   It might be possible to devise an elaborate system of regulation and inspection of the use of controlled drugs that would effectively deter abuse and would detect it whenever it occurred. However, the cost of such a system in terms of financial and human resources would be very great. I have not recommended such a system. Instead, I have sought to recognise the abuses and to recommend ways in which they may be countered without placing too great a strain on limited resources.

CHAPTER TWO

The Conduct of Phase Two, Stage Three of the Inquiry

Introduction

2.1   The Inquiry embarked upon the collection of evidence about all aspects of the regulation of controlled drugs. Apart from collecting the statutory materials, so as to trace the development of the legislation over the last 80 years, the Inquiry sought information from the Home Office (the Government Department with responsibility for controlled drugs) and from the Royal Pharmaceutical Society of Great Britain (RPSGB) (the pharmacists' regulatory body) about how the system of regulation is designed to work. The Inquiry also sought evidence from a large number of people and organisations about how the system works in practice. The Inquiry team examined in greater depth materials previously assembled relating to Shipman's methods of obtaining controlled drugs and sought evidence from those who had had dealings with him, in an attempt to discover why his illicit obtaining of drugs had not been detected earlier. The Inquiry looked closely at aspects of the systems of controlled drugs regulation in Northern Ireland and the Canadian province of British Columbia. Finally, the Inquiry consulted widely about ways in which the defects in the current system could be remedied.

The Collection of Evidence

2.2   Witness statements obtained from 67 witnesses and approximately 15,000 pages of documents were scanned into the Inquiry's image database in connection with Stage Three. Those statements and documents supplemented material from Phase One of the Inquiry (and some from Phase Two, Stage Four) that was relevant to the Stage Three issues. This material comes from the following sources.

Families

2.3   When providing their Inquiry witness statements for Phase One, the relatives of Shipman's patients were invited to give their suggestions for change, with a view to establishing additional safeguards for the future. Many provided considered views and positive suggestions as to how the procedures for regulating the use of controlled drugs might be improved. I have taken these suggestions into account. On the second day of the Stage Three hearings, I heard oral evidence from four relatives of patients of Shipman. Three of those patients were unlawfully killed by Shipman. All these witnesses had given careful thought to the issues under discussion and some brought to the Inquiry ideas from their own walks of life. I found their evidence thought provoking and helpful.

Local Pharmacies

2.4   In its attempt to identify all Shipman's sources of supply of controlled drugs, the Inquiry obtained and examined the controlled drugs registers (CDRs) from nine pharmacies in and around Hyde. Most contained no entries in Shipman's name and, from examination of them, it seems likely that all the diamorphine Shipman used to kill his patients was dispensed from the pharmacy at 23 Market Street, Hyde.

23 Market Street

2.5   The pharmacy premises at 23 Market Street are close to Donneybrook House, where Shipman practised between 1977 and 1992, and adjacent to the surgery at 21 Market Street, where he practised from 1992 until his arrest in 1998. Witness statements were obtained from 11 members of the pharmacy staff, some qualified pharmacists and some not. They included the former owner, Mr Peter Rothman, the pharmacist manager, Mrs Ghislaine Brant, and a number of others, including locum staff. Six of those members of staff gave oral evidence. The witnesses were asked about the dispensing procedures at the pharmacy, with particular reference to controlled drugs. They were asked about the system of inspection by police chemist inspection officers (CIOs) and by the RPSGB. They were asked for their opinions of Shipman and whether they had noticed anything unusual about his prescribing and use of controlled drugs. Some of the staff also gave evidence in connection with an unusual sequence of dispensing of diamorphine that took place during 1993.

Nupharm Chemist

2.6   Five diamorphine ampoules that Shipman stole in July 1998 (after he had killed his last victim) had been dispensed at Nupharm Chemist, Clarendon Street, Hyde, which is owned by Mr Richard Aucott. I have referred to this episode in paragraph 1.30. Mr Aucott gave oral evidence to the Inquiry about the arrangements and procedures for the obtaining, storing and dispensing of controlled drugs (especially diamorphine) in his pharmacy. He also gave evidence about his experience of police chemist inspections and RPSGB inspections and commented on the appearance of the diamorphine CDR held at 23 Market Street.

General Practitioners from Hyde

2.7   During the course of Phase One, it became clear to me that Shipman was able to divert controlled drugs during the whole of his career by purporting to collect them from a pharmacy on behalf of patients. I wanted to discover whether it was normal practice for a doctor to collect drugs on behalf of a patient. Accordingly, enquiry was made of 13 doctors who had been identified from the CDR held at 23 Market Street as having prescribed diamorphine or obtained it on requisition. Ten of those doctors responded, mostly by letter.

2.8   In Phase One of the Inquiry, 11 general practitioners who had at various times worked at the Donneybrook practice provided details of their arrangements (and of their knowledge, if any, of Shipman's arrangements) for keeping controlled drugs. In statements made either for Phase One or for Stage Four of Phase Two, some of those doctors also explained what Shipman had said, when interviewed for the position at the Donneybrook practice, about his intention not to keep a personal stock of controlled drugs in future.

Practice Staff

2.9   Members of the practice staff from Donneybrook House and 21 Market Street made statements concerning their knowledge of Shipman's arrangements for the use and storage of controlled drugs.

District Nurses

2.10   I have explained that, nowadays, many terminally ill patients are cared for at home, with the assistance of district nurses, who are responsible for the administration of a supply of diamorphine by means of a syringe driver. Much of the diamorphine obtained by Shipman was diverted from supplies prescribed for such patients. Witness statements were provided by four district nurses from the Tameside area, three of whom gave oral evidence. Mrs Diane Nuttall, Directorate Manager of the Community Care Directorate, Tameside and Glossop Primary Care Trust, also gave evidence. These witnesses explained their working arrangements, focussing upon the administration of diamorphine to terminally ill patients. They gave evidence about their experience of Shipman in general and they were also asked specifically about the cases of several patients whose diamorphine was diverted by him.

2.11   A demonstration of the operation of a syringe driver was provided by Mrs Carla Hartley, a Macmillan nurse and clinical nurse specialist.

Care Homes in Hyde

2.12   Some of the patients killed by Shipman lived in what are now known as 'care homes' or 'care homes with nursing'. Special requirements exist in respect of the keeping of controlled drugs for patients who live in such accommodation, and the Inquiry obtained statements from three persons occupying nursing or managerial positions in such homes.

The Royal College of Nursing

2.13   Mr Ian Hargreaves was, until 30th April 2003, Regional Director of the Royal College of Nursing. He retired on that date, although he has continued to represent the College during the remainder of the Inquiry. He gave evidence about nurses and their dealings with controlled drugs, about the special arrangements that apply for midwives (especially in the community) and about issues of diversion in general. He made some suggestions for improvement of the current systems. He outlined the procedures that apply in a hospital setting.

Expert Evidence

Mrs Kay Roberts

2.14   At an early stage, it became apparent that the Inquiry would need assistance in the form of evidence from an independent pharmacist with knowledge of the law and procedures relating to controlled drugs, together with personal experience of how they work in practice. Mrs Kay Roberts filled that role and was of great assistance to me. She is a former

Area Pharmacy Specialist in Drug Misuse, employed by the Greater Glasgow Primary Care NHS Trust. She is the Lead Pharmacist for the Royal College of General Practitioners (RCGP) National Drug Misuse Training Programme and, since 1999, has been a pharmacist member of the Advisory Council on the Misuse of Drugs. She also serves on the Scottish Advisory Committee on the Misuse of Drugs. Mrs Roberts qualified in pharmacy in 1961 and, during her distinguished career, has occupied hospital, community and administrative posts.

2.15   Mrs Roberts gave evidence on three days. She provided an invaluable explanation of the law applying to controlled drugs and community pharmacy and of the evolution of the relevant law. She provided an insight into the practical workings of a community pharmacy, in particular the procedures relating to controlled drugs. She also helped me to evaluate the unusual features of the sequence of dispensing of single 30mg ampoules of diamorphine that took place in 1993.

Professor Richard Baker

2.16   Professor Richard Baker is Director of the Clinical Governance Research and Development Unit at the University of Leicester. He has made important contributions at several stages of the Inquiry process. In the course of the Stage Three hearings, he gave oral evidence explaining the findings of a survey carried out by himself and colleagues from the University of Leicester, dealing with the quality and efficacy of local controlled drugs procedures. His evidence provided a useful insight into the arrangements for storing and dealing with controlled drugs by doctors, as well as by pharmacists.

Professor Henry McQuay

2.17   Professor Henry McQuay, Professor of Pain Relief at the University of Oxford and Honorary Consultant at the Oxford Pain Relief Unit, provided a written statement for Stage Three, setting out the various therapeutic uses of controlled drugs, in particular diamorphine.

The Home Office

2.18   The Home Office Drugs Branch is responsible for administering the statutory systems of control applicable to the production and distribution of controlled drugs, although routine community pharmacy inspections are carried out, not by the Home Office, but by the police. The Home Office Drugs Inspectorate (HODI) is responsible for investigating the suspected breach of certain controlled drugs regulations. Mr Alan Macfarlane, Chief Inspector of the HODI, gave oral evidence. He explained how the systems currently operate and, by reference to a large quantity of documentation supplied by the Home Office and various police forces, explained the history and purpose of the systems, from the inception of police pharmacy inspections in the early twentieth century to the present day.

2.19   The Inquiry obtained evidence about the investigation into the offences of which Shipman was convicted in 1976. A senior inspector from the Northern Regional Office of the HODI, who had been involved in the investigation, gave oral evidence. An inspector from the

Northern Regional Office provided a statement about his involvement in that investigation. In all, four HODI inspectors gave evidence about the way in which the Inspectorate operates.

2.20   The Inquiry also collected evidence about the procedures within the Home Office by which decisions were made to seek or not to seek directions under section 12 of the Misuse of Drugs Act 1971 (MDA 1971). The Home Secretary has the power to restrict the right of a doctor convicted of controlled drugs offences to prescribe, possess, supply or administer controlled drugs. In 1976, the Head of Division E4 of the Home Office (the Division that included the HODI) was Sir Geoffrey de Deney. It was he who decided that no direction should be sought from the Home Secretary in Shipman's case. Sir Geoffrey attended the Inquiry to give evidence about the policy governing directions that was in place at that time and to explain why no direction was sought. A witness statement was also obtained from a legal assistant at the Home Office. Twenty two case files relating to section 12 directions (or equivalent directions under the previous legislation) against doctors, dentists and pharmacists, spanning the period from 1969 to 1993, were also obtained.

The Royal Pharmaceutical Society of Great Britain

2.21   The RPSGB employs a number of full-time inspectors who carry out periodic inspections of all community pharmacies. One of the issues I had to consider was whether RPSGB inspections of the pharmacy at 23 Market Street and, in particular, inspections of the CDR held there, should have alerted the authorities to Shipman's acquisitions of diamorphine. For this reason, the Inquiry obtained witness statements from five past and present RPSGB inspectors, four of whom gave oral evidence.

2.22   I also heard oral evidence from Mr Stephen Lutener. Mr Lutener qualified as a pharmacist and then worked for Boots the Chemists for approximately seven years before joining the RPSGB as an inspector in 1987. He was appointed Head of the Ethics Division in 1991 and thereafter occupied a number of senior posts. When he gave evidence in June 2003, and at the time of his departure from the RPSGB in October 2003, his job title was Head of Professional Conduct. Mr Lutener's evidence covered many aspects of the work of the RPSGB and I found it invaluable.

Greater Manchester Police

2.23   It was also necessary for me to consider why the routine inspection of the CDR kept at 23 Market Street by the CIOs of the Greater Manchester Police (GMP) did not lead to the detection of Shipman's activities. I wished to know whether the failure to detect the diversion arose from individual or systemic failings (or both). I wished to compare the performance of the CIO responsible for inspection of the CDR with that of his fellow GMP CIOs. I also needed to compare the performance of the GMP CIOs with that of CIOs employed by other forces over the relevant period.

2.24   Detective Chief Superintendent (DCS) Peter Stelfox, the officer in charge of GMP Crime Investigation, gave oral evidence to the Inquiry, providing the perspective of a senior GMP officer. Witness statements were obtained from 11 past and present GMP CIOs, seven of whom (including Detective Constable (DC) Michael Beard, Chairman of the National Association of Chemist Inspection Officers (NACIO)) attended to give oral evidence. Their evidence shed valuable light on the various methods of diverting controlled drugs used by healthcare professionals. A witness statement was also obtained from a retired detective superintendent who had been in charge of the GMP Force Drugs Unit from 1993 until 2001 and who had prepared an internal report on GMP inspection of community pharmacists. DCS Bernard Postles, former Commander of the Investigative Support Branch, Crime Operations Department, GMP, also provided a witness statement.

Other Police Forces

2.25   The Inquiry obtained some general information from all 43 police forces in England and Wales about their CIO arrangements. More detailed information was obtained from 14 forces in England and Wales, from the Police Service of Northern Ireland and from six Scottish police forces. Senior officers from two forces gave oral evidence, as did four past and present CIOs from other forces. DC Diane Cooper, a trainer involved in the CIO training course at the West Yorkshire Police Training Centre, also gave oral evidence. DC Duncan White, a CIO and Secretary of the NACIO, provided a witness statement. He also attended the Inquiry's seminars. Further material was provided by the Association of Chief Police Officers.

The Department of Health

2.26   The last witness to give evidence before the Inquiry in Stage Three was Dr Jim Smith, Chief Pharmaceutical Officer for England at the Department of Health (DoH). Dr Smith, who also attended the Inquiry seminars, described the role of the DoH with regard to controlled drugs from 1974 to the present day, as well as explaining guidance and directions issued by the DoH on the MDA 1971 and the Misuse of Drugs Regulations 1973–2001. He also dealt with a number of issues related to diversion of controlled drugs into the community. The DoH provided a large quantity of written material for consideration.

Documents from Other Sources

2.27   Statements, correspondence and other material was received from a large number of other organisations. These included Government Departments and Agencies, among them the Department for the Environment, Food and Rural Affairs and the Medicines and Healthcare Products Regulatory Agency. Professional bodies supplying such material included the British Medical Association, the RCGP, the General Medical Council, the Medical Defence Union and the Dispensing Doctors' Association. The Nursing and Midwifery Council, the Association of Nurse Prescribing and the Royal College of Midwives also provided material, as did Macmillan Cancer Relief, Marie Curie Cancer Care and numerous individual hospices. The National Pharmaceutical Association, the British Association of Pharmaceutical Wholesalers and the Association of the British Pharmaceutical Industry provided further material.

2.28   In considering the systems in other jurisdictions, the Inquiry received material from Northern Ireland, Canada, the United States of America and Australia.

Evidence Relevant to Both Stages Three and Four

2.29   The Inquiry received some evidence that was relevant to both Stage Three and Stage Four. For example, evidence relating to the monitoring of prescribing by primary care trusts, relying on data provided by the Prescription Pricing Authority (PPA), was given during Stage Four but was relevant also to Stage Three. The evidence of Mr Michael Siswick, Director of Human Resources for the PPA, was particularly helpful.

Before the Oral Hearings

The Arrangements for the Distribution of Evidence

2.30   The arrangements for the distribution of evidence were the same for Stage Three as for Phase One and the earlier Stages of Phase Two. They are described at paragraphs 3.17 and 3.18 of my First Report. As in Phase One, all the evidence available to the Inquiry was released into the public domain via the Inquiry website, except where material had to be withheld in order to protect the identity of certain individuals unconnected with the enquiries into Shipman's activities.

The Public Meeting

2.31   On Monday, 17th March 2003, the Inquiry held a Public Meeting, at which I explained the arrangements for Stage Three.

Representation

2.32   Before and after the Public Meeting, I granted leave to various individuals and organisations to be represented before the Inquiry during the Stage Three hearings and, for some, recommended funding for that representation at public expense. A list of participants in Stage Three and their representation can be seen at Appendix B of this Report.

Salmon Letters

2.33   Before the Stage Three hearings began, the Solicitor to the Inquiry, Mr Henry Palin, sent letters (known as 'Salmon letters') to those persons and organisations whose conduct might become the subject of criticism by the Inquiry. The potential criticisms were clearly identified in those letters. In the event that any further potential criticisms came to light at or after the hearings, these were the subject of further Salmon letters. Recipients of Salmon letters were given the opportunity to respond to the potential criticisms in writing, as well as in the course of their oral evidence at the hearings.

Permission to Broadcast

2.34   I had given permission for the Stages One and Two hearings to be broadcast in accordance with a protocol prepared by the Inquiry and designed to ensure that Inquiry material would not be misused. Those arrangements caused no difficulties during Stages One and Two and I received no representations suggesting that they should be discontinued. I therefore gave permission to recognised organisations to broadcast during Stage Three, provided that they complied with a slightly amended protocol, clarifying the broadcasters' duties in respect of websites. During Stage Three, I received and granted one application from a witness that her evidence should not be broadcast.

The Oral Hearings

2.35   The oral hearings were held in the Council Chamber at Manchester Town Hall. The Stage Three hearings took place between Monday, 19th May and Wednesday, 2nd July 2003, and on Friday, 18th July 2003.

2.36   The arrangements for the oral hearings, and for the publication of evidence, were the same as for the Phase One hearings. They are described at paragraphs 3.28 to 3.36 of my First Report.

2.37   Volunteers from Tameside Victim and Witness Support attended to assist family witnesses at the start of the Stage Three hearings, but were not required during the remainder of these hearings. I remain most grateful to Tameside Victim and Witness Support for all the assistance they have given during the course of the Inquiry.

2.38   In general, witnesses who gave oral evidence during the Stage Three hearings were called by Counsel to the Inquiry. However, in the interests of fairness, those witnesses who had received Salmon letters were given the opportunity of making an opening statement of their evidence in response to questions by their own counsel or solicitor, before being questioned by Counsel to the Inquiry. In the event, none of the recipients of Salmon letters chose to avail themselves of this opportunity.

Submissions

2.39   Following the conclusion of the Stage Three hearings, representatives of a number of the individuals and organisations represented made written submissions. Counsel to the Inquiry also produced written submissions. I offered an opportunity to all representatives to make representations that I should hear oral submissions, but received no such representations.

The Inquiry's Consultations

The Discussion Paper

2.40   On 1st July 2003, before the end of the Stage Three hearings, the Inquiry published a Discussion Paper entitled 'The Use and Monitoring of Controlled Drugs in the Community'. The purpose of the Discussion Paper was to provide a focus for both written responses and oral discussion at a series of seminars held in January 2004. The Inquiry received written responses from 126 individuals and organisations. The views expressed in those responses were considered and discussed at the seminars.

The Seminars

2.41   Seminars were held in the Council Chamber at Manchester Town Hall on Monday, 12th, Wednesday, 14th and Friday, 16th January 2004. There were 16 participants, some representing organisations involved in the day-to-day operation of controlled drugs procedures, some being individuals with a particular interest in or knowledge of controlled drugs. The first day of the seminars was devoted to presentations about the systems of monitoring and inspection of controlled drugs in two other jurisdictions, Northern Ireland and the province of British Columbia, Canada.

2.42   On the second and third days, there was an exchange of views about the various issues raised in the Discussion Paper. The proceedings were led by Senior Counsel to the Inquiry. Participants in the seminars had submitted written responses to the Inquiry's Discussion Paper in advance and expanded on those responses during the course of the seminars. Persons attending the seminars as observers were able to raise points through Counsel for the consideration of seminar participants. After the seminars, the Inquiry received a number of further responses, both from participants who wished to confirm or revise views previously expressed and from people who had attended the seminars, or who had become aware of the discussions that had taken place and wanted to contribute their own opinions.

2.43   I found the seminars, and indeed the whole consultation process undertaken by the Inquiry, extremely valuable in clarifying my thoughts and helping me to formulate my recommendations for the future. A summary of the seminar discussions will be found in Chapter Fourteen.

CHAPTER THREE

A Brief History of the Regulation of Controlled Drugs

Introduction

3.1 In this Chapter, I shall examine the historical development of the regulation of controlled drugs in England and Wales. Some features of this development concern measures taken to deal with the problem of addiction to controlled drugs, a subject lying on the periphery of the Inquiry's remit. I have included them for the better understanding of the system as a whole.

The Origins of the Royal Pharmaceutical Society of Great Britain and the Passage of the Pharmacy Act 1868

3.2 From as early as the sixteenth century, the importance of maintaining standards in the supply of medicines was recognised. A body of physicians, later to become the Royal College of Physicians, received letters patent from King Henry VIII, entitling them to inspect the premises of apothecaries, i.e. persons who prepared and sold medicines. The inspectors were known as 'censors' and their role was to identify defective or impure medicines and to destroy them. Responsibility for fulfilling this role remained with the College until 1856. From the seventeenth century, the Society of Apothecaries also undertook inspections and paid particular attention to preparations containing opium, which were used for a wide variety of purposes.

3.3 Until the second half of the nineteenth century, medicinal drugs were supplied by apothecaries, chemists and druggists, as well as medical practitioners. They could also be sold by any general dealer and there were many 'quack' dispensers of potions and remedies. In due course, the chemists, druggists and apothecaries joined forces in an attempt to impose restrictions on the sale of drugs and to oppose the activities of the 'quacks'. The Pharmaceutical Society of Great Britain was established in 1841. It was granted a Royal Charter in 1843 and became the Royal Pharmaceutical Society of Great Britain (RPSGB) in 1988. Soon after the original formation of the Society, there were calls to restrict the right to practise pharmacy to those who were specially licensed, to promote professional standards of training and to establish controls on the sale of drugs.

3.4 These calls led to the passing of the Pharmacy Act 1868, which introduced a list of drugs, including opium, which could be sold only by 'pharmaceutical chemists'. Apart from the restrictions imposed by the 1868 Act, there was no legislative control of opiate drugs in the UK until 1916.

The Dangerous Drugs Act 1920

3.5 In 1916, a Regulation was introduced, under the Defence of the Realm Act, to curb the use of cocaine by soldiers in London on leave from war service. As the Government Department responsible for the Act, the Home Office acquired the custodianship of drug control legislation. The Regulation initially gave authority to an official of the Home Office to inspect retail pharmacists' premises and records. In 1917, this authority was extended to police officers not below the rank of inspector.

3.6   The UK had earlier become committed to a more extensive system of domestic control over narcotic drugs when it signed the International Opium Convention at The Hague in 1912 (the 1912 Convention). The 1912 Convention obliged the Government to take effective measures for the prevention of the traffic in, and abuse of, dangerous drugs. The term 'dangerous drugs' was used in all relevant domestic legislation until the Misuse of Drugs Act 1971 (MDA 1971), after which time such drugs were usually described as 'controlled drugs'. It was not until after the First World War that the Government was able to give effect to its obligations under the 1912 Convention (and, by then, also Article 29 of the Treaty of Peace) by the passage of the Dangerous Drugs Act 1920 (the 1920 Act).

3.7   The 1920 Act prohibited the importation and exportation of certain dangerous drugs (which included opium, cocaine, morphine and diamorphine) save under licence granted by the Secretary of State (in practice, the Home Secretary). It allowed for secondary legislation to provide for a licensing and regulatory framework governing the manufacture, sale, prescription, possession and distribution of dangerous drugs. The drugs to which the Act applied could be extended in future, by Order in Council, where such drugs were considered **'likely to be productive, if improperly used, of ill effects ... analogous to those produced by morphine or cocaine'**. Breaches of the Act or any regulation made under it would be criminal offences. The Act conferred on police officers and other authorised persons powers (but not duties) of inspection of the premises of producers, manufacturers, sellers and distributors of such drugs. It did not confer a power to inspect doctors' surgeries.

The Dangerous Drugs Regulations 1921

3.8   The secondary legislation was contained in the Dangerous Drugs Regulations 1921 (the 1921 Regulations). The production, supply, prescription and possession of dangerous drugs was made unlawful unless the person dealing with the drugs had a licence or was a medical practitioner, dentist or veterinary surgeon. Others were allowed to possess the drugs only when prescribed by a medical practitioner. This was the first statutory expression of the particular privileges of the medical practitioner in relation to dangerous drugs.

3.9   The 1921 Regulations laid down the formal obligations of doctors and pharmacists with regard to the prescribing and dispensing of dangerous drugs. Many of these obligations still exist today. The Regulations introduced the requirement that dangerous drugs be dispensed only on written prescription. Any person, authorised under the 1920 Act to manufacture, possess or supply a dangerous drug, who was convicted of any offence under the Act or Regulations might have that authorisation withdrawn by the Home Secretary.

3.10   Regulation 5 of the 1921 Regulations conferred on the Home Secretary the power to prescribe and issue an **'official form'** to be used by doctors when prescribing dangerous drugs. The intention was that the new **'official form'** would be used for the private prescribing of dangerous drugs. When issuing publicly funded prescriptions for dangerous drugs, doctors would use the same prescription form as for other medicines available on prescription. In the event, no **'official form'** for the private prescribing of dangerous drugs was ever introduced. It is perhaps of interest that, more than 80 years later, the Inquiry should be discussing this and other ideas that were current at the time that the 1921 Regulations came into effect.

3.11   The 1921 Regulations required all suppliers of dangerous drugs to record relevant transactions in a register, the form of which was prescribed by the Regulations. They also imposed an obligation of record keeping on a doctor supplying dangerous drugs to a patient. That duty was different from, and less onerous than, that imposed upon pharmacists. A doctor was required only to keep a daybook, which was less detailed than the pharmacist's register. This concession was removed in 1926, from which time a doctor was required to keep a dangerous drugs register.

3.12   It is interesting to note that a regulation, proposed in 1922, that doctors should not be permitted to prescribe a controlled drug for their own use was withdrawn by the Home Office following objections from the British Medical Association. A further proposal by the Home Office in 1923 to limit the right of a medical practitioner to possess, prescribe or administer dangerous drugs to those medical practitioners **'in actual practice'** (i.e. not retired or working in a non-clinical capacity) was also abandoned[1]. When similar proposals were raised in 2003 in the Inquiry's Discussion Paper, 'The Use and Monitoring of Controlled Drugs in the Community', they received support from a wide variety of organisations, including the Royal Colleges of Physicians of London and Edinburgh. The Royal College of General Practitioners supported the latter, though not the former, proposal.

Establishing Regular Police Inspection of Retail Pharmacies

3.13   In 1921, the police powers of inspection of retail pharmacies were extended to officers below the rank of inspector. A Home Office Circular issued to Chief Officers of Police explained the police role in ensuring compliance by pharmacists with the statutory requirements under the 1921 Regulations. The scheme was that the police would inspect pharmacies, the Home Office was to inspect the arrangements of pharmaceutical wholesalers and those licensed to manufacture or produce dangerous drugs, and the Ministry of Health was to be responsible for the inspection of the arrangements made by medical practitioners. The Ministry of Health assigned the duty of inspecting the arrangements of general practitioners (GPs) to the Regional Medical Service (RMS), which continued to perform this function until 1991.

3.14   In July 1922, the Commissioner of the Metropolitan Police wrote to the Home Office, questioning whether the inspection of pharmacies was a proper and worthwhile role for police officers and suggesting that these responsibilities might be better fulfilled by persons having some practical knowledge of the retail pharmacy business. (It is interesting to note that the Greater Manchester Police made exactly the same point to the

[1] Spear, Bing and Mott, Joy, *Heroin Addiction, Care and Control: The British System*, London: Drugscope, September 2002

Inquiry in 2003.) The Home Office response in 1922 was that the police were not expected to undertake elaborate examinations of the pharmacists' records. Their inspections would be a valuable stimulus to retail chemists, who might otherwise become slack, to maintain strict compliance with legislative requirements. Similar views about the value of a police inspection were expressed to the Inquiry in 2003.

The Rolleston Report 1926

The Appointment of the Rolleston Committee

3.15   From 1921 at the latest, the Home Office was concerned about the practice of prescribing dangerous drugs to addicts. It opposed the treatment of addiction to a dangerous drug by the prescribing of 'maintenance' doses, i.e. the continued prescribing of the quantity of the drug to which the patient had become accustomed, with the intention of maintaining the patient's stability. It did not approve even of the use of gradually reducing doses of the drug of addiction. Its position was that abrupt withdrawal from drug dependence was possible and that any other form of treatment was improper. For its part, in the years following the passing of the 1920 Act, the medical profession had become concerned about what it perceived as official intrusion into the sanctity of the doctor/patient relationship.

3.16   In 1924, as a result of its concerns, the Home Office approached the Ministry of Health, querying the propriety of the practice, followed by many doctors, of treating drug addiction by the gradual reduction of dosage. Following that approach, on 30th September 1924, a Departmental Committee was appointed, under the chairmanship of Sir Humphry Rolleston, to report on the problem. The Rolleston Committee, which was composed mainly of doctors, was required by its Terms of Reference:

> **'... to consider and advise as to the circumstances, if any, in which the supply of morphine and heroin (including preparations containing morphine and heroin) to persons suffering from addiction to those drugs may be regarded as medically advisable, and as to the precautions which it is desirable that medical practitioners administering or prescribing morphine or heroin should adopt for the avoidance of abuse, and to suggest any administrative measures that seem expedient for securing observance of such precautions'.**

The Main Findings of the Committee

3.17   On the main issue before it, the Committee found that the method of treatment favoured by the Home Office, namely sudden and complete withdrawal of the drug of addiction, was not practicable in the case of most addicts. They recommended that, in most cases, the steady reduction of the dosage of the drug of addiction was the method of treatment most likely to result in eventual withdrawal. Doctors had to be free to prescribe for the purpose of such treatment. There would be a few cases in which it would prove impossible to wean a patient from a longstanding addiction and in which it would be appropriate for the doctor to prescribe a small maintenance dose of the drug of addiction. The Committee stated that doctors must also remain free to prescribe controlled drugs for the treatment of organic disease.

A Useful Perspective on the Problems of the Day

3.18   The Report of the Rolleston Committee (the Rolleston Report) provides a useful perspective on the problems of the day. The Committee reported that the inspection of wholesale pharmaceutical suppliers and pharmacies had revealed cases in which very large quantities of dangerous drugs had been supplied to particular doctors and where individual patients had received unusually large quantities on prescription. Further enquiries had revealed a number of specific problems. Some doctors were prescribing dangerous drugs for addicts on a maintenance basis, without any attempt to reduce dependence. Some doctors had issued supplies of, or prescriptions for, large quantities of dangerous drugs to patients whom they saw only infrequently; in some cases, the drugs or prescriptions had been sent by post. Some doctors had supplied dangerous drugs or had issued prescriptions to persons previously unknown to them and without making any effort to communicate with those persons' usual medical advisers. There were cases in which persons had obtained supplies of dangerous drugs from several practitioners concurrently. Finally, it had been found that, in some cases, large supplies had been purchased or prescribed by practitioners for self-administration. I interpose to say that the same problems still exist today. These practices would now be described collectively as 'irresponsible prescribing' and some would involve the commission of criminal offences.

3.19   The Committee noted that cases of addiction to morphine or heroin were more prevalent in the **'great urban centres'**, among persons who had to handle those drugs for professional or business reasons and among persons especially liable to nervous or mental strain. Facility of access was said to be an important factor in the onset of addiction. Again, this observation would not be out of place if the Committee had reported 70 years later.

3.20   Even the ways in which the doctors' behaviour was addressed are familiar to those involved in monitoring the conduct of doctors today. It was said that an informal approach to the doctor, seeking to persuade him/her to pay due regard to the requirements of the legislation, had in many cases been followed by beneficial results. Some doctors might be prosecuted. In other cases, the Home Office might bring the case to the notice of the General Medical Council (GMC) if it appeared that the doctor's conduct had been such as might be regarded by the GMC as **'infamous in a professional respect'**.

Restricting Prescribing Powers

3.21   The Rolleston Report noted that the general authority to supply and possess dangerous drugs could, at the discretion of the Home Secretary, be withdrawn from individual practitioners who had been convicted of offences under the 1920 Act. As the Regulations stood at that time, withdrawal of authority had to be preceded by conviction in a police court. As a means of dealing with those problems of irresponsible prescribing which did not involve the commission of a criminal offence, the Committee recommended that the Home Secretary should have the power to withdraw the authority of a practitioner to possess, prescribe and supply dangerous drugs, if advised to do so by a suitably constituted medical tribunal. The question for the tribunal would be whether dangerous drugs had been supplied, administered or prescribed by the practitioner for purposes other than legitimate medical purposes. The tribunal would comprise three medical members and a legal assessor.

3.22 Some of the Rolleston Committee's recommendations were accepted by the Home Office and were introduced in the Dangerous Drugs Regulations 1926. However, although the statutory power to create the medical tribunal system was provided by those Regulations, the machinery for such a system was introduced only by the MDA 1971, almost half a century later.

The Evolution of the Chemist Inspection Officer's Role

3.23 In 1935, the League of Nations placed on national governments a duty to provide statistics about known drug addicts. In 1939, police forces were given the task of informing the Home Office about persons who were receiving regular supplies of dangerous drugs. It was the job of the chemist inspection officer (CIO) to gather this information during his/her inspections. This instruction was apparently contained in a Home Office booklet entitled 'Notes for the Guidance of Police Officers', published in 1939. No copies were available to the Inquiry.

3.24 In this way, the role of the CIO evolved from that described in the 1921 Circular (see paragraph 3.13), which focussed primarily upon compliance with the 1921 Regulations by pharmacists. Now, the police were also instructed to look at what individual patients were receiving and were seeking to identify addicts.

Continuing Problems with Diversion

3.25 The Dangerous Drugs Act 1951 consolidated the previous legislation and the Dangerous Drugs Regulations 1953 consolidated and updated previous Regulations.

3.26 In February 1956, the Home Office issued a publication giving guidance to doctors and dentists about dangerous drugs. Doctors were reminded of their obligations and of the limitation of their authority to possess and supply dangerous drugs. A practitioner could do so only **'so far as may be necessary for the practice or exercise of his profession'**. The publication warned that there had been cases in which doctors and dentists had been convicted of offences under the dangerous drugs legislation for having obtained drugs, ostensibly for use in their practices, and having subsequently diverted them **'to the gratification of their own addiction'**.

United Nations Conventions

3.27 Beginning with the 1912 Convention, successive international treaties had modified the systems of international control and the list of drugs controlled, notably by the addition of synthetic opiates and cannabis and cannabis resin. Whenever necessary, domestic law was amended to accommodate those changes. The 1961 United Nations Single

Convention on Narcotic Drugs (the 1961 Convention) replaced all the earlier international agreements governing the control of narcotic substances, including opiates, cocaine, cannabis and cannabis resin (but not lysergide (LSD) or amphetamines). It required national governments to place restrictions on particular narcotic drugs (including heroin, morphine, cocaine and cannabis), limiting their use to medical and scientific purposes. The UK ratified this Convention on 2nd September 1964 and the Dangerous Drugs Act 1964 enacted the provisions necessary for compliance. The Dangerous Drugs Act 1965 consolidated the Acts of 1951 and 1964.

3.28   Mr Alan Macfarlane is the current Chief Inspector of the Home Office Drugs Inspectorate. In evidence to the Inquiry, he explained that the 1961 Convention led very quickly to a much more organised approach to the licensing of the manufacture and wholesale supply of dangerous drugs and to improved compilation of statistical data for transmission to the United Nations (UN). The intention was for the UN to be in a position to monitor the use of dangerous drugs worldwide.

3.29   The problems arising from the misuse of LSD, amphetamines and other hallucinogens, which were outside the ambit of the 1961 Convention, were addressed domestically by the Drugs (Prevention of Misuse) Act 1964 (the 1964 Act). The 1964 Act provided a measure of control by rendering unlawful the possession of amphetamines and certain other drugs, although it did not impose any regulatory controls on their prescribing or storage. Restrictions similar to those contained in the 1961 Convention were required by the 1971 United Nations Convention on Psychotropic Substances. The UK ratified this Convention in 1986.

The Work of the Brain Committee

The Appointment of the Brain Committee

3.30   In the late 1950s, new synthetic opiates were being manufactured. Doctors began to use them for therapeutic purposes but it was soon found that they were capable of producing addiction. Accordingly, in 1958, again at the instigation of the Home Office, the Department of Health and Social Security (DHSS) set up an Interdepartmental Committee to review the policy of using dangerous drugs for the treatment of addiction.

3.31   Sir Russell Brain was appointed as Chairman of the Interdepartmental Committee on Drug Addiction. Its Terms of Reference required it to:

> '... **review, in the light of more recent developments, the advice given by the Departmental Committee** (*i.e. the Rolleston Committee*) **on Morphine and Heroin Addiction in 1926; to consider whether any revised advice should also cover other drugs liable to produce addiction or to be habit-forming; to consider whether there is a medical need to provide special, including institutional, treatment outside the resources already available, for persons addicted to drugs; and to make recommendations, including proposals for any administrative measures that seem expedient, to the Minister of Health and the Secretary of State for Scotland'**.

The First Brain Report

3.32   The Committee's Report (the first Brain Report) was published in 1961. Its conclusions effectively endorsed the main conclusions of the Rolleston Report and supported the principle that all doctors should be allowed to continue to prescribe addictive drugs as part of treatment for dependence. The Chairman reported that there was no need for any change in the British approach. Specifically, the Report concluded that the incidence of addiction to controlled drugs in Great Britain was still very small and traffic in illicit supplies (with the exception of traffic in cannabis) was almost negligible. Irregular prescribing of dangerous drugs by doctors was an infrequent occurrence and further statutory controls were not justified. There was no need for a medical tribunal system (such as that suggested by the Rolleston Report) to be set up to consider cases of improper use of dangerous drugs by doctors. Instead, the Report concluded, it would be sufficient for doctors to obtain a second medical opinion before embarking on the regular prescribing of dangerous drugs to a patient. No advantage would arise from the use of distinctive prescription forms for dangerous drugs. The Report was publicly criticised for failing to recognise the extent of the problems of addiction in Great Britain.

The Second Brain Report

3.33   In fact, by the beginning of the 1960s, heroin addiction in the UK had begun to increase and the pattern of use was changing. For the first time, CIOs reported that there were more people addicted to heroin than to morphine. Most of the 'new' addicts lived in London. The heroin used was pharmaceutically pure and was thought to be coming from the prescribing practices of a small number of doctors. It appears that the failings of a few weak, elderly, incompetent or dishonest doctors were being exploited by addicts. There was also concern that some doctors were exhibiting little or no inclination to make any attempt at a cure when prescribing for addiction.

3.34   In July 1964, the Brain Committee was reconvened to consider whether, in the light of recent experience, the advice given in its first Report required revision and, if so, to make recommendations. In 1965, the second Brain Report gave advice that was materially different from that contained in the Committee's first Report. The Committee concluded that there was a major problem with addiction to heroin and cocaine, that the main source of supply of these two drugs was over-prescribing by a small number of doctors and that further measures were required to deal with this problem. Evidence was cited in the Report that, in 1962, one doctor alone had prescribed almost 600,000 tablets (i.e. 6kg) of heroin for addicts. On one occasion, that doctor had prescribed 900 tablets to an addict and then, three days later, had prescribed another 600 tablets for the same patient **'to replace pills lost in an accident'**. The Committee commented that the evidence showed that the doctors who had over-prescribed in this way had acted **'within the law and according to their professional judgement'**. It might well have been right that the actions of the doctors did not contravene the letter of the law. However, if the Committee thought that doctors who over-prescribed in this way had done so **'according to their professional judgement'**, its members must have thought that doctors had a very wide professional discretion. To modern eyes, it seems surprising that the Committee did not attempt to lay down any standards as to how a responsible doctor should act. Instead, it recommended a drastic curtailment of the power of doctors to prescribe heroin and cocaine for the treatment of addiction.

3.35   The Committee recommended that the right to prescribe heroin and cocaine (but not other drugs) to addicts should be limited to doctors on the staff of special treatment centres. It should be a statutory offence for other doctors to prescribe these drugs to an addict for the treatment of addiction. Disciplinary measures against doctors alleged to have prescribed these drugs irregularly should be the responsibility of the GMC. All addicts should be formally notified to a central authority which would keep a register of addicts. Doctors should be under a statutory duty to notify the authority responsible for keeping the register of any addict with whom s/he had come into a professional relationship. There was still no need, in the opinion of the Committee, to introduce a different prescription form for dangerous drugs but, when prescribing dangerous drugs, a doctor should indicate the quantities by words as well as figures. An advisory committee should be set up to keep under review the whole problem of drug addiction, which was acknowledged to be a **'changing problem'**.

The Dangerous Drugs Legislation of 1967 and 1968

3.36   The Dangerous Drugs Act 1967, the Dangerous Drugs (Supply to Addicts) Regulations 1968 and the Dangerous Drugs (Notification of Addicts) Regulations 1968 implemented some of the recommendations of the second Brain Report.

3.37   Under the Dangerous Drugs (Supply to Addicts) Regulations 1968, practitioners were prohibited from prescribing, supplying or administering heroin or cocaine to addicts, except in the treatment of organic disease or injury, unless they were specially authorised to do so by the Home Secretary. In practice, authorisation was given only to doctors working in special treatment clinics. Doctors who contravened these rules might have their right to prescribe these drugs removed by direction of the Home Secretary.

3.38   The Addicts Index was set up and doctors were required to report to the Home Office any person whom they considered to be addicted to any dangerous drug. A person was to be regarded as addicted to a drug if, as a result of repeated administration, s/he had become so dependent upon it that s/he had an overpowering desire for its administration to be continued. The Addicts Index remained in operation until 1997, when the Regulations requiring notification were revoked.

3.39   The Dangerous Drugs Act 1967 gave the Home Secretary the power to make a direction restricting the right of a doctor to prescribe, supply, possess or administer any controlled drug if s/he were found, by a tribunal, to be in breach of certain regulations governing the handling of controlled drugs or the terms of a licence. However, this power could not be exercised until a tribunal had been set up to investigate the allegations and make the necessary findings. It appears that the tribunal system was not set up until the early 1970s.

The Medicines Act 1968

3.40   The Medicines Act 1968 was introduced by the DHSS following a review of legislation relating to medicines prompted by the thalidomide tragedy in the 1960s. It brought together most of the previous legislation on medicines and introduced a number of other legal provisions for the control of medicines. It did not deal specifically with dangerous drugs but many of the requirements of the Act applied to dangerous drugs.

3.41 The Act divided medicinal drugs into three categories, depending mainly on the dangers they posed and the risk of misuse. The categories are:

(a) prescription only medicines, which may be sold or supplied to the public only on a practitioner's prescription. They may be administered only by or in accordance with directions from an appropriate practitioner, which term includes a medical practitioner. With the exception of controlled drug preparations below a certain strength set out in Schedule 5 to the Misuse of Drugs Regulations (MDR) 2001, all controlled drugs are prescription only medicines.

(b) pharmacy medicines, which, subject to certain exceptions, may be sold or supplied only from registered premises by, or under the supervision of, a pharmacist. Most products listed within Schedule 5 are pharmacy medicines.

(c) general sales list medicines, which may be sold or supplied direct to the public in an unopened manufacturer's pack from any lockable premises. No controlled drugs are general sales lists medicines.

The Legislation of 1971 and 1973

3.42 The MDA 1971 and the Regulations made under it in 1973 provided a new statutory framework for the control and regulation of **'dangerous or otherwise harmful'** drugs which, from this time, usually became known as 'controlled' drugs. The new legislation came into force in July 1973. The Act remains in force today. It repealed almost all the previous legislation and re-enacted many of its substantive provisions. The Regulations relating to addiction, which had come into force in 1968, were retained. The MDR 1973 were amended on many occasions and were replaced by the MDR 1985, which were in turn amended several times before being replaced by the Regulations currently in force, the MDR 2001.

3.43 Essentially, the MDA 1971 made it unlawful to possess or supply a controlled drug unless an exception or exemption applied. A number of specific offences were created, such as unlawful possession of a controlled drug and unlawful possession of a controlled drug with intent to supply it to another. A controlled drug was defined as any drug listed in Schedule 2 to the Act. Under Schedule 2, controlled drugs were divided into Classes A, B and C. Upon this classification depended the severity of the penalties that could be imposed under the criminal law for an infringement of the Act. Drugs such as heroin and cocaine were in Class A and the penalty imposed for committing, say, an offence of unlawful possession of heroin was more severe than that which could be imposed for unlawful possession of a drug from Class B or Class C. Class B contained such drugs as amphetamines and cannabis and Class C contained such drugs as benzodiazepines.

3.44 Section 10 of the Act empowered the Home Secretary to make regulations to prevent the misuse of controlled drugs with particular reference to safe custody, documentation, record keeping, furnishing information, packaging and labelling, transportation, destruction or disposal, prescribing, dispensing, and notification of and prescribing for addicts. Section 18 of the Act made it a criminal offence to breach any of the Regulations made under the Act or the terms of a licence granted under the Act.

3.45   Section 7 of the MDA 1971 allowed the Home Secretary to authorise activities that would otherwise be unlawful under the Act. It specifically required him to make regulations to **'secure . . . that it is not unlawful'** for a doctor, acting as such, to possess, prescribe, administer or supply controlled drugs or for a pharmacist or person conducting a pharmacy business to supply controlled drugs. Without such regulations, doctors and pharmacists would not be able to deal with controlled drugs in any way.

3.46   Section 13(2) of the MDA 1971 gave the Home Secretary a new power to prohibit a practitioner from dealing with controlled drugs where s/he had been **'prescribing, administering or supplying ... any controlled drugs in an irresponsible manner'**. Section 14 provided for the setting up of a tribunal system by which cases of alleged irresponsible prescribing could be investigated and a recommendation made to the Home Secretary with a view to possible curtailment of a doctor's powers to possess or prescribe controlled drugs. The power of the Home Secretary to withdraw the authority of a doctor who had been convicted of offences under the relevant legislation was preserved by section 12. As I explained in paragraph 3.21, this power had been introduced in the 1921 Regulations.

3.47   The Act also provided for the setting up of a statutory Advisory Council on the Misuse of Drugs (ACMD) to replace a non-statutory Interdepartmental Advisory Committee on Drug Dependence, which had provided advice since 1968. The main duty of the ACMD was to keep under review the situation in the UK in relation to drugs liable to misuse and to advise on measures to deal with any social problems caused by such misuse.

3.48   The MDR 1973 provided a code of Regulations governing the conduct of those people who were permitted to possess, prescribe, supply or administer a controlled drug under an exception to or exemption from the main provisions of the Act. The Regulations divided controlled drugs into categories according to the degree to which their use was to be regulated. Somewhat confusingly, instead of utilising the three Classes A, B and C under Schedule 2 to the MDA 1971, the Regulations divided all controlled drugs into four Schedules. Schedule 1 contained drugs that required little regulation. Schedule 2 contained such drugs as heroin and cocaine, which could be held and prescribed by doctors, dentists and veterinary surgeons; they were subject to quite stringent regulation. Schedule 3 contained very few drugs, which, somewhat illogically, were less regulated than those in Schedule 2. Schedule 4 contained the drugs to be most closely regulated. They could be dealt with only by persons specifically licensed to do so by the Home Office.

3.49   The MDR 1973 contained many provisions, most of which remain in force today, albeit after some amendment and consolidation in the MDR of 1985 and 2001. I shall mention only those of particular interest to the Inquiry. Pharmacists and doctors, acting in their capacity as such, were authorised to possess any controlled drug, save those in Schedule 4, and supply it to anyone who might lawfully possess it. Regulation 6 authorised persons such as police officers, customs officers, post office employees and carriers, acting as such, to be in lawful possession of controlled drugs and to supply them to anyone who might lawfully possess them. Any person lawfully in possession of a controlled drug was authorised to supply it to the person for whom it was obtained. The Regulations laid down formal requirements for prescriptions for controlled drugs, save those in Schedule 1. These included the requirement that the information on the prescription should be written in the prescriber's own hand. A controlled drug prescription was to be valid for only 13 weeks after the date of issue. Any person with authority to supply to another a controlled drug from Schedule 2 or 4 was under a duty to keep a chronological record of all such transactions in a controlled drugs register (CDR). The specifications relating to CDRs were also laid down. Records relating to controlled drugs, such as CDRs, were to be kept for at least two years from the date on which the last entry was made. Regulation 24 provided that controlled drugs from Schedules 2 and 4 could be lawfully destroyed by doctors and pharmacists only in the presence of a person authorised by the Home Secretary and that a record of such destruction should be kept. In practice, Home Office inspectors, CIOs and inspectors appointed by the RPSGB were authorised to witness the destruction of controlled drugs.

3.50 The Misuse of Drugs (Safe Custody) Regulations 1973, which, with some amendment, remain in force today, prescribe the arrangements for the physical security of controlled drugs held by any person entitled to hold a stock. The requirements apply only to drugs within Schedule 2 (apart from quinalbarbitone and some other liquid preparations), and a few from Schedule 3, to the MDR 2001. The occupiers of pharmacies, nursing homes and private hospitals must, so far as circumstances permit, keep the relevant controlled drugs in a **'locked safe, cabinet or room which is so constructed as to prevent unauthorised access to the drugs'**. The Regulations also provide a specification for the type of cabinet in which controlled drugs are to be stored. The duty of a GP who keeps a stock of controlled drugs is provided by regulation 5. Any person keeping a stock of controlled drugs must ensure that, if the drugs are not kept in a locked safe, cabinet or room so constructed as to prevent unauthorised access to the drugs, they are, so far as circumstances permit, kept in a locked receptacle which can be opened only by that person or by someone acting with his/her authority.

Amendment of the Misuse of Drugs Regulations between 1973 and 2001

3.51 The MDR 1973 were the subject of minor modifications on eight occasions between 1973 and 1984. Most of these changes brought further drugs under control. In 1984, dipipanone was included with heroin and cocaine on the list of drugs for which a special authority was required for a doctor to prescribe to addicts.

3.52 The first major revision resulted in the MDR 1985. The main substantive change was the introduction of a specific authority to patients to return prescribed controlled drugs to a medical practitioner or pharmacist for the purpose of destruction. The practitioner or pharmacist was allowed to destroy the drugs without formality, i.e. without their destruction being formally recorded or witnessed. This was designed to achieve the safe removal from the community of controlled drugs that might otherwise be diverted to the illicit market. The change had been recommended by the ACMD in its 1983 Report entitled 'Security of Controlled Drugs'.

3.53 The Schedules to the MDR were also extended and re-organised. The number of Schedules was increased from four to five and the 'order of precedence' was rationalised. Schedule 1 drugs were those for which a licence was required. Schedule 2 contained such drugs as heroin, morphine and cocaine, which were strictly regulated. Schedules 3, 4 and 5 contained drugs which were progressively less regulated. Schedule 5 drugs included 'weak' preparations containing a controlled drug that could be sold over the counter.

3.54 Subsequent amendments to the MDR 1985 comprised the addition of various drugs to one or other of the Schedules. In 1996, controls were extended to 48 anabolic and androgenic steroids and to six similar products, all liable to misuse by sportsmen and sportswomen. Temazepam and flunitrazepam were transferred from Schedule 4 to Schedule 3 in 1996 and 1998 respectively. In 2001, 36 additional substances were brought within the controls for the first time. 'Ecstasy' became a Schedule 1 drug.

The Duthie Report

3.55 In 1988, the Joint Sub-Committee of the Standing Medical, Nursing and Midwifery and Pharmaceutical Advisory Committees published a report entitled 'Guidelines for the Safe and Secure Handling of Medicines: A Report to the Secretary of State for Social Services'. The Sub-Committee was chaired by Professor Robert Duthie. It was set up following advice from the ACMD that current guidelines on the security of controlled drugs in hospitals should be updated and consolidated.

3.56 The Sub-Committee's Report, known as the Duthie Report, suggested guidelines for the procedures governing controlled drugs in the hospital sector. They were adopted and are still in use today. Their premise is that the need for the **'three Rs'** (reconciliation, record keeping and responsibility) applies to controlled drugs as it applies to all medicines. It seems to me that the 'three Rs' are very sound principles on which to base the rules and systems which should govern the use of controlled drugs in the community as well as in hospitals.

Inspection Arrangements

3.57 I mentioned earlier that, since the 1920s, police CIOs have been responsible for the inspection of controlled drugs arrangements and CDRs in pharmacies. This continues to be the case, although there are some police areas in which there is no CIO in post. I also said that the RMS of the Ministry of Health (later the DHSS, then the Department of Health) was responsible for visiting GPs' surgeries and for examining, among other things, the arrangements made by GPs in connection with controlled drugs. The RMS ceased to make such visits in 1991. Since that time, many GPs have not had their controlled drugs arrangements inspected. Many primary care organisations arrange for a medical adviser or a clinical governance lead to carry out an annual practice visit, although this has not been universal practice. In the past, such visits have not focussed on the arrangements for controlled drugs. In a few areas, police CIOs visit the premises of GPs who also provide a dispensing service. They have no statutory power to do so and it appears that such visits occur mainly by invitation, when the practice wants a CIO to witness the destruction of 'out of date' controlled drugs.

Ideas for Improvement

3.58   No further significant changes had been made to the legislative framework relating to controlled drugs by the time Shipman's crimes came to light in August 1998. Since the extent to which he used and abused diamorphine has been understood, there has been much discussion about how the systems of control should be improved. There has also been much debate about ways to modernise the present systems. I shall describe those ideas and proposals later in this Report.

3.59   For the moment, I say only that this brief summary of the historical development of the regulation of controlled drugs has revealed several matters that are of particular relevance to the issues facing the Inquiry in 2004. The danger attaching to the freedom of medical practitioners to prescribe, supply and administer controlled drugs for therapeutic purposes has been recognised for more than 80 years. If that freedom is to remain, as it must, it should be circumscribed in ways that minimise the risk of diversion without compromising patient care. Two particular ways in which the risk might be reduced were recognised in the 1920s but not implemented, namely the suggestions that doctors should not be allowed to prescribe dangerous drugs for themselves and that they should be able to prescribe only while **'in actual practice'**.

3.60   Also, certain specific practical arrangements have been considered in the past, but rejected or abandoned. For the time being, I shall highlight only two. The provision in the 1921 Regulations, that all private controlled drug prescriptions should be written on special forms, was not implemented, possibly because it was thought that the advantage accruing would be slight. This proposal is worthy of reconsideration now, with the advent of the computerised analysis of prescribing data.

3.61   Second, from the very beginning of the routine police inspection of pharmacies, it was suggested by the police that it might not be a suitable body to carry out the task. As the nature of pharmacy practice has become more refined, it may be said that there is an even greater need now for some specialist expertise to be introduced into pharmacy inspection.

3.62   I shall return to all these issues in Chapter Fourteen of this Report.

CHAPTER FOUR

The Authority of a Medical Practitioner to Prescribe, Possess, Supply and Administer Controlled Drugs

Introduction

4.1 In the preceding Chapter, I have set out a brief historical background to the authority of medical practitioners to prescribe, possess, supply and administer controlled drugs. In this Chapter, I shall deal with a number of issues that arise from this authority.

4.2 The Misuse of Drugs Regulations (MDR) 2001 provide that doctors, acting in their capacity as such, may possess any controlled drug (save those in Schedule 1 to the MDR 2001), and may supply it to anyone who may lawfully possess it. That is subject to the rule that I mentioned in Chapter Three, to the effect that only doctors who have been specially authorised may prescribe, supply or administer cocaine, diamorphine or dipipanone for the treatment of addiction. Accordingly, any doctor who is registered with the General Medical Council (GMC), and who is not subject to any prescribing restrictions, has the general freedom to prescribe, possess, supply and administer controlled drugs. This is subject to the safe custody requirement and the requirement to keep a controlled drugs register (CDR), which apply to the stocks of some controlled drugs held personally. Doctors may lawfully prescribe any controlled drug (other than a Schedule 1 drug) in any quantity or strength, on either a private or a NHS prescription. The medical register kept by the GMC includes retired doctors, doctors who work in purely administrative posts, doctors who work in the pharmaceutical industry and doctors whose area of specialism may never require them to prescribe controlled drugs. In Chapter Three, I mentioned that, in the 1920s, it was suggested that only doctors **'in actual practice'** should be entitled to prescribe controlled drugs but this limitation was never enacted.

Guidance to General Practitioners on Good Practice in the Prescribing of Controlled Drugs

4.3 General practitioners (GPs) prescribe controlled drugs in a wide variety of situations. Schedule 2 drugs, which include the opiates such as diamorphine, are commonly used in the care of patients with terminal illness. The use of diamorphine for the relief of acute cardiac pain has decreased as a result of the improved care provided by the ambulance service. Nonetheless, there remain a wide variety of circumstances in which a GP might need to prescribe or use a controlled drug.

4.4 Only a minority of doctors (e.g. those working in the fields of addiction or palliative care) have received any specific training in the prescribing of controlled drugs or in their duties in relation to the Misuse of Drugs Act 1971 (MDA 1971) and the MDR 2001. However, some guidance on good practice is available. In 1999, for example, the Department of Health updated its 'Drug Misuse and Dependence – Guidelines on Clinical Management', previously issued in 1991. This document affirms that a doctor has an ethical responsibility to treat all patients and that GPs treating individuals for drug misuse have a right to support from their primary care organisation. It reminds doctors that treatment for addiction, when it involves the prescribing of controlled drugs, leads inevitably to the potential for diversion of the drugs and to the consequent tension between the health imperative and the need to reduce illicit drug use.

4.5   In setting out the responsibilities and principles for prescribing for drug dependence, the Guidelines recommend that doctors should keep good, clear, handwritten or computerised records of prescribing. Doctors are advised to liaise with the dispensing pharmacist about each patient and his/her prescribing regime. They are also advised that no more than one week's supply of drugs should be dispensed at a time, save in exceptional circumstances. The patient should be told that methadone and other controlled drugs must be kept out of reach of children. Special vigilance is urged with regard to the security of drugs, prescription pads and headed notepaper. The requirements of the MDA 1971 and MDR 2001 are explained.

4.6   The GMC does not currently provide guidance specifically related to controlled drugs, although it provides general advice on prescribing in its booklet 'Good Medical Practice'.

Problems with Controlled Drugs

4.7   The general freedom to prescribe reflects the desirable principle that doctors should enjoy clinical autonomy over their treatment of patients. However, it gives rise to undesirable consequences when doctors abuse that freedom and prescribe, supply and administer drugs unlawfully, inappropriately or irresponsibly. It may also give rise to a temptation for a doctor to prescribe for him/herself or for relatives and friends in circumstances where such prescribing may be unwise and not in the patient's best interest.

4.8   While the great majority of doctors behave honestly, appropriately and responsibly in their dealings with controlled drugs, there exists a minority which does not. Unlawful, irresponsible and inappropriate prescribing practices are damaging to the interests of patients, the medical profession and the public. In my view, it is important that any abuse of the doctor's prescribing privilege should be prevented where possible and detected and stopped when it occurs.

4.9   The Inquiry's focus is necessarily on doctors – GPs in particular. The law is changing, however, and some nurses and other healthcare professionals are now permitted to prescribe controlled drugs. There is no reason to believe that the problems posed by the doctor who prescribes dishonestly, irresponsibly or inappropriately will not also arise with the new categories of prescribers.

Dishonest Prescribing

4.10   While in Todmorden, Shipman repeatedly obtained supplies of pethidine for the purpose of self-administration. Because he was not acting in good faith in his capacity as a medical practitioner, he was in unlawful possession of the drug. When he wrote a prescription in the name of a patient who was not going to receive the drug, he obtained possession of the drug by deception. When he signed a false name on the back of the prescription, purporting to claim exemption from the prescription charge on behalf of the patient, he was guilty of forgery. In 1976, he was convicted of a range of offences. Every year, the courts and the GMC have to deal with a number of doctors who have behaved in a similar way. Some seek to obtain illicit supplies of controlled drugs to feed their own drug habit, as Shipman did in the 1970s. It seems likely that there will be very few indeed who, like Shipman, go on to obtain supplies for the purpose of killing patients. Some, however, make a living out of prescribing or supplying to addicts in breach of the law. The following are examples of the kind of unlawful conduct which has been brought to the Inquiry's attention.

Supplying Controlled Drugs for Monetary Gain

4.11   In 1998, Dr A was convicted of conspiracy to obtain controlled drugs, including Rohypnol (the so-called 'date rape' drug), by deception and to supply controlled drugs including Dexedrine and Seconal. Between January 1995 and February 1997, she wrote more than 70 private prescriptions for controlled drugs. Each prescription was for an amount that would have represented up to a year's normal supply of the drug. Each prescription was made out in the name of a different person and the drugs were collected from a pharmacy by the same third party in each case. This practice came to the attention of the police and, in interview, Dr A suggested that she habitually provided controlled drug prescriptions for her 'patients' without examining them. She did not keep any records for these 'patients'. Police enquiries failed to locate even one genuine patient. On one occasion, according to press reports of her trial, Dr A had written three bogus prescriptions and had received £250 in cash for each prescription. Evidence in the case suggested that the price payable by the patient for each tablet was about 20 pence compared to the 'street value' of up to £5. At the time of sentencing, Dr A was 63 and was described as a semi-retired GP who worked in the field of drug addiction. She was sentenced to a suspended term of imprisonment.

4.12   In 2002, Dr B was convicted of the unlawful supply of controlled drugs, including diazepam, Rohypnol and Dexedrine. He had been prepared to issue private prescriptions for a controlled drug on payment of £30. He did not examine the 'patient' in any way. He often issued prescriptions in a false name, thereby making detection less likely. He was also prepared to sell controlled drugs such as diazepam and Rohypnol from his own supplies to callers on demand. These callers could not, in any true sense, be described as patients. In 1988, Dr B had been visited by Home Office inspectors and warned about his prescribing of controlled drugs. Dr B had given up practice as a GP in 1992 but had returned to do locum work in 1993. He was working as a salaried assistant at the time of the offences but had agreed to see some former 'patients' on a private basis at his home. Over a period of four to five months before his detection, he was seeing about 20 to 25 'private patients' a week. Most of these were addicts recommended to him by other addicts.

4.13   In another case, the suspicion was that Dr C supplemented his living by selling temazepam capsules. His method was to select patients who were entitled to free medication on the NHS. He would write a prescription for the medication they required and include an order for 60 temazepam capsules. He would instruct the patient to go to the pharmacy and then to bring back the medication for him to check. He would then remove and keep the temazepam. It was found that he had done this on 16 occasions, thereby obtaining 960 capsules. At the time, these had a street value of about £3 to £4 each. In 1996, Dr C admitted his guilt and was sentenced to three months' imprisonment.

4.14   Another doctor, Dr D, supplied drug users with Diconal (dipipanone) tablets, methadone mixture and temazepam capsules and tablets. He also issued private prescriptions for controlled drugs, on demand, for a charge of £10 or £15. The names and the addresses on the prescriptions were fictitious. As a single-handed practitioner, he had a very small list of patients. Drug users from surrounding areas visited him, knowing that he would be prepared to supply drugs or issue a prescription without asking questions. A total of 174 patients (half his list) were being prescribed controlled drugs. Dr D was warned about his conduct by a Home Office Drugs Inspector. Three months later, the doctor was found to be continuing in his old course of conduct. He was arrested but not prosecuted. The case was reported to the GMC and he was erased from the medical register in 1994. It was suggested by Counsel for the GMC that the doctor had acted with the intention of increasing his patient list and not with the best interests of his patients in mind.

Obtaining Controlled Drugs to Feed the Doctor's Addiction

4.15   It has long been recognised that the ease of access of doctors to controlled drugs gives rise to an increased risk of addiction. Doctors who become addicted to a controlled drug usually obtain their supplies either by prescribing it for themselves or by using supplies taken from the practice stock. In research carried out by Brooke, Edwards and Taylor, reported in 'Addiction as an Occupational Hazard'[1], the records of 144 doctors who had been treated for drug and alcohol problems at two London hospitals were analysed. It was found that 83 of the 144 had been addicted to a controlled drug. Only four of the 83 had resorted to black market supplies. The usual means of supply were self-prescribing, prescribing for self but in the name of another, taking practice supplies and keeping 'patient returns'. On average, the doctors had misused the controlled drug for over six years before seeking treatment.

4.16   The Inquiry learned of several cases of GPs who had become addicted to a controlled drug and had been brought before the criminal courts. Dr E was a GP who, in 2000, pleaded guilty to six counts of unlawful possession of diamorphine, and seven counts of obtaining property by deception. Over 400 offences of a similar nature were taken into consideration. He had offended, over a period of seven years, for the purpose of feeding his own addiction. In the early days, he obtained diamorphine on requisition and took possession of unused drugs when a patient died. Later, he began to prescribe diamorphine and morphine in the names of genuine patients who, in some cases, were terminally ill. He obtained the drugs without payment by using a NHS prescription form and signing on the reverse, claiming that he was the patient's representative and the patient was entitled to free medication. All three of these methods of obtaining were also used by Shipman. Dr E was made the subject of a probation order. When the case was referred to the GMC, Dr E entered the voluntary health procedures and was allowed to

---

[1] published in the *British Journal of Addiction* 1991; 86:1011–1016

continue in practice, subject to conditions. From 2003, he was allowed to practise without restriction.

4.17 Dr F was dependent on diamorphine. He obtained his supplies by writing NHS prescriptions in the names of patients and arranging for the drugs to be delivered to his surgery. The patients did not need, and did not receive, the drugs. There were no entries in the patient records. The doctor also kept and used a quantity of the controlled drug dihydrocodeine, returned to him by a patient for destruction. In 2003, he pleaded guilty to a large number of offences of deception and unlawful possession.

4.18 Dr G was addicted to pethidine. Using signed orders, he obtained the drug in both tablet and ampoule form from four pharmacies in the area in which he practised. After his activities had come to the notice of the police chemist inspection officer (CIO), he was interviewed by the Home Office Drugs Inspectorate (HODI). He claimed that the drugs he had bought had been used on patients. He was advised about his duty to keep a CDR. He continued to obtain pethidine on signed orders and this came to the attention of the CIO. In the course of a police interview, Dr G admitted that the drugs were for his own use. In 1999 he pleaded guilty to two charges of unlawful possession of pethidine and asked for 32 further cases to be taken into consideration. He was put on probation for 12 months.

Irresponsible Prescribing

4.19 I have dealt so far with doctors who prescribed dishonestly and broke the law. Others abuse their privilege by prescribing drugs in a way that complies with the law but is irresponsible. Sometimes, a doctor will prescribe on the basis that s/he is treating a patient for organic disease while carelessly turning a blind eye to the fact that the patient is addicted. In other cases, the doctor will prescribe in quantities far in excess of those reasonably needed by the patient, who then sells the excess on the black market to finance his/her next supply. Private patients have to pay for the prescription, as well as for the drugs, and will sometimes sell part of their supply in order to finance their next prescription. Patients will sometimes obtain supplies from more than one source (e.g. from one doctor on the NHS and from another privately), a practice known as 'double scripting'. There is no legal duty on a doctor providing a private prescription to ascertain whether the patient is already receiving drugs on the NHS or whether s/he can afford to pay for the prescription and the drugs to be dispensed. Connivance with, or turning a blind eye to, this kind of conduct is irresponsible. Mr Stephen Lutener, former Head of Professional Conduct of the Royal Pharmaceutical Society of Great Britain (RPSGB), said that such practices cause considerable problems in London, where most private GPs practise.

4.20 The Inquiry heard about a number of such cases. Typically, the doctor would be prescribing prescriptions for controlled drugs for 'patients' who attended the surgery but who were not receiving real medical attention. A fee would be charged but there would be virtually no examination of the 'patient' and no records would be kept. Nor would the doctor make any attempt to contact the usual medical practitioners of the 'patients'. There would be no clear breach of the MDR but such prescribing would be highly irresponsible.

4.21 Such doctors appear to make a business out of irresponsible prescribing. Others behave irresponsibly as the result of naïveté rather than bad faith. Some doctors, particularly when old or frail, become the prey of drug addicts, who soon learn when it is possible to persuade a doctor to prescribe controlled drugs. Addicts will often approach a doctor with a plausible story about the urgent need for a controlled drug for the relief of pain. If the doctor believes the story of one addict and provides a prescription, other addicts soon learn where to go. One is bound to feel some sympathy for the doctor who unwittingly finds him/herself in a situation that might well become quite intimidating. Such cases, when discovered by the authorities, are usually dealt with by the giving of advice as to how to avoid the problem. Only the more serious cases of irresponsible prescribing would be the subject of any formal disciplinary proceedings for serious professional misconduct before the GMC.

4.22   The Inquiry has also become aware of concern that some doctors prescribe drugs such as benzodiazepines in larger quantities than is either necessary or appropriate. Guidance was issued by the Committee on Safety in Medicines in 1988, advising GPs not to prescribe these drugs for long-term use but to limit them to the short-term treatment of patients with distressing symptoms of anxiety or insomnia. The main reason behind this guidance was that it was realised that benzodiazepines are addictive and can be dangerous. However, there is now another cause for concern. It appears that some patients who receive a regular supply on prescription sell part of their stock; in effect the drugs go onto 'the street'. Although the prescribing of benzodiazepines has declined substantially since 1988, it appears that many GPs still do not heed the 1988 guidance and continue to prescribe substantial quantities of benzodiazepines over a long period. In the Chief Medical Officer's 'Update 37', issued to all doctors in January 2004, he estimated that 14% of substance misusers attending drug treatment centres reported benzodiazepine use subsidiary to their main drug use. The DoH is planning to introduce instalment dispensing of benzodiazepines for addicted patients in order to minimise access to large quantities.

Unwise Prescribing

The Doctor Who Self-Prescribes or Prescribes for Family and Friends

4.23   Although it is discouraged by the GMC, it is not unlawful for a doctor to treat him/herself or members of his/her own family. The doctor has the right to prescribe, supply or administer all controlled drugs to any person, including him/herself and members of his/her family, for the treatment of organic disease. It appears that s/he can also prescribe or administer the usual range of controlled drugs to such persons for the treatment of addiction. I have already mentioned in Chapter Three that it was proposed in the 1920s that doctors should not be allowed to prescribe controlled drugs for themselves and that the proposal was shelved in the face of opposition from the British Medical Association (BMA).

4.24   The legal position under the MDR 2001 is that a doctor is authorised to possess any controlled drug provided that s/he does so **'when acting in his**(*/her*) **capacity as such'**, i.e. in his/her capacity as a medical practitioner. In the leading case of R v Dunbar[2], a doctor was convicted of the unlawful possession of a quantity of pethidine and

---

[2] [1982] 1 All ER 188

diamorphine which he had obtained from a pharmacy on a signed order, stating that it was required for 'professional purposes'. He had admitted to the police that he had obtained the drugs for self-administration. It was alleged by the prosecution that the doctor had told the police that he had obtained the drugs with the intention of killing himself but, in evidence, he denied saying that and claimed that he had obtained them in order to treat himself for depression. The trial judge directed the jury to convict on the basis that any obtaining with the intention of self-administration was unlawful. The Court of Appeal held that the trial judge's direction had been wrong. Under regulation 10(1) of the MDR 1973, a doctor who, in good faith, prescribed or obtained on signed order a controlled drug for his/her own treatment was entitled to have the drug in his/her possession. The Court of Appeal decided that the issue whether, on that occasion, the doctor had acted in good faith in his capacity as a medical practitioner (as opposed to having obtained the drug for the purpose of committing suicide or for some other unlawful purpose) was an issue for the jury to decide.

4.25   It should be noted that, on the facts of the case of Dunbar, there was no question of the doctor treating himself for addiction. It appears that the courts have never considered this issue. However, it seems to me that such a practice is not unlawful, although I hope that the GMC would take a serious view of it. Nor is it unlawful for a doctor to prescribe controlled drugs for members of his/her family or for friends, whether for the treatment of organic disease or for the treatment of addiction, provided that s/he is acting in good faith in his/her capacity as a medical practitioner.

4.26   Although that is the legal position, there are good reasons to suggest that it is unwise for a doctor to prescribe for him/herself, friends and family. The GMC, the Royal College of General Practitioners and the BMA all regard such prescribing of any drugs as poor practice. The BMA guidance on prescribing, which is not limited to controlled drugs, appears in 'Medical Ethics Today', the BMA's handbook of ethics and law (2nd edition) in the following terms[3]:

> **'The BMA and the GMC advise doctors against prescribing for themselves or for family, friends and colleagues. There are clearly some cases, such as in an emergency situation, in which such action would be reasonable but as a general rule it should be avoided. There is a risk that doctors who self treat may ignore or deny serious health problems or may simply treat symptoms without taking steps to identify the underlying cause. There is also a risk that self-prescribing could lead to drug abuse or addiction; ...**
>
> **Treating family, friends, and colleagues could raise questions about the objectivity of the advice provided and, although the same duty of confidentiality would apply, raises issues of privacy for the family members and friends. One-off prescribing for family and friends, except in exceptional circumstances, is also to be avoided because this could interfere with care or treatment being provided by the patient's usual**

---

[3] published 2004 by BMJ Books

doctor. There is also a risk that, if the patient is harmed by the medication, the doctor's motives could be called into question.'

4.27   It seems clear that it is sensible for a doctor to ensure that any controlled drug required by him/herself or by a friend or family member is prescribed by a doctor who is at 'arm's length' and in a proper professional relationship with the patient. I can see that it might not be appropriate to prohibit a doctor altogether from prescribing such drugs for him/herself, family or friends. If this were not permitted in an emergency, it might give rise to unacceptable delay in treatment. However, it seems to me that such prescribing for the treatment of chronic organic conditions and, worse still, for the treatment of addiction is extremely undesirable. I shall consider in Chapter Fourteen whether and to what extent the present position should be changed.

Prescribing for 'Casual' or Occasional Patients

4.28   The current legal position is that there need be no formal relationship between a doctor and the patient for whom s/he prescribes controlled drugs. Accordingly, a doctor is entitled to prescribe any drug, including a controlled drug, to any patient whom the doctor is willing to see, even on an entirely isolated occasion. In most cases, there will be nothing improper or unwise about such a consultation, even when it results in the prescription of a controlled drug. However, at present, there is no way in which the doctor can readily acquaint him/herself with the patient's previous medical or drug history. In future, when (as it is intended) all NHS records will be accessible to all NHS doctors on a national electronic system (the NHS Care Record), the position will be easier. However, at present, a doctor who prescribes a controlled drug to an unknown patient, without first speaking to the patient's usual GP, risks not only prescribing something that might interact badly with other drugs being taken by the patient but also the possibility that the patient is obtaining a controlled drug from two doctors concurrently or, in other words, is double scripting.

4.29   In the current edition of 'Good Medical Practice', the GMC advises doctors to:

> **'... prescribe drugs or treatment, including repeat prescriptions, only when you have adequate knowledge of the patient's health and medical needs'**.

It seems to me that the GMC and/or the BMA might think it appropriate to include special advice in their respective guidance about the particular dangers of prescribing a controlled drug without adequate knowledge of the patient's history.

Powers to Restrict the Rights of a Practitioner in Respect of Controlled Drugs

The Power of the Home Office to Restrict a Doctor's Rights Following Conviction

4.30   In Chapter Three, I explained the historical background to the power of the Home Secretary to restrict the right of a doctor to deal with controlled drugs. In brief, since 1921, if a doctor has been convicted of certain criminal offences involving controlled drugs, the Home Secretary has had the power to make a direction restricting the doctor's right to possess, prescribe, supply or administer any controlled drug or type of controlled drug named in the direction. The current power is to be found in section 12 of the MDA 1971. The power to make a direction does not apply where the doctor has been cautioned but not prosecuted, despite the fact that a caution cannot be issued unless the doctor has admitted an offence. Nor does the power apply where the doctor has been found guilty of an offence but has been given an absolute or conditional discharge or put on probation. In the past, the power was used to prevent doctors who were convicted of offences involving unlawful possession or supply of controlled drugs or obtaining such drugs by deception from prescribing or having any dealings with such drugs while the direction remained in force.

4.31   On receiving notification of a conviction, a Home Office official would prepare a case for possible submission to the Home Secretary. As part of that preparation, the Home Office would consult with the Department of Health and Social Security (DHSS) and would enquire of the GMC as to what action, if any, it intended to take upon the doctor's registration. If the GMC did not intend any positive action and if the DHSS was against the making of a direction, it would be very unlikely that one would be made, although the discretion remained with the Home Secretary.

4.32   It would have been open to the Home Secretary of the day to make a direction under this section against Shipman in 1976, but, for reasons that I shall explain in Chapter Ten, none was made. The Home Office provided the Inquiry with a number of files relating to cases in which section 12 directions (or directions made under previous legislation) had been made against doctors between 1969 and 1986. The evidence suggests that such directions were made from time to time until 1976, when there was a policy change. Up to that time, they were being made in cases where a doctor had, on a number of occasions, obtained a controlled drug unlawfully, whether in order to feed his/her own addiction or in order to make money through improper supply to others. However, it appears that, after 1976, as a result of the policy change, only doctors convicted of offences involving the supply of drugs to others were made the subject of a section 12 direction. Doctors who offended only in order to feed their own addiction, and in whose cases there was no evidence of any adverse impact on patients' well-being, were not subjected to any official restriction.

4.33   Thereafter, very few directions were made and it appears that the provision has not been used at all since about 1994; it was last used against a doctor (as opposed to a pharmacist or other healthcare professional) in 1986. Mr Alan Macfarlane, Chief Inspector of the HODI, explained that there is little point in the Home Office exercising this power now that the GMC has the power to impose conditions and restrictions upon a doctor's right to prescribe. The GMC usually becomes aware of any relevant conviction and the view is taken by the Home Office that the GMC is in a better position than the Home Office to make a decision. Few, if any, section 12 directions now remain in force.

The Power of the Home Office to Restrict a Doctor's Rights by Reason of Irresponsible Prescribing

4.34   As I explained in Chapter Three, it was recognised as early as 1926 that some power was needed to control the activities of doctors who abused their privilege of prescribing controlled drugs. From 1967, the Home Secretary had the power to make a direction restricting the right of a doctor to prescribe, supply, possess or administer any controlled drug if s/he were found to be in breach of certain regulations governing the handling of controlled drugs or the terms of a licence. This power was not exercised until after the passage of the MDA 1971, section 13 of which extended it to include any doctor who was found by a tribunal to have been prescribing **'in an irresponsible manner'**. There was no statutory definition of **'irresponsible'**. During a House of Commons debate on the Misuse of Drugs Bill in 1970, the then Home Secretary spoke of the measure as being designed to deal with **'careless, negligent or unduly liberal prescribing'**. In the 20 years during which the section 13 provision was applied, it was never considered by the courts and, as a result, there was never any authoritative definition of irresponsible prescribing.

4.35   Setting in motion the tribunal proceedings that were a necessary preliminary to a section 13 direction was always an option of last resort for the Home Office. The first response to a suspicion of irresponsible prescribing was to contact the doctor and seek to persuade him/her to alter his/her prescribing practice. Only if such measures failed would section 13 proceedings be commenced, and the authority of a senior official was required before this could be done. The proceedings were extremely cumbersome. Mr Macfarlane described the process as 'tortuous'. The Home Office was, in effect, the prosecutor of the proceedings before the tribunal. Preparation of the evidence and making the arrangements for a hearing might well take up to a year. When a date had been set, there were often adjournments for one reason or another. Why the processes of evidence gathering and setting a date should have taken so long is not clear but the evidence to the Inquiry was that they did.

4.36   When the case eventually came before the tribunal, all involved were handicapped by the absence of any statutory definition of what constituted prescribing **'in an irresponsible manner'**. It was, according to Mr Macfarlane, necessary to consider the detail of many individual prescribing transactions in order to establish 'beyond argument' a pattern of prescribing that was susceptible to only one conclusion, namely that it was irresponsible. If an adverse finding was made, the tribunal could recommend to the Home Secretary that a section 13 direction should be made. The Home Office had to give notice to the doctor of the intention to make a direction, setting out its proposed terms. The doctor could then make representations. If s/he did not, the direction could be made but, if s/he did, the Home Office had to refer these representations to a specially constituted advisory body. That body would advise the Home Secretary as to the exercise of his powers. On receipt of that advice, the Home Secretary could make a direction but he might or might not direct that the case be remitted to the tribunal or to a differently constituted tribunal. I understand why Mr Macfarlane described the process as 'tortuous'.

4.37   Mr Macfarlane said that only 14 section 13 orders were made between 1974 and 1993. He believes that about 25 to 30 cases went before a tribunal in the period between 1973, when section 13 came into force, and 1997, when the last case was concluded. The final nail in the section 13 coffin was a case that became very protracted owing to adjournments and concurrent police investigations. When eventually the case came before a tribunal, the tribunal made a limited recommendation that was contested by the doctor. The proceedings became yet more protracted and eventually failed on the ground of excessive delay.

4.38   Since the early 1990s, the Home Office has not instituted any new applications under section 13. Not only was the procedure slow and ineffective, it was considered by the Home Office that the GMC was better placed to provide effective control over doctors who had prescribed irresponsibly. Mr Macfarlane is satisfied with the way in which the GMC has handled such cases.

The Power of the General Medical Council in Respect of a Practitioner Convicted of a Criminal Offence

4.39   I shall consider the role of the GMC in the Fifth Report. For the present, it suffices to say that, where a doctor is convicted of offences concerning controlled drugs, or where there is evidence before the GMC that a doctor has prescribed controlled drugs irresponsibly or even unwisely, s/he is at least potentially liable to disciplinary action. This might result in the imposition of conditions or restrictions upon his/her continued practice or even, in a really serious case, in erasure from the medical register.

4.40   In the 1970s, when Shipman was referred to the GMC, its powers were very limited. It could erase or suspend a doctor from the medical register but could not impose any restriction or condition upon a doctor while allowing him/her to continue in practice. Since 1980, the GMC's powers have increased and the imposition of restrictions on the right to possess, prescribe, supply or administer controlled drugs, or a particular class of controlled drug, is not uncommon. In some cases, where a doctor is addicted to a drug, s/he will enter the GMC health procedures and will usually give undertakings as to the conditions under which s/he can continue to practise. These might well include a restriction on the right to prescribe or possess certain controlled drugs.

The Power of a Primary Care Organisation to Restrict a Doctor's Right to Prescribe Controlled Drugs

4.41   Since 2001, a primary care organisation has had the power, under the provisions of sections 49F and 49G of the National Health Service Act 1977 (as amended), to remove a GP from its medical list or to impose conditions upon the doctor's continued inclusion on the medical list. The power to impose conditions on inclusion can be invoked only on the ground of prejudice to efficiency or fraud. At least in theory, these powers could be used to restrict the right of a doctor to prescribe controlled drugs following a relevant conviction or a finding of irresponsible prescribing, although the Inquiry is not aware of any case in which this has occurred.

Notification of Restrictions to Pharmacists

4.42   Although the Home Office and the GMC have for a long time had the power to make orders restricting a doctor's right to prescribe controlled drugs, the Inquiry was told that the arrangements by which information about doctors who are made subject to such restrictions is disseminated to pharmacists are not satisfactory. The MDA 1971 provides for publication of directions made under sections 12 and 13 in the London, Edinburgh and Belfast Gazettes, thereby recognising the need for proper notice to be given to the public. Not only have section 12 and 13 directions fallen out of use, publication in the Gazettes can no longer be regarded as a satisfactory means of bringing such matters to public notice. Until about ten years ago, the RPSGB used to publish periodically a cumulative list of doctors who were subject to section 12 and section 13 directions. This practice came to an end in unfortunate circumstances. The prohibition on one doctor whose name was on the list was removed after the draft had been sent to the printers. He was not pleased that his name still appeared when the list was published. Thereafter, the RPSGB, realising that it could not keep its list fully up to date, abandoned the publication and now publishes the telephone number of the Home Office so that pharmacists can check the current status of an individual prescriber. However, this is not satisfactory, as the telephone line is not manned continuously and pharmacists cannot access the information at night or at weekends.

4.43   The GMC does not circulate information to pharmacists about GMC restrictions upon a doctor's prescribing rights. If a pharmacist is in doubt about the status of a doctor who has signed a prescription, s/he can telephone the GMC and will be given the necessary information. However, this service is available only during working hours. Out of hours, the pharmacist can obtain some information from the GMC website or by means of an automated answering service, but these do not provide information about restrictions or conditions attached to a doctor's registration. For that information, it is necessary to speak to a GMC caseworker. It seems to me that these difficulties must be resolved.

Conclusion

4.44   It is an almost inevitable corollary of the doctor's general freedom to prescribe controlled drugs that some will abuse that freedom. Some do so dishonestly and/or to feed their own habit; others may do so out of naïveté or weakness. The potential for significant harm is present whatever the motive or state of mind of the practitioner in question. Some cases have come to light where abuses have continued for many years before they were detected. Some abuses may never be detected. Better systems are needed to deter, prevent and detect such behaviour. In Chapter Fourteen, I shall consider ways by which these objectives might be achieved.

CHAPTER FIVE

Arrangements for Dealing with Controlled Drugs in General Practitioners' Surgeries

Introduction

5.1 In Chapters Three and Four, I mentioned some of the requirements imposed upon general practitioners (GPs) by the Misuse of Drugs Act 1971 (MDA 1971), the Misuse of Drugs Regulations (MDR) 1973–2001 and the Misuse of Drugs (Safe Custody) Regulations 1973 (the Safe Custody Regulations). I shall describe them in a little more detail in this Chapter. They are set out in tabular form at Appendix C to this Report.

Legislation

5.2 Regulation 5 of the Safe Custody Regulations requires a GP who keeps stocks of certain controlled drugs (otherwise than in a locked safe, cabinet or room which is so constructed as to prevent unauthorised access to the drugs) to store them in a locked receptacle, which can be opened only by the GP or someone acting on his/her authority. The regulation applies to all controlled drugs in Schedule 2 to the MDR 2001 (except quinalbarbitone) and to a small number in Schedule 3. The receptacle is usually the 'doctor's bag'.

5.3 Regulation 19 of the MDR 2001 requires GPs who keep a stock of Schedule 2 drugs to maintain a controlled drugs register (CDR) detailing the particulars of every such drug obtained and supplied by him/her. A separate CDR or a separate part of it has to be used for each controlled drug. The form of the CDR is illustrated in Schedule 6 to the Regulations. However, this Schedule shows only a blank table with a series of unidentified columns. Regulation 20 requires that the class of drugs to which the entries on a given page relate shall be specified at the top of that page. Every entry must be made on the day of the supply or, if that is not reasonably practicable, on the following day. Corrections must be indelible and made by a note in the margin or as a footnote. Cancellations, obliterations and alterations are not allowed. The CDR is not to be used for any purpose other than the purpose of the Regulations.

5.4 Under regulation 27 of the MDR 2001, GPs who keep a stock of Schedule 2 drugs may not destroy or cause to be destroyed any such controlled drugs except in the presence of, and in accordance with any directions given by, a person authorised by the Home Secretary to witness such destruction. The date of destruction, the quantity destroyed and the signature of the witness should all be recorded in the CDR. Those authorised include police constables, Home Office Drugs Inspectorate inspectors and Royal Pharmaceutical Society of Great Britain (RPSGB) inspectors. This provision applies to 'out of date' and contaminated drugs but not to 'patient returns', which, by virtue of regulation 6, can be destroyed without formality.

5.5 The practical arrangements made by practitioners in order to comply with these requirements vary from one practice to another. To an extent, this is understandable and reflects the existence of a wide variety of practice styles. However, this variability is partly attributable to a lack of knowledge and understanding of the requirements on the part of many GPs and to the absence of any mechanism for inspecting or approving the arrangements made at GPs' surgeries. As will become clear from the rest of this Chapter, ignorance of and failure to comply with the requirements is widespread among GPs. Arrangements are often informal, and staff and doctors sharing premises may not be aware of the arrangements made by individual colleagues.

The Arrangements in the Practices where Shipman Worked

5.6   Shortly after his arrival at the Abraham Ormerod Medical Centre in Todmorden in 1974, Shipman took over responsibility for the ordering of controlled drugs for the practice. The doctors in the practice shared the use of a controlled drugs cabinet and only one CDR was kept. Shipman was responsible for recording in the CDR any Schedule 2 controlled drug obtained by the practice, and each doctor was responsible for making an entry in the 'drugs supplied' section when s/he removed a quantity of drug from the cabinet for supply or administration to a patient. Shortly after his arrival, Shipman began to order large quantities of pethidine and to divert them for his own use. Initially, he made entries in the 'drugs obtained' section of the CDR but made no entries in the 'drugs supplied' section. In July 1975, after suspicion had been aroused by the quantities of pethidine purchased for the practice, the police and a Home Office drugs inspector visited the practice. Shipman and his partners were advised of their obligation to complete both sides of the register. Thereafter, Shipman continued to order supplies of pethidine on requisition and to divert them for his own use, but ceased making any entries at all in the CDR. In September 1975, Shipman's actions came to light. He was dismissed from the practice and he was prosecuted.

5.7   After he left Todmorden, Shipman never again kept a CDR and never officially used a **'locked receptacle'** for controlled drugs. Provided he was not holding any stock of Schedule 2 drugs or the relevant Schedule 3 drugs, there was no requirement for him to do so. When being interviewed by members of the Donneybrook practice, Hyde, prior to his appointment to the practice in October 1977, Shipman said that he did not intend to keep controlled drugs but would use Fortral (which was not then a controlled drug) for pain relief. In fact, he usually did have a secret stock of diamorphine. It is not clear where this was kept. It seems likely that he usually kept his supplies in a bag or box in his motor vehicle. He probably also kept some in a secret place in his consulting room. After his arrest, some diamorphine was found at his home. But, when anyone asked him whether he kept controlled drugs – as a regional medical officer (RMO) and a medical adviser employed by the Family Health Services Authority (FHSA) did – he told them that he did not. Had a search taken place (which it did not until he was under suspicion of murder) and had any controlled drugs been found, he would no doubt, at least after 1985 (when the relevant provisions were introduced), have claimed that they were patient returns, which he was entitled to receive for the purpose of destruction without keeping any record.

5.8   In Phase One of the Inquiry, 11 GPs, who had at various times been at the Donneybrook practice, provided details of their personal arrangements for holding the relevant Schedule 2 and Schedule 3 controlled drugs. Most kept their own stock in their doctor's bags and maintained their own CDRs. One of them, Dr Ian Napier, used to have his record of drug acquisitions in the CDR witnessed by a pharmacist. Two said that they did not keep a stock of controlled drugs; they could use non-controlled drugs for emergency pain relief and wished to avoid the risk of theft inherent in carrying a controlled drug.

5.9   Staff at the Donneybrook practice were not aware that any controlled drugs were kept on the premises. Mrs Vivien Langfield, the practice manager, said that, for security reasons, drugs were not usually kept on the premises. Drugs returned by, or on behalf of, patients were stored in a cupboard in reception prior to being sent for use in the Third World.

5.10   The staff at the Market Street Surgery, to which Shipman moved in 1992, were unaware of the arrangements Shipman made as regards controlled drugs. They were unaware too of the statutory requirements which would have applied if he were to have kept a stock of controlled drugs. Mrs Carol Chapman, who started working as a receptionist for Shipman in 1992, recalled that she twice saw a 'drugs bag', which Shipman kept in his motor vehicle. She said that she did not know whether diamorphine was regularly kept on the premises but she recalled that, on one occasion, probably Saturday, 27th December 1997, when she was suffering from acute back pain, Shipman gave her an injection of diamorphine at the surgery. He did not leave his room to obtain the drug, so it was clear to her that it must have been kept there. Neither Mrs Chapman nor the other staff to whom she mentioned the episode expressed surprise that Shipman should have been able to give her such an injection. They are not to be criticised for that. They had had no training in the requirements relating to controlled drugs.

The Position Today

5.11   At the present time, many GPs do not keep controlled drugs either in their bags or at their surgeries. They are, therefore, under no obligation to keep a CDR. There are a number of reasons why doctors do not keep controlled drugs. Many doctors practising in urban areas are fearful that carrying controlled drugs would make them a target for theft or robbery. Doctors in such areas would, in any event, have ready access to a pharmacy. It appears that doctors in rural areas are more likely to carry a supply of controlled drugs. However, many doctors find that there is no need to carry controlled drugs, as non-controlled alternatives are available. The Royal College of General Practitioners (RCGP) provides advice to doctors about the contents of an emergency bag. Some form of analgesia is required but this need not be in the form of a controlled drug. The British Medical Association pointed out to the Inquiry that changes in the arrangements for the provision of out of hours services and the increased provision of care by paramedics in the ambulance service may also account for a reduction in the number of GPs carrying controlled drugs.

5.12   In those practices where doctors do keep a stock of controlled drugs, the methods of record keeping and stockholding vary. In some cases, a central cupboard and CDR are kept; in others, the doctors make their own personal arrangements.

Lack of Inspection

5.13   Until 1991, RMOs visited GPs' premises periodically. The purpose of the visit was mainly pastoral; advice could be given on any matter of concern. The RMO would inspect the GP's arrangements for keeping controlled drugs and the CDR and give advice, if necessary. If a GP failed to heed advice given by the RMO about such matters as the excessive prescribing of any drugs, s/he might be referred to the local medical committee (LMC). However, it appears that this occurred only very infrequently and that, when it did occur, the focus was on discouraging unnecessarily costly prescribing, rather than on preventing diversion of controlled drugs.

5.14   In 1991, the task of inspecting GPs' premises passed to the NHS body with responsibility for the local provision of primary care services. Initially, this was the FHSA; it is now the primary care trust (PCT). Medical advisers were appointed by the FHSAs and a system of annual surgery visits was developed. However, it appears that these visits did not focus on the arrangements for keeping controlled drugs. As a result, most practices have not had their arrangements inspected for many years.

Lack of Compliance and Understanding

5.15   The effect of this lack of inspection and support has been clearly demonstrated in the report of a survey completed in January 2002 by Professor Richard Baker, Director of the Clinical Governance Research and Development Unit, University of Leicester, and colleagues, entitled 'Reducing Leakage of Prescribed Drugs'[1]. The study was commissioned by the Leicester, Leicestershire and Rutland Drug Action Team and was undertaken to assess the risk in Leicestershire and Rutland of leakage of prescribed controlled drugs. Leakage was defined as the use of controlled drugs for purposes other than those for which they were prescribed. It was recognised that shortcomings in the systems of control and in their day-to-day application could increase the risk of leakage.

5.16   The study had two phases. Initially, a number of GPs and community pharmacists were selected for interview and their arrangements for storing and recording the use of controlled drugs were examined. The findings from these interviews were used to devise questionnaires that were sent to all GP practices and community pharmacists not previously interviewed. The questionnaires sought information about their procedures and arrangements for storage of controlled drugs, for keeping of CDRs and for handling of patient returns and out of date drugs. The questionnaires sought views on the strengths and weaknesses of the present systems and also sought ideas as to how the systems could be improved.

5.17   Professor Baker explained the study findings to the Inquiry. So far as GPs were concerned, the arrangements for storage were variable; controlled drugs might be stored in a doctor's bag, a secure practice store or the practice dispensary. Several types of CDR were in use and doctors said that they were uncertain or confused as to their duties in this respect. Many said that they lacked any source of help or advice.

---

[1] published in abbreviated form in *Quality & Safety in Health Care* 2004; 13:21–25

Most GPs reported that their arrangements had not been inspected for many years, and many said that they would welcome an inspection.

5.18 As I have explained, the legislation allows a GP or pharmacist to accept the return of unused controlled drugs from patients for the purpose of destruction, without imposing any duty to record either the receipt or the destruction. The survey found that some practices accepted and encouraged the return to the practice of unused controlled drugs. The remainder would not accept them; they perceived problems with disposal and issues of ownership. Their policy was to advise patients or carers to return the drugs to a pharmacy.

5.19 The report recommended the provision of a local source of advice about good practice to pharmacists and GPs. It suggested that inspection arrangements should be put in place. It also encouraged greater support for police chemist inspection officers (CIOs).

5.20 Other witnesses giving evidence to the Inquiry confirmed that many GPs are uncertain about their duties and responsibilities with respect to controlled drugs. Dr Geoffrey Roberts, a former member of the Donneybrook practice and now Medical Director of a mental health trust in Warrington, told the Inquiry that, in his capacity as secretary of the LMC for Tameside, he had often received requests for advice about such matters as the destruction of unused controlled drugs following the death of a patient.

5.21 In 2001, Dr Clare Gerada, a Lambeth GP and Director and Chair of the RCGP National Advisory Group for Drug Misuse, while on secondment to the Department of Health (DoH), prepared a 'scoping study' entitled 'Controlled Drugs in Clinical Practice – Summary of Use and Controls'. In it, she reported that most practitioners are unclear about their roles and statutory responsibilities under the MDA 1971. As a result, compliance is poor, particularly in respect of the records kept of items administered personally from the doctor's bag. The position is made worse where several different doctors use the same emergency bag.

5.22 Mr David Young, an inspector for the RPSGB, confirmed that GPs have difficulty in understanding their responsibilities. He described an occasion when he was asked for advice by a group practice in Sheffield. The senior partner was concerned about the practice's arrangements for controlled drugs. They had had no guidance and did not know to whom to turn. They asked Mr Young to help them set up a CDR and to advise them on safe custody arrangements. Their existing arrangements would have permitted anyone working in the building, including cleaners, to have access to the drugs cupboard. Mr Young gave the help requested, although to do so was not part of his duties as a RPSGB inspector. When the system was set up, the senior partner asked Mr Young when he would come back to inspect its operation. That was not within his brief either and it is likely that the practice remains uninspected.

5.23 Very recently, in May 2004, the National Prescribing Centre published a preview edition of a new guide to good practice in the management of controlled drugs in primary care in England. This is a useful and comprehensive guide for general practitioners, pharmacists and others. The guide seeks to explain the current legal and regulatory frameworks and goes on to state what is regarded as good practice within those frameworks. The publication of the guide is a very welcome development. It will be available on the DoH website and will be subject to regular revision in the light of future developments.

Dispensing Doctors

The Separation of Prescribing and Dispensing

5.24 The usual practice in respect of all prescription only medicines, including controlled drugs, is for a GP to write a prescription, which is taken by the patient or his/her representative to a pharmacy for dispensing. In general, the view has been taken that it is preferable for doctors to prescribe and for pharmacists to dispense. In that way, the pharmacist brings his/her separate expertise to bear upon the questions of whether the drug has been appropriately prescribed and whether the dosage is within normal limits.

5.25 There are two sets of circumstances in which this usual separation of functions does not apply. The first follows from the fact that all doctors are permitted to supply and administer prescription only medicines, including controlled drugs, to their patients for immediately necessary treatment, pursuant to regulation 19 of the National Health Service (Pharmaceutical Services) Regulations 1992 (the 1992 Regulations). These Regulations allow a doctor to provide emergency medication from his/her bag or practice stock. Regulation 19(b) permits a doctor to supply to a patient any appliance or drug that is personally administered.

5.26 The second set of circumstances arises because, under the 1992 Regulations, some doctors, practising in rural areas, are permitted to dispense as well as to prescribe drugs, even in circumstances where there is no emergency. This is a source of additional income for such doctors, which may be of some importance to a rural practice with a small patient list.

5.27 The 1992 Regulations provide that a PCT may authorise a GP to provide pharmaceutical services under the NHS to patients living in a **'controlled locality'** who would have serious difficulty in reaching a pharmacy. A controlled locality is a rural area. In a dispensing practice, the dispensing of medicines will take place on the practice premises under the authority of the GP. However, the GP usually delegates the work of dispensing to a pharmacist or dispenser (who may or may not be qualified) employed by the GP or the practice. In England, there are about 4800 dispensing GPs, about 15% of all practising GPs. Scotland, despite its geographically dispersed population, has only about 290, which represents about 8% of GPs in practice there.

5.28 All applications to provide NHS pharmaceutical services from a community pharmacy in England must be approved by the local PCT and, if the application relates to a controlled locality, it may be opposed by the local dispensing doctors. By regulation 4(4) of the 1992 Regulations, the application is to be granted only if the PCT is satisfied that it is necessary or desirable to do so in order to secure the adequate provision of services of the type proposed in the neighbourhood in which the pharmacy would be situated.

5.29　Regulation 4(4), which, in respect of a controlled locality, effectively places the onus on the applicant pharmacy to overcome any objections raised by the dispensing doctors, appears rather surprising. On the face of it, the determining factor is whether the existing pharmaceutical services are adequate. It seems that these include the pharmaceutical services provided by dispensing doctors. The fact that those pharmaceutical services may not be as safe for patients as those provided by a pharmacist independent of the prescribing doctor does not appear to be taken into account. It is generally recognised that the scrutiny that can be applied to a prescription by a qualified pharmacist, independent of the prescribing doctor, provides a better potential clinical safeguard than that provided by a dispenser or even a pharmacist who is employed by the prescribing doctor. These issues may be said to be beyond the scope of the Inquiry. However, there is another public interest reason, which does lie within the remit of the Inquiry, why pharmaceutical services provided by pharmacists may be preferable to those provided by dispensing doctors. An independent pharmacist is or should be a safety check on malpractice by a GP in connection with drugs of potential abuse. If Shipman had been a dispensing doctor, it would have been even easier than in fact it was for him to obtain his illicit supplies. It would have been extremely difficult for an employed dispenser to challenge any irregularity of which s/he became aware. I am not suggesting that there is any evidence that dispensing doctors are any more prone to acts of dishonesty in relation to controlled drugs than any other doctor. However, I do consider that there is a significant potential for abuse, particularly since CIOs have no authority routinely to inspect the dispensaries of dispensing GPs.

Conclusion

5.30　I have explained that, at present, many GPs are not complying with their duties under the MDR 2001, often as the result of ignorance, confusion and lack of advice rather than with any intention to default. Does this matter and, if it does, what should be done about it?

5.31　The general policy of the current legislation is that the keeping and use of controlled drugs should be subject to safe custody and record keeping requirements and that the arrangements and records should be subject to periodic inspection. That being so, there seems every reason why GPs, including dispensing doctors, should be subject to the same standards of inspection and enforcement as pharmacists. To achieve this, there must be improved sources of advice for GPs and a new or improved system of inspection. However, it is clear that the existing safe custody and record keeping requirements, even if fully enforced, will not deter or detect the activities of a doctor who, like Shipman, is determined to keep a secret supply of a controlled drug. Shipman did not keep a CDR but, even if he had kept one, it would not have contained entries relating to his illicit supplies. However good a system of inspection of his CDR and of his arrangements for keeping any legitimate supplies had existed, his illicit supplies would not have been found. In Chapter Fourteen, I shall discuss the improvement of inspection arrangements and the feasibility of measures that would detect activities such as Shipman's.

CHAPTER SIX

Prescriptions and Requisitions

Introduction

6.1 In this Chapter, I shall examine the existing statutory rules and requirements governing the issue of prescriptions and requisitions for controlled drugs and the way in which they operate in practice. I will rehearse the evidence from various sources as to whether these rules should be changed. In Chapter Fourteen, I will weigh the competing arguments for and against change.

The Current Position

6.2 The current rules and requirements governing the issue and dispensing of prescriptions for prescription only medicines are laid down in the Medicines Act 1968 and secondary legislation made under the Act. Additional requirements exist for some but not all controlled drugs and these are set out in the Misuse of Drugs Regulations (MDR) 2001.

6.3 Regulation 15 of the Prescription Only Medicines (Human Use) Order 1997 lays down the requirements for a prescription for all prescription only medicines, including controlled drugs. The regulation requires that a prescription issued by a practitioner must bear the practitioner's signature in ink. The other parts of the prescription must be written in ink or otherwise so as to be indelible, although NHS prescriptions may be carbon-copied. The prescription must give the practitioner's name, address and profession and the date of issue. It must give the patient's name and address and age, if under 12. There is no legal limit to the volume or quantity of any drug that may be prescribed on one prescription. The drugs prescribed may not be dispensed more than six months after the date of issue of the prescription.

6.4 Regulation 15 of the MDR 2001 imposes additional requirements for all controlled drugs in Schedule 2 to the Regulations and for almost all those in Schedule 3. First, the prescription must specify the dose, the form, the strength (where appropriate) and either the total quantity (in both words and figures) or the number of dosage units (in both words and figures) to be dispensed. The Royal Pharmaceutical Society of Great Britain (RPSGB) advises its members on the interpretation of the statutory requirements affecting these controlled drugs. The advice is that dosage must be specifically stated and that a statement, for example, that medication is to be 'taken as directed' is unacceptable. Also, prescriptions for controlled drugs to be used in a syringe driver must specify the number of ampoules or the amount of controlled drug to be used over a specified period of time. The requirement to specify the form of the drug prescribed means that, even where only one form of the drug exists or where the form is implicit in the proprietary name (e.g. MST, which is the standard abbreviation for morphine sulphate tablets), the prescription must contain a specific direction as to the form in which the drug is to be dispensed (e.g. the words 'tablets' or 'tabs'). The use of abbreviations such as 'T' for tablets and 'C' for capsules is regarded by the RPSGB as unacceptable. The strength of the preparation must be specified if more than one strength of the drug is available. In the case of drugs to be supplied in instalments, detailed instructions are required. Since 1998, it has been possible for a practitioner to issue a prescription for a controlled drug to be dispensed in instalments. Special rules apply to such prescriptions.

6.5   Second, except in the case of phenobarbitone, all this information must be entered in the prescriber's own handwriting. Doctors may not, therefore, issue typewritten or computer generated prescriptions for controlled drugs. Where a prescription requires amendment, the amendment must be made in indelible ink in the handwriting of the original prescriber. If that doctor is not available, a new prescription must be issued. Moreover, RPSGB guidance suggests that prescription details cannot be amended by a covering letter from the prescriber, purporting to give authorisation. Nor is a carbon copy or faxed amended prescription acceptable.

6.6   A doctor, such as one working on a community drugs team, who makes out a large number of Schedule 2 and 3 prescriptions can apply to the Home Office for exemption from the handwriting requirement. If exemption is granted, the doctor may use computer generated prescriptions. Each year many such exemptions are granted.

Changes in General Practice

6.7   The special handwriting requirements have not changed since 1973. In the intervening period, there has been a radical change in the administrative systems used in general practice. Until the late 1980s or early 1990s, all patient medical records were written on cards kept in an envelope or folder and named 'Lloyd George cards' (after the Rt Hon David Lloyd George who was Minister of Health in the early twentieth century). All NHS prescriptions were written, usually by hand, on a NHS prescription form. Starting in the late 1980s, most general practices installed computer systems on which patient records are kept. Most prescriptions are now drafted automatically when the doctor enters the prescribing information into the patient record; s/he then prints the prescription onto the NHS prescription form and signs it. Much time is saved by this method of creating a prescription but there are also other advantages that I shall refer to later. However, prescriptions for controlled drugs that attract the special handwriting provisions cannot be prepared in this way. The doctor must still make out the controlled drug prescription by hand although s/he will almost certainly have already entered the prescribing information into the patient's record on the computer. This makes the task of prescribing a controlled drug much more time-consuming for the doctor. Questions have arisen as to whether the special handwriting rules are now necessary or worthwhile.

6.8   It seems to be generally accepted that change is desirable. In 1997, the Advisory Council on the Misuse of Drugs (ACMD) gave its approval in principle to computer generated controlled drug prescriptions. The Home Office issued a consultation paper on this topic in May 2003. It now appears likely that the handwriting rules relating to controlled drug prescriptions will be relaxed in future. These potential changes are of interest to the Inquiry because it is charged with making recommendations for the future safety of patients. In order to form a view as to whether the relaxation of the existing requirements would compromise patient safety or make it easier for a dishonest doctor to obtain illicit supplies of controlled drugs, I must examine the purpose for which each restriction was intended and the effect of its removal. I shall include an examination of the requirements relating to private (i.e. non-NHS) prescriptions for controlled drugs. So far as it is known, Shipman did not use private prescriptions and, to that extent, it might be said that consideration of them lies outside the Inquiry's remit. However, in my view, I should recommend changes that will improve the safety of all patients, not just those treated under the NHS.

The Advantages and Disadvantages of Handwritten Prescriptions for Controlled Drugs

6.9   The requirement that the essential information on a controlled drug prescription should be written by hand appears to have two purposes. First, it ensures that the doctor writes the whole prescription him/herself rather than delegating the task (save for signature) to a member of staff. This requires the doctor to apply his/her own mind to the details of the prescription. Second, it reduces the risk of forgery. The more handwriting there is, the more difficult it is for the forger to imitate and the greater the chance that a pharmacist will spot the forgery. The requirement that numbers should be written in words as well as figures must also be intended to reduce the risk of forgery and mistake.

6.10   It is impossible to judge the extent to which the handwriting requirement produces the desirable effects intended. However, it does appear that it gives rise to several problems. Mr Alan Macfarlane, Chief Inspector, Home Office Drugs Inspectorate, described the requirement as 'antediluvian' and told the Inquiry that it leads to all sorts of difficulties.

6.11   I have already mentioned one disadvantage, namely, that to write a controlled drug prescription by hand is time-consuming for the doctor. The simultaneous entry of the prescribing information onto the prescription and into the patient records saves much time for the doctor. Of course, I recognise that general practitioners (GPs) are very busy and any measure that saves time must have some attraction. However, if the handwriting requirement increases patient safety, I would say that the saving of time should not be a determinative factor.

6.12   The main disadvantage of the handwriting rule appears to be that the incidence of errors is far greater when prescriptions are handwritten than when they are generated by computer. In her evidence, Mrs Kay Roberts, Lead Pharmacist for the Royal College of General Practitioners National Drug Misuse Training Programme and pharmacist member of the ACMD, emphasised that many handwritten prescriptions are technically incorrect and do not comply with the Regulations. One advantage of computer generation is that the computer should ordinarily prompt the prescriber to comply with every technical requirement. Mrs Roberts explained that technical prescribing errors can give rise to great inconvenience, frustration and anger at the pharmacy. If an error is detected at the pharmacy, the pharmacist has to explain to the patient or his/her representative that s/he cannot dispense the prescription and that the prescription form must be returned to the prescriber for amendment and signature. This is so even where the prescriber's intention is clear, as, for example, on a prescription for MST, where the prescriber has forgotten to state that the 'form' of the drug is 'tablets'. On occasions, pharmacists will 'take a chance' and dispense a drug even though the technical requirements have not been complied with, because they know that a refusal to do so will cause distress and they are confident that the doctor will, on request, provide a correct prescription.

6.13 Errors on the prescription can also give rise to a risk that the patient might be given a drug that is contraindicated or that s/he might be directed to take the drug in too large a dose. If a computer is used to generate the prescription, the software should produce an 'alert' signal if the doctor tries to prescribe a drug that is contraindicated for a patient by reason of an allergy or on account of incompatibility with another drug that the patient is currently taking. There should also be an alert if the doctor seeks to prescribe a dosage that is outside the normal range. However, research published in May 2004[1], while this Report was being written, suggests that computer systems currently in operation do not satisfactorily draw attention to many contraindicated drugs or hazardous drug interactions. The authors have suggested ways in which such systems might be improved and this work is to be taken forward by the National Patient Safety Agency.

6.14 Mrs Roberts said that many prescribing errors made by GPs occur because the legal requirements are not fully understood; she would like to see improved training on these issues. Also, she is of the view that the incidence of errors would be much reduced if all prescriptions were generated by computer. These advantages present a strong argument in favour of computer generated prescriptions for controlled drugs.

6.15 Would the switch to computer generation make it easier for dishonest people, whether healthcare professionals, drug addicts or drug dealers, to obtain illicit supplies? The evidence presented to the Inquiry suggested that it would probably not make a great deal of difference, and it was pointed out that, with electronic transmission, there might be a reduced danger of the theft of prescription pads. However, these views were based on the assumption that GPs' computer systems could be made secure. It is beyond the scope of the Inquiry to examine whether secure systems can be achieved in practice. Two types of problem spring to mind. First, can the systems be protected from 'hackers'? That is a difficult question and is not for me to consider. Second, can access to the prescribing facility be limited to those doctors and nurses with prescribing rights, to the exclusion of other members of the practice staff and staff employed by the primary care trust (PCT) with which most GP computer systems are now linked? I know, of course, that it is technically possible to do these things; access to parts of a system can be restricted to authorised people. However, I do have some concern that, in reality, security might not be as tight as it should be. For example, in Shipman's practice, all the staff had access to all parts of the computer system; everyone used the same password.

6.16 It seems to me that there are sensible arguments both for and against permitting the computer generation of controlled drug prescriptions. I realise that it might be thought advisable to move to computer generated prescriptions on the grounds of patient safety even though this might give rise to an increased risk of forgery and fraud. There is, however, a way to get the best of both worlds. The Inquiry heard evidence about a general practice where the doctors have found a way of combining the advantages of computer generation with compliance with the handwriting requirement of the MDR. They print out the prescription in a format that allows space for the doctor to write, in his/her own hand, beneath the printed words. In this way, the computer provides the prompts that ensure compliance with all the technical requirements and the alerts that avoid contraindicated

[1] 'Prescribing Safety Features of General Practice Computer Systems: Evaluation Using Simulated Test Cases', *British Medical Journal* 2004; 328:1171

drugs or excessive dosages. The writing provides a safeguard against forgery and mistake. The prescription complies with the MDR. The whole process does not take longer than the present processes whereby the doctor types the prescribing information into the computer and then writes the prescription by hand. It seems to me that this idea is worthy of serious consideration.

6.17 Whether or not computer generated prescriptions are permitted for controlled drugs, there will, at least for the foreseeable future, be some circumstances, such as a home visit, in which it will not be possible to use a computer, or at least not one that complies with the necessary security arrangements. No witness suggested to the Inquiry that, for a controlled drug prescription generated without the assistance of a computer, the existing special requirements should be lifted.

The Monitoring of Controlled Drug Prescriptions Issued under the NHS

6.18 Most prescriptions written for a patient being treated on the NHS are written on a standard prescription form, known as a FP10. Pads of such forms are issued to GPs by the local PCT. The same form, printed on white paper with blue and green shading, is used for all drugs, including controlled drugs, unless the controlled drug is being prescribed for dispensing by instalments, in which case a different form is used. All the prescriptions in the pads bear the name of the issuing PCT. They also bear a serial number unique to each individual prescription printed. If a pad is stolen, a warning can be issued to pharmacists not to dispense prescriptions within the range of numbers covered by the pad. The prescription pad also bears the name of the GP to whom it is issued and the GP's individual prescriber code. This code is not the GP's General Medical Council (GMC) registration number. Not all doctors working in general practice currently have an individual prescriber code. For example, locums and GP registrars (trainees) use the prescription pad of the GP principal for whom they are working. Such doctors are required to endorse the prescription with the letter 'D' to indicate their status as deputies or 'T' as trainees. However, I understand that it is intended that, at some stage in the future, all doctors who are entitled to prescribe will be allocated an individual prescriber code and pad.

6.19 The reverse of the FP10 requires the patient or the patient's representative to provide certain information at the time the prescription is presented. The collection of this information is designed to combat prescription charge fraud.

The Prescription Pricing Authority

6.20 All NHS prescriptions are sent to the Prescription Pricing Authority (PPA), which is a special health authority established under the National Health Service Act 1977 (as amended). Its principal functions are to price NHS prescriptions, to reimburse dispensers (i.e. pharmacists and dispensing doctors) and to collect and analyse information derived from these activities. It records details of all NHS prescriptions.

6.21 Prescription forms are received in batches from pharmacists and reimbursement is calculated according to the applicable Regulations. In the year to September 2003, more than 600 million prescription items were reimbursed following the receipt and processing of more than 350 million prescription forms. The process of entering data into the computer is currently performed manually by PPA employees but computer scanning and reading of the prescription forms is to be introduced between 2005 and 2007.

6.22 Because the details of individual drugs dispensed are recorded, the PPA is able to provide prescribing and cost analysis (PACT) data and related information to strategic health authorities, PCTs and a range of other NHS bodies. Information can also be provided to individual GPs and their practices. The PPA produces its information in paper and electronic format. The information is analysed by reference to the individual prescriber code on the FP10. In theory, this means that the prescribing habits of any doctor can be examined, down to the level of each individual drug. This is a very valuable tool. The doctor can audit his/her own prescribing habits. Also, a PCT can monitor the prescribing practice of any individual doctor or of the doctors within a particular practice. However, the accuracy of the prescribing data is limited as a result of three factors. First, as I indicated above, at present a locum or registrar does not have his/her own prescription pad and instead uses the pad of one of the principals in the practice. As I have said, this arrangement is set to end in the future. Each individual doctor will have his/her own individual prescriber code and will be permitted to prescribe only under that code. The second factor that has reduced the accuracy of individual prescribing data is the very common practice whereby doctors sign repeat prescriptions for medication initially prescribed by a colleague. They often do so without either seeing the patient concerned or giving much thought to the appropriateness of the choice of medication. If a doctor signs a lot of repeat prescriptions, using his/her own prescription pad, the PACT data will not accurately reflect his/her own prescribing practice nor that of the doctor(s) who initially prescribed the medication. Third, doctors working for a deputising service or co-operative use prescription forms on which the prescribing doctor's individual prescriber code does not appear, only the code for the practice with which the patient is registered. Thus, the cost of the drug is attributed to the right cost centre but, in the PACT data, the prescription is not attributed to the prescribing doctor. If these three problems can be resolved, it should be possible in future for accurate information about any GP's NHS prescribing practice to be provided.

6.23 The usefulness of prescribing data has recently been confirmed in a report entitled 'Audit of Controlled Drugs Prescribing in England for the Financial Year 2002/3', published by the Prescribing Support Unit (PSU) of the Department of Health. The PSU examined the prescribing of controlled drugs, based on the prescribing data from the PPA, and found a number of cases where GPs were repeatedly prescribing large quantities of controlled drugs. It appears that some of these had not been picked up by the routine surveillance carried out by PCTs. The circumstances of each case have now been investigated by the PCTs in whose areas these doctors practise. In most cases, a reasonable explanation has been provided but, in some, there has been cause for concern about the doctor's conduct or competence.

6.24 Prescription forms are normally kept by the PPA for 14 months 'post-pricing', although this period is flexible and may be extended in individual cases where, for example, irregularity is suspected. Police chemist inspection officers (CIOs) often request the production of old prescription forms for the purpose of their investigations. The PPA was able to provide relevant 'in date' prescription forms issued by Shipman at the request of the prosecuting authorities. However, the PPA's inability (for reasons of lack of storage space) to keep prescription forms for a longer period limits the use that can be made of them in investigations. Mr Barry Lloyd, an independent prescribing information consultant, who provides training for PCT employees in the analysis of PACT data, expressed the hope that, in future, it will be possible to keep an electronic archive of prescriptions and prescribing data for much longer.

Private Prescriptions

6.25   The overwhelming majority of GPs in this country work within the NHS. However, many have a few private patients and a few work exclusively, or almost exclusively, in the private sector. All prescriptions, whether issued under the NHS or privately, have to comply with the statutory requirements that apply to the kind of drug being prescribed. Whereas NHS prescriptions must be written or printed on form FP10, there is no special form for a private prescription. Most private prescriptions are written on a sheet of the doctor's headed notepaper. However, a pharmacist is obliged to dispense drugs on a private prescription written on any paper, provided that s/he is satisfied that the document is genuine, that the signatory is entitled to prescribe and that the technical requirements are satisfied. A private prescription carries no individual prescriber code such as appears on NHS prescriptions, and the prescriber is not required, as a matter of course, to provide his/her unique GMC registration number. A doctor seeing a patient privately may charge the patient a prescription fee, in addition to any consultation fee, and the pharmacist may charge a dispensing fee.

6.26   When a private prescription for a controlled drug is dispensed at a pharmacy, the pharmacist must enter the particulars of the prescription in a private prescriptions book unless the drug in question is a Schedule 2 drug and its supply has already been entered in the controlled drugs register (CDR). Private prescriptions must be kept on the pharmacy premises for two years after dispensing, unlike NHS prescriptions, which are sent to the PPA at the end of each month. A CIO or RPSGB inspector is entitled to examine private prescriptions and the private prescriptions book during a periodic inspection. However, RPSGB inspectors rarely look at them. Their brief is to ensure that the pharmacy as a whole is being properly conducted. Most CIOs do examine private prescriptions, as well as the CDR, and, from time to time, they notice signs of unlawful or irresponsible prescribing. In particular, by visiting several pharmacies in a locality, a CIO might notice a pattern of prescribing by a particular doctor which had not been apparent to any individual pharmacist.

6.27   Because private prescriptions for controlled drugs are not sent to the PPA, there is no way, at present, whereby the totality of a doctor's prescribing of controlled drugs can be monitored or audited. His or her prescribing on NHS prescriptions can be analysed by the PPA and monitored by the PCT but his/her private prescribing cannot be included in that scrutiny. Dishonest doctors know that they can evade scrutiny by prescribing privately. The Inquiry heard evidence of a GP who had been prescribing large amounts of controlled drugs on the NHS and sending an agent to collect them from the pharmacy. When he realised that his activities had come under suspicion, he switched to private prescribing, which did not show up on the PACT data received by the PCT. Accordingly, it appeared that he had heeded advice to reduce his prescribing of controlled drugs, although all he had in fact done was reduce his NHS prescribing. Mr Michael Siswick, Director of Human Resources for the PPA, told the Inquiry that it would be quite possible for the PPA to process information from private prescriptions, as well as NHS prescriptions, provided that the prescription was written on a form that could be 'read' by the new scanning equipment that will shortly be in use. In practice, the form and layout of the prescription would have to be very similar to the FP10 form used in the NHS. Mr Siswick said that a 'more holistic picture of prescribing' would be obtained if information about private prescriptions were provided to the PPA. He believed that the PPA would welcome any step that enhanced the level of prescribing information available to doctors and NHS bodies.

Requisitions or Signed Orders

6.28   At present, any doctor can obtain supplies of a controlled drug by presenting a signed order or requisition either to a pharmacy or to a wholesaler. In effect, a signed order is very similar to a private prescription, save that it is not made out in the name of an individual patient and will normally be endorsed by the doctor with words such as 'for practice use'. In England, there is no requirement that a signed order should be presented in any particular form. In Scotland, a signed order has to be made out on a special form, akin to but distinguishable from the FP10. In England, most doctors or practices order their supplies on headed paper but this is not compulsory. The transaction is a private one and the doctor or practice pays the commercial price for the drug. If the drug is administered to a patient under the NHS, the doctor or practice is entitled to be reimbursed the cost of the drug and an administration fee. If the treatment is given privately, the patient will pay the cost of the drug.

6.29   When a requisition is presented, the pharmacist makes an entry in the CDR (when necessary) and should keep the requisition for at least two years. The CIO might well inspect it. For the great majority of doctors, these arrangements are perfectly satisfactory. However, it is possible for a doctor who is addicted to drugs to obtain supplies on requisition from different pharmacies and for his diversion to escape the notice of a CIO. If a doctor repeatedly obtains controlled drugs on requisition from the same pharmacy or even from several pharmacies within the area of one CIO, a pattern of obtaining should be noticed. But, if the doctor obtains his/her supplies from pharmacies in different areas, the entries are unlikely to appear significant to the CIO. Such requisitions are not sent to the PPA and do not form part of its analysis of the doctor's usage of controlled drugs.

Conclusion

6.30   I mentioned in Chapter Three that, more than 80 years ago, the Dangerous Drugs Regulations 1921 conferred on the Home Secretary the power to prescribe and issue an official form for the private prescribing of controlled drugs. The proposal was never implemented. I can understand why it was not thought necessary. The abuse of controlled drugs was not such a grave problem then as it is today. In the 1960s, the Brain Committee twice decided against the introduction of such a form. It was thought that the additional safeguard to be provided by the use of such a form would be slight. However, in modern times, the use of an official form for the private prescribing and/or requisitioning of controlled drugs would provide a significant safeguard against abuse, principally because it would allow the PPA to analyse the whole of a doctor's use of controlled drugs, both private and NHS. This is an issue to which I will return in Chapter Fourteen. I shall also consider the need for additional information, such as some means of identification more informative than just a signature, to be included on a private prescription.

6.31 In Chapter Fourteen, I shall also return to consider whether, in the light of the responses to the Discussion Paper and the views of participants in the seminars, I should recommend the abolition of the handwriting rule and the introduction of computer generated forms for the prescribing of controlled drugs.

CHAPTER SEVEN

Pharmacists and Pharmacies

Legislation

7.1 The statutes governing the practice of pharmacy are the Pharmacy Act 1954, the Medicines Act 1968 and the Poisons Act 1972. The Misuse of Drugs Act 1971, the Misuse of Drugs Regulations (MDR) 2001 and the Misuse of Drugs (Safe Custody) Regulations 1973 (the Safe Custody Regulations) govern the way in which pharmacists deal with controlled drugs.

7.2 The legal basis for the provision of NHS pharmaceutical services in the community, including the dispensing of NHS prescriptions, is set out in sections 41 and 43 of Part II of the National Health Service Act 1977 (as amended), and in the NHS (Pharmaceutical Services) Regulations 1992, as amended. These Regulations require primary care organisations (then health authorities now primary care trusts (PCTs)) to provide NHS pharmaceutical services, mainly by contractual arrangements with pharmacists.

The Royal Pharmaceutical Society of Great Britain

7.3 The Royal Pharmaceutical Society of Great Britain (RPSGB) is the professional and regulatory body for the pharmaceutical profession in Great Britain. As I said in Chapter Three, the RPSGB was originally granted a Royal Charter in 1843. In 1953, a Supplemental Charter was granted which still governs the Society today. The Council of the RPSGB has recently petitioned the Privy Council for the grant of a new Royal Charter. The objects of the RPSGB are to advance chemistry and pharmacy, to promote pharmaceutical education and the application of pharmaceutical knowledge, to maintain the honour and to safeguard and promote the interests of its members in their exercise of the profession of pharmacy and to provide relief for distressed persons in certain circumstances.

7.4 As a professional body, the RPSGB leads and develops the profession. As a regulator, it is responsible for maintaining the register of pharmacists, for assuring competence and fitness to practise, for setting standards for education and practice and for disciplining pharmacists who breach the standards set. It combines these functions with a statutory enforcement role, exercising law enforcement functions under the Medicines Act 1968 and the Poisons Act 1972.

7.5 Pharmacy is the only self-regulated profession with its own inspectorate. The RPSGB employs 18 full-time inspectors, who operate on a regional basis and carry out periodic inspections of all community pharmacies. I shall explain their role in the inspection of community pharmacies in Chapter Nine.

7.6 The Inquiry received valuable assistance from the RPSGB and, in particular, from two of its officers. Mr Stephen Lutener, who was Head of Professional Conduct when he left the Society in 2003, gave oral evidence and provided the Inquiry with much relevant material. Miss Mandie Lavin, Director of Fitness to Practise and Legal Affairs, represented the RPSGB at the seminars and I was greatly assisted by her contributions.

7.7 Most of the income of the RPSGB comes from membership subscriptions and the profits from its publications. The 2004 annual retention fee for a full-time pharmacist is £205 and for pharmacy premises is £125 per year. The Society receives a contribution from the Department of Health (DoH) towards the cost of enforcing certain provisions of the Medicines Act 1968.

The Register of Pharmaceutical Chemists

7.8 The Pharmacy Act 1954 imposes a duty on the RPSGB to maintain a register of pharmaceutical chemists, and to determine eligibility for admission to the register by setting examinations and determining the conditions and qualifications required for registration. A 'pharmacist' is defined in section 132(1) of the Medicines Act 1968 as a person being on the register maintained under the Pharmacy Act 1954. All pharmacists wishing to practise in Great Britain must, therefore, be on the register.

7.9 The RPSGB publishes on its website a list of all pharmacists on the register, with information about their professional status. Some 23,000 members work in community pharmacies, with about 6000 employed in hospital pharmacies and about 2000 in the pharmaceutical industry. All registered pharmacists have a registration certificate issued by the RPSGB, which must be displayed in the community pharmacy where the pharmacist is working. All registered pharmacists are subject to the RPSGB Code of Ethics, the standards of professional performance to be observed by its members and its disciplinary jurisdiction.

Training and Qualifications of Pharmacists

7.10 The educational and training requirements for pharmacists have increased significantly over the last three decades. Prior to 1970, many pharmacists gained their qualification by undertaking a period of apprenticeship and college training and by passing the RPSGB examinations. With the expansion of tertiary education in the 1960s, it became increasingly common for aspiring pharmacists to undertake a degree course in pharmacy. In 1970, the RPSGB made entry to the profession conditional upon such a qualification. After 1970, pharmacy graduates were additionally required to undertake 12 months' experience in a pharmacy prior to registration.

7.11 By the early 1980s, the RPSGB had begun to specify the content of the pre-registration training, and quarterly reporting by tutors on trainees' progress was introduced. Since 1993, all applicants have been required to pass a formal written examination on completion of their approved pre-registration training. In 1997, the total qualification requirement was increased from four to five years, achieved through a four-year Master of Pharmacy degree and one year's pre-registration training culminating in the registration examination.

7.12 The syllabus for the registration examination is practice-based. Candidates are required to demonstrate knowledge of a wide range of medicinal drugs, including their properties and uses, their manufacture, procurement and storage. They must show a working knowledge of the legal framework of the practice of pharmacy, including the requirements in respect of controlled drugs. They must understand the ethics of the profession. One unit of the course deals with the supply of items against prescriptions and signed orders from practitioners. Trainees are required to demonstrate a thorough knowledge of the checks to be carried out before a prescription is dispensed. They learn how to assess a prescription, identifying any aspect that is unusual or clinically inappropriate and, if necessary, querying it with the prescriber. The trainee's skills, behaviour and knowledge are assessed in the workplace by an appointed tutor, as well as by examination. Once qualified, pharmacists are required to undergo continuing professional development.

Enforcement Functions of the Royal Pharmaceutical Society of Great Britain

7.13   The RPSGB has responsibility for the enforcement of certain provisions of the Medicines Act 1968 and of the Regulations made thereunder. Broadly speaking, these provisions deal with the adulteration and mis-labelling of medicines and the conditions under which some products may be sold.

7.14   The RPSGB also has enforcement duties under the Poisons Act 1972 relating to the sale of poisons. Certain poisons may be sold only on registered pharmacy premises under the supervision of a pharmacist. Moreover, before any lawful supply of certain poisons can be made, the seller must cause the purchaser to make an entry in the poisons book and sign it, giving particulars of the transaction. This requirement is more onerous than the requirements governing the supply of controlled drugs, which do not demand that any record be made of or by the person collecting the drugs. RPSGB inspectors routinely check pharmacy poisons books.

7.15   Breaches of the Medicines Act 1968 or the Poisons Act 1972 may result in prosecution in the courts. The RPSGB acts as prosecutor. However, the RPSGB has no power or duty to enforce any provision of the Medicines Act 1968 against a medical practitioner.

'Medicines, Ethics and Practice – A Guide for Pharmacists'

7.16   The professional standards to be observed by pharmacists are set out in the RPSGB booklet entitled 'Medicines, Ethics and Practice – A Guide for Pharmacists' (the MEP Guide). The MEP Guide, which is published annually, brings together the essential legal, professional and practical guidance needed by a pharmacist. In its current edition, it comprises four sections.

7.17   Section One describes the legal provisions relating to the sale or supply of medicinal products and poisons. It includes a subsection dealing with the requirements of the controlled drugs legislation.

7.18   Section Two is entitled **'Code of Ethics and Standards'**. Part 1 of this Section, entitled **'Pharmacists' ethics'**, highlights the pharmacist's ethical responsibility to act in the interests of patients and other members of the public, and to seek to provide the best possible health care for the community, in partnership with other healthcare professionals. It stresses the duty of a pharmacist to keep his/her knowledge up to date and emphasises that disreputable behaviour or breach of a professional responsibility or of a requirement identified in the Code of Ethics could form the basis of a complaint of professional misconduct. Part 2 sets standards of professional performance under the headings **'Personal responsibilities'**, **'Professional competence'** and **'Confidentiality'**. Examples of the standards of **'Personal responsibilities'** include the pharmacist's duty to report to the prescriber and to the relevant authorities any adverse drug reaction experienced by a patient. Another example given is that, if a pharmacist becomes aware that anyone has received pharmaceutical care of a standard less than s/he had a right to expect, the pharmacist must, if possible, provide an explanation of what happened, whether or not the pharmacist is the person responsible for the substandard care. A pharmacist must report to the RPSGB any concerns s/he may have that **'a pharmacist's professional competence or ability to practise may be impaired and put the public at risk'**. The responsibilities of pharmacists, pharmacy owners and superintendent pharmacists in relation to the running of a pharmacy business are set out. I think that pharmacists must find it helpful that these important duties are pointed out in clear terms. Under the heading **'Professional competence'**, there is a requirement that a pharmacist should undergo at least 30 hours' continuing professional education each year. Under **'Confidentiality'**, the rules relating to the disclosure of confidential information without a patient's consent are clearly set out. Part 3 sets out Service Specifications on 23 aspects of the pharmacist's work, including dispensing procedures, patient medication records (PMRs) and prescription collection services.

7.19   Section Three provides practice guidance on a wide variety of topics, including, for example, the disposal of pharmaceutical waste, the provision of domiciliary oxygen services, and needle and syringe exchange schemes. This Section is a positive mine of information useful to pharmacists.

7.20   One topic of particular interest to the Inquiry was the advice given to pharmacists about their duties in relation to controlled drugs and other substances liable to misuse. Pharmacists are advised to be alert to the possibility of patients obtaining prescriptions for excessive quantities of controlled drugs and should question the prescriber where it appears that an inappropriate supply has been requested. Advice is given about the detection of forged or altered prescriptions. Since May 2000 there has been no specific warning to pharmacists of the need to be alert to the risk of drug dependency in healthcare professionals although such a warning did appear previously.

7.21   Section Four provides a telephone enquiry guide and a section providing advice for pharmacists in difficulty.

7.22   At the time of writing, the current edition of the MEP Guide is the 27th edition, which was published in July 2003. In considering Shipman's acquisition of controlled drugs in 1993, it was necessary for the Inquiry to look at the MEP Guide current at that time. The relevant provisions are examined in detail in Chapter Eleven and are not considered further here.

Disciplinary Function of the Royal Pharmaceutical Society of Great Britain

7.23   Breaches of the Code of Ethics and Standards contained in the MEP Guide, and disreputable behaviour generally, might lead to a complaint of professional misconduct to the RPSGB, resulting in disciplinary action. Such complaints are usually investigated initially by a local RPSGB inspector. When the investigation is complete, the investigator submits a report to the RPSGB Directorate and, if it is decided that further action may be needed, the details of the case will be put before the Infringements Committee.

7.24 The Infringements Committee consists of pharmacists and lay members of the RPSGB Council. The Committee will receive a description of the case, in an anonymised form, on the basis of which its members will decide what action to take. The options are to take no action, to send an advice letter, to issue a formal warning, to order a prosecution or to refer the case to the Statutory Committee.

7.25 Allegations of professional misconduct are finally determined by the Statutory Committee, which also deals with pharmacists convicted of a criminal offence and with other matters related to the registration of pharmacists. The Statutory Committee sits as a formal tribunal. It may decide to take no further action, to admonish or reprimand the pharmacist or to direct that the pharmacist's name be removed from the register. Bodies corporate and partnerships may also be disqualified from operating a pharmacy. An appeal from a decision of the Statutory Committee lies to the High Court. The RPSGB is currently seeking statutory authority to widen its powers to include the imposition of a requirement that a pharmacist should practise only while under supervision.

The Operation of Community Pharmacies

7.26 There are more than 10,000 community pharmacies in England and Wales, of which about one half form part of a chain with four outlets or more. All community pharmacies must be registered in the RPSGB's register of pharmaceutical premises. Section 69(1) of the Medicines Act 1968 provides that the business of a community pharmacy may lawfully be conducted either by an individual pharmacist, by a partnership of pharmacists or by a 'body corporate'. Not all community pharmacies are contracted to provide NHS pharmaceutical services, although the great majority are.

Personal Control

7.27 Prescription only medicines and pharmacy medicines (see paragraph 3.41) can be dispensed in a community pharmacy only by registered pharmacists or by pharmacy technicians (also known as dispensers) working under the supervision of a registered pharmacist. Such medicines can be sold only from registered retail pharmacy premises, either by a pharmacist or by a person acting under the supervision of a pharmacist. At least one pharmacist should be on duty at all times when a community pharmacy is open. The RPSGB takes the view that temporary absence for about three quarters of an hour at lunchtime is regarded as acceptable, although no prescription only or pharmacy medicines can be supplied during such absence.

7.28 If a pharmacy is conducted by a body corporate, that part of the business concerned with the retail sale or supply of prescription only medicines and pharmacy medicines must be under the 'personal control' of a superintendent pharmacist, or of another pharmacist who is subject to the direction of the superintendent.

Locum Pharmacists

7.29   In its publication entitled 'A Vision for Pharmacy in the New NHS', issued in July 2003, the DoH stated that there is a shortage of pharmacists. This results in heavy reliance (especially in community pharmacies) on locum pharmacists and on pharmacists still working beyond the normal retirement age. Mr David Slater, an inspector employed by the RPSGB, told the Inquiry that, although many pharmacies are able to engage permanent staff, he and his colleagues encounter the increasing use of locum pharmacists. Locum work is quite well paid and, apparently, attractive to newly qualified pharmacists.

7.30   The availability of locum pharmacists is plainly important to the running of pharmacy businesses but some disadvantages are bound to accrue from their employment. A locum pharmacist cannot be expected to acquire the same degree of personal knowledge of customers or prescribers as is usually developed by permanent staff.

Keeping Records of Controlled Drugs Supplied by Pharmaceutical Wholesalers

7.31   Most community pharmacies purchase their supplies from wholesalers. Wholesalers of controlled drugs are required to keep records of all supplies to customers. When a sale is made, an invoice is prepared which records the quantity of each drug to be supplied and the name and address of the pharmacy to which the drug is to be delivered. The driver collects two copies of a delivery note with the drugs from the wholesaler's controlled drugs store. On receipt of the drugs, this document is signed by a representative at the community pharmacy and one copy is returned to the wholesaler as proof of delivery. The wholesaler will keep the signed delivery note for six months and a copy invoice for seven years. Wholesalers balance their actual stock of controlled drugs against book stocks following the completion of each shift, to check for discrepancies. All documentation relating to controlled drugs is subject to inspection by Home Office drugs inspectors.

7.32   Community pharmacies are required to keep invoices and copy delivery notes of all controlled drugs received. Pharmacists also have to enter a record of each drug received into the appropriate section of the pharmacy controlled drugs register (CDR), which, like its counterpart in the doctor's surgery, is intended to record receipts and supplies of controlled drugs. I shall discuss the CDR in detail later in this Chapter. As I will explain in Chapter Nine, the CDR should be inspected twice a year by a police chemist inspection officer (CIO), who also has the power to call for and inspect invoices and copy delivery notes. However, it seems that most CIOs do not routinely carry out a reconciliation of the quantities of controlled drugs arriving at the pharmacy with those entered into the pharmacy CDR. As a result, if a pharmacist were to order a greater amount of a controlled drug than was required by the business and keep part for him/herself, this would probably not be detected by a CIO, so long as the over-ordering was not immoderate and the CDR appeared to be technically in order. Nor would a CIO be likely to detect the activities of a pharmacist who diverted the whole of a supply obtained from a wholesaler but who made no corresponding entry in the CDR.

The Misuse of Drugs (Safe Custody) Regulations 1973

7.33   The Safe Custody Regulations regulate the conditions under which certain controlled drugs must be kept on certain types of premises. I have described their general application in Chapter Three. The Safe Custody Regulations apply to a few drugs in Schedule 3, and all drugs in Schedule 2, save quinalbarbitone and some other liquid preparations. In short, these provisions are directed against the drugs most liable to misuse.

7.34 Regulation 3 of the Safe Custody Regulations requires pharmacists, so far as circumstances permit, to keep all relevant controlled drugs in a locked safe, cabinet or room, which should be so constructed as to prevent unauthorised access. Every such safe, cabinet or room must either comply with the various structural requirements set out in Schedule 2 to the Safe Custody Regulations or, in the case of a retail pharmacy, be covered by a current certificate of adequacy issued by a chief officer of police following an inspection.

Dispensing Controlled Drugs in the Community Pharmacy

The Legal Requirements

7.35 Regulation 16 of the MDR 2001, which does not apply to drugs in Schedules 4 or 5, sets out the conditions which must exist before a controlled drug can validly be dispensed on prescription by a pharmacist. The prescription must comply with the requirements of regulation 15 (which are set out in detail in Chapter Six). The issuer's address must be specified and must be in the UK. The dispensing pharmacist must either be acquainted with the prescriber's signature and have no reason to suspect that it is not genuine or must have taken reasonably sufficient steps to satisfy him/herself that it is genuine. The drug should not be dispensed prior to the date specified on the prescription. The supply (or the date of first supply in the case of instalment prescriptions) must not take place more than 13 weeks after the date specified in the prescription. The supplier of the drugs has to mark on the prescription the date of supply or, in the case of instalment prescriptions, the dates of supply.

7.36 According to the MEP Guide, where the signature of the prescriber is not known, the prescriber should be contacted by the pharmacist and asked to confirm that the prescription is genuine. The Inquiry was told that, with the increasing use of locum pharmacists and locum doctors, it was becoming more difficult for a pharmacist to recognise the signature of a prescriber. If a prescription is presented out of hours and the signature of the prescriber is not familiar to the pharmacist, s/he is unlikely to be able to contact the prescriber. In such circumstances, if the prescription is dispensed, the pharmacist may well be acting in breach of the strict letter of the law and of RPSGB guidance.

Patient Medication Records

7.37 Nowadays, although there is no obligation on them to do so, virtually all pharmacies keep a computerised record of the drugs dispensed to each individual patient. This record is known as a PMR. The pharmacy computer will store details of all items previously dispensed to the patient, identifying the drug prescribed, the date of the prescription and the name of the prescriber. The purpose is to provide as complete a medication history as possible, in order to inform the future dispensing of drugs to the patient. In general, PMRs are kept by individual pharmacies and are not linked with other pharmacies. I understand that Boots the Chemists (Boots) has an integrated system connecting all its pharmacies. Because many people have their medication dispensed at a variety of different pharmacies, the PMR kept by any one pharmacy is likely to be an incomplete record of the patient's drug history.

The Usual Practice

7.38   The procedure for dispensing medicines varies to some extent from pharmacy to pharmacy. Mr Richard Aucott, the owner of Nupharm Chemist in Hyde, who is himself a pharmacist, described the procedures in operation at his pharmacy and I have no reason to think that they are atypical. The RPSGB intends to introduce, by 2005, a requirement for pharmacists to operate according to written standard operating procedures (SOPs). These will cover the dispensing process and the transfer of prescribed items to patients. Mr Aucott produced for the Inquiry the SOPs which have been in use at his pharmacy since 2003.

7.39   The essentials of dispensing a controlled drug are the same as for any prescription only medicine although there are some additional procedures to be completed. Usually, when the customer/patient presents a prescription for any medication, a pharmacy technician will assemble the medicine(s), packaging and labelling required. This process may involve the counting of tablets or the measuring of liquids. The preparation of a label, with instructions as to dosage, will, nowadays, entail the entry of the prescribing information into a computerised PMR; when the entry has been made, a label will be printed. Once the technician has assembled the medication, it is passed to the pharmacist on duty in its container, with the label and the prescription. The pharmacist will then check that the label and contents of the container correspond with the prescription. He or she will also consider the nature of the drug prescribed, the dosage, the age of the patient and the possibility of any interaction with any other drug being taken by the patient. This last consideration is possible only if the patient is a regular customer and all his/her recent prescriptions have been recorded in the PMR. If all is in order, the medication, suitably packaged and labelled, will then be handed to the customer/patient. The pharmacist must ensure that the patient receives sufficient information and advice to permit the safe and effective use of the medication. In that way, the pharmacist will have performed his/her duty, although the performance of much of the task will have been delegated.

7.40   On receipt of a prescription for a controlled drug, the pharmacist will first examine the prescription to assess its compliance with the MDR 2001. If all is in order, the pharmacist will give the technician the key to the safe, cabinet or room where the controlled drugs are stored, and the technician will assemble and label the medication in the usual way. At Nupharm Chemist, a second technician checks that the medication has been correctly dispensed, although this is not universal practice. The pharmacist will then make a final check in the way described above.

7.41   If satisfied, the pharmacist will then take the dispensed controlled drug to the counter and hand it over to the patient or the patient's representative. Mr Aucott said that he would give an explanation to ensure that the patient knew the nature of the medication, that it is a 'strong drug', that it should not be used by anybody else, that it should be taken exactly as directed on the label and that it should be kept in a safe place. Mrs Ghislaine Brant, the pharmacist manager at 23 Market Street, Hyde, said that she would explain that it was a 'strong drug'. As a rule, she would give no warning as to the risk that the drug might be attractive to drug addicts or drug dealers; nor would she tell the patient or his/her representative that the drug was a 'controlled drug'. She was concerned that giving such warnings might worry patients.

7.42   At the time of supply or shortly afterwards, an entry recording the supply is made in the CDR. If no entry was required in the CDR (as would be the case with a Schedule 3 or 4 controlled drug, for example) and the prescription was a private prescription, an entry would be made in the private prescriptions book. I will explain the relevant requirements for an entry in a CDR in detail later in this Chapter.

Assessing the Appropriateness of the Prescription for the Patient's Needs

7.43   Nowadays, it is recognised that an important aspect of a pharmacist's duty is to assess every prescription in order to determine not only that it complies with any legal requirements but also that it is suitable for the patient. The SOPs to be introduced by the RPSGB will include a requirement that all prescriptions be assessed by pharmacists for safety and clinical appropriateness. The appropriateness of the drug for the patient's condition and the compatibility of the drug with other medication being taken will have to be considered.

7.44   This duty is alluded to in 'A Vision for Pharmacy in the New NHS', which I mentioned in paragraph 7.29. In that publication, the Chief Pharmaceutical Officer of the DoH identified, as a key role for pharmacists, the promotion of patient safety by **'preventing, detecting and reporting adverse drug reactions and medication errors'**. It seems to me that, with the growing complexity of the range of drugs available to doctors, pharmacists have an increasingly important role to play in the clinical treatment of patients. In general, they have a wider and more detailed knowledge of drugs, their properties, dosages and side effects than most general practitioners. That is their speciality. It must be in the interest of patients that pharmacists should be able to apply their expertise so as to carry out a proper assessment of the prescription issued by the doctor. Although it is the aim of all good pharmacists to carry out such an assessment, it appears that, at present, the extent to which this can be achieved is limited by the inadequacy of the information at the pharmacist's disposal. There are two aspects to the problem.

7.45   First, the pharmacist will probably not know for what condition the doctor has prescribed the medication. This does not appear on the prescription. Some drugs have such a specific application that the pharmacist can infer the condition for which a given drug has been prescribed. Some pharmacists know a lot about their regular customers and some customers will readily talk about their condition if given the opportunity. However, the customer is not necessarily a reliable source of information.

7.46   Mr Lutener said that pharmacists feel that the present situation is unsatisfactory. He stressed that the need for information is even greater in the case of controlled drugs than with other medication. By way of example, he mentioned that benzodiazepines are very widely prescribed for a range of conditions. Without knowledge of the condition for which they are being prescribed, the pharmacist will not be able to tell whether they are being properly prescribed. If given on a long-term basis, they can easily lead to addiction. They should not be used in the long-term treatment of insomnia or for the relief of anxiety. However, if used in the control of epilepsy, long-term continuous treatment may be appropriate.

7.47   Second, for the reasons I have explained, the PMRs kept at a pharmacy may well not present a complete picture of the medication the patient is currently taking. Even if the PMRs are meticulously kept, they will be incomplete if the patient obtains medication from more than one pharmacy. Mr Lutener explained that, if the information is incomplete, it is difficult for the pharmacist to carry out an adequate assessment. The same point was made in written evidence submitted by the Oldham, Tameside and Glossop Local Pharmaceutical Committee.

How Could These Problems Be Overcome?

7.48   The problem of satisfying the pharmacist's need to know for what condition the medication has been prescribed was regarded by many witnesses to the Inquiry as virtually insoluble, at least for some time to come. Many regarded the idea that the patient's medical diagnosis should be recorded on the prescription as unacceptable, for reasons of patient confidentiality. It was, however, recognised that, if the NHS is soon to introduce a centralised electronic network of patient medical records (the NHS Case Record), to which all doctors could obtain access, pharmacists could also be given access to that network. In that way, both of the problems I have mentioned would be resolved. However, such a network may not be available for some time and, in any event, there are some who consider that access to such records by pharmacists would give rise to problems of patient confidentiality. This issue was raised for discussion at the Inquiry's seminars and I will return to consider it further in Chapter Fourteen.

The Controlled Drugs Register

Form and Format

7.49   Regulation 19 of the MDR 2001 requires pharmacists to maintain a chronological register (the CDR) detailing the quantities of every Schedule 2 controlled drug obtained or supplied. There is no such requirement for controlled drugs in Schedules 3–5. A separate CDR, or a separate part of the CDR, has to be used for each different Schedule 2 controlled drug. Regulation 27 provides that, when pharmacists destroy contaminated or 'out of date' stocks of such drugs, they should record in the CDR details of the date of destruction and of the quantity destroyed. The entry has to be signed by the authorised person in whose presence the drugs are destroyed. Unused drugs returned by a patient to a pharmacist for the purpose of destruction are specifically exempted from this provision.

7.50   The maintenance of a CDR is intended to permit the monitoring of stocks held at the pharmacy and to afford to CIOs the opportunity to identify prescribing or dispensing that gives cause for concern.

7.51 The format of the CDR is prescribed by the MDR 2001. Regulation 19 provides that each page of the register should take the form illustrated in Schedule 6 to the Regulations. However, the illustration which appears there is not at all detailed and shows only a number of unmarked columns (four in the case of the 'drugs obtained' pages and five in the case of the 'drugs supplied' pages). Regulation 20 requires that the class of drugs to which the entries on a given page relate should be specified at the head of that page. Every entry should be made on the day when the transaction takes place or, if that is not reasonably practicable, on the following day. Thus, entries do not have to be made contemporaneously with the transaction. Corrections must be indelible and made by a note in the margin or footnote; cancellations, obliterations or alterations are not allowed. All these requirements are designed to reduce the risk of forgery and diversion of drugs. The CDR is not to be used for any purpose other than the purpose of the Regulations. The CDR is specific to one set of premises only and has to be kept at those premises.

7.52 The physical form of the CDR is a matter for individual pharmacists. Many pharmacists use CDRs produced in a ring binder by the National Pharmaceutical Association (NPA). Some of the larger retail pharmacy chain stores and supermarkets, such as Boots and ASDA, have produced their own form of CDR for use in their pharmacies. The NPA ring binder contains a number of separately bound registers in the form of rectangular soft-backed stapled booklets, each designated for a different controlled drug. The first pages in each register contain records of drugs obtained and the remaining pages record drugs supplied. Coloured dividers separate the individual registers. The ring binders also contain a brief description of the drugs requiring an entry in the CDR.

7.53 At Appendix D, three sample pages from this CDR (which complies with the MDR 2001) are reproduced. The first page is the front cover of the diamorphine register, the second is a sample 'drugs obtained' page and the third is a sample 'drugs supplied' page. The record of 'drugs obtained' shows the date of receipt, the name and address of the person or firm from whom the drug was obtained and the amount and form in which it was obtained. The record of 'drugs supplied' shows the date of the relevant transaction, the name and address of the person or firm supplied and the amount and form supplied. The name and address of the patient, or (where the supply is on requisition) of the doctor or practice, are entered in the columns seeking details of the person or firm supplied. The next column requires the entry of **'Particulars as to licence or authority of person or firm supplied to be in possession'** and this is the column in which the prescriber's name is entered.

7.54 The entering of data into the CDR is a time-consuming business and the registers themselves are unwieldy. Some pharmacists may make as many as 200 entries in the CDR in a day, depending on the number of drug dependent patients they serve. At present, the Regulations do not permit the keeping of an electronic CDR. If pharmacists were permitted to keep their CDRs electronically, they could integrate the PMR with the CDR. Then, an entry could automatically be made in the CDR when the prescribing information was entered into the PMR. In this way, a great deal of time would be saved. The Home Office issued a Consultation Paper in May 2003, seeking views on a proposal that legislation be passed to allow the keeping of electronic CDRs and this met with the general approval of pharmacists. The Inquiry heard many other expressions of dissatisfaction about the form of CDR currently in use. I shall now mention several of their perceived inadequacies.

Running Balances

7.55 The NPA has construed regulations 19 and 20 strictly, and has not provided space for the insertion of any additional information into the register besides that which is compulsory. Although many pharmacists have recognised that it would be advantageous to keep a running balance of the amount of each Schedule 2 controlled drug that is or should be in stock at any one time, most have felt unable to record this information in the CDR because there is no provision for it in the Regulations and no space in the NPA register.

7.56 In hospital pharmacies, the keeping of a running balance in CDRs is standard practice. According to the report entitled 'Reducing Leakage of Prescribed Drugs', to which I referred in Chapter Five, 80% of the community pharmacists surveyed in the study would support the maintenance of a running balance. The recording of such a balance is an elementary stock control measure. It would enable a pharmacist or superintendent pharmacist to make a regular check on stocks of controlled drugs and would act as a disincentive to diversion. It would be of great help to the CIO.

7.57 Some pharmacists have been so aware of the advantages of a running balance that they have devised a CDR which incorporates this feature. Mrs Kay Roberts, Lead Pharmacist for the Royal College of General Practitioners National Drug Misuse Training Programme and pharmacist member of the Advisory Council on the Misuse of Drugs (ACMD), devised one in the 1980s, while working in a community pharmacy in Harrow. She showed a draft to her local CIO and RPSGB inspector who were entirely content that it should be used. The CDR used by the ASDA chain of pharmacies is another case in point. It records all the information required by the Regulations and also requires a running balance to be recorded. It enables pharmacists to record the details of the drugs obtained alongside the corresponding record of drugs supplied. They can easily be cross-matched. An additional column to the right details the running balance. Pharmacists are instructed to calculate and enter the running balance after each transaction. At the end of each week, and before prescriptions are sent to the Prescription Pricing Authority (PPA), pharmacists are instructed to check the recorded balance against the quantities physically held in the controlled drugs cabinet. Thus, elementary stock control is achieved. This register was introduced with the knowledge and approval of one of the CIOs working in the Greater Manchester area, Detective Constable (DC) Michael Beard. He told the Inquiry that the feedback from pharmacists using this type of CDR was universally positive and the Home Office has not raised any objection. As I shall explain in Chapter Fourteen, ASDA has said that this CDR has caused very few problems. ASDA staff do not carry out an audit every time they change shift but check the running balance every week. In that way any discrepancy is discovered and corrected quickly. ASDA reported that the keeping of a running balance has resulted in the detection of a locum pharmacist who was manipulating the records and had stolen a large number of amphetamine tablets from a number of different ASDA pharmacies.

7.58 Historically, the RPSGB and the NPA have been reluctant to agree to a requirement that running balances be maintained. The proposal was rejected in 1990, when the Home

Office asked the RPSGB to consider the matter following discussion of the subject at the annual meeting of police CIOs. The RPSGB Community Pharmacy Sub-Committee noted that the keeping of running balances had been considered by the Council of the RPSGB on previous occasions and had been rejected. The fear had been expressed that an over-zealous CIO might take too strict a line with pharmacists for slight discrepancies beyond their control. This might occur, for example, where the container in which methadone (a liquid) is supplied to a community pharmacy is slightly overfilled, resulting in a small residue after the dispensing of a number of doses that would normally exhaust the supply. Mr Lutener, although supporting the introduction of running balances, was also concerned that failure to ensure an exact balance might be met with inappropriate criticism, or worse. I am puzzled by this concern. While I can understand that pharmacists might be concerned that an over-zealous CIO might seek to bring a prosecution for a trivial infringement, they might be equally concerned that that could happen in the event of an infringement of any of the existing requirements. In fact, the evidence I have heard suggests that CIOs do not prosecute for minor infringements. They see their role primarily as giving advice and support. Only if a pharmacist were doing something quite seriously wrong would they take legal action.

7.59   The NPA remains concerned about the burden on its members that would result from the keeping of a running balance. I shall discuss these concerns further in Chapter Fourteen.

Recording the Pharmacist's Name

7.60   There is no requirement under the MDR 2001 for the pharmacist responsible for a transaction to identify him/herself in the CDR. In a small pharmacy, using permanent staff, the handwriting of the individual pharmacists will be recognisable by other staff and by the local CIOs. However, this is not always the case in a large pharmacy or in a pharmacy where locum staff are used, some of them for only short periods. Although the Regulations do not provide for it, the ASDA CDR also records the name of the person responsible for entering each transaction. This may be vital information if it later becomes necessary to investigate a particular transaction.

Recording Who Collects Controlled Drugs

7.61   Regulation 14 of the MDR 2001, which does not apply to drugs in Schedules 4 or 5, is designed to prevent a controlled drug which has been ordered on requisition (as opposed to on prescription) from falling into unauthorised hands. If the drugs are to be collected by anyone other than the person who has ordered them, the pharmacist must be satisfied that the collector has been authorised in writing to collect the drugs. By contrast, there is no provision requiring a pharmacist who intends to supply a controlled drug, dispensed in accordance with a prescription, to a person other than the named patient to require the person collecting the drug to produce an authority signed by the patient. This proved to be a significant *lacuna* in Shipman's case. He was able to collect drugs, ostensibly on behalf of a patient, without the patient's knowledge.

7.62   Moreover, there is no requirement that the identity of the person who collects a controlled drug from the pharmacy should be recorded, either in the CDR or anywhere else. I have already mentioned that anyone collecting certain poisons has to sign the poisons book. When a NHS prescription is presented, the person presenting it must sign the reverse side to state whether or not exemption from the prescription charge is claimed and whether any fee has been paid. However, the person presenting the prescription is not necessarily the same as the person who collects the drug. Moreover, no such statement is required in the case of private prescriptions. Thus, in the case of both private and NHS prescriptions, there is no formal record of the identity of the person who collects the drug.

7.63   Evidence before the Inquiry suggests that a record of who has collected a controlled drug would be useful. It also suggests that there are many other doctors, apart from Shipman, who have diverted controlled drugs by collecting them from community pharmacies, purportedly on behalf of their patients. Mrs Rose Smith, the niece of Mrs Lucy Virgin (who was unlawfully killed by Shipman in March 1995), was, until about two years ago, the manageress of Nupharm Chemist, Hyde. This pharmacy, like many others, runs a prescription collection and medication delivery service. Mrs Smith explained that, although it was a requirement that the person to whom the drugs were delivered should sign for the drugs, there was no corresponding requirement for those persons collecting drugs from the pharmacy to sign for them. She did not foresee any problem if patients or their representatives were required to produce identification and to sign their name when collecting controlled drugs.

7.64   If the identity of the person collecting a controlled drug were noted in the CDR, the pharmacist and the CIO would be likely to notice a name which occurred with any frequency. If the person were to use several pharmacies in the same area, the CIO might notice that. In 1993, when Shipman collected a series of 30mg ampoules of diamorphine from the pharmacy at 23 Market Street, it is likely that the CIO, DC Patrick Kelly, might have noticed the frequency with which Shipman's name appeared as a collector, even though he was not struck by the appearance of Shipman's name as the prescriber of the drugs. Certainly, in any later investigation, such entries would have been extremely useful in proving that Shipman had collected the drugs in question. Shipman might well have been discouraged from behaving as he did, had he known that his collection of the drugs would be recorded.

7.65   ASDA pharmacists are instructed to record the name of the person collecting controlled drugs and the ASDA CDR contains a column in which such entries should be made. This arrangement was adopted only shortly before the time when DC Beard attended to give evidence but he told the Inquiry that the feedback from one pharmacy where it was used was good. ASDA has since confirmed that it has caused very few problems.

Recording Batch Numbers in the Controlled Drugs Register

7.66   One of the ideas considered by the Inquiry in its quest to improve the recording of controlled drugs transactions was whether it would be possible to identify and record in the CDR the actual product supplied under each prescription. If a controlled drug were found in the hands of someone who appeared not to be entitled to possession of it, it would be of great value to the police or Home Office if its origin could be traced.

7.67   The Inquiry team had in mind the use of batch numbers. The standard labelling requirements for all medicinal products for human use, as prescribed by European Union Council Directive 92/27, also apply to controlled drugs. The manufacturer's batch number must appear on the label. However, when the Inquiry was considering the value of recording the batch number in the CDR, or using it as a part of any audit trail, it was discovered that the size of a production batch might be very large indeed, up to millions of unit doses. To record the batch number in the CDR would not, therefore, be very useful. Moreover, it would be time-consuming, particularly as the digits on the label can be very small or faint and difficult to read. If, in time, batch numbering or other coded information is applied to smaller numbers of unit doses or even to individual packets, or blister packs, this may become practicable and worthwhile. In Chapter Fourteen, I shall consider the possibility of creating an audit trail for controlled drugs by the use of bar coded products.

Bringing All Controlled Drugs within the Controlled Drugs Register

7.68   As I have explained, transactions involving controlled drugs in Schedule 2 have to be recorded in the pharmacy CDR. Pharmacists are also required to record details of the dispensing of all private (but not NHS) prescriptions of prescription only medicines, including prescriptions for controlled drugs, in a private prescriptions book, unless the transaction is recorded in the CDR. The RPSGB recommends that private prescriptions for Schedule 2 controlled drugs should be entered in both the private prescriptions book and the CDR.

7.69   It follows that all supplies of Schedule 2 controlled drugs will be recorded in the CDR; supplies relating to controlled drugs in Schedules 3–5 will be recorded in the private prescriptions book if they are dispensed on a private prescription. However, the great majority of supplies of controlled drugs in Schedules 3–5, which are dispensed under a NHS prescription, will not be recorded in any document or system that remains on the pharmacy premises and is available for inspection. It appears to me that this is not an ideal situation, if a serious attempt is to be made to monitor the use of controlled drugs through local inspection. A more satisfactory inspection could be achieved if transactions (whether private or NHS) in all controlled drugs in Schedules 2–4 were required to be recorded in the CDR. While CDRs are kept in paper form, this would be impracticable. If they were kept electronically, however, it might be feasible. I shall consider this further in Chapter Fourteen.

Retention of Records

7.70   Regulation 23 of the MDR 2001 provides that requisitions and private prescriptions for controlled drugs and CDRs must be retained for two years either from the date on which the last delivery under the prescription or requisition was made, or, in the case of CDRs, from the date on which the last entry was made. Insofar as private prescriptions are concerned, the provision under the MDR 2001 is otiose, as, under the Medicines (Sale or Supply) (Miscellaneous Provisions) Regulations 1980, all private prescriptions must be retained by the pharmacist for two years. Regulation 23 does not apply to prescriptions issued under the NHS, which are sent to the PPA on a monthly basis.

Destruction of Controlled Drugs

Out of Date and Contaminated Drugs

7.71 All controlled drugs are marked with a date by which they should be used. A pharmacist is not permitted to dispense a drug which is out of date and nor, of course, should drugs that become contaminated in some way be dispensed. Because such drugs might be attractive to thieves, they must be kept secure until they can be destroyed. By virtue of regulation 27 of the MDR 2001, no pharmacist may destroy or cause to be destroyed any Schedule 2 controlled drugs except in the presence of, and in accordance with any directions given by, a person authorised by the Home Secretary to witness such destruction. Those authorised include Home Office inspectors, police constables (most commonly CIOs), RPSGB inspectors, Chief Executives of NHS Trusts, some PCT personnel and certain area managers of large pharmaceutical chain stores. The date of destruction, the quantity destroyed and the signature of the witness should all be recorded in the CDR. This provision applies to out of date and contaminated drugs but not to 'patient returns', which are exempt by virtue of regulation 6(2).

7.72 Problems arise when an opportunity for destruction does not occur for many months. At present, CIOs try to visit all pharmacies in their area twice yearly but this is often not achieved. In any event, there are some areas where there is no CIO in post. RPSGB inspectors are currently visiting each pharmacy about once every two years. Thus, opportunities for destruction are limited. The problems have become more acute in recent years as larger quantities of controlled drugs are being prescribed. The problems relate to security, storage capacity and the need to keep separate those drugs that are 'in date' from those that are out of date.

7.73 There is a degree of tension between the various bodies as to the allocation of resources to the task of destruction, which can be extremely time-consuming. The RPSGB, which receives no specific funding for the destruction of drugs, expects CIOs to perform this task, although, as I have said, CIO coverage is not universal. Standing instructions to RPSGB inspectors are that they should not carry out the destruction of controlled drugs as a matter of routine, although, if a pharmacist has accumulated a large volume of drugs and is obtaining no assistance from any other quarter, a special visit will be arranged for the purpose.

7.74 It is not within the remit of this Inquiry to make anything more than passing reference to such tensions, but they must be borne in mind when considering the alternatives for the safe and secure disposal of drugs which have been dispensed and have to be destroyed in the community.

Informal Destruction of Controlled Drugs: Patient Returns

7.75 It is generally recognised that the return and safe disposal of unwanted medicines is in the public interest and, in recent years, there have been several successful campaigns to encourage the public to return them to community pharmacies. In 1983, the ACMD recommended that patient returns of controlled drugs should be allowed to be destroyed without formality. The thinking behind this relaxation of the legislation was that it was desirable to remove controlled drugs from the community in as swift and simple a way as possible. In consequence of this recommendation, regulation 6(2) of the MDR 1985 (now regulation 6(2) of the MDR 2001), permitting the informal destruction of patient returns by doctors and pharmacists, was passed.

7.76   Mrs Roberts drew to the attention of the Inquiry Government figures suggesting that more than 523 tonnes of unwanted medicines were returned to community pharmacies for disposal in 2003. This demonstrates the magnitude of the problem faced by pharmacists when they have to sift a large 'mixed bag' of drugs returned to them, some of which are controlled drugs and some of which are not.

7.77   All patient returns originally dispensed on NHS prescriptions must be destroyed. Drugs dispensed on private prescriptions can be put back into stock if they are still in date, although pharmacists are advised against this. RPSGB guidance to pharmacists with respect to the disposal of controlled drugs returned by patients is that they should be destroyed as soon as possible, for security reasons. NPA guidance suggests that the pharmacy should keep a record of destruction in the private prescriptions book and that destruction should be witnessed by a second member of staff who should sign the record.

7.78   The evidence from the pharmacists at 23 Market Street, Hyde, indicates that they did not follow this practice until after Shipman's arrest. Mrs Brant said that she usually destroyed patient returns by dissolving them in boiling water and flushing them down the lavatory. Mrs Brant did not ask anyone to witness this process, nor did she make a record. I think it likely that most pharmacists follow this type of procedure, which is not unlawful. However, I observe that pharmacists could very easily take such returned drugs for their own use with little, if any, risk of detection. According to Mr Lutener, many pharmacists feel uncomfortable about the informality of these arrangements. Consideration must be given to the issue of whether such destruction should be witnessed and recorded.

Conclusion

7.79   Many issues warranting further consideration have arisen in this Chapter. Pharmacists seek changes that would enable them better to carry out their important task of assessing the appropriateness of a prescription. There is a general view that CDRs should contain more information than at present. The destruction of controlled drugs gives rise to practical problems and there is a view that the destruction of patient returns should be witnessed and recorded. I will deal with these issues in Chapter Fourteen.

CHAPTER EIGHT

Controlled Drugs in the Community

Introduction

8.1 In the preceding Chapters, I have examined the Regulations governing the prescribing and dispensing of controlled drugs. When controlled drugs are dispensed at a community pharmacy, the person who collects them is not normally required to provide his/her name or address and, consequently, no record is made of such information. Once a controlled drug has been dispensed and any necessary entries made in the controlled drugs register (CDR) (or, in some cases, in the private prescriptions book), there is no legal requirement to keep any further record of any kind. In most cases, therefore, any possible audit trail ceases at the time of dispensing. There is an exception to this general rule in that there are record keeping and custody requirements in relation to controlled drugs prescribed to patients living in a care home. I shall refer to them again later in this Chapter.

8.2 Apart from cases in which a patient is living in a care home, there are two types of situation in which a record is commonly made in relation to a controlled drug after dispensing. In these cases, the records are made, not in order to comply with a legal duty, but as a matter of good practice or to comply with advice or instructions given by an employer or a professional association. First, a district nurse will keep a record, on a patient drug record card (PDRC), of controlled drugs administered through syringe drivers by him/her to a patient in accordance with the instructions given by a doctor on the prescription, and will also make a record of any controlled drug that s/he destroys after a patient's death. He or she will do so to comply with his/her professional duty and, probably also, with the instructions of his/her employer. Second, a general practitioner (GP) or pharmacist might make a record of the destruction of controlled drugs returned to him/her for the purpose of destruction. Pharmacists are advised to do so by the Royal Pharmaceutical Society of Great Britain. Many doctors and pharmacists ask a colleague to witness the destruction of controlled drugs. However, there is no legal obligation to do so; the drugs can be destroyed without any formality.

8.3 The position of a district nurse is to be contrasted with that of a community midwife who keeps a supply of controlled drugs for administration to patients during childbirth. Regulation 21 of the Misuse of Drugs Regulations 2001 imposes specific record keeping requirements on midwives. They have to keep a book for recording the details of any Schedule 2 drugs obtained; the details include the date, the name and address of the supplier and the amount and form of the drug obtained. On administering such a drug to a patient, the midwife must enter, as soon as practicable, the name and address of the patient, the amount administered and the form in which the drug was administered.

The Administration of Controlled Drugs by District Nurses

8.4 For many years, district nurses have administered controlled drugs to patients suffering severe pain in the course of a terminal illness. Until recent years, it was common for a patient to take an oral preparation, containing an opioid analgesic, sometimes known as the Brompton mixture or Brompton cocktail. If this became insufficient, a doctor or district nurse would give periodic injections of diamorphine. Nowadays, methods of pain control are much improved. Initially, the pain will be controlled by the ingestion of a slow release tablet containing morphine sulphate, or by the application of a fentanyl patch, which allows the gradual absorption of fentanyl, an opioid analgesic. District nurses are not usually involved in the patient's daily care at this stage. However, when these measures become insufficient, and the patient needs stronger analgesia, the most usual solution is the provision of a syringe driver. A syringe driver is a portable battery-operated pump. Over a 24 hour period, it ensures the gradual release of diamorphine, administered in combination with an anti-sickness drug. Usually, by this stage, the patient will require general nursing care; the district nurse will set up the syringe driver and will refill the syringe each day, in accordance with the doctor's instructions as to dosage.

8.5   The introduction of syringe drivers has enabled terminally ill patients who choose to be nursed at home, rather than in a hospital or a hospice, to remain at home in far greater comfort than previously. The syringe driver avoids the soreness associated with repeated injections and achieves a steady flow of analgesia. According to Mr Ian Hargreaves, retired Regional Director of the Royal College of Nursing (RCN), adequate pain control was often not achieved prior to the introduction of syringe drivers. In his view, it is impossible to overstate their value. In Tameside, the first syringe drivers were purchased in 1993. The evidence before the Inquiry suggests that their use is increasing.

8.6   It is often necessary for a patient with terminal cancer to be given quite large amounts of diamorphine through a syringe driver. Not only will the pain worsen, but the patient will become habituated to the drug and increasing amounts will be required to provide adequate relief. Large quantities are prescribed and are usually collected by a relative or carer and kept at the patient's home. Sometimes, particularly if a patient is being cared for by an elderly person, it may be difficult for the carer to go to a pharmacy. In such circumstances, GPs and district nurses will sometimes collect medication from the pharmacy as an act of kindness.

8.7   After the drug has been brought to the house, the district nurse will enter the amount into the receipt column of the PDRC. The dosage, as authorised by the doctor, is entered on the card and signed by the doctor. Any alteration to the dosage is recorded by the doctor during a visit. This provides the nurse's authority to administer the drug. The nurse will keep a continuous record of drugs received and administered, including a running balance of stocks held at the house.

The District Nurses in Tameside

8.8   Mrs Diane Nuttall, Directorate Manager of the Community Care Directorate of the Tameside and Glossop Primary Care Trust (T&G PCT), successor body to Tameside and Glossop Community and Priority Services NHS Trust (T&G CPST), described the district nursing service as it is provided in Tameside. About 120 persons are employed; some are qualified district nurses, some are registered nurses and some are care assistants. They operate from 14 bases in the Tameside area with teams of between five and seven nurses working from each base. They provide a service seven days a week. The general role of district nurses is to ensure that patients of their allocated GP obtain all necessary nursing assessments and nursing care. This, of course, includes palliative care for terminally ill patients living at home.

8.9　In 1995, Shipman joined a fundholding consortium of small general practices, known as the Tameside Consortium, which negotiated an arrangement whereby district nurses based at a clinic in Dukinfield were allocated to serve the patients of members of the Consortium. From April 1995, Shipman's patients were attended by Mrs Marion Gilchrist, who became the 'named nurse' for his practice. Mrs Gilchrist had qualified as a registered general nurse in 1974, and had begun working for the T&G CPST in 1990 as a relief district nursing sister. She worked as a district nurse until her promotion to district team leader in 1998 and became a senior district nurse in September 2001. When Mrs Gilchrist was on holiday or otherwise unavailable, other nurses would cover for her and visit her patients.

8.10　Mrs Gilchrist gave oral evidence to the Inquiry. Understandably, this was a distressing experience for her, given the close working relationship she had once enjoyed with Shipman. Mrs Gilchrist used to meet Shipman weekly to discuss those patients of his whom she was responsible for nursing. She held him in high regard. According to her, he seemed to know all his patients and their extended families. She had the impression that he really cared about them. She felt that he was an 'old-fashioned' GP, which she clearly intended as a compliment. She said that he treated her as a fellow professional and listened to her ideas and suggestions. He made her feel a valued member of the team. From 1995, Mrs Gilchrist was responsible for setting up and replenishing syringe drivers for Shipman's patients. She said that Shipman seemed to be more interested than other doctors in the care of his terminally ill patients. He visited them more frequently and was more willing than other doctors to prescribe diamorphine.

Shipman's Diversion of Diamorphine Prescribed for Use in Syringe Drivers

8.11　As I have explained in Chapter One, Shipman sometimes collected drugs from a pharmacy, ostensibly out of kindness to the patient's family, but in fact to give himself an opportunity to steal some or all of the patient's drugs. He well knew that, if he prescribed the drug, presented the prescription for dispensing and then delivered the drug, no one would notice if he delivered an amount smaller than he had prescribed. He did this on several occasions. For example, on 3rd July 1997, Shipman prescribed 2300mg diamorphine for Mrs Maureen Jackson; he delivered only 1500mg to her house. Mrs Gilchrist entered the amount of 1500mg on the 'receipt' side of the PDRC; she had no means of knowing that a larger amount had been prescribed and dispensed.

8.12　On other occasions, Shipman attended at a patient's house soon after the patient had died and took possession of the unused stock of diamorphine, saying that he would destroy it. For example, he did this in the case of Mr Raymond Jones in 1993, and in the case of Mr James Arrandale in 1995. Sometimes, he would make a note on the PDRC, to the effect that he had taken the drug for destruction. Provided that the deceased's family consented, as they did, he appeared to be acting lawfully. It never occurred to Mrs Gilchrist that Shipman might be doing wrong. In fact, he was acting unlawfully, because the law allowed him to take the drug for destruction, not to keep it for himself. However, his intentions remained secret and his failure to destroy the drug was not detected.

8.13   On one occasion, in 1998, Mrs Gilchrist had occasion to question Shipman about the amount of diamorphine in stock at the home of a patient, Mr John Henshall, who was suffering from cancer and had a syringe driver. On Monday, 6th July 1998, Mrs Gilchrist found that there was a difference between the stock balance, in which Shipman had made the last entry, and the actual stock. There was a deficit of five 10mg ampoules. Mrs Gilchrist asked Shipman about this. At first, he suggested that the PDRC was correct and sought to explain why this was so. Mrs Gilchrist could not understand his explanation and began to feel foolish. However, she asked him specifically about the five 10mg ampoules and he then said that he had given them to a colleague from whom he had previously borrowed a similar quantity of the drug. Mrs Gilchrist accepted this explanation. She thought Shipman's practice in this respect was poor, but she did not for a moment think that Shipman had stolen the drug, as I am sure he had. Nor did she think seriously about reporting him. In that respect, she behaved differently towards a doctor from the way in which she would have behaved to a nursing colleague. She told the Inquiry that, had a nursing colleague 'borrowed' and 'repaid' a controlled drug, she would have made a report to her employers. Following Shipman's arrest, Mrs Gilchrist's failure to report Shipman's unorthodox practice to her employers was 'noted' on her personnel records. This was a minor form of disciplinary action. She was advised that she had failed to comply with her employer's policy that all such irregularities should be reported. I have no doubt that this policy is correct and that it is important that all irregularities should be reported. However, in the context of Mrs Gilchrist's working relationship with Shipman, I find it wholly understandable that she did not report him to her employer. By this time, Shipman had already killed his last victim.

Attempts to Improve the System of Control in Tameside

8.14   Shipman exploited to the full the lack of any regulation of controlled drugs after dispensing. Since his activities came to light, those with responsibility for the district nursing service in Tameside have sought to devise ways of improving their procedures in the hope of deterring or detecting any possible repetition of Shipman's conduct.

Conveying Controlled Drugs to a Patient's Home

8.15   As I have said, it is usual for drugs for use in a syringe driver to be collected from a community pharmacy by a relative or carer of the patient. However, this is not always possible. Some pharmacies offer a delivery service, but not all. On occasions, the healthcare professionals caring for the patient may perceive a need to collect the drugs from the pharmacy. Mrs Gilchrist explained that such a need arises most often in the case of elderly couples, without friends or family able to assist, where the spouse of the patient is unable to drive.

8.16   Mr Hargreaves told the Inquiry that most primary care trusts (PCTs) have a policy that district nurses should not collect medicines of any description for their patients; the prohibition applies particularly to controlled drugs. The T&G CPST had such a policy during the 1990s. However, it appears that, from time to time, the district nurses 'bent the rules' in cases where they felt that it was necessary, for the welfare of patients, for them to collect medication. Recently, the policy has been formally relaxed, as the result of pressure from the district nurses. The policy now recognises that, in exceptional circumstances, it will be acceptable for a nurse to collect controlled drugs, provided that prior notice is given by the district nurse to a senior staff member. The present policy is that:

> **'... where there is an urgent need for medication and every avenue for delivery and collection has been explored to no avail, a Registered Nurse may contact his/her manager or senior nurse on duty and may subsequently carry medication from the community pharmacy directly to the patient's home'**.

8.17   I can see no objection to this practice, provided it remains the exception rather than the rule. It seems to me that the safeguard imposed by the Tameside policy is a sensible one. It protects the district nurse from possible criticism and permits the employing trust to supervise its employees. However, in my view, a more important general safeguard would be a requirement that the pharmacist should record in the CDR the name of any healthcare professional who collects Schedule 2 controlled drugs on behalf of a patient.

The Patient Drug Record Card

8.18   I have already explained that the PDRC contains the doctor's authority for the district nurses to administer the drug prescribed. The primary purpose of the PDRC, which has equivalents in hospital practice, is clinical. It exists to ensure that a proper record of drug administration is maintained. It is not primarily intended to provide a record of the movement of drugs for audit purposes. Nor is its purpose the recording of the disposal or destruction of a controlled drug, although it is sometimes used to that end.

8.19   The version of the PDRC in use in Tameside during Shipman's time contained spaces for recording the identities of the patient, the GP and the district nurse. It also contained a number of columns and rows for the recording of the nature and amount of drug obtained and the amount administered. It required the administering nurse to sign each entry and to record the stock balance following each administration. GPs would not usually administer the drug. The only entries that a GP would usually make related to the dosage as initially directed and as subsequently revised. The PDRC contained no space specifically designated for the recording of this information.

8.20   In the light of the lessons learned since the discovery of Shipman's crimes, a revised version of the PDRC has been introduced in Tameside. One face of the card is intended exclusively for completion by the GP and specifically provides for entries covering the dosage, frequency and route of administration of the drug prescribed. The other face, for use by the district nurse, is in the same format as the old card. The new PDRC is plainly an improvement. However, there is still no system by which anyone can check that the amount of the drug dispensed by the pharmacy is the same as the amount entered on the PDRC. A doctor could still perpetrate the deception employed by Shipman in, for example, the case of Mrs Jackson. Mrs Nuttall told the Inquiry that the district nurses in

Tameside would welcome a document issued by the dispensing pharmacist that recorded what had been dispensed so that they could be sure that each entry on the acquisition side of the card reflected what had left the pharmacy.

8.21 At the moment, following the patient's death or following cessation of district nurse involvement, PDRCs are archived by the T&G PCT. They are not 'married up' with the GP or pharmacy records. Nor, until recently, was there any audit or review of their contents. Mrs Nuttall explained that samples of PDRCs are now reviewed for legibility and accuracy and 'benchmarked' against records provided by other trusts. She said that an audit of every PDRC would be feasible and that it might well be worth giving consideration to reviewing every PDRC.

8.22 Mr Hargreaves, on behalf of the RCN, made the suggestion that a new drug administration record card could be opened by the dispensing pharmacist and could accompany every supply of the drug to the patient's home. That arrangement would deter anyone from removing part of the consignment. Administrations of the drug would then be entered onto the card until either the drug was exhausted or the patient died. If there were unused drugs after death, the destruction of the excess would have to be entered on the card and witnessed by another healthcare professional. Used cards could be reviewed by an officer of the PCT and, if all was found to be in order, could be 'married up' with the patient's medical records. In this way, the cards could provide a complete audit trail for the drugs, and the patient's medical records would be complete in this important respect.

8.23 Under this system, it would not be permissible for a doctor to remove controlled drugs from the patient's house; they would have to be destroyed in the presence of another healthcare professional and the destruction recorded. Even if the rule permitting a doctor to take drugs away with him/her for destruction were to be retained, a record that s/he had done so would be useful. A review of comments written by Shipman on the PDRCs kept for some of his patients would have given rise to concern. For example, the mutually inconsistent entries that he made on the PDRC of Mr Keith Harrison, saying **'All Drugs Destroyed'** and **'returned to Chemist for destruction'**, might have been queried.

8.24 I shall consider the RCN's suggestion further in Chapter Fourteen. It may provide a useful additional safeguard, at least in connection with injectable drugs such as diamorphine, which are usually administered by a doctor or district nurse. I do not think it would be practicable in the case of other controlled drugs that are usually administered by the patient or a carer.

The Administration of Controlled Drugs by a Single District Nurse

8.25 When considering Shipman's methods of diverting controlled drugs, the Inquiry also heard evidence that other healthcare professionals, such as nurses, are sometimes found to have committed offences of a similar kind. Some nurses fear accusations of misconduct of this type and feel vulnerable to possible criticism, even when behaving with complete integrity. In Tameside, the district nurses have suffered a deep sense of shock on learning that a doctor whom they trusted implicitly should have been so profoundly dishonest. It is entirely understandable that they should feel the need for additional procedures that will enable them to demonstrate that they have behaved properly.

8.26   The policy in hospitals used to be that, in the interests of patient safety, two nurses should be present at the administration of all drugs. The policy now applies only to controlled drugs, and the justification is no longer patient safety but the prevention of diversion. There has never been such a general rule in the district nursing service. In Tameside, such a policy has recently been introduced for both the administration and destruction of controlled drugs. I was told that the district nurses feel more secure operating in this way. I can understand why, given the particular sensitivities in Tameside, it has been thought appropriate to introduce such a requirement there. In most areas, however, there is no such policy.

8.27   Mrs Nuttall said that the adoption of this policy had had no adverse impact on human resources. The nurses planned their visits so that they could work in pairs when necessary. However, one of the district nurses, Mrs Barbara Sunderland, said that they would rarely otherwise work in pairs, and I cannot see how the imposition of such a restriction could fail to have significant resource implications. Certainly, the weight of opinion of those who contributed to the Inquiry's seminars was that it would have such implications. Given the shortage of nurses at the present time, it would seem to me that such a policy could be justified only if it had advantages for patient safety (for example, by reducing medication error), as well as providing a safeguard against diversion. Mr Hargreaves said that there was no evidence that attendance by two nurses did reduce medication error. It had been found that there was no significant increase in medication error when the policy in hospitals was abolished for drugs other than controlled drugs. While that might appear surprising, I can see that, when a nurse is routinely required to check a colleague's performance of a procedure, which will almost always be correctly carried out, s/he might well cease to give the process the attention required to provide a real check. Also, I can see how a nurse who knows that his/her procedures will always be checked might be less careful than one whose work is not routinely checked.

8.28   Finally, Mr Hargreaves explained that, in areas of dispersed population, it might be extremely difficult to achieve the implementation of such a policy. I can readily see that it might be wasteful of resources if two nurses had to travel long distances together, when the only purpose of the journey for one of them was to witness the work of the other.

Storage and Security

8.29   The exacting storage and security requirements that apply to controlled drugs in pharmacies are immediately relaxed when controlled drugs are released into the community. At first sight, this seems surprising and even alarming. I heard evidence that controlled drugs such as diamorphine are often kept on a table or in a cupboard in the room where the patient is being nursed. It may be said that this does not matter greatly because the quantities taken into the patient's home are much smaller than those stored in a pharmacy. I appreciate that a locked cabinet will not always be available in a patient's home although it might be worth considering the feasibility of providing one on loan to any patient for whom a syringe driver is supplied. I do accept that strict rules for the custody of controlled drugs in a patient's home would not be practicable or enforceable.

8.30   That said, it does appear to me that more could be done to educate patients and their relatives about the need to keep controlled drugs as securely as possible. I am sure that most pharmacists advise patients or their relatives to keep such drugs out of the reach of children. However, I was concerned to hear that pharmacists do not usually explain that the drugs are vulnerable to misuse. Their justification is that they fear that patients might be worried by the responsibility they are taking on and might not use the drugs. I find this attitude rather condescending. I think that most patients and their families are capable of understanding that a drug which is appropriate to their particular needs might be a temptation or a danger to others, and that it should be looked after accordingly. I think that there is a need for greater frankness with patients and for a heightened awareness of the potential of such drugs for diversion.

The Destruction of Controlled Drugs after Death

The Legal Position

8.31   An unexpected issue arose in the course of the Inquiry's consideration of the various procedures adopted to dispose of unused controlled drugs following the death of the patient for whom they were prescribed. It concerned the right of a district nurse or doctor to remove drugs from a patient's home following the death. By virtue of the provisions of section 52 and section 58 of the Medicines Act 1968, the dispensing of pharmacy medicines and prescription only medicines (including controlled drugs) by a community pharmacist is regarded as a retail sale of the drug, even though the patient might not have paid for the drug, or even paid a contribution by way of prescription charge. The legal effect of the transaction is that the drug becomes the property of the patient. There are, of course, limitations on what the patient can do with a controlled drug; for example, s/he might commit a criminal offence if s/he supplied it to someone other than to a doctor or pharmacist for the purpose of destruction. However, if the patient dies, ownership of drugs passes to his/her estate. In the immediate post-death period, that will mean that the drugs become the property of the executor or the personal representative of the deceased. There are limitations also on what that person can lawfully do with the drugs; in practice, s/he can only give them to a doctor or pharmacist for destruction. If, however, that person leaves them in the deceased's house, it is doubtful whether s/he is committing any offence. He or she is, however, creating a risk that the drugs will find their way into the wrong hands.

8.32   In Tameside, the district nurses usually offer to destroy any excess diamorphine as this can easily be done within the home. The legality of this procedure is uncertain, as nurses (unlike doctors and pharmacists) do not have a statutory right to receive controlled drugs for the purpose of destruction. However, it is not unlawful for a district nurse (or indeed anyone) to destroy a controlled drug on behalf of the person legally entitled to its possession. The district nurses in Tameside find that the families of deceased patients are content for them to destroy excess drugs and I am sure that many wish this service to be performed on their behalf. Perhaps the niceties of the legal position do not greatly matter, as the executor or personal representative would not be able to make use of the drugs and it is plainly in the public interest that the drugs be destroyed as soon as possible. However, the district nurses cannot lawfully insist on destroying any excess controlled drugs, or on taking them away for destruction by a pharmacist, in the face of objection from the family. Mrs Kay Roberts, Lead Pharmacist for the Royal College of General Practitioners National

Drug Misuse Training Programme and pharmacist member of the Advisory Council on the Misuse of Drugs, explained how, in one case in Glasgow, difficulties were encountered by a district nurse where the offspring of a deceased patient were drug abusers.

8.33   The present legal situation is anomalous and unsatisfactory. This problem does not arise where drugs are provided to a patient in hospital because, in that situation, the drugs never become the property of the patient. I would urge that consideration be given to changing the law to avoid this potential difficulty. I will address the question in greater detail in Chapter Fourteen.

Practical Problems Connected with Disposal

8.34   It is clear that the informal arrangements relating to the destruction of unused controlled drugs are open to abuse by dishonest doctors, pharmacists or nurses. However, other, quite separate practical problems arise in connection with the disposal of controlled drugs. The Inquiry learned that doctors and pharmacists who are completely honest experience problems arising from the safe and secure disposal of such drugs. They would welcome an improved system, not necessarily imposing rules and regulations, but providing a method of safely discharging the responsibility that is put upon them when they receive 'patient returns'. District nurses are not under any legal responsibility to dispose of returned drugs but find themselves having to deal with the problem. The Department of Health acknowledges these problems and is considering whether to impose on PCTs a duty to establish a scheme for the secure collection and disposal of controlled drugs.

8.35   Following the death of a patient who has been nursed at home and who has used a syringe driver, the patient's GP is often called out to confirm that death has occurred and to certify its cause. That was the occasion that Shipman would exploit in order to take drugs away if, as was often the case, a district nurse was not present. As a general rule, doctors do not remove excess drugs unless specifically asked to do so by a member of the patient's family. More usually, the drugs will be dealt with by the district nurse who will attend, probably within 24 hours of the death, to dismantle and remove the syringe driver and possibly other items of equipment lent to the family for the patient's use. The district nurse will often deal with the excess drugs as part of his/her professional responsibility towards the patient.

8.36   District nurses do not always perform this service. The Association for Nurse Prescribing produced to the Inquiry the policy of one PCT that directs district nurses to advise patients' families to return unused controlled drugs to the dispensing pharmacy. Some NHS trusts advise district nurses not to accept drugs for return to the pharmacy in order to avoid accusations of diversion and to reduce the risk of attack.

8.37   In Tameside, district nurses are permitted to destroy controlled drugs at a patient's home and, according to Mrs Nuttall, this is what they prefer to do. This avoids the risk that the drugs might be stolen while being taken to a pharmacy for destruction.

8.38   The most common method of destruction of diamorphine within a patient's home is for the ampoules to be broken open and the contents flushed down a sink or lavatory. The powder is very soluble. There are no legal restrictions on putting drugs into waste water or sewage systems from domestic premises. However, such a process is probably not ideal from an environmental point of view. Some nurses put the ampoules into a tamper-proof container for surgical waste, which is then taken for incineration, and this is probably preferable.

8.39   The practice in Tameside is for the destruction to take place at the patient's home in the presence of a witness, with a signed record being made on the PDRC. Until recently, there was no requirement that the witness should be a nurse or other healthcare professional and, in practice, it was often a relation of the deceased. Now, however, the T&G PCT requires that any destruction of controlled drugs by a district nurse should be witnessed by a second registered nurse, who should sign a record of the destruction. The initiative for this change came from the district nurses, who felt that the person who acted as a witness to the destruction should be a person who fully understood the process and its purpose. Family members might be very distressed and quite unable to exercise an effective check on what was happening. A doctor or nurse, intending to divert drugs for his/her own purposes, could easily 'pull the wool over the eyes' of a family member, either by sleight of hand or by the misleading use of language. In any event, according to Mrs Nuttall, families do not always wish to be involved in witnessing the process and I do not think that they should be required to do so. Mrs Nuttall said that, in the past, destruction was sometimes witnessed by a neighbour who had a key and had let the district nurse into the house. Not only would a neighbour be unable to confirm in an informed way what the doctor or nurse had actually done by way of destruction, s/he would have no authority to sanction the destruction.

8.40   I have already mentioned that there is no special place on the PDRC for the recording of the details of destruction. Even the most recent guidance in Tameside specifies only that a record of destruction be made and signed by a second nurse; it does not specify what the record should comprise. According to Mrs Nuttall, the nurses know that they must state exactly what has been destroyed but they would be complying with the strict wording of the current policy if they were simply to record, as Shipman sometimes did, 'all remaining drugs destroyed' or something similar. In Chapter Fourteen, I shall consider whether there should be a requirement that a formal, detailed record be made of the destruction of leftover drugs.

8.41   I have already discussed the resource implications of the requirement that two nurses be present at the administration of diamorphine in a patient's home. Similar consequences would follow the requirement that two nurses attend to witness destruction although, of course, administration takes place daily, whereas destruction would normally occur only once in the case of each patient.

Care Homes

8.42   At the beginning of this Chapter, I mentioned that there are special requirements in respect of the keeping of controlled drugs for patients who live in care homes. The Inquiry has not considered these requirements in any detail, as there was no evidence of poor practice in the homes occupied by Shipman's patients. The Care Standards Act 2000 and associated Regulations (which became operational in April 2002) require the person in charge of registered care homes to **'make arrangements for the recording, handling, safekeeping, safe administration and disposal of medicines received into the care home'**. The Act also confers on the Secretary of State for Health the power to produce statements of national minimum standards which are to be taken into account by the regulatory authorities when exercising their powers under the Act.

8.43   Statements of minimum standards have now been published. Among other things, these state that care homes must comply with the requirements of the Misuse of Drugs Act 1971. Certain homes providing nursing care have to comply with the Misuse of Drugs (Safe Custody) Regulations 1973. In addition, the administration of a controlled drug by a member of staff must be witnessed by another member of staff. A CDR must be kept recording the receipt, administration and disposal of controlled drugs. Responsibility for ensuring compliance has now passed from the National Care Standards Commission (NCSC) to the Commission for Social Care Inspection (CSCI), which is required to carry out at least two statutory inspections annually.

8.44   Before 2002, it appears that some local authorities and primary care organisations laid down guidelines on good practice in connection with the keeping of medication in care homes. I have seen one such set of guidelines promulgated by Tameside Metropolitan Borough Council and the Tameside Family Health Services Authority in 1995. These guidelines were eminently sensible. They included a requirement that the receipt, administration and return of controlled drugs should be recorded in a CDR. Although these guidelines did not have the force of law, the local authority had the power to inspect care homes and was able to enforce compliance through its power to grant or withhold a licence to keep the home.

8.45   I received evidence from Mr Mark Shockledge, Director of Care Services at the Laurel Bank Residential Care Home, where a number of Shipman's patients lived. He told the Inquiry that the home complied with the guidelines to which I have referred and now complies with the applicable standards. He explained that all drugs prescribed by residents' GPs are dispensed at a designated pharmacy. All controlled drugs prescribed for residents are kept in a cabinet, to which only team leaders have access. On receipt of the controlled drug, details are entered in a bound book known as the Controlled Drugs Record of Administration, which has pages similar in layout to the Tameside PDRC. Each page is specific to a particular resident. Mr Shockledge said that, at the time when he made his statement, there were twice-yearly inspections of the premises by the NCSC, which monitored compliance with procedures at the home and had the power to issue compliance notices. Also, the pharmacist from the home's designated pharmacy regularly monitored the home's compliance with its procedures. It appears to me that these arrangements should keep the risk of diversion to a minimum. Similar arrangements apply at the Hyde Nursing Home. The Inquiry considered several deaths that took place there and at the Laurel Bank Residential Care Home. There is nothing to suggest that the procedures in operation there were in any way unsatisfactory.

8.46   In February 2004, a letter was received by the Inquiry, from a NCSC inspector, expressing concern about the potential for diversion of controlled drugs that exists in children's homes, residential homes, younger adult placements, boarding schools and secure units.

It is beyond the scope of the Inquiry to examine compliance with standards in such establishments. The CSCI has also recently raised certain concerns, which I readily understand, connected to issues of storage and disposal of controlled drugs in the premises that they visit. Again, however, these concerns do not fall within my remit.

8.47 For the sake of completeness I mention that, if a care home wishes to keep a stock of controlled drugs (as opposed to drugs prescribed for an individual patient), the manager must obtain a licence from the Home Office.

Conclusion

8.48 In this Chapter, I have highlighted the almost complete absence of any regulation of controlled drugs once they have left the pharmacy. Shipman took advantage of the informality of the current arrangements. So, no doubt, do other dishonest doctors and healthcare professionals. In my view, it is necessary that there should be some improvement in the methods of tracking controlled drugs from the pharmacy until the point where they are consumed or destroyed. I shall discuss the means by which this might be achieved in Chapter Fourteen.

CHAPTER NINE

The Inspection and Monitoring of the Arrangements for Controlled Drugs

Introduction

9.1   In this Chapter, I shall describe the ways in which various bodies inspect the storage arrangements and standards of record keeping for controlled drugs in community pharmacies. I shall also consider the extent to which the use of controlled drugs is monitored through the inspection of pharmacies. I have already explained, in Chapter Five, that there is very little inspection of the practical arrangements in general practitioners' (GPs') surgery premises. There is some monitoring of GPs' prescribing. This will be described more fully in the Fifth Report.

The Legislation

9.2   Section 23 of the Misuse of Drugs Act 1971 (MDA 1971) provides the statutory basis for the inspection, by the Home Office Drugs Inspectorate (HODI) and police chemist inspection officers (CIOs), of the premises of those who carry on business as producers or suppliers of controlled drugs. The section permits CIOs and HODI inspectors to enter the premises of a pharmacist or manufacturer or wholesaler of controlled drugs and to inspect the arrangements for the keeping of the drugs and the records of controlled drugs transactions. This includes the power to inspect the controlled drugs register (CDR). Since the power extends only to 'business premises' it does not allow the routine inspection of GPs' surgeries.

9.3   Regulation 26 of the Misuse of Drugs Regulations (MDR) 2001 requires doctors and pharmacists to provide to authorised persons such particulars or documents as may be requested in respect of the production, obtaining or supplying of controlled drugs or of any stock of controlled drugs in their possession. Such doctors and pharmacists are also required to produce such stock for inspection when requested to do so. However, by regulation 26(3), this requirement does not extend to personal records held in confidence. It was in the exercise of powers conferred upon HODI inspectors by regulation 26 that Mr Graham Calder, a HODI inspector, accompanied by Detective Constable (DC) Michael Beard, the Greater Manchester Police (GMP) CIO for Tameside, visited Shipman at his surgery on 14th August 1998, asking to see his CDR. By this time, Shipman had come under suspicion of murdering Mrs Kathleen Grundy by administering an opiate drug. Shipman said that he did not keep a CDR.

Home Office Inspections

9.4   The Home Office Drugs Branch is responsible for administering the statutory systems of control applicable to the production and distribution of controlled drugs. The role is performed by two units within the Drugs Branch, the HODI and the Licensing Section. Mr Alan Macfarlane is the Chief Inspector in charge of the HODI. He reports to the Head of the Drug Legislation Enforcement Unit. The role of the Drugs Branch is to implement international convention obligations through the licensing of the manufacture and wholesale supply of controlled drugs. The Licensing Section issues the necessary licences and authorities to manufacture, possess and supply controlled drugs, together with licences to import and export such drugs. The main focus of activity of the HODI is the inspection of licensed manufacturers and wholesalers and the giving of advice to the Licensing Section on the grant of licences.

The Organisation of the Home Office Drugs Inspectorate

9.5   Apart from the Chief Inspector, the HODI has three senior inspectors and 11 inspectors. The HODI Headquarters and the South Eastern Regional Office are in London and there are two small regional offices located outside London. The Northern Regional Office, which was relocated from Bradford to Leeds in 1990, covers the North of England and Scotland. It is staffed by a senior inspector, three inspectors, a full-time clerk and a part-time administrative assistant. The Inquiry heard oral evidence from Mr Macfarlane and four inspectors from the Northern Regional Office. These were Mr Alan Stears (an inspector from 1972 and a senior inspector from 1987 until his retirement in May 2003), Mr Calder (an inspector since 1989, with responsibility for Greater Manchester since the late 1990s), Mr John Scullion (an inspector since 1985) and Mr Frank Eggleston (an inspector from 1969 and a senior inspector from 1974 until 1981).

The Qualifications and Training of Inspectors

9.6   HODI inspectors are not pharmacists or doctors and they have no specialist training in pharmacy or medicine. The inspectors who gave evidence to the Inquiry had all worked previously as Home Office immigration officers. Their initial training is provided 'on the job'. Understanding of such issues as irresponsible prescribing is gained in an *ad hoc* manner, by learning from the experience of colleagues, listening to them recount details of previous cases and reading old case files. It is, however, clear that, as they gain experience, they become knowledgeable about trends in the uses and abuses of controlled drugs. They have access to textbooks and use for reference the Department of Health (DoH) guidelines for doctors on the treatment of addiction, entitled 'Drug Misuse and Dependence – Guidelines on Clinical Management', to which I have referred in Chapter Four. They may also seek help from the Royal Pharmaceutical Society of Great Britain (RPSGB) inspectors or from primary care trust (PCT) medical or prescribing advisers. According to Mr Macfarlane, they also have access to advice from a Controlled Drug Adviser at the DoH. From time to time, HODI inspectors meet consultant psychiatrists or pharmacists who have a special interest in the treatment of drug addiction.

The Types of Inspection Undertaken by the Home Office

9.7   Apart from the core function of inspecting the arrangements of manufacturers and wholesalers of controlled drugs, a function which occupies about 80% to 90% of its inspectors' time, the HODI also carries out routine inspections of the arrangements in private hospitals and in other premises licensed to hold controlled drugs, such as drug treatment clinics and some care homes. NHS hospitals do not require a licence and are not inspected by the HODI unless their pharmacies supply controlled drugs to other hospitals or units. The HODI also has overall responsibility for enforcing the statutory provisions relating to retail pharmacies and GPs' surgeries, but the routine inspection of retail pharmacies is delegated to the police. HODI inspectors examine the arrangements in GPs' surgeries and dispensaries only when a problem is brought to their attention.

9.8   As well as examining the safe custody arrangements made by manufacturers and wholesalers, HODI inspectors also routinely examine stock and stock records which, unlike those held at community pharmacies, are often kept electronically and include running balances. They also examine records of supply, such as invoices and delivery notes. As I mentioned in Chapter Seven, however, these records of supply, whether in electronic or paper form, are not routinely compared, even on a sample basis, with records (such as the CDR) held at community pharmacies or at GPs' practices.

The Involvement of the Home Office Drugs Inspectorate with General Practitioners and Community Pharmacies

9.9   Although it does not routinely inspect community pharmacies or GPs' surgeries, the HODI may become involved in the investigation of any problem or concern that arises in a retail pharmacy and which suggests that there might have been a breach of the MDA 1971 or of the MDR in force at the material time.

9.10   The HODI also issues detailed written guidance notes, called 'Notes for Chemist Inspection Officers', to CIOs for the purpose of informing their routine inspections of community pharmacies. HODI inspectors are sometimes involved in the training of CIOs and are available to give advice over the telephone on controlled drugs matters to CIOs, PCT prescribing advisers and others. According to its guidance notes, the HODI expects CIOs to report to it any supply of controlled drugs by a community pharmacy which appears to be unlawful or in breach of the Regulations or which suggests that a doctor might be prescribing irresponsibly, for example by over-prescribing in such a way as to give rise to the danger of leakage of drugs onto the illicit market. The same is true of cases where a doctor issues prescriptions for controlled drugs, naming him/herself as patient, or where a doctor regularly presents prescriptions for controlled drugs in the name of patients and collects the drugs him/herself. Mr Stears said, however, that the HODI would not necessarily expect CIOs to report all such cases. He suggested that if, for example, there was concern that the doctor was likely to move around the country, then the HODI might become involved so as to ensure that people were aware of his/her past history. Otherwise, he did not take the view that the HODI had to be informed about each and every criminal offence coming to the attention of the police or of a NHS authority involving the diversion or abuse of controlled drugs by a doctor.

9.11   The HODI inspectors also receive expressions of concern about unlawful or improper practice from RPSGB inspectors and, sometimes, from pharmacists and GPs. They liaise with PCT medical and prescribing advisers in the investigation of concerns about a GP's irresponsible prescribing. Until 1997, CIOs were expected to notify to the HODI the name of any drug addict of whom they had recently become aware, for incorporation into the Home Office Addicts Index. After 1997, the Index was no longer kept.

9.12   If, on investigation of a reported concern, it is found that a doctor has been prescribing irresponsibly or has breached one of the technical requirements of the MDR 2001, but has not apparently committed a serious crime, a HODI inspector will often issue a warning or advice to the doctor and enlist the help of the PCT prescribing adviser in re-educating the doctor or in monitoring the doctor's future conduct. If the doctor's conduct does not improve, the inspector may refer the case to the General Medical Council (GMC) with a view to disciplinary action. However, if, on investigation, the conduct in question appears to amount to an offence under the MDA 1971 or a serious or continuing breach of the MDR 2001, the case will be taken over by the police for further investigation and possible prosecution. As I explained in Chapter Four, the Home Secretary's powers (which used to be instigated by the HODI) to restrict a doctor's use of controlled drugs following a drugs-related conviction or a finding of irresponsible prescribing have fallen into disuse.

Police Inspections

9.13   In Chapter Three, I explained that, in 1917, police officers not below the rank of inspector were given the power to inspect the arrangements made for controlled drugs in community pharmacies and that, in 1921, the power was extended to officers below the rank of inspector. A Home Office Circular, issued to Chief Officers of Police, described the role that the police were to fulfil. However, the police were not placed under a statutory duty to inspect community pharmacies. Police officers had the power to enter and inspect, but were under no duty to do so. The position remains the same today. As I said in Chapter Three, in 1922, the Commissioner of the Metropolitan Police queried whether the task of inspection could not more appropriately be performed by persons with practical knowledge of the retail pharmacy business. Today, although the Association of Chief Police Officers (ACPO) values the work of the CIO and encourages its members to ensure that the job is performed by properly trained officers, there remains a body of opinion among senior officers that pharmacy inspection is not 'police work'. Not all police areas employ a CIO and, in many areas where there is a CIO, the post is not accorded the prominence or resources that its incumbent might wish.

The Changing Purpose of Police Inspections

9.14   In 1922, the object of a pharmacy inspection appears to have been to check that the safe custody and formal prescription requirements for controlled drugs were being complied with and that the relevant records were being properly kept. No special expertise was required for the work. It appears that, prior to 1939, the CIO was not expected to examine the contents of the records (then the dangerous drugs register) in detail, only to check that the pharmacist was complying with the Regulations. The CIO would not be expected to notice the names of the prescribing doctors or their patients; nor would s/he be expected to notice the quantities of controlled drugs prescribed or supplied. After 1939, however, it appears that the scope of the inspection widened. CIOs were then asked also to identify persons who were receiving regular supplies of dangerous drugs and to report back to the HODI. This information was required to enable the Government to comply with its international obligations.

9.15 During the 1960s and 1970s, the duties of the CIO increased again. Following the Brain Committee's second Report, the Government brought in measures designed to control irresponsible prescribing by doctors. Section 13 of the MDA 1971 permitted the Home Secretary to restrict the right of a doctor to deal with controlled drugs following tribunal proceedings at which irresponsible prescribing had been proved. Consequently, after the passing of the MDA 1971, CIOs were encouraged to report, not only supplies to known or suspected drug misusers, but also supplies that suggested irresponsible prescribing or diversion. That remains the position today, despite the fact that directions under section 13 of the MDA 1971 are no longer made.

Home Office Guidance Notes for Chemist Inspection Officers

9.16 The nature of the duties of a CIO and the types of knowledge and understanding required for the position can be inferred from an examination of the guidance notes for CIOs issued by the Home Office. The purpose of CIO inspections, as described in 'Notes for Chemist Inspection Officers', has remained essentially the same for more than 15 years. The 1988 edition of the guidance notes, which was still current in 1993, when the GMP CIO inspected the CDR held at the pharmacy at 23 Market Street, Hyde (which inspection I shall describe in Chapter Eleven), states:

> **'The inspections are intended to ensure that controlled drugs are not being supplied to unauthorised persons and that proper records are kept, and to bring suspicious supplies to the attention of the Home Office. The efficient supervision of the arrangements for storing and distributing controlled drugs from retail pharmacies is an essential part of the machinery of drugs control. The inspection of retail pharmacies can also provide valuable intelligence about overall drug abuse, especially in relation to the type of drugs being abused, the incidence of drug addiction, irresponsible prescribers and those practitioners who are failing to notify drug addicts to the Home Office.'**

9.17 That passage gives some indication of the wide scope of the duties of the modern CIO. He or she is not merely an examiner of records and safe custody arrangements and a witness to the destruction of 'out of date' controlled drugs (which would be fairly routine tasks), s/he is also an intelligence officer who is expected to sniff out all manner of wrongful practices which would not necessarily be apparent from a CDR. The duty to notify the Home Office of addicts no longer exists, as I have explained, although the current guidance notes still mention it.

9.18 The CIO is expected to look out for irresponsible prescribing. The 1988 guidance notes attempted to define this concept, which is not easy. There has never been either a statutory or a judicial definition. The 1988 guidance notes stated that a doctor would be guilty of irresponsible prescribing if s/he prescribed controlled drugs in a way that resulted in the recipient selling the drugs on the black market, or where there was a real risk of this happening or where there was a risk that the recipient was misusing the drugs. To help with the CIO's assessment of a particular prescription, a small table was annexed to the guidance notes, showing the levels of periodic supply of certain drugs which might suggest that a doctor was prescribing irresponsibly. To make proper sense of this table and to apply it intelligently, the CIO needed knowledge of a range of controlled drugs, of the proper uses to which they were put and of the ways and means by which they were sometimes abused.

9.19   The 1988 guidance notes also contained advice on detecting signs of suspicious practice. For example, Note 9 said:

> **'Any large or regular supplies by doctors should be reported. Details of any instances where a doctor issues prescriptions for CDs naming himself as the patient, or where the doctor regularly presents prescriptions for controlled drugs in the names of patients and collects the drugs himself, should also be reported.'**

9.20   And again, Note 10 stated that:

> **'A practitioner may act as a patient's agent in cashing a prescription and taking the drugs to the person he has specified as the recipient on the prescription. ... This obviously enables the unscrupulous practitioner to obtain CDs by deception. He may do this rather than obtain CDs lawfully through written requisition in an attempt to conceal his own drug use or to avoid having to pay for drugs which he intends to use in his practice, and at the same time to claim reimbursement from his Family Practitioner Committee ....'**

9.21   This advice would certainly help a CIO to recognise the kind of features that might be present when a doctor was obtaining illicit supplies of a controlled drug. However, even armed with this advice, a CIO would not necessarily become aware of instances of a doctor collecting controlled drugs. As I said in Chapter Seven, the CDR provides for the name of the prescribing doctor to be recorded but not the name of the collector of the drugs. The CIO would, therefore, be dependent almost exclusively on information received from the pharmacist if s/he were to learn of cases where a doctor regularly presented prescriptions for controlled drugs in the names of patients and collected the drugs him/herself.

9.22   The most recent edition of the guidance notes, issued in June 2002, describes the obligations of doctors and pharmacists and the organisation of the Home Office Drugs Branch. It states that inspections should be carried out at least twice a year. The guidance notes advise how a routine inspection should be undertaken and recorded. Among other things, it is said that the CIO should check each section of the CDR for compliance with the Regulations and should then sign and date the last entry in each section. The CIO must be satisfied that all drugs that should be kept in the controlled drugs cabinet are in fact kept there. He or she must check for over-stocking and the presence of out of date stocks. Guidance is given about the destruction of out of date controlled drugs, which is an important part of the CIO's role.

9.23   CIOs are still required to report to the HODI any concerns that controlled drugs are being prescribed unlawfully or irresponsibly. A 'new' definition or description of irresponsible prescribing has been provided. The guidance notes say that the definition used by the HODI is that used by the then Home Secretary in the House of Commons debate on the relevant provisions of the Misuse of Drugs Bill 1970, i.e. **'careless, negligent or unduly liberal prescribing ...'**. The guidance notes also suggest that experience has given the Home Office some understanding of the factors that a tribunal or the GMC will take into account when considering an allegation of irresponsible prescribing. The reference to a tribunal is puzzling, as the tribunal system instituted by the MDA 1971 has been defunct for about ten years. Also, I am unsure how the experience of the Home Office in respect of GMC proceedings will be of assistance to a CIO when examining a CDR. It may be intended that the CIO should telephone the HODI for advice if s/he sees something that might be suspicious. The current edition of the guidance notes repeats the warning about doctors who collect controlled drugs, ostensibly for their patients.

9.24   One aspect of the CIO's duty is to gather intelligence about drug addicts and the practice of those who prescribe for them. The guidance notes provide some advice on these issues. They quote extracts from the DoH guidelines for doctors on the treatment of addiction, entitled 'Drug Misuse and Dependence – Guidelines on Clinical Management', to which I referred in paragraph 9.6. To understand some of these guidelines, the CIO would need a considerable depth of knowledge of the subject. I suppose that any CIO will understand the point when told that doctors should avoid prescribing methadone tablets which, if crushed and injected, are dangerous. However, other advice contained in the guidelines, such as that recommending the use of long-acting rather than short-acting benzodiazepines when treating benzodiazepine dependence, may be beyond the understanding of many CIOs. CIOs will not, of course, be able to glean from the CDR for what condition the drugs have been prescribed and nor will pharmacists necessarily be in a position to tell them.

9.25   Annex A to the guidance notes contains a list of the controlled drug preparations commonly encountered on CIOs' inspections. This sets out the name of each drug, the proprietary or other preparations in which it is normally found and the purpose for which it is normally used. This information is obviously useful for the CIO. However, nothing is said about the normal dose or the quantities that should usually be prescribed. So the CIO must rely on his/her own experience when assessing whether it appears that the drug has been prescribed appropriately.

9.26   In short, to be done well, the duties of a CIO require a good working knowledge of the quite complex statutory requirements, the acquisition of considerable knowledge about the proper and improper usage of a wide variety of controlled drugs, the establishment of good confidential relations with pharmacists (while still maintaining an objective view of the pharmacists' own honesty, conduct and performance), a knowledge of what is happening on the 'drug scene' in the area and a sensitive 'nose' for detecting all manner of different types of illegal and unethical behaviour. Perhaps the most difficult aspect of the job is the detection of irresponsible prescribing. Where the CIO has to cover a large number of retail pharmacies, the job requires dedication and enthusiasm. However, as I shall later explain, some CIOs become very experienced in examining CDRs and develop a very sensitive 'nose' for bad prescribing practices of all kinds.

The National Protocol

9.27   The ACPO Drugs Sub-Committee's National Protocol for Chemist Inspecting (*sic*) Officers, published in 1997, describes the functions and responsibilities of CIOs. The functions are summarised as inspection, investigation, intelligence gathering, crime prevention and liaison. According to the Protocol, the CIO's role **'is often viewed as esoteric and somehow standing apart from mainstream** *(police)* **activity'**. The general description of the investigative elements of the role correlates broadly with what is said in the Home Office guidance notes.

Coverage by Chemist Inspection Officers

9.28   All 43 police forces in England and Wales provided general information to the Inquiry about their CIO arrangements. The Inquiry obtained detailed information from the Metropolitan Police Force and from forces in West Yorkshire, Avon and Somerset, Lancashire, Merseyside, Northumbria, South Wales, North Wales and Northern Ireland, as well as from all the Scottish police forces. A number of forces which have no CIO coverage (or had none until recently), such as Cumbria, Essex, Cleveland, Warwickshire and North Yorkshire, also provided information. Chief Superintendent John Taylor, from Cumbria, and Detective Superintendent Wilson Kennedy, from Essex, gave oral evidence to the Inquiry, as did former or current CIOs, Detective Sergeant (DS) Raymond Humphreys and retired DS Arthur Kilner from the Metropolitan Police and DC Neville Hanley and retired DS William Barker from the West Yorkshire Police. Further material was provided by ACPO. DC Diane Cooper, a trainer involved in the course for CIOs at the West Yorkshire Police Training Centre, gave evidence, as did several GMP CIOs and Detective Chief Superintendent (DCS) Peter Stelfox. A witness statement was provided by DC Duncan White, a CIO and Secretary of the National Association of Chemist Inspection Officers (NACIO), who also participated in the Inquiry's seminars in that capacity.

9.29   Although police officers have been inspecting community pharmacies since 1917, coverage has never been universal across the country and, even now, there are several areas where there are no pharmacy inspections by police officers. This variability of coverage arises because the decision as to the appointment of a CIO is an operational matter for the chief constable for the area concerned. The Home Office and ACPO can only encourage such appointments. So, for example, the Warwickshire Police undertake no pharmacy inspections. They take the view that the appointment of a CIO would involve an inappropriate use of scarce police resources.

9.30   The practice of appointing a dedicated CIO began in some areas in the 1960s. However, more than half the current CIOs also perform other duties. In some areas, an officer will combine the duties of a CIO with that of a chemical liaison officer (CLO). A CLO's duty is to visit manufacturers of chemicals that are capable of being used in the production of controlled drugs. The purpose of such visits is to advise the management of the company about the illicit purposes to which its products might be put and to monitor the destinations of those products. The duties of a CLO fit well with those of the CIO. However, in many areas, the CIO has to combine his/her duties with quite unrelated work. In 2003, only about 11 police forces had an officer employed exclusively either on CIO duties or on CIO-related and CLO-related work. In other areas, the work was undertaken on a part-time basis. I heard evidence about CIOs being seconded to other criminal investigations and spending very little time on the duties of pharmacy inspection. Those senior police officers who regard the task as an inappropriate use of police time will readily transfer the CIO to other duties when they are short-staffed. An officer in that position has little opportunity to acquire the necessary experience and expertise to carry out the job competently. However, I accept that it is better that there should be a part-time CIO in post than none at all. When Derbyshire Police reintroduced a dedicated CIO in 2001, DC Beard assumed a mentoring role towards the new appointee. He told the Inquiry that, on carrying out the first visits with the new CIO, he saw abysmally low standards of record keeping and security in pharmacies. This was, no doubt, a result of the lack of inspection previously.

9.31   The number of community pharmacies in each police area varies significantly. According to data obtained by the GMP in 2000, the Metropolitan Police area had the greatest number; the Metropolitan Police undertook the inspection of 1510 pharmacies. It now covers about 1900. The police in the other large conurbations have several hundred each; in 2000, the GMP area had 611, West Midlands had 650 and West Yorkshire had 480. Eleven police areas covered between 300 and 400 and six covered between 200 and 300. Fourteen areas contained fewer than 200, but more than 100, and five areas had fewer than 100. It appears that there is no obvious correlation between the number of CIOs in post and the number of pharmacies to be inspected. So, whereas, in 2000, County Durham had one CIO/CLO with 117 pharmacies to inspect, the sole CIO in Hampshire had 303 pharmacies to inspect and the CIO for Sussex had 358.

The Quality of the Work of Chemist Inspection Officers

9.32   It appears to me from the evidence before the Inquiry that, in many police forces, though not all, the work of a CIO is regarded as unimportant and unrewarding. The position is not seen as a useful part of an officer's career progression; rather the reverse, it is more likely to be seen as a backwater. The work does not fit closely with other police functions although in some forces there is an association between the CIO and the Drugs Squad. In general, the status accorded to a CIO is not high. According to DC Cooper, some senior police officers have the perception that the main responsibility of the CIO is the destruction of controlled drugs which can be done 'as and when needed'. As I have explained, the duties are far more complex and onerous than that, although the destruction of controlled drugs is an important function. In most forces, the position of CIO is occupied by a police or detective constable who rarely has the advantage of guidance or supervision by a senior officer with any real understanding of what the job entails. Another problem is that there is a tendency for an officer to be moved from his/her position as a CIO onto other work after only two or three years in post. If this happens, the valuable experience and specialised knowledge the officer has gained is lost for good.

9.33   The evidence suggested that the quality of CIOs' work was, at least in the past, very variable. Some CIOs were undoubtedly conscientious and enthusiastic about their duties and became extremely knowledgeable. Others appeared to regard the job as a 'soft option'. I heard that, on entering a pharmacy, some officers would ask the pharmacist whether 'everything was all right' and, on being told that it was, would ask to be shown where to sign the CDR. This was plainly unsatisfactory. Others would be less cavalier about their duties, but might still rely too heavily on what the pharmacist told them. From a conscientious pharmacist, no doubt the CIO would learn a great deal, but over-reliance on a pharmacist is not satisfactory, as it is one of the CIO's duties to inspect the pharmacist's practice with respect to controlled drugs.

9.34 Until recently, there had been no organised form of training for a CIO. Until 1999, the usual arrangement in Greater Manchester was for a new appointee to spend a few weeks working alongside an experienced CIO and to learn by a brief 'apprenticeship'. The quality of an apprenticeship can only be as good as the individual officer providing it. No doubt some were good and some less good. A new CIO could also read the guidance notes provided by the Home Office, to which I have referred. If a CIO post was being created in a force for the first time, a CIO from a neighbouring force might provide the training. Some CIOs would take it upon themselves to spend time at a regional office of the HODI, to learn what was required.

9.35 In 1997, the need for a training course for CIOs was recognised. Since 1999, such a course has been provided at the West Yorkshire Police Training Centre, Wakefield, which is open to CIOs from all over the country. The course takes place annually and up to 16 students can attend. A distance learning pack, including a workbook, is sent out to students for completion in advance of the course. The course itself, which lasts for four and a half days, covers all the relevant topics, including a half day on basic pharmacology. DC Cooper said that, even with the benefit of the training course, it takes about two years for a CIO to build up a sufficient reservoir of knowledge to be competent in the job; she thinks that four to five years represents the minimum satisfactory period of tenure.

9.36 The evidence suggests that the existence of the training course has done much to improve the commitment and quality of work of many CIOs. Another improvement has been the formation, in 2000, of the NACIO. The NACIO was founded by a group of enthusiastic CIOs. It circulates advice as to best practice and makes possible the discussion of common problems. It provides peer support to newly appointed officers. The organisation has been very well received by CIOs and the Home Office.

9.37 Notwithstanding these improvements, I fear that, in police areas where there is no dedicated CIO, standards are not high. It must be tempting for an officer with other pressing work and a limited time in which to carry out inspections to rely entirely on what a pharmacist reports. Mr Calder said that, in the North of England, the area for which he is responsible, there is a wide divergence of commitment to the job even where there is a dedicated CIO. Much depends on the attitude of the police force and the enthusiasm of the individual post-holder. In two police areas of which he has detailed knowledge, there is a theoretical commitment to the provision of dedicated CIOs, but in practice this is very limited. In these two areas, pharmacies are not routinely inspected and the officers are not sure of what they are supposed to be inspecting. This does not surprise me. If officers are to perform well, most will need management and supervision. Even after attending a training course, it must be an exceptional police officer who can motivate him/herself without direction and support from above. That some CIOs are highly motivated and very successful is much to their individual credit.

The Position of a Chemist Inspection Officer Seeking to Detect Irresponsible Prescribing

9.38 Without training and experience, it must be very difficult for a CIO to detect irresponsible prescribing. Even with training and experience, it seems to me that the CIO is not ideally placed for this particular aspect of the work. Recognition of irresponsible prescribing requires not only a good deal of knowledge about the uses and abuses of drugs, but also considerable medical knowledge. In order to assess the reasonableness of any prescription, the CIO needs to know the general properties and uses of the controlled drug and the dosage in which it is usually prescribed. Ideally, s/he should also know the condition for which it has been prescribed in the individual case, but that information is not available. When in need of advice or assistance, some CIOs liaise with the local PCT's medical or prescribing advisers or the regional RPSGB inspector. However, even with access to such advice, it seems to me that the CIO is not well equipped for this type of work. It appears to me that a person qualified in either medicine or pharmacy would be far better equipped to detect irresponsible prescribing than a CIO, however well trained and conscientious s/he may be.

Should Chemist Inspection Officers Be Civilians?

9.39   I have mentioned that some chief constables of police are not prepared to expend resources on the work of pharmacy inspection. In some areas, the duties of a CIO are undertaken by police civilian workers. Such personnel do not have the powers of entry and inspection granted to a constable under the MDA 1971 but the Home Office can and does authorise named civilians to exercise those powers. One advantage is that the contractual arrangements for such personnel are more flexible than those of a police officer and the cost of employment is much less. Also, a civilian employee can concentrate on the specific duties of a CIO, possibly remaining in the same post for many years. This allows the development of experience and expertise. There are those who say that a civilian CIO does not have the same deterrent effect against slackness as does a police officer. Official ACPO policy is that the duties of CIOs should be carried out by police officers. However, it was clear from the evidence I heard, particularly from DCS Stelfox, that there is a view that, if the police are to continue to be responsible for pharmacy inspection, they will almost inevitably have to deploy civilian personnel for the purpose.

Greater Manchester Police Inspections

The Background

9.40   The first Manchester CIO was DC John Galt, who took up the post in 1967 when serving with what was then Manchester City Police. Upon the formation of the GMP in 1974, another detective constable was appointed to assist in covering the pharmacies in the enlarged police area. The target of the two CIOs was to inspect each pharmacy twice a year. This situation continued until the number of pharmacies had increased so that it became impossible for two officers to do the job. A third CIO was appointed in 2001. DC Galt was succeeded by DC Alan Jackson in 1988. DC Jackson was in turn succeeded by DC Patrick Kelly in 1993. He was succeeded by DC Stefan Bidolak in 1997. The second post, created in 1974, was occupied by a succession of four officers until 1987, when DC Robert Peers was appointed. DC Peers occupied the post until 1997, when he was succeeded by DC Beard. DC William Graham was appointed as the third GMP CIO in 2001.

9.41   The GMP developed the job description of the two officers in accordance with the terms of the ACPO National Protocol for Chemist Inspecting Officers. My overall impression, gathered from the evidence of GMP officers, is that the position of a CIO is not accorded much status or priority. I also suspect that the work has been regarded by some within the GMP as undemanding and easy. I do not think appointment as a CIO has been seen as a good career move. That is a pity, because the effectiveness of the role and the job satisfaction to be derived from it are dependent upon the effort and enthusiasm invested in it. However, some of the GMP CIOs have been diligent and enthusiastic about their work.

9.42   Prior to 1999, the training offered to GMP CIOs was, as I described in paragraph 9.34, limited to a short apprenticeship with an existing CIO. The training period was not always spent with the 'retiring' CIO and, therefore, did not always include a handover period in which the new CIO was introduced to at least some of the pharmacists on his/her patch. DC Kelly said that, when his training was complete, he felt ill equipped for the job and lacked the confidence necessary to discuss issues with the pharmacists he was visiting for fear of revealing his own lack of knowledge. He said that he gradually gained experience and confidence while working in the job. Nowadays, a new CIO will spend a short period with an experienced CIO and will attend the Wakefield course as soon as is practicable. This might be several months after s/he has taken up his/her duties. All three of the current GMP CIOs have now attended the course. CIOs are also able to discuss problems with their colleagues and with their Drug Squad supervisor if the need arises. That will often be of only limited value because the supervisor will rarely, if ever, have performed CIO duties. DCS Stelfox acknowledged that it is difficult to monitor the quality of the work of CIOs. Although they are asked to submit reports, he said that '... in terms of looking at the judgements they have made in individual cases and assessing whether they were ... the appropriate judgements, that does not go on'. He added that there is no one to whom DC Beard can report; no one within the GMP knows more than he does about pharmacy inspections.

The Purpose and Form of Greater Manchester Police Inspections

9.43   Inspections by GMP CIOs take place at intervals of approximately six months. They are unannounced and the CIOs attend in plain clothes. In recent years at least, the Force Instruction Book has contained directions very similar to the Home Office guidance notes. For example, in 1990, the Instruction Book said:

> **'47. Any irregularity by a pharmacist or doctor etc., or any suspicion that a doctor or any other person is purchasing large quantities of drugs, or is prescribing excessively either for himself or for a patient, or that an excessive stock is being carried having regard to the quantity dispensed and that kept by other pharmacists in the district, must be made the subject of a report to the Home Office Drugs Branch.'**

9.44   The CIOs are generally aware that, apart from ensuring that pharmacists comply with the requirements imposed upon them, it is also part of their responsibility to detect irresponsible prescribing or diversion of controlled drugs by prescribing doctors.

9.45   DC Beard described his role and a typical visit of inspection. He said that his main task was to keep the pharmacist interested in controlled drugs issues. My understanding of his evidence is that, if the pharmacist is encouraged to maintain an interest in these issues, s/he may (provided s/he is honest) achieve a high standard of personal compliance with the Regulations and may also become a very useful source of intelligence for the CIO. In order to foster this interest, DC Beard will spend the first part of any inspection, possibly up to an hour, listening to any concerns that the pharmacist may have. During that time, he will keep an eye open to ensure that the pharmacist is complying with his/her professional obligations and, if he suspects that the pharmacist is not, he may alert the RPSGB inspectors. He then empties the controlled drugs cabinet or safe and sorts out any drugs that are out of date. He will try to reconcile the stock with the CDR. However, this is difficult because there is usually no opening stock entry and no running balance. He will examine each section of the CDR and sign and date the last page of each section. He will look out for signs of unusual prescribing and other features such as the cessation of a previous pattern of prescribing. If he were to notice that a patient who used to receive methadone had not collected his/her supply for some time, he would enquire why; the failure to collect might signify that the patient had returned to the use of illicit drugs. He might ask the pharmacist for information about who had collected a particular supply of drugs. Together with the pharmacist, he will undertake the destruction of any out of date stock. After a visit, DC Beard will record on his laptop computer any information of significance, including any advice or warning he has given to the pharmacist.

9.46   Until about 1997, the CIOs recorded the results of their visits in writing. A leather-bound book was kept, in which to record the times and dates of inspections, whether drugs were destroyed and whether any particular problems had arisen. Space in this volume was limited, so it did not usually contain information about individual patients or doctors. More detailed records were kept on a series of cards, with one card or set of cards being kept for each pharmacy. This system was initiated in the 1970s and was designed to maintain a record of any supply of controlled drugs that might give rise to concern. The names of all patients to whom drugs were being prescribed for addiction were recorded; they had to be reported to the Home Office. The names of patients who began to receive diamorphine were also recorded. The CIOs would then follow the patient's prescribing history. Usually, patients on diamorphine would be terminally ill; their supplies would increase and then stop suddenly. That would be a normal pattern and would not give rise to concern. If that pattern was not seen and the supplies continued, suspicion might arise that the drugs were being diverted. The card system seems to have worked well. It enabled a CIO to refresh his/her memory when preparing for a visit. It would also enable him/her to make a cross-check if s/he noticed a name in the CDR of one pharmacy and suspected that s/he might have seen the name in the record of another. It would enable him/her to discuss the precise details of any odd features with colleagues. Unfortunately, the card system was abandoned in 1997 (possibly as a result of the removal of the requirement to notify the Home Office about addicts), and the cards and the leather-bound books have all been destroyed.

9.47   DCS Stelfox accepted that, at least until 1999, the training provided by the GMP for its CIOs had been unsatisfactory. He also accepted that the CIOs were not adequately supervised and pointed out that it was almost impossible to find a more senior officer who had a real understanding of the work of a CIO. In essence, his view was that the police should not be involved at all in the routine inspection of retail pharmacies. He considers that this function is not appropriate for police forces. He would like to see the duty of routine inspection taken away from the police and given to a dedicated independent inspectorate which would benefit (in the way that CIOs do not) from inspecting the broad range of individuals and organisations involved in the production and supply of controlled drugs intended for therapeutic use. The police could then receive any complaints or concerns about possible criminality and could investigate them with a view to prosecution in the usual way. He was not impressed by the suggestion that regular contact with pharmacists through routine inspection provided a valuable source of intelligence to the police. He accepted that this contact was of some value, but considered that it did not justify the expenditure of police resources involved.

Inspection by the Greater Manchester Police of the Controlled Drugs Registers in Hyde

9.48   Since about 1974, a CIO has inspected the pharmacies in the Hyde area on a regular basis. This is usually achieved twice yearly. In the CDRs available to the Inquiry, the signature of the CIO in each section of the CDR can be seen as evidence of these visits.

9.49   Mrs Ghislaine Brant, who, since October 1991, has been the pharmacist manager of the pharmacy at 23 Market Street, Hyde, where most of Shipman's controlled drug prescriptions were dispensed, confirmed that inspections took place regularly. The CIOs were entirely satisfied that Mrs Brant was efficient in her work and they had no complaints about her conduct of the pharmacy in any respect.

9.50   The CDR kept by the pharmacy was produced to the Inquiry. It dated from 1991. The earlier CDRs were no longer available. In the CDR, Shipman's name appears as prescriber rather more frequently than that of any other doctor. In the period between 1991 and 1998, 83 out of a total of 188 supplies of controlled drugs were made on prescriptions issued by Shipman. However, with the exception of a period in 1993, his prescribing does not stand out as unusual or remarkable. I would not have expected a CIO to notice Shipman's name particularly or to suspect that he was obtaining drugs from the pharmacy by illicit methods. Mrs Brant did not tell the CIO that Shipman used to collect diamorphine prescribed for patients. Without this additional information, the CIO would have had no reason to notice Shipman's name in the CDR.

9.51   I have already said that Shipman's prescribing of diamorphine in 1993 was unusual. I shall consider that prescribing and the actions of the pharmacist and CIO concerned in Chapter Eleven.

Royal Pharmaceutical Society of Great Britain Inspections

The Inspection Function

9.52   In Chapter Three and Chapter Seven, I described the origins and functions of the RPSGB. Mr Stephen Lutener, whose position as Head of Professional Conduct included responsibility for the Inspectorate and Enforcement Division of the RPSGB, gave oral evidence to the Inquiry.

9.53   The RPSGB has no specific inspection or enforcement role under the Misuse of Drugs legislation, although its inspectors are authorised to possess and to witness the destruction of controlled drugs in the course of their duties. This position contrasts with the situation under the Medicines Act 1968, where (as I explained in Chapter Seven) the RPSGB has a statutory inspection and enforcement function with regard, for example, to offences relating to the adulteration or mis-labelling of medicines.

The Inspectors

9.54   The RPSGB employs 18 full-time inspectors who are all qualified pharmacists. They are based in different regions of the country and carry out periodic inspections of all retail pharmacies and of those hospital pharmacies that are registered with the RPSGB and have a retail pharmacy on the premises. However, they do not inspect doctors' surgeries or dispensing doctors' premises. The Society also employs eight inspectors who are not qualified pharmacists; their duties are to inspect the premises of distributors of agricultural pharmaceutical products. These inspectors also carry out test purchases in retail pharmacies because, unlike their pharmacist colleagues, they will not be recognised by the pharmacy staff.

9.55   The Inquiry received evidence from five RPSGB inspectors, Mr David Young, Mr Stanley Brandwood, Mr Graham Pickup, Mr David Slater and Mr Peter Greenwood. All save Mr Greenwood gave oral evidence. Mr Pickup and Mr Greenwood are now retired.

9.56   In Chapter Seven, I set out the educational and vocational requirements for qualification as a pharmacist. Pharmacists seeking appointment as a RPSGB inspector must have at least three years' experience as practising pharmacists. They must then undergo training as an inspector. There is no formal training course, although there is a structured training programme. The turnover of inspectors is low and the numbers to be trained are too small to justify a training course. Initially, a trainee spends two weeks at the RPSGB Headquarters in Lambeth, south London, where s/he is shown the workings of the governing body and the relevant committees and is introduced to office procedures. This is followed by two weeks spent accompanying one or two experienced inspectors on their rounds. Finally, trainees spend two further weeks with senior staff at Headquarters.

9.57   Inspectors also undergo continuing professional development. This focusses on such matters as interview technique, the gathering of evidence and personal safety. There are two inspectors' meetings each year. One lasts for three days and is devoted to training; the other comprises two days devoted to training and policy. There are also two one-day meetings each year, held at regional level, at which difficult or topical issues are discussed.

9.58   There is no continuing education on clinical pharmacy specifically focussed on controlled drugs, although inspectors are trained in the regulatory provisions of the MDA 1971 and the MDR 2001. Both Mr Brandwood and Mr Young told the Inquiry that they could not hold themselves out as being clinically up to date.

The Nature and Purpose of Royal Pharmaceutical Society of Great Britain Inspections

9.59   RSPGB inspectors have two main functions. They carry out routine inspections of pharmacies and they investigate complaints against pharmacists. Mr Slater said that he investigates about 30 complaints a year and this occupies about half his time.

9.60   The purpose of routine inspections is the promotion of good and safe pharmaceutical practice. This is achieved by ensuring compliance with the legislative requirements and the professional Code of Ethics. In the main, compliance is achieved by the giving of advice although, in the case of serious shortcomings, an inspector will make a report to Headquarters, for consideration by the Infringements Committee, or even a report to the police. Such serious matters are found only rarely on routine inspection and, in recent years, there has been a shift in the emphasis of these visits towards an advisory or pastoral role. Mr Young said that the most valuable aspect of his work was the time he spent talking to pharmacists about their continuing professional development, the introduction of standard operating procedures and other developments in pharmacy. In effect, the inspectors supplement the guidance and direction given in the RPSGB publication 'Medicine, Ethics and Practice – A Guide for Pharmacists'.

9.61   In the 1980s, all visits were unannounced, but nowadays about 75% of visits are made by prior arrangement. Prior arrangement allows a pharmacist to ensure that the most appropriate persons are present in the pharmacy on the day in question and enables him/her to prepare in advance any questions s/he might wish to discuss. However, the inspectors acknowledged that a poorly performing pharmacist is more likely to be 'caught out' by an unannounced inspection and that is why a proportion of inspections are not arranged in advance. In general, a pharmacy will be inspected about every two years, although this could be more frequent if any cause for concern arose.

9.62   There is no set format to an inspection. The focus of the inspection and the time spent on particular aspects of pharmacy practice will vary from one pharmacy to the next. I was told, for example, that, in the case of a pharmacy which is a member of a large retail chain, there is often no need to check that the dispensary is being kept tidy; an area or regional manager will routinely ensure that the dispensary is in good order. Such pharmacies often provide pre-registration training for new graduates, so the inspector might spend more time checking on the quality and arrangements of the pre-registration training being given. A pharmacy with a poor track record will warrant a longer visit than will one that is obviously well run. Some visits take as long as three hours. The inspector might wish to observe the procedures for dispensing and for the sale of medicines over the counter.

Controlled Drugs

9.63   It is implicit in what I have said that, in the course of a routine inspection, the RPSGB inspector is not expected to focus on the arrangements for controlled drugs. Not unreasonably, the inspectors regard this as the job of the CIO. However, an inspector would almost certainly notice if there did not appear to be proper arrangements for the safe custody of controlled drugs. He or she might also look at the CDR from time to time, not so as to study it, but in order to satisfy him/herself that it appeared to be properly kept.

He or she would not look at the entries in detail. He or she might notice if something were obviously wrong. For example, s/he might well notice a marked imbalance between the amounts of a controlled drug acquired and the amounts dispensed. As I have mentioned in Chapter Seven, a RPSGB inspector might also help out a pharmacist who could not find anyone to witness the destruction of out of date controlled drugs. Mr Lutener confirmed that the description given by the inspectors of their duties in relation to controlled drugs was as he would have expected. One of the inspectors described his role, in relation to controlled drugs, as providing 'an extra pair of hands and eyes'.

9.64   Thus, nowadays at least, RPSGB inspectors do not look at CDRs with a view to identifying prescribing patterns that might give rise to concern or might suggest irresponsible prescribing by a doctor. Under the present arrangements, I cannot see how they could be expected to perform such a task. However, it appears that, in the past, they did look out for cases of over-prescribing and, according to Mr Pickup, had a special form on which to report it. This practice seems to have fallen into disuse by about the end of the 1980s. Nowadays, the RPSGB inspectors are so busy that the various aspects of an inspection have been prioritised. Some tasks must be undertaken at every inspection; others are optional and should be undertaken only if time allows. The inspection of arrangements for controlled drugs is essentially optional. Broadly speaking, the inspectors said that, if they were unable to look at the CDR on one visit, they would make a point of doing so on the next or the one after that. In other words, six years might pass between inspections of the CDR. In general, the inspector would notice only problems that were gross and obvious; s/he would not notice that a pattern of prescribing was unusual.

9.65   According to the inspectors, they would expect pharmacists to raise any concerns they had about the prescribing practice of particular doctors. This would not be limited to the prescribing of controlled drugs. If a pharmacist raised a concern about excessive prescribing of a controlled drug, the inspector would look at the CDR and would advise the pharmacist what should be done.

9.66   The inspectors said that, if they came across evidence of improper prescribing by a doctor, they might liaise with the CIO or the HODI or with a PCT's medical or prescribing adviser. Thereafter, the matter would be reported, either to the police or to the GMC. If the case also gave rise to a potential breach of the Code of Ethics by the pharmacist (e.g. where the pharmacist had failed to report a case of obviously irresponsible or dangerous prescribing), the inspector would report the pharmacist to the RPSGB. I accept that RPSGB inspectors are not under a duty to look out for signs of irresponsible prescribing. However, in my view, this is a pity, as it seems to me that, by reason of their professional background, they are very much better equipped than CIOs to detect such signs.

9.67   The RPSGB inspector responsible for the Manchester area during the 1990s was Mr Young. He visited the pharmacy at 23 Market Street, Hyde, on a regular basis and formed the view that Mrs Brant was a competent and conscientious pharmacist. The CDR appeared to be well kept and he felt no concern about any aspect of the business or the practice of any prescribing doctor in the area. In Chapter Eleven, I shall consider the position of Mr Young, in relation to the CDR that reveals Shipman's unusual pattern of prescribing of diamorphine in 1993.

Inspection of General Practitioners' Surgeries by NHS Bodies

9.68   In the Fifth Report, I shall deal fully with the monitoring of GPs and the inspection of their premises by NHS organisations. Here, I shall explain briefly the scope of such activities with specific reference to the keeping and prescribing of controlled drugs. I shall deal first with the position nationally and then with the position locally in Tameside.

The Nationwide Position

9.69   As I explained in Chapter Three, prior to 1991, the officers of the Regional Medical Service (RMS) visited general practices periodically. The regional medical officer (RMO) would discuss the doctors' prescribing and would usually examine the practice's CDR and its arrangements for storing controlled drugs. Such visits were not regarded as inspections; rather they were an opportunity to advise the practice about good prescribing and the right methods of compliance with the requirements of the legislation. In 1991, the RMS ceased to undertake these visits. Responsibility for visiting GPs passed to the NHS body with responsibility for administering primary care services in the locality.

9.70   From 1991, family health services authorities (FHSAs), the NHS bodies responsible for the administration of primary care services, began to appoint medical advisers. These advisers were doctors; many had been in general practice; some were former RMOs. One of their roles was to inspect GPs' surgeries, including their equipment and facilities. Some medical advisers were given authority to inspect GPs' CDRs and their arrangements for the storage of controlled drugs. Inspection of CDRs and storage arrangements has been patchy ever since, and many GPs have not had their controlled drugs arrangements inspected for more than ten years.

9.71   Another function of the medical adviser was to monitor the prescribing practice of GPs and to promote rational and cost-effective prescribing. When appropriate, GPs were to be discouraged from prescribing expensive drugs of a proprietary brand and were to be encouraged to prescribe a cheaper generic equivalent. The medical advisers received prescribing data provided by the Prescription Pricing Authority (PPA) and used this to inform their discussions with GPs. Little attention was paid to controlled drugs; indeed, until fentanyl patches came into common use, controlled drugs were not of particular interest to the medical adviser as most are not expensive. According to Dr Jim Smith, Chief Pharmaceutical Officer for England at the DoH, controlled drugs were not regarded as presenting a problem and so were not given any special attention.

9.72   During the 1990s, there was a gradual change in the purpose and focus of the monitoring of prescribing. Instead of being concerned almost entirely with cost factors, FHSAs (and later the health authorities (HAs) that took over their responsibilities for general practice in 1996) sought to promote good and therapeutically effective prescribing practice. To this end, they began to appoint pharmaceutical advisers (usually part-time) to advise on the more technical aspects of prescribing. They also began to employ community pharmacists to go into general practices on a regular basis to advise the doctors on the prescribing needs of particular patients or groups of patients. The PPA provided FHSAs and HAs with increasingly sophisticated prescribing data. This data came in paper and, later, electronic form. From 1995, FHSAs were additionally able to send requests to the PPA for more detailed data analysis. However, until 1999, it was difficult and time-consuming for a medical or pharmaceutical adviser to analyse prescribing practice in respect of a particular drug or class of drugs. Mr Peter Welsby, Pharmaceutical Adviser for the West Pennine Health Authority (WPHA) in the 1990s, said that this task would be undertaken only if a concern had been expressed. The process of analysis became easier when prescribing data became available on-line from June 1999.

9.73 Neither the pharmaceutical advisers nor the community pharmacists were intended to examine a doctor's prescribing practice critically; their role was advisory. Nor did they have the authority to inspect GPs' CDRs and controlled drugs stocks. Dr Smith said that, during the 1990s, it was thought that the routine inspection of community pharmacies by CIOs provided a sufficiently robust system of control in respect of controlled drugs. It was not until 1998 or 1999, when it became clear how Shipman had obtained and kept controlled drugs for his own purposes, that it was realised that the assumptions underlying the existing policy had been mistaken.

The Position in Tameside

9.74 The bodies successively responsible for organising primary care in Tameside were unaware until 1998 of the fact that Shipman had convictions associated with the misuse of controlled drugs. They were unaware that he presented any particular risk, either with regard to controlled drugs or at all.

9.75 The RMOs covering the Tameside area made regular visits to GPs between 1977 and 1990. The Inquiry received evidence from three former RMOs. It appears that prescribing was one of the topics that would be discussed at such visits, as was the question of whether the doctor kept a CDR. When Dr David Edwards, working as a RMO in the 1980s, visited Shipman at Donneybrook House, Shipman told him that he did not keep an emergency supply of controlled drugs and, therefore, did not keep a CDR. Such a claim would not have caused any surprise. It was rather more common in those days than now for doctors to keep controlled drugs for use in emergencies, but the practice was by no means universal. Shipman obtained his diamorphine supplies illicitly and kept them well hidden. No regular inspection of GPs' arrangements for keeping controlled drugs and CDRs could reasonably have been expected to detect Shipman's illicit supplies. The practice of a RMO inspecting a GP's patient records had ceased long before Shipman arrived in Hyde. In any case, the purpose of the inspection was to ensure that records were being kept, not to carry out any routine comparison of patient records with prescriptions or other records held at community pharmacies.

9.76 During the 1990s, Shipman's use of diamorphine increased. He had several patients who were terminally ill and required substantial amounts of diamorphine for pain relief. His theft of drugs from patients after dispensing and his retention of unused supplies after a patient's death went unnoticed. During a routine practice visit, he told Dr Roger Freedman, Medical Adviser to the Tameside FHSA from 1991 to 1993, that he kept neither an emergency supply of controlled drugs nor a CDR. He said that keeping controlled drugs gave rise to a risk of theft. He also said that, if a patient telephoned the surgery complaining of chest pain, it was his practice to admit the patient to hospital immediately rather than go to the house himself. Thus, he had little need of emergency analgesia. In fact, this was quite untrue but Dr Freedman had no reason to disbelieve him.

9.77   The increasing use of diamorphine occasioned by the introduction of syringe drivers in 1993 would have shown up on the prescribing data provided by the PPA. However, this never gave cause for concern. Ms Carol Abdulezer, the pharmacy consultant employed by the Tameside Consortium (the GP fundholding Consortium of which Shipman was a member), told the Inquiry that, in 1995 or early 1996, she had occasion to speak to Shipman about his prescribing of diamorphine. She did so, not because diamorphine was a controlled drug or because Shipman was suspected of any wrongdoing. On examining the Consortium's prescribing data, she had noticed that his diamorphine prescribing for the relevant quarter was high. She spoke about it to Shipman, not to investigate the reason for his prescribing or to persuade him to reduce it, but to ascertain for how long the current level of need for diamorphine was likely to continue. She assumed that it was being used for the treatment of a terminally ill patient and wanted to know whether she should request special provision in the Consortium's prescribing budget. Shipman immediately identified the patient concerned, got out the medical records and showed Ms Abdulezer a letter from the consultant at the hospital where the patient was being treated. This confirmed that a high dosage of diamorphine was indeed necessary. Shipman told her that the drug would not be required for long, as the patient was in the terminal stages of illness. When Ms Abdulezer next came to review the prescribing data, she noticed that the diamorphine usage had returned to its previous level. She had no reason to doubt Shipman's explanation for the short-term increase.

9.78   I have mentioned that there was a period in 1993 when Shipman's prescribing of diamorphine was unusual in that, over a period of seven months, he prescribed 14 single 30mg ampoules of diamorphine in the names of 13 different patients. In Chapter Eleven, I shall consider whether this prescribing should have been identified as unusual by the dispensing pharmacist and by the local CIO. However, I am quite satisfied that these prescriptions would not have shown up as unusual on routine examination of prescribing data. Prescribing data was in its infancy in 1993 and it was less easy to analyse than it is now. Not even the most conscientious or suspicious pharmaceutical adviser could have been expected to notice this series of prescriptions from the prescribing data.

Analysis after Shipman's Arrest

9.79   In October 1998, following Shipman's arrest, Dr Alan Banks, then Medical Adviser to the WPHA, asked the PPA to analyse Shipman's prescribing of 100mg diamorphine injections during the two previous years. Data from further back was not available. The analysis revealed, first, that Shipman was only the sixth highest prescriber of diamorphine in the area of the WPHA. I am not sure whether, if diamorphine prescribing had been subject to analysis and monitoring at that time, a doctor in the sixth highest position would have been regarded as an outlier. Second, it was found that the pattern of Shipman's prescribing was not quite as would be expected. It is usual to find a sporadic pattern of prescribing of diamorphine. From time to time, the doctor will have a terminally ill cancer patient. Gradually increasing supplies of diamorphine will be needed but will cease abruptly on the death of the patient. There may then be a period when the doctor does not prescribe diamorphine at all. Shipman's pattern of prescribing showed more frequent, relatively low level, prescribing than would be expected. However, examination of the other high volume prescribers also showed some unconventional patterns. Nevertheless, had the data been available earlier, the patterns revealed by the analysis would probably have given rise to some concern about Shipman's prescribing of diamorphine. I think it highly likely, however, that, had Shipman been questioned about his prescribing of diamorphine, he would have been able to offer plausible explanations, by reference to individual terminally ill patients, as to why he had prescribed as he did.

Conclusion

9.80   At present, the inspection and monitoring of the use of, and the arrangements for, controlled drugs are spread between three agencies: the Home Office, the police and the PCTs. RPSGB inspectors are also involved. Each agency seeks to do a good professional job and each co-operates with the others when appropriate. However, the overall result is less than satisfactory. The HODI appears to function well, but it cannot and does not attempt to cover the inspection of retail pharmacies. Coverage by CIOs is patchy. In general, the work of the CIOs is under-resourced. Moreover, even where a dedicated CIO is in post and even now that some training is available, most CIOs are left to their own devices. To be done properly, the job requires enthusiasm and the development of knowledge and experience over a substantial period. It also requires proper management. Even the longest serving and most able CIOs are not ideally placed to recognise irresponsible prescribing of controlled drugs. The RPSGB inspectors appear to me to be well trained, highly motivated and effective. Their professional knowledge equips them well to detect signs of irresponsible prescribing, but they are so few in number that they can visit a pharmacy only about once every two years and often do not have time to pay much attention to controlled drugs issues. Primary care organisations have many other tasks and the monitoring of controlled drug usage is but a small part of their responsibility for promoting good prescribing practice. They have limited resources to devote to the inspection of GPs' surgeries; as a result, the controlled drugs arrangements of many GPs have not been inspected for many years. In Chapter Fourteen, I shall consider how the work done by these various agencies might be rationalised and co-ordinated.

CHAPTER TEN

Shipman's Abuse of Controlled Drugs in Todmorden

The Obtaining of Drugs in 1974 and 1975

10.1   Shipman began his career in general practice in March 1974 when he joined the Abraham Ormerod Medical Centre, Todmorden. About ten months later, in January 1975, an inspector from the Northern Regional Office of the Home Office Drugs Inspectorate (HODI) in Bradford carried out a routine inspection of the records of a pharmaceutical wholesaler in the North of England. The inspection revealed that unusually large and regular supplies of pethidine ampoules were being delivered to the Todmorden branch of Boots the Chemists (Boots).

10.2   That information was passed to West Yorkshire Police (WYP), who attended and checked the records of all the pharmacies in the Todmorden area. It was found that, on nine separate occasions, between 8th April 1974 and 12th December 1974, Shipman had purchased ten 100mg ampoules of pethidine injections, a total of 9000mg. He had presented signed orders at Boots, claiming that the drugs were required for 'practice use' and had collected the drugs himself. In addition, it was found that, on 11 occasions between November 1974 and January 1975, Shipman had collected ten 100mg ampoules of pethidine, ostensibly on behalf of a patient in whose name he had prescribed the drug. On nine of those occasions, he had presented the prescriptions at Boots; on the other two occasions, he had presented them at another pharmacy in the town. During this period, Shipman also prescribed pethidine for two other patients, who presented and collected the drugs themselves. Thus, in a period of eight or nine months, Shipman had collected 20,000mg pethidine in injectable form.

10.3   When carrying out these enquiries, the police were told that Shipman was held in high regard by the local pharmacists. It appeared that Shipman had told the pharmacists that the signed orders were for use by the local midwifery service, which was based at the Abraham Ormerod Medical Centre, and that the prescriptions were for a terminally ill patient who was too unwell to collect the pethidine himself. No further action was taken at that time but a watch was to be kept on Shipman's activities.

10.4   Shipman's prescribing of pethidine, as revealed in the controlled drugs register (CDR) held at Boots, was reviewed by a Home Office inspector who visited Boots on 4th July 1975. He saw from the CDR that, between January 1975 and May 1975, Shipman had obtained ten pethidine ampoules on requisition on a further 11 occasions. The CDR also showed that, since 3rd April, Shipman had issued 31 further prescriptions, each for 1000mg pethidine, in the name of the same patient for whom Shipman had previously prescribed the drug. According to the pharmacist, Shipman had collected the drugs every time, explaining that the patient had cancer and that he was prescribing on the advice of a hospital consultant. It is not clear whether Shipman had collected drugs in the name of this patient during February and March 1975.

10.5   On 17th July 1975, two inspectors from the HODI Northern Regional Office, a senior inspector, Mr Frank Eggleston, and his junior colleague, Mr Donald McIntosh, together with Detective Constable Harrison from the WYP, visited Shipman at his surgery and asked him to account for his use of pethidine. By this time, Shipman had collected pethidine for the same terminally ill patient on a further three occasions since 4th July (most recently on 16th July, the day before the visit). All previous enquiries had been made without informing Shipman and it is unlikely that he had become aware of them.

10.6 Shipman explained that Mr A, the patient for whom he had collected the drugs, was 82 and lived with his elderly wife in an inaccessible part of Todmorden. He suggested that the patient found it difficult to collect his prescriptions, that the district nurses were not authorised to carry controlled drugs and that, as a favour to his patient, he had delivered the pethidine for him. Shipman said that the drugs were self-administered by the patient and he produced a hospital letter relating to the patient, confirming that he was suffering from cancer. Shipman mentioned that he had also had an informal conversation with the treating surgeon, who had agreed with Shipman that treatment with pethidine was appropriate. Although it may have been true that Mr A had cancer, he was not in fact being treated with pethidine. Shipman was later to explain that the patient had had only five doses of pethidine before changing to a different analgesic drug because the pethidine made him **'sleep all the time'**. As for the requisitions, Shipman explained that he had had to collect these because he had assumed the responsibility for ordering controlled drugs on behalf of the practice.

10.7 When questioned about the practice CDR, Shipman produced a register in which he had entered the practice's acquisitions of pethidine but not the amounts of the drug supplied or administered to patients from the practice stock. He said that he and his colleagues would **'help themselves'** to drugs from the cabinet as and when they required them. He professed ignorance of the need to maintain a record of drugs taken from the cabinet. He was asked whether he could recall any patients to whom pethidine from the surgery cabinet had been administered. He gave the names of four patients who he suggested had required at least one injection. When the cabinet was examined, it was found to contain no pethidine; this was despite the large quantities obtained on requisition and the small number of occasions on which Shipman could recollect having personally administered the drug. It was decided that the absence of any record of supplies meant that tracing the drugs was impossible. No contact was made with the four patients Shipman had named and no request was made to examine their medical records.

10.8 Shipman was asked whether he had ever taken pethidine himself and he said that he had, at a party when he was a student. He said that he had never done so before or since. The Home Office inspectors decided to take no further action at that time but to keep Shipman's use of controlled drugs under review. They asked the police to provide a report on Shipman in six months' time. On 7th August, Mr McIntosh spoke to Shipman and his fellow doctors at the practice. They were advised of the requirements of the law governing record keeping and destruction of controlled drugs.

Shipman Is Caught Out and Referred for Treatment

10.9 A few weeks later, on Monday, 29th September 1975, the HODI was informed that Shipman had resigned from the Abraham Ormerod Medical Centre after it had come to the attention of his partners that he was obtaining drugs illicitly. He had admitted abusing pethidine. During the previous week, the practice had been alerted to the presence of numerous further suspicious entries in the Boots CDR in Shipman's name.

10.10   Inspection of the pharmacy CDR revealed that, since 17th July, there had been a further seven occasions when Shipman had obtained 1000mg pethidine on requisition. Moreover, there had been nine occasions when he had prescribed 1000mg pethidine in the name of patients: two in the name of the same patient as previously, Mr A, and seven in the name of Mr M, a patient who lived in a residential care home. The pharmacist said that, on each occasion, Shipman had collected the drugs himself. Thus, in the ten-week period prior to 29th September, Shipman had collected 16,000mg pethidine from the pharmacy.

10.11   Examination of the practice CDR revealed that a new register had been used since 1st August but neither in that register nor in the old register was there any entry relating to the recently obtained pethidine. Since the HODI visit, therefore, Shipman had ceased making any record of controlled drugs obtained. One of the other doctors at the practice explained, when asked, that he was sure that, of the two patients whose names appeared in the pharmacy CDR, one had not received the drugs recorded as having been prescribed for him.

10.12   On 29th September 1975, Dr Philip Humberstone, a consultant physician at the Halifax Royal Infirmary, saw Shipman and arranged for him to be referred to Dr Hugo Milne, a local consultant psychiatrist and Director of the Regional Drug Unit, based at the Leeds Road Hospital in Bradford. Dr Humberstone had previously seen Shipman on 18th August for **'blackouts'** or **'seizures'**, which he had attributed to **'idiopathic epilepsy'**, i.e. epilepsy of unknown cause. It seems almost certain in hindsight that those episodes had been caused by Shipman's pethidine abuse. For some weeks before this abuse came to light, Shipman's wife had been driving him to his home visits. Dr Milne saw Shipman on 30th September. Shipman told Dr Milne that he was depressed and had been abusing pethidine for some time. It is not clear whether he said that the abuse had begun 18 months or two years previously. On Dr Milne's recommendation, Shipman was admitted to a private hospital, The Retreat, in York, under the care of Dr Ronald Bryson, also a consultant psychiatrist. He was to remain there for about three months. In the meantime, both Dr Bryson and Dr Milne notified the Home Office of his 'addict' status as the law required them to do.

Shipman Is Interviewed about His Abuse

10.13   On the evening of Friday, 28th November 1975, Shipman was interviewed at The Retreat by Detective Sergeant (DS) George McKeating of the WYP and Mr McIntosh. By this time, the police investigations had uncovered the possibility that Shipman had forged signatures on the back of the prescriptions issued in the name of Mr M and the police had also come to suspect that he had taken the whole or part of the supplies of pethidine obtained in the names of other patients. At the start of the interview, Shipman said that he intended to say nothing, on advice from the Medical Defence Union. However, when he learned that the officers might speak to his patients in the course of their enquiries, he said that he would tell them what he had done. He said that he had first taken pethidine about 18 months previously, shortly after joining the practice. He had become depressed and had not got on well with his partners; taking pethidine made him feel better. He had been injecting pethidine intravenously into his arms and legs. He bared his arms to his interviewers to reveal that his veins had collapsed through repeated injection. He said that he had used about 600–700mg pethidine a day. Since beginning treatment, he had taken no pethidine and had suffered no withdrawal symptoms; he claimed that he was considered by Dr Bryson to be a drug abuser (rather than a drug addict).

10.14   When asked about the prescriptions for pethidine issued in the name of Mr M, Shipman admitted that he had taken all the pethidine for himself. Also, he admitted that he had forged, on the back of the prescriptions, the signatures of various members of staff at the residential home where Mr M lived. He had done this in order to claim exemption from prescription charges. When asked about a patient named Mrs WS, who suffered from cancer, Shipman admitted that he had collected and kept the pethidine from three of the four prescriptions issued in her name. In respect of a patient named Mrs ES, for whom he had issued two prescriptions for pethidine, he accepted that he had forged her signature on the back of the prescriptions, in order to avoid the prescription charge, and had taken almost all the drug for himself. He had also prescribed pethidine for a maternity patient; he had forged her signature on the back of the prescriptions. He had given the patient a small amount of pethidine while she was in labour and had taken the rest for himself. For patients named Mrs LC and Mr SH, he said he had prescribed for their needs but had given them only a small amount of pethidine, keeping the rest for himself. For Mrs GE, a patient with a renal stone, he said he had prescribed pethidine but had taken some for himself. He added rather flippantly, **'... shall we say half for her and half for me?'** In respect of one patient, Mrs JR, for whom he had issued a prescription for pethidine, Shipman said he had no recollection at all. He agreed that he had deliberately selected certain patients, knowing that the prescribing of pethidine for them would have appeared, on superficial enquiry, to be reasonable treatment.

10.15   Shipman also agreed that he had failed to enter into the surgery CDR various amounts of pethidine that he had obtained on requisition. He said that he had been **'in a bit of a state'** at the time. He then made a written statement in which he repeated the admissions he had made orally. He was charged with eight offences in connection with obtaining pethidine.

10.16   Examination of the contemporaneous documents has revealed that, in addition to obtaining pethidine, during February and March 1975, Shipman also obtained 20 ampoules of 30mg injectable morphine on requisition. DS McKeating (now retired) recalled in his statement to the Inquiry that, during the interview in November 1975, Shipman was asked whether he had ever injected himself with morphine. He said that he had tried it but had not liked it. He was not charged with any offence in connection with morphine. It seems to have been assumed that the acquisition of morphine was for genuine practice purposes. However, that quantity was enough to kill about ten opioid-naïve patients, and I cannot rule out the possibility that some of it was used to kill Mrs Eva Lyons (the patient whom I found in my First Report Shipman had killed while in Todmorden) and one or more of the of the six Todmorden patients about whose deaths I was suspicious.

Court Proceedings

10.17   On 26th January 1976, Dr Milne saw Shipman again and provided a psychiatric report for use in the criminal proceedings before the Halifax Magistrates' Court. On 29th January, Dr Bryson provided a report for the same purpose. Both reports were very supportive of Shipman. Dr Bryson said that the trigger for Shipman's abuse of pethidine had been depression, which Shipman had treated by **'unwise self-medication'**. Although he had become addicted to pethidine, his addiction had not reached the stage of total compulsion or constant need. After his discharge from hospital at the end of December 1975, he had shown insight into his condition and approached his problems with **'great courage, common sense and determination'**. Dr Bryson said that he thought the chances of relapse into drug dependence or anything similar **'extremely unlikely'**. He thought that, if Shipman were to suffer a recurrence of his depression, this would be recognised immediately and the strength of his basic personality was such that he would be able to avoid a repetition of his drug abuse.

10.18   On Friday, 13th February 1976, Shipman pleaded guilty at the Halifax Magistrates' Court to the eight offences with which he had been charged. These were no more than a representative sample of the offences he had committed. He pleaded guilty to three charges of obtaining ten ampoules of 100mg pethidine by deception, three corresponding charges of unlawful possession of pethidine and two charges of forgery of NHS prescriptions. The forgery charges reflected Shipman's conduct in endorsing the back of the prescriptions with what purported to be the signature of the person responsible for the care of the patient for whom the drug had been prescribed. He agreed to have 74 other charges taken into consideration. Although the relevant police and court files have been destroyed, it is clear from contemporaneous press reports that 67 of the 74 offences concerned the obtaining of pethidine by deception. It was said by the prosecution that the investigating police officers believed that Shipman had not supplied drugs to any third party; nor had he deprived any patients of drugs that they needed. It was also confirmed that he had recently obtained a post in the Durham area in which he would have no need to use controlled drugs. Shipman was fined a total of £600 and was ordered to pay £58.78 in compensation to the local Family Practitioner Committee.

The Procedure under Section 12 of the Misuse of Drugs Act 1971

10.19   In earlier Chapters, I have described the power conferred on the Home Secretary by section 12 of the Misuse of Drugs Act 1971. Following Shipman's conviction, the Home Secretary had the power to make a direction prohibiting Shipman from possessing, prescribing, supplying or administering controlled drugs. The initiative for the making of any such direction would originate with the HODI.

10.20   The HODI was based in London and was part of Division E4 of the Home Office. From June 1975 until about July 1978, the Head of Division E4 was Sir Geoffrey de Deney. In 1976, the Chief Inspector in charge of the HODI was Mr Charles Jeffrey and his deputy was Mr Bing Spear. Drugs policy was the responsibility of a separate department of Division E4. The Head of Drugs Policy was Mr Derek Turner.

10.21 Sir Geoffrey explained to the Inquiry the procedure for making a section 12 direction at that time. When a doctor was convicted of drugs offences, the case file would be sent to London from the regional office involved. The file would be considered by the Chief Inspector or his deputy. If it appeared to him that a direction might be appropriate, he would probably consult the Department of Health and Social Security (DHSS), although there was no standard procedure requiring this to be done. In the case of a general practitioner, a regional medical officer with knowledge of the offending doctor would provide an opinion on the doctor's general abilities and prospects for rehabilitation. It is not clear to the Inquiry upon what evidence this opinion would have been given, although in one case the regional medical officer spoke to the doctor's treating psychiatrist and, having received a favourable report, advised against a direction and none was made. Also, the Home Office would find out what the General Medical Council (GMC) intended to do about the doctor. Sir Geoffrey explained that the Home Office paid considerable heed to the views of the DHSS and the intentions of the GMC, as they had greater expertise in the field of drug misuse by doctors than did the Home Office, whose main interest and expertise lay in uncovering illegal supplying of drugs.

10.22 Having taken these steps, the Chief Inspector would refer the papers to the policy side of Division E4 with a proposal either to seek or not to seek a direction. If the Head of Drugs Policy approved a proposal that a direction should be sought, the papers would come to the Head of Division – in 1976, Sir Geoffrey. Once the case came to Sir Geoffrey's attention, he would make a decision on the basis of the material before him. If he agreed that a direction should be sought, the relevant official documents and a submission to the Home Secretary would be drafted and approved by legal advisers. The papers would then be sent to the Home Secretary. If the Chief Inspector and the Head of Drugs Policy were of the view that a direction should not be sought, the papers would not be sent to the Home Secretary and might not reach even the Head of Division. Sir Geoffrey said that, if a direction was made, it would usually be revoked after about two years, provided that there were no further reports of misconduct.

10.23 It appears from the small number of cases examined by the Inquiry that, in the years before 1976, section 12 directions were made not only in cases in which a doctor had unlawfully obtained controlled drugs for the purpose of supplying them to others but also in cases where the doctor's purpose had been to obtain the drugs for self-administration. As I shall explain below, this situation was to change in 1976. The number of convictions coming to the attention of the Home Office was not great and it appears that they were dealt with on a case by case basis, with no clear criteria being established to inform the decision whether to recommend a direction. However, it is clear that significant weight attached to what was perceived to be in the doctor's best interest. So, for example, if it was thought that the making of a direction would cause the doctor to lose confidence in his/her professional abilities, with a resultant impact upon his/her prospects of rehabilitation, this would be taken into account and might result in a doctor being given a second chance. In one case, a direction was lifted after only two months when supportive reports from treating doctors were considered. A direction was much more likely to be made and to remain in force where the doctor did not co-operate with any treatment offered.

The Section 12 Issue in Shipman's Case

10.24   On 4th March 1976, the WYP sent a report of the criminal proceedings to the Northern Regional Office of the HODI. It described the circumstances in which the offences had been committed and said that the police were satisfied that Shipman had been taking the pethidine himself. It summarised what Shipman had said in interview, namely, that he had not got on well with his partners, had become depressed and had consequently begun taking pethidine in June 1974. (I pause to observe that the date of Shipman's first obtaining of pethidine was April 1974, only a few weeks after he had started work in Todmorden in March 1974.) It said that the police were satisfied that Shipman had not supplied the drug to anybody else and that none of his patients had suffered as a result of his actions. In fact, it is probable that there had been no investigation into whether any had suffered, but certainly no evidence had been produced that they had. Sir Geoffrey said that he would not have expected the HODI inspectors to enquire whether patient care or safety had been affected by Shipman's drug taking. Such matters would, he said, have fallen more within the remit and expertise of the DHSS or the GMC. All the information in the WYP report was already known to the HODI inspectors in Bradford. Mr McIntosh noted in Shipman's file that the Home Office was going to have to decide whether to make a section 12 order against him.

10.25   At the same time, the GMC was notified of the conviction. On 17th March, a member of staff wrote to the WYP and to the HODI in London, asking for a brief account of the circumstances leading up to the offences, together with any additional information that might assist the GMC's Penal Cases Committee when it came to consider Shipman's case the following month. The police replied that it was contrary to their practice to provide reports or to allow their officers to provide witness statements, although they did offer DS McKeating for interview.

10.26   Shipman's Home Office file was considered by Mr Eggleston. Although those working in the Northern Regional Office played no formal role in deciding whether a section 12 direction should be made, Mr Eggleston was entitled to send a note of his views on the issue to London and, on 16th March 1976, he did so. He expressed concern about the seriousness and duration of Shipman's abuse but was also conscious of the impact that a direction might have upon his ability to make a living. He wrote:

> **'I have confirmed that no appeal against sentence has been lodged in this case and so we should now consider whether a direction should be issued under Section 12 of the MDA. My own view is that a direction would be appropriate, since Dr Shipman has on his own admission, taken up to 600mg of pethidine per day, and has used the drug for a period of about eighteen months. Both doctors who have attended him since his addiction was discovered, Dr Milne, of Lynfield Mount Hospital, Bradford and Dr Bryson, of The Retreat, York, have notified him as an addict to pethidine.**
>
> **I do not know whether DHSS will be able to provide an assessment of Dr Shipman since I understand that he is no longer working as a general practitioner, but as an Area Medical Officer with the NCB** *(National Coal*

Board), **at Doncaster. A point to bear in mind, although it need not influence our decision unduly, is that Shipman may have responsibility for stocks of Omnopon injections held by the NCB and I understand that area medical officers are expected to hold stocks of analgesic drugs in case they are called to serious accidents at mines. It is conceivable, therefore, that a direction prohibiting his possession etc of those drugs in Part 1 of Schedule 2 to the MDA might seriously hamper his ability to carry out his present work.'**

10.27 Shipman's file was then sent to London where, on 18th March 1976, a junior Home Office Drugs Branch officer, Mrs Susan Powrie, wrote to the GMC asking for the view taken on the case by its Penal Cases Committee. Until 1980, the Penal Cases Committee was the GMC committee that decided whether a case should be referred to the Disciplinary Committee for a public hearing. Mrs Powrie wrote:

> **'We are now giving consideration to the question of whether action should be taken under Section 12 of the Misuse of Drugs Act 1971 to remove Shipman's authorities to possess, supply, prescribe, administer, manufacture ... controlled drugs and we should be glad if in this connection you would let us know the view taken by the Penal Cases Committee.'**

10.28 Mrs Powrie's memorandum confirms that, at that stage, she was not excluding the possibility of a section 12 direction being made. It also confirms the evidence of Sir Geoffrey that the approach taken by the Home Office would have been influenced by the attitude of the GMC.

10.29 On 19th March, Mr Eggleston noted in the file that Shipman either had not taken the NCB post or had been discharged from it and was thought to be working at a health clinic somewhere in the North East of England.

10.30 On 26th March, Mr Spear wrote to the DHSS seeking the Department's advice on the section 12 issue. He wrote:

> **'We are now faced with the problem of whether or not to advise the Secretary of State to issue a direction under Section 12 of the Misuse of Drugs Act and should be grateful for your advice on this aspect. We understand that Dr Shipman did receive treatment in the Retreat, York, under Dr Bryson and he was in fact, notified as an addict. We are not certain of his exact whereabouts but have heard he is working at a health clinic somewhere in the north east of England but have no address for him other than that quoted above.'**

No reply to this letter has been found. The Department of Health (DoH) has been unable to shed any light on whether its predecessor, the DHSS, ever responded to it. However, the fact that it was written suggests that the usual practice was followed in Shipman's case.

10.31 On 21st April, Hempsons, the solicitors acting for Shipman, wrote to the GMC to make representations to the Penal Cases Committee, which was shortly to consider his case.

They enclosed the medical reports obtained for the purpose of the criminal proceedings. Their letter expanded upon what was said to be the background to Shipman's drug abuse. It was said that Shipman had first taken pethidine following a back strain in 1974. This was the first time that this had been suggested on his behalf. It was almost certainly untrue but it was also no doubt the kind of thing that many doctors in a similar predicament used to say and still say now. On 23rd April, Dr Michael O'Brien, the Area Medical Officer of the Durham Area Health Authority (AHA), wrote to the GMC confirming that Shipman's current employer (Durham AHA) knew of his behaviour and that he seemed to be doing well in his new post. On 27th April, Hempsons wrote to the GMC again, enclosing a further letter from Dr Milne. This suggested that it would be **'catastrophic'** were Shipman not to be allowed to continue in practice.

10.32 On 28th April, the Penal Cases Committee decided not to refer Shipman's case to the Disciplinary Committee but to close the case with a warning against any repetition of his conduct. By letter dated 3rd May, this decision was conveyed to the Home Office. The letter said that:

> **'... in all the circumstances, and particularly in the light of a number of reports received on the practitioner's condition ... it would now be sufficient to conclude the case'**.

I shall deal with this decision in greater detail in the Fifth Report when I consider the role of the GMC. The GMC did not enclose the medical reports and letters it had taken into consideration. It was not usual practice for it to do so. As a result, the Home Office did not have access to these materials, which were in any event favourable to Shipman.

10.33 It appears that a few weeks then elapsed before any further step was taken. It may be that the Home Office was waiting for a reply to its request for an opinion from the DHSS; as I have said, no response from the DHSS was found in the Home Office file and it may be that none was sent. Another possibility is that the Home Office delayed its decision on Shipman because a change in policy on section 12 directions was imminent.

A Change in the Policy Governing the Making of Section 12 Directions

10.34 In Chapter Four, I explained that, until 1976, section 12 directions were made in cases in which a doctor had obtained controlled drugs solely for his own use. In 1976, there was a change of policy and directions were no longer made in such cases. Directions were made only in cases in which the doctor's activities were thought to have created a risk to the public. This risk was usually evidenced by the fact that the doctor had wrongfully supplied drugs to others. Under the new policy, the thinking was that, if a doctor had obtained drugs for his/her own use, his/her conduct did not create a risk to the public and there was no need for a direction. Sir Geoffrey had no recollection of this change of policy and, unfortunately, the Home Office has not been able to shed any light on why or how it happened. Nor has the DoH been able to assist.

10.35 This change of policy would have made good sense for the Home Office (whose primary interest in relation to controlled drugs was to prevent leakage onto the illicit market) if the GMC had been in a position to protect patients by restricting the prescribing rights of a doctor, either on account of a drug-related conviction or for serious professional misconduct related in some way to the abuse of controlled drugs. However, in 1976, the GMC had no such power and the change of policy by the Home Office at that time left a *lacuna* in the power of the authorities to protect patients from a drug-abusing doctor who was not suspended or struck off.

The Decision in Shipman's Case

10.36   It appears that Shipman was an early (possibly the first) beneficiary of this new policy. An entry in Shipman's HODI file, made by Mrs Powrie on 1st July, states:

> **'In view of the recent policy decision that the S of S is not empowered to make directions purely for a doctor's own protection, and of the GMC's decision, there is no action for us to take...? no action at present.'**

10.37   Sir Geoffrey explained that a more accurate statement of the position would have been to say that the Home Secretary remained empowered to make a direction but that these were not circumstances in which it would be normal to do so. It seems likely that the policy decision was reached in May or June 1976. As I have already said, the reason behind it remains obscure. Sir Geoffrey speculated that it had been provoked by the difficulties thrown up by a particular case but he could offer no more assistance.

10.38   The entries in the file continue with a memorandum to Sir Geoffrey, dated 1st July 1976, signed by Mr Turner, setting out the arguments to be considered:

> **'Any considerations of the public interest in this case are extremely marginal; in the area of possible risk of harm to patients from a doctor who may be addicted to narcotic drugs. In doc 14** (DS McKeating's report of 4th March 1976) **however, the police report that there was no evidence that Dr Shipman's patients suffered as a result of his irregularly obtaining pethidine, and the GMC have now taken the view that there are no grounds for stopping him practising as a doctor. In the circumstances ? agree, no further action.'**

10.39   Sir Geoffrey saw the file on 1st July and approved the decision that no section 12 direction should be sought. In his oral evidence to the Inquiry, he agreed that, without the change of policy, it would have been 'perfectly on the cards' that a section 12 direction might be made against Shipman. I am unable to reach any firm conclusion as to whether, absent the change of policy, a direction would have been made in Shipman's case. Certainly, the GMC's letter did not suggest that one was necessary. It is not known what view the DHSS expressed, if any, although his treating doctors and his employers were sympathetic. It is quite possible that he would have been given a second chance. Even if he had not been given a second chance, it is equally possible, that, with the support of his employers and treating doctors, he would, by the time he came to apply for the vacant position at the Donneybrook practice, have been able successfully to apply for a lifting of the direction. In my view, there can be no criticism of Sir Geoffrey or the other Home Office officials who advised him. They were acting in accordance with what was plainly the new Home Office policy. I feel unable to comment on the wisdom of the new policy, as I do not know why it was introduced.

Conclusion

10.40 It is reassuring that Shipman's abnormal acquisition of pethidine was identified by a Home Office inspection of the records of a pharmaceutical wholesaler; it is also reassuring that a watch was kept on Shipman and that steps were taken to explain to Shipman and his partners their duties and responsibilities relating to controlled drugs. It is also reassuring that when, later in the year, it was realised that the abnormal usage was continuing, the facts were promptly reported to the police.

10.41 Someone unaware of the arrangements that exist for policing controlled drugs might, however, be surprised that the HODI inspectors did not act more decisively when they saw the state of the Abraham Ormerod Medical Centre's CDR in July 1975. Also, the Home Office inspectors appear to have accepted without question Shipman's claim that he did not know that he was supposed to keep a record of drugs leaving the practice's controlled drugs cabinet. However, Shipman might well have claimed that, in the short time he had been in practice, he had not had the CDR checked and that he (like many doctors) was not aware of the extent of his obligations concerning the maintenance of a register. The Home Office inspectors may have been understandably prepared to give him the benefit of the doubt, since he was a young doctor and they may have believed that their 'low level' intervention would be likely to lead to an improvement in his ways.

10.42 The responsibility of the Home Office for section 12 directions was and remains anomalous. Today, section 12 remains in force but the power has not been exercised for a decade. The primary focus of attention for the police and the HODI is the prevention of crime and the leakage of controlled drugs from the wholesaler, pharmacy or surgery to 'the street user'. They do not have the expertise to assess whether an individual doctor should be prevented from prescribing or possessing controlled drugs. It is not surprising therefore that, in the past, the Home Office relied so heavily on the advice of the DHSS in making decisions in respect of section 12. Nor is it surprising that the Home Office should have made a policy decision in 1976 that section 12 directions should be sought only where there was evidence of illicit supply to a third party and not for the doctor's own protection. It might have been better to postpone such a decision until 1980, when the GMC acquired the relevant powers.

10.43 Had a section 12 direction been made in 1976, I doubt that it would have had a significant impact on Shipman's subsequent career or criminality. It was usual for such a direction to be lifted within about two years, or sometimes less, provided that there were no further reports of misconduct. Whenever Shipman decided to return to general practice, it was open to him to apply for the lifting of the direction. With support from his employers and treating doctors he might well have secured the lifting of the direction in time to allow him to apply for the position at the Donneybrook practice in the summer of 1977. If not, he would certainly have found a position in general practice somewhere else, and I am sure he would have pursued a course of conduct similar to that which he followed in Hyde.

10.44 The events of 1976 demonstrate the need for proper and regular inspection of the records and security arrangements related to the keeping of controlled drugs in a general practitioner's surgery. They also demonstrate the need for the monitoring of wholesalers' and pharmacists' controlled drugs arrangements. Also needed is a system for ensuring that, in appropriate cases, the right of a doctor to possess, supply, prescribe and administer controlled drugs can be restricted. According to Mr Alan Macfarlane, the present Chief Inspector of the HODI, the power under section 12 is in disuse (even in relation to doctors who unlawfully supply drugs to others) and is likely to be abandoned in the near future. It is thought that the GMC is better placed to exercise the necessary powers. Provided that the GMC carries out an adequate investigation of the past circumstances and the past and potential effects of the doctor's misuse of controlled drugs upon patient safety and welfare and provided it ensures that the interests of patients are given due weight in the decision-making process, I recognise the force of that argument.

CHAPTER ELEVEN

Shipman's Use of Controlled Drugs in Hyde from 1977 to 1993

Introduction

11.1   Shipman commenced practice at Donneybrook House in Hyde on 1st October 1977. He became one of seven doctors in the practice. At interview, earlier in the year, Shipman had told some of the Donneybrook doctors that he had had a problem with controlled drugs and had been convicted of controlled drugs offences. He had also said that he did not intend to use controlled drugs in future. They were no longer necessary for analgesia as there was a new drug on the market called Fortral (pentazocine) which was not controlled and provided a suitable alternative to the opioid drugs in common use.

11.2   Before Shipman was offered the position, Dr Geoffrey Roberts, one of the members of the practice, telephoned the General Medical Council (GMC) and the Home Office to satisfy himself that there was no current restriction on Shipman's prescribing rights. The Donneybrook doctors would not have invited Shipman to join the practice if his prescribing rights had been fettered in any way. They operated in the main as single-handed practitioners, sharing premises and staff. Dr Roberts was told that Shipman was not subject to any restrictions.

11.3   During the 14 years for which he practised at Donneybrook House, Shipman killed 71 patients, and the deaths of 30 other patients give rise to suspicion. On 1st January 1992, he set up in practice as a fully independent single-handed practitioner, albeit still from rooms within Donneybrook House. On 24th August 1992, he moved to his new premises at 21 Market Street. During the years 1992 to 1998, he killed 143 patients and the circumstances of a further nine deaths give rise to suspicion. Shipman usually killed by giving an intravenous injection of diamorphine. I have already explained in Chapter One how Shipman was able to obtain his supplies of diamorphine. In this Chapter and the next, I shall examine his actions in greater detail and will consider why the systems of regulation and inspection then in force failed to detect his activities. I shall concentrate in particular upon a sequence of single 30mg ampoules of diamorphine that Shipman obtained in 1993. That sequence was unusual and might have been expected to arouse suspicion on the part of the pharmacist dispensing the drugs and the chemist inspection officer (CIO) who examined the controlled drugs register (CDR) at the pharmacy concerned.

11.4   In an attempt to identify all Shipman's sources of supply of controlled drugs, the Inquiry examined the CDRs from nine pharmacies in and around Hyde. Although a pharmacy is required to keep its CDR for only two years after the last entry, some had been kept for much longer. One extended back as far as 1967. Examination of the CDRs revealed that the great majority of controlled drugs prescribed by Shipman had been dispensed at the pharmacy at 23 Market Street. Only very occasionally were entries relating to Shipman found in the CDRs of other pharmacies. This is not surprising, as 23 Market Street was conveniently located close to both the Donneybrook and the 21 Market Street practices.

11.5   The first entry in the surviving CDR for the pharmacy at 23 Market Street was made on 1st October 1991. From the registers of other pharmacies, some of which go back much further, it appears that no other pharmacy had dispensed ampoules of diamorphine prescribed by Shipman before that date. It seems reasonable to infer that, even before he moved to the Market Street premises, diamorphine prescriptions written by Shipman were dispensed mainly, if not exclusively, at 23 Market Street. Because so few entries in Shipman's name were found in CDRs from other pharmacies, I consider that the CDR from 23 Market Street provides a virtually complete picture of Shipman's prescribing of diamorphine after 1991.

The Period Prior to October 1991

11.6   Having seen the methods by which Shipman obtained large quantities of pethidine in Todmorden and the similar means that he employed to acquire diamorphine in the 1990s, I have inferred that he probably used similar methods during the intervening years. In the First Report, I explained my belief that, during the 1980s, Shipman obtained most of his supplies by over-prescribing for the needs of his terminally ill patients and retaining any supplies that were left over after their deaths. I noted a disturbing correlation between the periods during which he would have had access to supplies prescribed for a patient with cancer and the occasions on which he killed. I think it unlikely that he ever ordered diamorphine on requisition. That was the method that had resulted in his detection in 1975. I think he would have been very anxious to avoid being detected for a second time. By taking possession of drugs left over after a patient's death, he would not be vulnerable to detection. He would have known that there was no continuing record of drugs, even injectable controlled drugs with a high black market value, once they left the pharmacy. It is probable that, on occasions, Shipman also obtained supplies by collecting a patient's drugs from the pharmacy and retaining part of the consignment for himself. Probably, he would have hesitated to do that in the early days, as it was known to the authorities that he had used that method in Todmorden. However, as time went by, I am satisfied that he resumed that practice. His willingness to collect drugs from the pharmacy for a patient and to remove excess supplies after the death fitted well with his carefully created reputation as a caring doctor, who would 'go the extra mile' for his patients.

11.7   Between 1978 and 1983, Shipman did not kill frequently. However, from 1984 until 1989, he killed between eight and twelve times a year with no long intervals between the deaths. He probably obtained his supplies of diamorphine from cancer patients. For example, two patients died in January 1985; both had been taking diamorphine for their cancer pain. In one case, there is evidence that he took away the unused drugs; I think it likely that he did so in the second case too. There followed a spate of four killings during February 1985 and six during the rest of the year. Similar connections can be traced during the next four years, during which time Shipman killed 39 patients. For reasons that I do not fully understand, Shipman killed only one patient between November 1989 and October 1991. During that time, he had decided to leave Donneybrook House and to set up on his own at 21 Market Street, next door to the pharmacy at 23 Market Street.

The Pharmacy at 23 Market Street, Hyde

11.8   The pharmacy at 23 Market Street is a busy retail pharmacy. For many years it traded under the name Battersby's and this continued following its acquisition, in September

1991, by Mayfair Chemists (Hyde) Limited (Mayfair), a company owned by Mr Peter Rothman and his wife. In October 1991, Mr Rothman engaged Mrs Ghislaine Brant as the pharmacist manager at Battersby's. He had the premises refurbished and provided a well-equipped dispensary. He installed a computerised system of keeping patient medication records (PMRs).

11.9   Mr Rothman's company had two other pharmacies; one was located in Chadderton, near Oldham, and the other at premises in The Square, Hyde. Mr Rothman was based at the Chadderton pharmacy, although he would visit the other two shops once or twice a week. During the early 1990s, he was the superintendent pharmacist for Battersby's. As well as his managerial duties, Mr Rothman, who had qualified as a pharmacist in 1955, liked to keep up an active interest in dispensing. He would provide cover when one of his pharmacists was off sick, on holiday or having a day off. In 1993, he underwent heart surgery and decided to reduce his business activities. He told the Inquiry that the company owned the premises and business until 1st September 1995 when all three businesses were sold to United North-West Co-op Healthcare Limited.

Mrs Ghislaine Brant

11.10   Mrs Brant graduated in pharmacy at the University of Manchester in 1977. She underwent a one-year pre-registration course with Boots the Chemists (Boots) and obtained her professional qualification in July 1978. She then worked as a relief or second pharmacist at Boots pharmacies throughout Greater Manchester. In about July 1979, she left Boots' employment and began working as a self-employed locum pharmacist. Within about a year, she was offered full-time employment by the proprietor of a pharmacy in Salford and she worked there until 1991, when the business was sold to a pharmacist who intended to manage the pharmacy himself and so had no need for her services.

11.11   At Battersby's, Mrs Brant worked a 40 hour week, which allowed her to take one day off in the working week. On her days off, and during her holidays, her position would be taken either by Mr Rothman himself or by one of the pharmacists working at Mayfair's Chadderton pharmacy. Occasionally, a locum would be employed. All the evidence suggested that Mrs Brant ran the pharmacy in Market Street very well. The premises were well kept; her dispensing was very efficient and there was no reason to question her managerial or professional abilities. Under the new ownership, Mrs Brant continued as manager of the pharmacy and still occupied this position at the time of the Inquiry hearings. So far as I am aware, she continues to give satisfaction to her employers.

11.12   It was Mrs Brant's misfortune that, within 12 months of her appointment, Shipman moved into the surgery premises next door to the pharmacy. As a result, Mrs Brant was responsible for dispensing the great majority of Shipman's prescriptions for diamorphine during the following six years. In particular, she was responsible for dispensing all but one of a series of 14 prescriptions for single ampoules of 30mg diamorphine that Shipman wrote between February and August 1993. The other prescription was dispensed by Mrs Janice Beesley, who usually worked at the Chadderton pharmacy. As I have indicated, this series of prescriptions was very unusual and must be closely scrutinised.

The Other Staff

11.13   A number of other staff were employed at Battersby's in the early 1990s. Mrs Christine Williamson was a very experienced dispensing assistant who, in 1984, had returned after a maternity break to work full-time at Battersby's. She was still working at the pharmacy in 2003. Mrs Elizabeth Pilkington began working at Battersby's in 1984. She was employed as a counter assistant. She was to qualify as a dispensing technician in 1998. She left the pharmacy in September 2001. Mrs Beesley was based at the Chadderton pharmacy but, in common with others who worked there, also worked at 23 Market Street as an occasional relief pharmacist between 1991 and November 1996. Mrs Karen Barham worked as an occasional relief pharmacist between 1990 and 1992. All held Mrs Brant in high regard and none had any reason to doubt her professional integrity or competence in any way.

Diamorphine Stocks and the Appearance of the Controlled Drugs Register from October 1991 to February 1993

11.14   Later in this Chapter, I shall have to consider whether Mrs Brant or Detective Constable (DC) Patrick Kelly (then recently appointed as CIO) should be criticised for not making a report to an appropriate authority about the series of prescriptions for single 30mg ampoules of diamorphine dispensed on prescriptions issued by Shipman during 1993. In order to make that assessment, I shall have to compare the appearance of the diamorphine section of the CDR in the period between October 1991 and February 1993 with its appearance in the following seven months. Copies of the relevant 'drugs supplied' pages (but not the 'drugs obtained' pages) appear at Appendix A.

11.15   The CDR from 23 Market Street is well kept, neat and legible although much of the handwriting is very small. It was in the standard printed form issued by the National Pharmaceutical Association and complied with the requirements of the Misuse of Drugs Regulations 1985, then in force. The periodic visits of the CIO are recorded, at which times 'out of date' drugs were often destroyed.

11.16   On 1st October 1991, twenty 30mg ampoules and five 5mg ampoules of diamorphine were received from the wholesaler; on the same day twenty 30mg ampoules were dispensed to a patient on the prescription of a general practitioner (GP), whom I shall call Dr A. Mrs Brant said that the drugs must have been specially obtained on request, probably for a patient with cancer. She explained that, in the early 1990s, it was not her practice to keep a stock of any drug that was not often called for. The pharmaceutical wholesalers that supplied the pharmacy responded very quickly to any order. There could be up to four deliveries a day.

11.17   The CDR shows that, on 13th November 1991, some diamorphine linctus was dispensed for a patient of Dr B and, the following day, a delivery was received replacing the diamorphine powder that had been used in the linctus. On 3rd December 1991, DC Alan Jackson (DC Kelly's immediate predecessor) attended and witnessed the destruction of four out of date 10mg ampoules.

11.18   On 18th February 1992, Dr A purchased five 5mg ampoules on requisition. Either some of those ampoules obtained on 1st October 1991, or some others previously held in stock, must have been supplied to him.

11.19   On 6th March, twenty five 30mg ampoules were dispensed for a patient on a prescription written by Dr C, and on 10th March, the same quantity was dispensed for the same patient, this time prescribed by Dr D, who worked in the same practice as Dr C. It appears likely that the patient in question was terminally ill. Fifteen of the 50 ampoules dispensed had been obtained by the pharmacy on 5th March, probably because one of the doctors then informed the pharmacy that supplies were going to be needed. Twenty more were obtained on 6th March and 25 more on 10th March, making 60 in total. The 'spare' ten ampoules were not dispensed for the patient in question (it is possible that s/he had died) and they remained in stock. This is important to note, because they probably represent the stock (or part of the stock) which was later to be dispensed on prescriptions written by Shipman for single 30mg ampoules. On 11th March, the pharmacy also obtained ten 100mg ampoules but the CDR shows that these were returned to the wholesaler on the same day. On 16th March, some linctus was dispensed on a prescription issued by Dr B.

11.20   Shipman's name had not appeared as the prescribing doctor in the CDR by this time. It appears likely that he was not caring for any patients needing diamorphine. Significantly, I have not found that he killed any patients during this period, although I am suspicious about the death of Mrs Annie Powers, who died on 10th January 1992.

11.21   On 16th March 1992, a prescription written by Shipman for two 30mg ampoules of diamorphine was dispensed. This is the first time his name appears in the CDR. The drug was prescribed in the name of a male patient who subsequently transferred to another doctor and has since died. The Inquiry has obtained the patient's medical records; they do not show that he was prescribed diamorphine in March 1992. Nor do they reveal any condition that would have justified such a prescription. It seems likely, therefore, that Shipman obtained the drugs for his own purposes. Mrs Brant could not remember whether Shipman collected the drugs on behalf of this patient, although she thought he had not because her recollection was that she did not meet him until after he had moved into 21 Market Street, when he held an opening for the surgery. She thought that these two 30mg ampoules might have been collected by a nurse or a member of the surgery staff. I think that Mrs Brant is almost certainly wrong about this. It is highly unlikely that a district nurse would have collected drugs other than at the specific request of the patient. These drugs were not needed by the patient and the prescription for them was not recorded in the patient's medical notes. They were plainly intended for Shipman's personal use. It would have been quite out of character for Shipman to allow anyone else to collect his illicit supplies of diamorphine.

11.22   On 19th March 1992, the Royal Pharmaceutical Society of Great Britain (RPSGB) inspector, Mr David Young, witnessed the destruction of five out of date 10mg ampoules of diamorphine. It is not possible to tell whether any more remained in stock because the CDR does not provide for an opening stock or a running stock balance.

11.23   Between May 1992 and February 1993, there was very little activity recorded in the CDR. On 15th May 1992, five 10mg ampoules of diamorphine were purchased and the same quantity was supplied on a requisition signed by a GP, Dr E, presumably for his emergency supply. On 21st October 1992, a prescription for diamorphine in solution was dispensed for a patient of Dr F. In December 1992, a pack of 5mg ampoules was purchased and the same quantity was supplied to a GP, Dr G, apparently for emergency use. There were no purchases or supplies of 30mg ampoules.

11.24   In summary, during the 16 months before February 1993, the diamorphine section of the CDR showed ten dispensings. The names of eight different doctors appeared; no doctor's name appeared more than twice, whether as prescriber or as having sought a supply on signed order. The quantities and form of the drug dispensed were variable.

The Abnormal Pattern of Prescribing and Dispensing of Diamorphine in 1993

11.25   The diamorphine section of the CDR from 23 Market Street shows that, between 22nd February and 27th August 1993, Shipman issued 14 prescriptions (in the names of 13 different patients), each for a single 30mg ampoule of diamorphine. This is a most unusual amount to be prescribed as a single dose for therapeutic purposes. The dose was far too large to be intended for use in the treatment of acute pain and far too small to be intended for the relief of chronic pain in terminal illness. As one of the RPSGB inspectors observed, it is 'neither one thing nor the other'. For an opioid-naïve patient, 30mg would be a fatal dose.

11.26   Mrs Brant accepted that she was responsible for dispensing the drug and making the entry in the CDR in each case save one. The relevant entries are made in her distinctive hand. Although the CDR does not record who collected the drugs, Mrs Brant accepted that Shipman usually collected them himself and I think that he did so in each case. Mrs Brant said that her understanding was that Shipman wanted the drugs for the relief of cardiac pain suffered by patients. She said that it did not occur to her that Shipman's prescribing practice was unusual or suspicious and she did not think of reporting it to anyone or drawing it to the attention of the CIO.

11.27   As I observed in the First Report, for several months during 1993, Shipman's pattern of killing his patients was very closely related to his obtaining of diamorphine. Six of the 14 prescriptions were dispensed within a few days after the death of the patient in whose name they were issued. Four of the 14 prescriptions were issued on the day of the death of the patient in question. Two patients in whose names prescriptions were dispensed told the court at Shipman's trial that they were not aware that the prescriptions had been issued and that they had had no need of diamorphine. Of those GP records of the deceased patients which are still available, none contains any reference to the administration of diamorphine, although three sets of records (those of Miss Mary Andrew, Mrs Edna Llewellyn and Mrs Amy Whitehead) refer to the intravenous administration of 10mg morphine sulphate or morphine on the day of the death. I have explained in the First Report how I came to find that, in those cases, Shipman misrepresented in the notes the amount and the type of opiate given. Diamorphine is two or three times as strong as morphine and morphine sulphate.

11.28 It is clear that, during that year, Shipman used these single 30mg ampoules of diamorphine to kill patients. I say that with the benefit of hindsight. The question I must now address is whether, without the benefit of hindsight and in the light of what was known to her at the time, Mrs Brant should have noticed this unusual pattern of prescribing and have been suspicious about it. Later, I shall consider what would have happened if this pattern of prescribing had been noticed and investigated.

Mrs Brant's Professional Obligations

11.29 In Chapter Seven, I summarised the contents of the current edition of the booklet published by the RPSGB, entitled 'Medicines, Ethics and Practice – A Guide for Pharmacists' (the MEP Guide). Mrs Brant was shown extracts from the edition current in April 1993 and agreed that she was familiar with it. It set out the professional duties of pharmacists in a Code of Ethics, which comprised both principles and more detailed obligations. The Code was supplemented by guidance on interpretation.

11.30 The first principle of the Code was that:

> **'A pharmacist's prime concern must be for the welfare of both the patient and other members of the public.'**

11.31 Obligation 1.7 under that principle said that:

> **'A pharmacist must exercise professional judgment to prevent the supply of unnecessary and excessive quantities of medicines and other products, particularly those which are liable to misuse, or which are claimed to depress appetite, prevent absorption of food or reduce body fluid.'**

11.32 Mrs Brant accepted that it was her duty to check that the dosage of medicine prescribed was not excessive for the patient. That, she said, would be her approach when handing over medicine to a member of the public, but she considered that, when medication was being handed over directly to a GP, she was entitled to assume that s/he would use the drug appropriately. I cannot accept the distinction she sought to draw. The main reason why a pharmacist should check that the dosage of a drug is appropriate is that the prescribing doctor might have ordered an inappropriate dose. If s/he has, s/he might have done so because s/he made a slip of the pen or, alternatively, s/he might have made the error through ignorance of the appropriate dosage range. The pharmacist is quite likely, by reason of his/her training and expertise, to have a greater technical knowledge of the drug than the doctor. I do not think therefore that a pharmacist should be excused from exercising his/her professional judgement simply because s/he is handing the drug to a doctor rather than to a member of the public. However, if, on enquiry by the pharmacist, the doctor were to say that s/he knew that the quantity prescribed was greater than should be administered and that s/he intended to use only part of the drug prescribed and throw away the rest, it would, in my view, be reasonable for the pharmacist to assume that the doctor would give the patient an appropriate dose. In any event, even though the pharmacist might be satisfied that the patient would not come to harm, s/he still had a duty to **'prevent the supply of unnecessary and excessive quantities of medicines'**.

11.33   Guidance on Obligation 1.7 was in the following terms:

> **'Drug Misuse.**
>
> **Many prescription only medicines and Controlled Drugs have a potential for misuse or drug dependency. Care should be taken over their supply even when it is legally authorised by prescription or signed order. A pharmacist should be alert to the possibility of drug dependency in health care professionals and patients and should be prepared to make enquiries to ensure that such medicines are to be used responsibly.'**

11.34   Mrs Brant said that, in 1993, she was aware of the possibility of drug dependency among doctors. However, I accept that she was not aware, and had no reason to suspect, that Shipman had a history of drug abuse. I accept that Mrs Brant and all the staff shared the widely held view that Shipman was a competent, conscientious and caring practitioner.

Mrs Brant's Understanding of the Appropriate Dosages of Diamorphine

11.35   I have explained that a single 30mg dose of diamorphine was a very unusual quantity to prescribe; it was 'neither one thing nor the other'. The Inquiry wished to know what Mrs Brant's understanding was of the usual dosages of diamorphine for various purposes. Her attention was drawn to the British National Formulary (BNF) for 1993, which gave guidance as to the appropriate dosages of diamorphine for the various conditions for which it can be prescribed. The guidance read:

> **'Acute pain, *by subcutaneous or intramuscular injection*, 5 mg repeated every 4 hours if necessary (up to 10 mg for heavier well-muscled patients)**
>
> **By slow intravenous injection**, quarter to half corresponding intramuscular dose
>
> **Myocardial infarction, *by slow intravenous injection* (1 mg/minute), 5 mg followed by a further 2.5–5 mg if necessary; elderly or frail patients, reduce dose by half**
>
> **Acute pulmonary oedema, *by slow intravenous injection* (1 mg/minute) 2.5–5 mg**
>
> **Chronic pain, *by mouth or by subcutaneous or intramuscular injection*, 5–10 mg regularly every 4 hours; dose may be increased according to needs, intramuscular dose should be approximately half corresponding oral dose, and quarter to third corresponding oral *morphine* dose ...'**

11.36   Mrs Brant accepted that this guidance was consistent with her understanding of the properties of diamorphine and her experience of the quantities of diamorphine that had been requested by doctors for their personal stocks. She confirmed that, for a patient with myocardial infarction or symptoms suggestive of it, appropriate treatment for the pain would be the administration of 2.5mg to 5mg diamorphine, or less in the case of a less well-muscled patient, but possibly more if necessary. Larger doses would be appropriate for cancer pain.

11.37 Mrs Brant was asked whether she realised that 30mg diamorphine was a far greater dose than would be needed to treat a patient with acute pain. At first, her response was that Shipman was an experienced doctor who knew what dose he needed to give and that he could work out how much he should give from a larger ampoule. She then said that other doctors were prescribing 30mg ampoules for acute pain and that, in some patients, that was the necessary dose. She agreed, however, that it was 'pretty unusual' as a single dose. When asked whether these other doctors were using 30mg as a single dose for opioid-naïve patients, she replied that she did not know whether the patients in question were opioid-naïve. I am quite sure that Mrs Brant knew that 30mg diamorphine would be an excessive dose for an opioid-naïve patient suffering an acute episode of pain.

The Events of 1993 in Detail

11.38 I will now deal with the events in 1993 in some detail. I shall examine them from the point of view of Mrs Brant, bringing into account only the information that was, or should have been, available to her. Pharmacists do not have access to a patient's medical records and a prescription does not carry any indication of the condition for which the medication has been prescribed. In Chapter Seven, I explained the difficulties that this can create for pharmacists when assessing the appropriateness of a particular prescription. Pharmacists do, in general, have access to the PMRs kept by the pharmacy where they work. If the patient uses a particular pharmacy exclusively, a very useful picture can be built up in such records. The Inquiry has obtained the PMRs for some of the patients for whom Shipman prescribed a single ampoule of diamorphine in 1993. No record is available in some cases. That may be because no record was ever created in that patient's name. It is possible that a record was created but is no longer available. However, in each case where a PMR was kept and is available to the Inquiry, it has been found that these single ampoule prescriptions for diamorphine were not entered into the record.

The Week of 22nd to 26th February 1993

11.39 On Monday, 22nd February, Shipman presented two prescriptions for single 30mg ampoules of diamorphine. One was in the name of Mrs Louisa Radford and the other in the name of Mr Harold Freeman. The pharmacy held a PMR for Mr Freeman but this prescription was not entered. For the reasons explained in paragraphs 11.19 and 11.21, Mrs Brant must have had more than eight 30mg ampoules in stock at this time, because, before ordering any further supplies on 1st July, she was to supply Shipman with 12 single ampoules and to dispense ten more on a prescription for a patient of another doctor on 30th June.

11.40 When giving oral evidence to the Inquiry, in May 2003, Mrs Brant said that the first time she dispensed a diamorphine ampoule for Shipman was probably on 22nd February 1993, although as I have said in paragraph 11.21, it is highly likely that she dispensed two 30mg ampoules for him on 16th March 1992. She recalled that Shipman came into the pharmacy, saying that he had to make an emergency visit to a patient who had suffered a suspected heart attack, for which he needed an ampoule of diamorphine. If Mrs Brant's recollection is right, that patient would have been Mrs Radford, for whom no PMR is available. Mrs Brant thought that Shipman initially asked for a 5mg ampoule but she told him that she had none in stock so he then asked for a 10mg ampoule. She told the Inquiry that she understood, from the fact that he was seeking a 5mg or 10mg ampoule, that Shipman did not keep an emergency stock of his own. She said that she went to the controlled drug cabinet, where she found that she had only 30mg ampoules in stock. She told the Inquiry that she believed that she had had no stock of 10mg ampoules since the destruction carried out by Mr Young in March 1992. She claimed that she had had no requests for 10mg ampoules since her arrival in Hyde and that, when the existing stock had gone out of date, she would not have replaced it. In fact, she supplied five 10mg ampoules to Dr E on 15th May 1992 and purchased the same quantity on the same day. It is quite possible that she purchased these ampoules specifically for Dr E because she did not have any in stock but it is also quite possible that she supplied existing stock to Dr E and replaced the ampoules with new stock. This would be sensible stock rotation. However, I accept that there is no evidence to contradict her belief that she had no 5mg or 10mg ampoules in stock on 22nd February 1993.

11.41   Mrs Brant said that, because she had only 30mg ampoules, she had to give Shipman one of those. She said that there could not have been any 5mg or 10mg ampoules in her stock, because, if there had been, that is what she would have given him. She emphasised that it was open to Shipman to use less than the full 30mg, if appropriate, and to throw away the rest. She could not remember whether, at the time of making his request, he had already written a prescription for 5mg or 10mg. She said that he might have had an empty prescription pad in his hand or he might have brought her a prescription. She was sure, however, that he had written out a prescription for a 30mg diamorphine ampoule before he left the shop.

11.42   When providing a statement for the police in 1999, Mrs Brant identified each of the 14 entries in the CDR covering the single 30mg ampoules. She then said:

> **'I can recall that when I asked Dr Shipman about these prescriptions he stated that the drugs were being used for patients with suspected chest pain and heart attacks which** (sic) **he was going to visit.'**

11.43   At the trial, in 1999, Shipman's counsel asked Mrs Brant whether she had any independent recollection of the individual occasions on which Shipman had prescribed diamorphine or whether she was dependent for her recollection on the CDR. She said that she was dependent on the CDR. She was asked specifically whether she remembered the prescription for Mrs Radford and she said that she did not.

11.44   In 2002, when Mrs Brant provided a statement for the Inquiry, she was asked about the series of single ampoules prescribed in 1993. She did not say that she had any recollection of what Shipman had said to her at the time. She explained that she had not noticed any particular pattern to Shipman's prescribing. She said that it was not her practice to look for a pattern. Each prescription would be examined individually and, if it was correctly presented and there were no other concerns about it, it would be dispensed.

11.45   In oral evidence to the Inquiry, Mrs Brant said that she could not remember Shipman coming in for a second time on 22nd February with a prescription for Mr Freeman. She postulated that he might have come in later in the day and issued a prescription to 'replenish' his stock, having already administered a quantity of diamorphine to the patient from that stock, although she could not remember that he had done so. When a doctor administers a drug from his/her own stock to a NHS patient, s/he ought to reclaim the cost of the drug, which s/he has paid for, from the Prescription Pricing Authority. He or she is also entitled to claim an administration fee. It appears that some doctors cannot be bothered to go through this procedure and prefer to issue a prescription in the name of the patient and keep the drug to 'replenish' their own stocks. The practice of 'replenishing' is unlawful, because the actual drugs dispensed under a prescription ought to go to the patient in whose name they are prescribed. However, I was told that 'replenishing' is not uncommon. It seems to me a relatively minor offence and I understand that some pharmacists turn a blind eye to the practice. I think Mrs Brant did so. At one stage in her evidence she implied that it was acceptable; at another, she said that she knew that the correct procedure was for the doctor to buy his/her own stock on a signed order. She did not know what the procedure was for the doctor to reclaim the cost of the drugs if and when s/he had administered them to a patient. It was clear from her evidence that she did not think that the practice was dishonest.

11.46   I find it strange that Mrs Brant should claim to remember the first supply on 22nd February but not the second. She said that she could not think 'back that far' but, since both supplies took place on the same day, and since the two were so similar, I think that she would be bound to remember the second supply if she could remember the first. I am driven to conclude that she could in fact remember neither. In my view, her evidence as to what she could recollect is unreliable. I think that, by the time she was about to give oral evidence to the Inquiry, she knew how unusual Shipman's demands for single 30mg ampoules were and felt vulnerable to criticism. Also, she had come to realise for the first time that she might well not have had any 5mg or 10mg ampoules in stock. She realised this because her legal representatives had, very carefully and quite properly, analysed both the receipt and the supply sides of the CDR in preparation for the Inquiry hearing. I think that, when she realised that, she persuaded herself that she had given Shipman 30mg ampoules that day because that was all she had. I am quite satisfied that she gave Shipman 30mg ampoules that day because that is what he had prescribed. We know now that Shipman would not have wanted 5mg or 10mg ampoules. He wanted 30mg ampoules for the purpose of killing patients. Mrs Brant could not know that, of course, but I am entitled to take that knowledge into account when assessing the reliability of her evidence as to the events of 22nd February. If her recollection of this day is faulty, as I find it to be, I cannot be satisfied that Shipman came in twice. He might have come in only once and asked for two ampoules for different patients.

11.47   Mrs Brant accepted that she dispensed a 30mg ampoule of diamorphine on a prescription issued in Mr Freeman's name and did not make an entry in his PMR. She could not explain why normal practice had not been followed in this respect. As a rule, the making of an entry in the PMR is an integral part of the dispensing process. The prescribing information is typed into the PMR and the computer is then used to print out a label for the drug package.

Mrs Brant claimed that she would have put a printed label on the packet containing the drug she gave Shipman but accepted that no entry was made by her or by the dispenser in the PMR. She said that it was possible to use the computer system to print a label without making an entry in the PMR. I wondered why a pharmacist would want to do that. It was explained to me that, sometimes, after the prescription had been entered into the PMR, the printer might malfunction. In that event, the pharmacist would wish to make a second attempt at printing without making a second entry in the record. That makes sense but it does not explain what happened on that occasion because there was no entry in Mr Freeman's PMR for that day.

11.48   There must have been some reason for this departure from the usual use of the PMR system. It is possible that Mrs Brant believed that, in writing a prescription in Mr Freeman's name, Shipman was 'replenishing' his own stock because he had given Mr Freeman some diamorphine earlier in the day. However, that explanation would be inconsistent with Mrs Brant's claim that Shipman had come in earlier in the day asking for an emergency supply for Mrs Radford, which, she said, led her to believe that he did not keep a stock of his own. However, as I have concluded that her recollection of the events of this day is unreliable, it is quite possible that she believed that Shipman usually kept a stock of one ampoule of diamorphine for emergency use and that he had had to replace it twice in one day. If that were so, Mrs Brant might well have realised that the ampoule that she dispensed, ostensibly for Mr Freeman, was not going to him but was going into Shipman's stock. If so, it is possible that she might have thought it unnecessary or inappropriate to make an entry in Mr Freeman's PMR. However, she denied that that would have been her practice. She said that, if a doctor told her that s/he was replenishing stock of a drug that had been used on a patient by prescribing the drug in the name of that patient, she would enter the prescription into the patient's PMR. The only explanation I can think of for Mrs Brant's failure to enter this prescription into the PMR is that she did not make out a printed label and therefore did not use the computer system at all. It may well be that she just put an ampoule into a package and wrote on it the name of the drug and nothing more.

11.49   On Friday, 26th February, two more prescriptions for single 30mg ampoules of diamorphine were presented, in the names of Mrs Olive Heginbotham and Mrs Lillian Ibbotson. The Inquiry does not have a PMR for Mrs Heginbotham and the PMR for Mrs Ibbotson does not cover 1993. Mrs Brant said that she had no recollection of either of these transactions. She could not even remember whether Shipman himself came in. She stressed that Fridays were usually very busy. That I accept. However, she must have approved the dispensing of these ampoules and she must have found time to enter them in the CDR.

11.50   Mrs Brant was questioned closely about her thought processes when agreeing to dispense two more 30mg diamorphine ampoules only a few days after the first two. She claimed that she trusted Shipman completely and that it had never occurred to her to think that there might have been any reason not to dispense the prescriptions he presented. She also described the nature of her professional relationship with Shipman. She said that she had formed a very favourable view of him even before she met him, from what her customers said about him. This view was confirmed when she got to know him. She found that he was always willing to take the time to explain the reasons for his choice of medication. Sometimes, he would ask her advice about the availability of different types of drug. Once, he asked her to remind him if ever he prescribed a proprietary brand of drug when he could have prescribed a generic product.

11.51   Mrs Brant said that she was confident in Shipman's competence; she thought he knew what he was doing. She said that it had not occurred to her that Shipman's requests for single 30mg ampoules were strange. She said that, from time to time, they spoke about the patients for whom these drugs were prescribed and Shipman always gave her a plausible explanation for what he was doing. She could not now remember what these explanations were. When asked whether she recognised the use of a single 30mg ampoule as strange and inappropriate prescribing, she said that she did not and that she had trusted Shipman's judgement. In my view, had she thought about it at all at the time, she would have recognised that his prescribing was strange and inappropriate.

The Period from March to June 1993

11.52   On 22nd March, Shipman obtained a single 30mg diamorphine ampoule in the name of Mrs Whitehead and another, on 12th April, in the name of Miss Andrew. No PMRs have been found for these patients.

11.53   By this time, the diamorphine supplies page of the CDR must have had a most unusual appearance. Instead of a variety of doctors' names appearing in the prescriber's column, Shipman's name appeared in six consecutive rows. Mrs Brant said that she now recognises that this was a strange pattern of prescribing, although at the time she had not seen it as such; she had seen it simply as a treatment that Shipman was using at the time. That is not in my view a satisfactory answer, as to give 30mg of diamorphine to a patient who is suffering from cardiac pain (which is what she maintained she believed was the use to which the drugs were put) is not a reasonable course of treatment. A much smaller dose should have been given. If Shipman was repeatedly taking 30mg ampoules but using only about 5mg, this was wasteful and the dispensing of it contrary to Obligation 1.7 of the RPSGB Code of Ethics. Mrs Brant should have suggested that he should prescribe a smaller ampoule, which she would obtain for him. It seems that she never suggested this. The records suggest that she did not purchase any diamorphine ampoules during this period.

11.54   Mrs Brant maintained that it was not her practice to look out for prescribing patterns; she said that, if an individual prescription was satisfactory and there were no other causes for concern, a pharmacist should dispense the drug. I do not accept that opinion as it is not consistent with a pharmacist's duty, as set out in the MEP Guide, to be aware of the possibility that doctors might seek to divert drugs to their own use. Indeed, I think that a pharmacist is under a duty to look out for any sign of potentially unlawful or unethical prescribing by doctors. However, Mrs Brant pointed out that one or two single 30mg ampoules is not a large quantity of diamorphine and would not immediately give rise to the suspicion that the doctor was addicted or was supplying to someone who was. I accept that that is so. I also accept that Mrs Brant had no other reason to suspect Shipman of drug addiction. The question is whether, by reason of the frequent repetition of the requests for 30mg ampoules, not interspersed with any other requests more typical of a GP's use of diamorphine, Mrs Brant should have realised that his pattern of prescribing was very odd. I accept that, in fact, she did not realise that it was.

11.55 Mrs Brant said that Shipman always gave her plausible explanations but she has not been able to recall what any of them were. I do wonder if he perhaps told her that he liked to keep a 30mg ampoule about him in case of emergency, acknowledging that, if it was a cardiac case, he would have to throw some away but also ensuring that, if more than 5mg or 10mg was ever necessary, he would have enough. Mrs Brant has not suggested that as an explanation. However, I had the impression for much of her evidence that she was not thinking very clearly. I think she found the experience of giving evidence very stressful and I am not unsympathetic about that. Plainly, she was flustered because she could see clearly by that time how obvious and unusual the pattern of prescribing was and that she had failed to appreciate it at the time. I do wonder whether she was also embarrassed because she did not wish to admit that she knew that these single prescriptions were not in fact going to the named patients but were for Shipman's personal stock. If she knew that this was not the correct procedure, she might have been reluctant to admit to it, even though it was not the most serious matter.

11.56 On 17th April, Shipman prescribed an ampoule in the name of Mrs Sarah Ashworth. This was dispensed by Mrs Beesley, who was working as a relief in Mrs Brant's absence. I shall consider her position in greater detail below. She made no entry in Mrs Ashworth's PMR.

11.57 On 27th April, Shipman obtained two more single ampoules, in the names of Mrs Fanny Nichols and Mrs Marjorie Parker. A PMR was available for Mrs Parker, although it is not known whether there was one for Mrs Nichols. Mrs Brant made no entry in Mrs Parker's record. She said that she had no recollection of dispensing these two ampoules.

11.58 On 5th May, Mrs Brant dispensed two more single 30mg ampoules on prescription in the names of Mrs Llewellyn and Mrs Nellie Mullen. There was a PMR for Mrs Llewellyn but Mrs Brant did not make an entry in it. No PMR for Mrs Mullen has been found. Mrs Brant appeared to have no recollection of the events of this day. She maintained that it still did not occur to her that either the individual prescription or Shipman's pattern of prescribing was unusual.

11.59 On 20th May, Shipman obtained another ampoule in the name of Mr Ernest Ralphs. There is no PMR for Mr Ralphs. When Mrs Brant entered the transaction in the CDR, the page was almost full. Only one line remained at the bottom. Every line on that page save the first recorded the dispensing of a single 30mg ampoule prescribed by Shipman in the name of a different patient. Yet Mrs Brant did not notice anything unusual. The bottom line was filled on 30th June 1993, when a box of ten 30mg ampoules of diamorphine, prescribed by another GP, Dr H, was dispensed for a patient who appears to have been terminally ill. To replenish her stock of 30mg ampoules, Mrs Brant ordered five more on the following day.

The Period from July to August 1993

11.60 At the beginning of July, five 10mg ampoules of diamorphine were purchased for the pharmacy. However, their arrival did not cause Shipman to switch to that size of ampoule. This confirms my view that he had never wanted 10mg ampoules at all.

11.61 The next entry in the supply side of the diamorphine register recorded the visit of DC Kelly, the CIO, on 12th July. He signed at the top of a new page to indicate that the CDR had been inspected. It is common ground that DC Kelly did not notice anything unusual about the previous page of the diamorphine register and that Mrs Brant did not draw his attention to it. Nor did she tell him that Shipman had personally collected all the supplies recorded on that previous page.

11.62 In the CDR, there then followed three entries relating to large amounts of diamorphine prescribed by Dr C for a patient who appears to have been terminally ill. Then, on 14th and 27th August, Shipman prescribed the last two single 30mg ampoules in the names of Mr Ralphs (again) and another patient. There is a PMR for the latter patient, but Mrs Brant did not make an entry in it when she dispensed an ampoule of diamorphine in his name.

11.63 Thereafter the CDR resumed a more normal appearance. Shipman's name continued to appear but was interspersed with entries relating to other GPs. After this time, when Shipman prescribed diamorphine, he did so in a much more usual way, typical of the treatment of terminal illness. There was no reason why Mrs Brant should have been concerned about those entries. The abnormal pattern had ceased.

Mrs Brant's Failure to Report This Sequence of Prescriptions

11.64 Ought Mrs Brant to be criticised for her failure to notice or to be concerned about the pattern of Shipman's unusual prescribing and collecting of diamorphine in 1993? It is common ground that, if she had noticed it and had realised that it was unusual, she should have reported it to an appropriate authority.

11.65 I am satisfied that, as a pharmacist, Mrs Brant was under a duty to keep a lookout for abnormal prescribing patterns that might suggest illegal or irresponsible prescribing of controlled drugs. A number of witnesses with experience of examining CDRs told the Inquiry that the series of entries in 1993 was obviously or strikingly unusual. I think even Mrs Brant found it difficult to explain how she had not regarded it as odd. Mr David Young, an inspector from the RPSGB, initially said that he did not notice anything unusual about the record but then said that, on further reflection, he did. On Mrs Brant's behalf, it was said that everyone who now sees the record has the benefit of knowing that it relates to a mass murderer who was using the individual ampoules to kill his patients. I recognise the power of hindsight, but I have been careful to look at these issues in the light of what was known to Mrs Brant at the time and in the light of the impression of Shipman that it was reasonable for her to have formed.

11.66 My own view is that the series was unusual, and conspicuously so. First, because, for the individual patients, the amount of the drug prescribed was 'neither one thing nor the other'; it was too much for acute pain and too little for terminal care. Each entry save one related to a different patient. This would not make sense as, usually, patients who need diamorphine in such a quantity continue to need it for some time. Second, the appearance of the CDR during these few months was quite unlike its previous appearance and quite unlike any diamorphine supplies page that I have seen in any other CDR examined in the course of the Inquiry. On the previous page of the CDR in question, the record showed prescriptions for a variety of quantities and sizes of ampoules of the injectable form of diamorphine, interspersed with prescriptions for a different form of the drug, e.g. in solution for oral administration. In the series under examination, entry after entry was for the same number of the same size of ampoule containing the same injectable form of the drug. I recognise that doctors have their own styles of prescribing, but, if the use of single 30mg ampoules of injectable diamorphine was to be regarded as Shipman's style, it appears to have been a very unusual one. As it happened, the unusual appearance of the register was emphasised by the absence of any entries in the names of other doctors. Had the Shipman entries been interspersed with entries relating to other doctors, its unusual appearance would have been less obvious.

11.67   In my view, the CDR would have looked odd even at the end of the week beginning 22nd February but, by July, when there was a column of 12 similar entries, the appearance was quite remarkable, especially when compared with the previous page. Other witnesses said that they had never seen a CDR with this appearance before and Mrs Brant did not suggest that she ever had. Mrs Brant also knew that Shipman himself had collected each of the ampoules. That in itself was an odd feature. Of course, doctors do call into pharmacies to collect emergency supplies from time to time but, if that was what Shipman was doing, he was doing it with unusual frequency.

11.68   I have sought to make full allowance for the advantage of hindsight that everyone now has in commenting on this page of the CDR. I have also borne in mind Mrs Brant's reputation as a competent and careful pharmacist. Nonetheless, I have come to the conclusion that this series of entries was sufficiently unusual to call for enquiry and explanation. In my view, in failing to notice the unusual nature of this series of transactions, Mrs Brant fell below the standard to be expected of a competent and conscientious pharmacist.

11.69   Why did Mrs Brant not notice this series of entries? She was under a duty to watch out for abnormal patterns that might suggest illegal or irresponsible prescribing of controlled drugs. Being an honest person, she would have reported any such signs that she noticed. I think the explanation for her failure to notice this series of prescriptions lies partly in her own attitude towards her work and partly in the influence Shipman had over her.

11.70   First, Mrs Brant did not regard it as part of her duty to look out for unusual prescribing patterns. In her Inquiry statement, she said that, provided a prescription was correctly presented and there were no other concerns about it, it would be dispensed. Second, I think that Mrs Brant was careful and conscientious about her own direct responsibilities but was less concerned about ensuring that those about her also complied with theirs. I am satisfied that she had a proper regard for her duty towards patients. She would look carefully at a prescription to ensure that the dosage was appropriate. She was plainly conscientious about her duties in relation to the CDR. It is carefully completed. I think she would also be careful to ensure that she did not dispense a controlled drug prescription unless all the statutory requirements were met. I think she was quite strict with her staff; she 'ran a tight ship'. However, I do not think it would have worried her if she had thought that a doctor was 'replenishing' his/her stocks by prescribing in the name of a patient whom s/he had already treated. She knew that this practice was not technically correct but thought that it was convenient and not dishonest. Provided that she did not know for a fact that the doctor was replenishing, her own conduct could not be criticised. I do not believe that she would have been greatly concerned to think that a doctor was prescribing much more of a drug than was needed for the patient and throwing away what was unused. I do not think she saw it as an important part of her duty to be responsible for the actions of her fellow professionals.

11.71 It follows that, to some extent, the explanation for Mrs Brant's failure lies within her own approach to her job. However, in my view, of far greater effect upon her was Shipman's personal influence. Shipman was an extremely devious man. In 1992, when he met Mrs Brant, he probably had no terminally ill patients who would have been a means for him to obtain diamorphine. When he decided that he wanted some diamorphine, he would not at that time have been able to follow his usual procedure of over-prescribing for, and stealing from, a cancer patient. He must have realised that he would have to devise a new method. He would, I am sure, have been wary of obtaining the drug on requisition. That had led to his detection in 1975. Also, he had claimed to the medical adviser of the Tameside Family Health Services Authority (FHSA) that he did not keep stocks of controlled drugs or a CDR. For this reason, he devised a method of obtaining diamorphine that was intended to appear lawful and inconspicuous. The individual prescriptions were not for large amounts and, if interspersed in the CDR with a variety of prescriptions for other forms of diamorphine prescribed by other GPs, would not be very noticeable. The practice of collecting drugs on behalf of a patient would be seen as usual for him, although unusual for other doctors. However, I am quite certain that he would have recognised that he could be vulnerable to detection if the pharmacist noticed anything unusual. It would have been important to him to ensure that the pharmacist had complete confidence in him. It may be that Shipman recognised that Mrs Brant was not inclined to ask probing questions. Whether or not he did so, I think it highly likely that Shipman set out to win Mrs Brant's trust and confidence and to erode such professional objectivity as she had towards him. I am sure he would have been particularly pleasant towards her. He would, as he often did, have talked about the principles on which he conducted his practice in such a way as to inspire admiration and respect. He would always have had time to explain to Mrs Brant why he was prescribing as he was. He would have asked her advice. She might well have found this flattering. I think he was capable of being very charming when it suited him; I have little doubt that it suited him to be charming to Mrs Brant. I think she came to trust and admire him to the extent that she lost all professional objectivity and, when Shipman came into the pharmacy, she treated him as a friend. I think they probably chatted about this and that. Sometimes, the conversation would have included Shipman telling her a tale about a patient he was going to see or had just seen. The tales might or might not have been based on truth. Mrs Brant did not question what he was doing or why. In my judgement, she is to be criticised for losing her professional objectivity but must be excused to a large extent because she was the victim of a deliberate deception by an accomplished liar.

Mrs Janice Beesley

11.72 I mentioned earlier that, on 17th April, Mrs Beesley dispensed one of Shipman's prescriptions for a single 30mg diamorphine ampoule in the name of Mrs Ashworth. She said that she could not remember the transaction and this is not surprising. In her written statement, she said that she would not have thought that the prescription for a single 30mg ampoule was in any way unusual. However, in oral evidence, she said that the dose was unusually large as a single dose. In her experience, doctors usually took 5mg ampoules for emergency use and prescribed a box of 30mg ampoules for treating cancer pain. She said that she thought she would have wanted to know from Shipman why he had prescribed a 30mg ampoule and claimed that he must have given her a satisfactory explanation. That is possible, although it is hard to think what he might have said to justify the request for a single ampoule as large as 30mg. However, Mrs Beesley said that, if Shipman had said that the patient was having a heart attack and if he had persisted in requesting 30mg, she would probably have let him have it.

11.73   Mrs Beesley did not enter this prescription in Mrs Ashworth's PMR. She claimed that it would have been her usual practice to do so and could not explain why she had not done so in this case. She agreed that, had she looked at Mrs Ashworth's PMR, she would have seen nothing that would have suggested that Mrs Ashworth might need strong analgesia. She said that it was possible that, if Shipman had come into the pharmacy himself, she might not have looked in the PMR. I cannot understand why the presence of the doctor would prevent her from following her normal practice, unless perhaps Shipman claimed to be in a desperate hurry and encouraged her to hand over the ampoule without making an entry in the PMR or printing a label. Either at the time of dispensing the ampoule or later, Mrs Beesley entered the transaction in the CDR but said that she did not notice the column of six similar transactions immediately above her own writing. Owing to my own familiarity with the record, I find that surprising but I accept the truth of Mrs Beesley's assertion.

11.74   I have the impression that Mrs Beesley is a competent and well-organised pharmacist. I accept that she would have recognised that 30mg diamorphine was a very unusual single dose and would have been likely to ask Shipman what it was for, unless he volunteered an explanation in advance of any enquiry from her. I think that is quite likely to have happened. I think he might well have said that he needed the drug very urgently and that he had written a prescription for 30mg 'to be on the safe side' or something of that nature. I do not criticise Mrs Beesley for dispensing one single 30mg ampoule on that one occasion.

Mr Peter Rothman

11.75   In 1993, Mr Rothman was the joint owner (with his wife) of Mayfair, which owned the pharmacy at 23 Market Street. All retail pharmacies operated by a body corporate have to have a superintendent pharmacist. In 1993, Mr Rothman was the superintendent of the pharmacy in Market Street. The question arose whether, in his capacity as superintendent, Mr Rothman was under a duty to make a regular inspection of the CDR and whether he should, in so doing, have noticed the entries relating to the unusual series of prescriptions for single 30mg diamorphine ampoules.

11.76   Under section 71 of the Medicines Act 1968, the supply of medicinal products in a pharmacy business must take place either under the personal control of the superintendent (who must be a pharmacist) or subject to the direction of the superintendent and under the personal control of a manager or assistant who is a pharmacist. As Mrs Brant (or in her absence another pharmacist) was in personal control of the supply of medicinal products from the premises, the duties of Mr Rothman, as superintendent, were limited to the giving of 'directions' for the proper running of the business.

11.77 Mr Rothman expressed the opinion that his position as superintendent did not require more than that he should be satisfied that the business was properly run. He said that this would include being satisfied that the CDR was properly kept. He said that he visited the premises once or twice a week and was satisfied with the way in which Mrs Brant exercised personal control. He said that he did not inspect the CDR, although he knew that it was properly kept because, from time to time when working as the pharmacist on duty, he would have to make entries in it himself. He said that he did not notice the page of the diamorphine section on which the unusual series of entries was written. Unless he inspected the CDR, it is apparent that he would be very unlikely to notice that series, as he had had no occasion to write on that page.

11.78 Mr Stephen Lutener, former Head of Professional Conduct at the RPSGB, agreed with Mr Rothman that the duty of a superintendent to give directions would not normally be expected to include a regular inspection of the CDR. That evidence does not surprise me and I accept it without hesitation. Indeed, it would seem very surprising if the giving of 'directions' were to include such a routine task. Strictly speaking, it should be enough for the superintendent to tell the pharmacist manager to keep the CDR properly. In the early stages of a new manager's employment, it might well behove a superintendent to look at the CDR quite carefully to ensure that the manager was completing the register with apparent care and accuracy. However, once satisfied that that was being done, I would have thought it impossible to criticise a superintendent pharmacist for making no further inspections of the contents of the CDR, provided that, from time to time, s/he checked to ensure whether or not the CDR was still being kept. I am quite satisfied that Mr Rothman did that and he is not to be criticised for not noticing that one page of the diamorphine section contained a series of very unusual entries.

Detective Constable Patrick Kelly

11.79 DC Kelly of the Greater Manchester Police (GMP) was appointed as a CIO in April 1993. As I have explained in Chapter Nine, his duties included the inspection of pharmacies in Tameside. Before his appointment, he had worked in the GMP Drug Squad but this entailed mainly the keeping of observations on drug dealers. Otherwise, he had no training in, or experience of, controlled drugs or the work of retail pharmacies. DC Jackson, the previous occupant of the post, had retired before DC Kelly's appointment. Accordingly, DC Kelly's training for the post was to accompany DC Robert Peers, an experienced CIO, for half of each working day over a period of about three weeks. DC Peers was available for only half of each working day because he was also a police 'sniffer dog' handler. He started work very early in the mornings, before the pharmacies had opened, and finished in the early afternoon. Accordingly, DC Kelly's opportunity to make accompanied visits to pharmacies was limited. Also, DC Peers' work was not entirely typical of the work to be done by DC Kelly. DC Peers was responsible for the pharmacies in the city centre, where a substantial number of drug addicts obtained their supplies. DC Kelly was to be responsible for the outer areas, where addicts were less in evidence.

11.80   DC Kelly told the Inquiry that, as a result of his training with DC Peers, he understood that the most important features of the job were to audit the supplies of controlled drugs held at the pharmacies, to supervise the destruction of out of date supplies and to monitor the use of methadone by addicts. He had read the Home Office guidance notes and knew that his duties included the policing of the pharmacists themselves and also that he should keep a watch for irresponsible prescribing by doctors. However, I think that the guidance notes did not mean a great deal to him until he had had several months' or even a year or two's experience in the job. Initially, he seems to have thought that irresponsible prescribing was prescribing wastefully, so that the patient had a lot of drugs that would never be used. It would not be surprising, therefore, if he regarded this aspect of his work as less important than the supervision of drug addicts. He was, in any event, ill equipped to recognise a case of irresponsible prescribing if he saw one. He knew very little about the properties of individual controlled drugs or the quantities in which they might be used for therapeutic purposes. He had read in the guidance notes that he was to look out for doctors who collected drugs from pharmacies but did not understand why he should do so, even though the notes explain the reason for this advice.

11.81   DC Kelly started inspecting on his own in May 1993. He was responsible for inspecting over 400 pharmacies. He estimated that, by July, he had probably visited about 150. He said, and I accept, that, in the first few months, he was very dependent upon the information given to him by pharmacists. Also, he was so conscious of his own lack of knowledge that he would hesitate to question a pharmacist, other than in general terms.

11.82   DC Kelly agreed that he inherited the card index system operated by his predecessor. I do not think that he had a very clear idea of what he was supposed to enter on these cards, besides the names of drug addicts. One might have expected that DC Kelly would have followed the practice of DC Peers, who had taught him the job. DC Peers said that, as well as recording the names of drug addicts, it was his practice to record the name of every patient who was prescribed diamorphine (even in a modest amount) on the first occasion the drug was prescribed. DC Jackson (whose cards DC Kelly inherited) initially said that he did not record every first prescription of diamorphine but, on further reflection, thought that he must have done. I do not think that DC Kelly had a clear recollection of what he recorded in respect of patients who were not drug addicts. It appears to me that the primary purpose of these cards was to record the names of all known drug addicts, so that the Home Office could be notified and enter the names on the Index of Addicts. In other respects, I think that the rules were not clear.

11.83   DC Kelly made his first visit to the pharmacy at 23 Market Street on 12th July 1993. Although he cannot remember doing so, he accepted that he had examined and signed the diamorphine section of the CDR. He signed at the top of a new page. The previous page was the one recording the series of Shipman's 12 prescriptions for single 30mg ampoules. Every line, save the first and last, recorded a similar transaction. DC Kelly said that he did not notice anything unusual about that page. It is common ground that Mrs Brant did not mention it to him or suggest that there was anything unusual about it. DC Kelly said it would not have struck him that it was unusual for a doctor to prescribe exactly the same amount for a lot of patients. Nor would he have known that 30mg was a large ampoule for a single dose of diamorphine. Although he had a copy of MIMS (a reference book similar to the BNF, which provides information about drug dosages) with him, he did not look at it on this occasion. He knew that diamorphine was used to relieve severe pain in terminal cancer cases and said that he would have expected to see several entries of prescriptions for the same patient. He said that what 'threw' him was seeing the names of so many different patients. However, he did not ask Mrs Brant about the entries. He did not think that he would have entered the name of each patient on the card for that pharmacy. (It is not possible to check this as the cards have been destroyed.) Nor, so far as he could remember, did he ask Mrs Brant whether the doctor had collected any or all of the drugs. I am quite sure that he did not.

11.84   It appears to me that, at least at this early stage of his appointment as a CIO, DC Kelly was not capable of recognising the unusual features of this CDR. He was completely dependent upon the pharmacist in charge to draw any unusual matters to his attention. He was also diffident about asking the advice of a pharmacist or raising any matter that puzzled him, because he did not wish to reveal his lack of knowledge. Because Mrs Brant did not say anything to him about this page of the CDR, this opportunity for Shipman's illicit practice to be detected was lost.

11.85   Is DC Kelly to be criticised for his failure to recognise that there was something unusual about this page of the CDR? Every other CIO who gave evidence about these CDR entries said that he believed that he would have recognised the unusual nature of the entries. In general, the CIOs said that they would have asked Mrs Brant about the transactions and that any further course of action would have depended upon her response to their questions. I recognise that all the CIOs had the benefit of some years' experience when giving evidence to the Inquiry, as well as the benefit of hindsight. However, even DC Kelly agreed that, to an experienced CIO, the CDR would appear very unusual and would call for some enquiry. In fact, he was at something of a loss to explain how he could have failed to notice it.

11.86   At the time, DC Kelly was undoubtedly very inexperienced as a CIO. He had not had the benefit of a very satisfactory training or induction for his new position. In my view, he cannot be criticised for his failure to realise that a single 30mg ampoule of diamorphine was an inappropriate dose. However, he must, in my view, be criticised for his failure to notice that the appearance of this page of the register was quite unlike any page of a diamorphine section of a CDR that he had seen, either with DC Peers during his training or in the 150 pharmacies he had inspected since starting work on his own two months earlier. It should have appeared highly unusual even to someone who knew nothing about the properties and usual doses of diamorphine. In my view, a reasonably competent police officer, with only two months' experience as a CIO, if conducting him/herself with reasonable diligence, should have noticed that this page was very unusual. Although I am critical of DC Kelly, his failure is mitigated by the inadequacy of the training he had received before being put to work unaccompanied.

11.87   Assuming that he did not do so, ought DC Kelly to have recorded every patient's name in the 1993 sequence on a card? If he had done so, would the unusual nature of the entries have been more likely to strike him? I think the answer to the second question must be that it would. It must have been unusual for him to enter more than three or four names onto the cards in the course of a single visit; to enter more than ten would have been remarkable and rather burdensome. He might well have shown the cards to his colleague, DC Peers, who would, I think, have recognised that Shipman's prescribing was unusual. Having said that, I am not persuaded that the rules relating to the card system were quite as clear cut as DC Peers (in particular) suggested. As I have said, I think that the main purpose of the card system was to record the names of addicts and perhaps also to check that the pattern of prescribing diamorphine to patients with terminal illness followed a 'normal' course; in other words, that the amounts prescribed increased and then stopped. I do not think that it was ever mandatory to record the name of every patient who received a single dose of diamorphine. In practice, it would be rare to see a prescription for a single dose of diamorphine and I think DC Peers probably thought that he recorded every patient who received diamorphine, when, in fact, he might not have done. In short, I think there was an element of discretion for the CIO not to record the occasional small or single prescription. I do not specifically criticise DC Kelly for his probable failure to record the names of these patients as a matter of routine. I criticise him only for his failure to recognise that they were unusual in the sense of being different from anything he had seen in his short experience as a CIO.

11.88   What would have happened if DC Kelly had asked Mrs Brant about these entries? I think her first reaction would have been to tell him that she had no concerns about Shipman; he was a very good GP and well respected and popular with patients. If she had said something like that, I think DC Kelly would have accepted her opinion and would probably have put the matter from his mind. It is quite possible that Mrs Brant might have mentioned to DC Kelly that Shipman had called into the pharmacy to collect these single ampoules. A reasonably competent and moderately experienced CIO would then have heard the ringing of a powerful alarm bell. However, I doubt that DC Kelly would have recognised the significance of that information. He said that, in the early days, he did not understand why the guidance notes said that CIOs should look out for doctors who collected drugs. Nonetheless, it is quite possible that he might have asked DC Peers about the significance of a doctor collecting drugs from a pharmacy. DC Peers would have explained and, in the ensuing discussion, might well have come to realise that the CDR that DC Kelly had seen was most unusual. By that means, it is quite possible that an investigation might have been set in train.

11.89   If DC Kelly had asked Mrs Brant about Shipman's single ampoule entries, it is quite possible that, while giving reassurance at the time, Mrs Brant would later have reflected more carefully about Shipman. It is possible that she might have realised that his prescribing and collecting was odd, even though she trusted him completely. She might have resolved to speak to him about it on the next occasion that he requested a 30mg ampoule, although I think she would have found it difficult to do so in a challenging way. She might have shown the register to Mr Rothman, the superintendent of the pharmacy. She might have sought advice from Mr Young, the RPSGB inspector for the area. Had she spoken to either of those people, I think it likely that some investigation of Shipman's conduct would have been initiated.

Greater Manchester Police

11.90   I have said that the training of DC Kelly left him poorly equipped to undertake his duties as a CIO. For that shortcoming, the GMP must be responsible. It is clear that the GMP did not appreciate the specialist nature of the role of CIOs, requiring, as it did, training in the ability to recognise excessive or unusual prescribing and dispensing of controlled drugs. To be properly equipped, a CIO needs some knowledge of the uses and abuses of the most common controlled drugs and some understanding of the signs to look out for in order to detect bad or illegal practice. Thus, a combination of theoretical knowledge and supervised experience is needed.

11.91   At least until 1999, none of the GMP CIOs was adequately trained at the start of his/her employment in that capacity. I have the impression that, with experience, they all became competent. Since 1999, the CIOs have been better trained. Some of them, such as DC Michael Beard, have the combination of enthusiasm and ability necessary to make outstandingly good CIOs. However, the situation is not entirely satisfactory. All the CIOs are left very much to their own devices. Even those who, through experience, become competent would in my view benefit from better management and direction from senior officers.

11.92   In criticising the GMP for the inadequacy of the training provided to its CIOs and the lack of direction given subsequently, there are two important points mentioned in Chapter Nine that mitigate such criticism. First, so far as CIO services are concerned, the GMP appears to be one of the better police forces in the country. It has for many years had two dedicated CIOs and, in recent years, has increased the number to three. It is unusual for these officers to be taken off their CIO duties, although it does happen from time to time. Since the Wakefield course began in 1999, all three of the current CIOs have attended. Second, the GMP has applied significant resources to the work of the CIO, despite the fact that some of its senior officers, at least in recent years, have been of the opinion that the functions of a CIO are not proper police work. Detective Chief Superintendent Peter Stelfox considers that the work could well be done by civilians and that it does not bring benefit to the police commensurate with the resources expended on it. As I have said, as long ago as 1922, the Commissioner of the Metropolitan Police expressed the view that pharmacy inspection should be carried out by those with practical knowledge of the retail pharmacy business. That point of view is even more valid today than it was then. The scope of the duties of the CIO and the range of controlled drugs with a potential for abuse have both greatly increased. In the light of these factors, it is to the credit of the GMP that it devoted resources to the work of the CIOs to the extent that it has done.

Mr David Young

11.93   In Chapter Nine, I explained that the main purpose of the pharmacy inspections carried out by the RPSGB is the promotion of good and safe pharmaceutical practice by checking compliance with the statutory requirements and the Society's Code of Ethics. Thus, their scope is far wider than that of CIO inspections; in particular, they do not focus on controlled drugs, save to satisfy the inspectors that the pharmacist appears to be complying with the legislative requirements.

11.94 During an inspection, the usual practice of the RPSGB inspectors, including that of Mr Young, was to examine a CDR to ensure that it was being kept, that the entries were legible and that there were no worrying alterations. To check for these matters, most of the inspectors said that they would usually look at the morphine register, which they would expect to be the most heavily used. They might or might not look at the diamorphine register. In the course of such an examination, an inspector would not be looking out for signs of irresponsible prescribing; s/he might notice such signs but, if s/he did, it would be more by luck than design. One inspector spoke of an occasion when he happened to notice a marked imbalance between the quantity of drugs acquired and that supplied. Of course, if a pharmacist expressed concern about entries that suggested irresponsible or illegal prescribing, the inspector would look at them and discuss with the pharmacist what course of action should be taken. He or she might undertake to report the matter to the relevant primary care trust or to the Home Office Drugs Inspectorate (HODI).

11.95 In paragraph 11.22, I mentioned that Mr Young visited the pharmacy at 23 Market Street on 19th March 1992. It is not clear now whether that was a routine visit of inspection or a visit at the request of the pharmacist for the purpose of witnessing the destruction of controlled drugs. In any event, he signed the diamorphine register to say that he had witnessed such destruction. He might possibly have noticed that a doctor called Shipman had prescribed two 30mg ampoules for a patient three days earlier but there would have been no reason why that should have struck him as odd. The patient might well have just begun to need the drug for palliative care. It is not entirely clear when Mr Young next visited the pharmacy. His records are no longer available. He might have visited again in November 1992. A record of his presence in another pharmacy in Hyde has been found and Mr Young says that he might have visited the pharmacy at 23 Market Street on the same day. Otherwise, it appears that he did not visit the pharmacy until April 1994. He cannot say whether he would have looked at the CDR at all on that occasion. Certainly, there is no reason to think that he looked at the diamorphine section. He cannot be criticised for not doing so. Nor can the RPSGB be criticised for not requiring their inspectors to pay closer attention to the content of CDRs. It has never been their duty to do more than ensure that the pharmacy is being properly run and the legislation complied with.

The Home Office Drugs Inspectorate

11.96 Elsewhere in this Report, I discuss the question of whether the arrangements whereby retail pharmacies are inspected by CIOs is satisfactory. I have described those arrangements in Chapter Nine. In short, taking the country as a whole, the arrangements operated to a variable degree of satisfaction. It might be said that the HODI should have recognised the shortcomings of the existing system and should have sought to improve it. It might have pressed for improved training and complete coverage across the country. It might have drawn attention to the difficulty that many CIOs experienced in detecting irresponsible prescribing. It might have suggested that this task should be undertaken by inspectors with greater clinical knowledge of controlled drugs. It might equally be said that the Advisory Committee on the Misuse of Drugs or the Association of Chief Police Officers should have recognised the shortcomings of the system and done something about it. However, the fact is that improvements cost money, resources are always tight and there was no pressing reason to think that any great harm was being caused by the imperfections in the existing system.

11.97   The discovery of Shipman's crimes has shown that, in Tameside, in 1993, the arrangements did not work as well as they should have done and that, if DC Kelly had had better training or more experience, it is possible that Shipman's illicit obtaining of diamorphine might have been detected. However, in 1993 and in previous years, the HODI had had no particular reason to be concerned about the way in which the system operated in Greater Manchester. The GMP had CIOs in post and the HODI inspectors in the Northern Region would have known that in, say, 1992, the GMP CIOs were efficient. They might also have known that, in the summer of 1993, when DC Kelly was new in post and very inexperienced, coverage in the outer areas of Greater Manchester was not as good as it had been. That is not to say that they were under a duty to do anything about it. They would expect that time and experience would put matters right, as I think to a large extent they did. In my view, the HODI is not to be criticised because the system of pharmacy inspection failed to detect Shipman's unusual prescribing pattern in 1993.

What Would Have Happened?

11.98   What would have happened if either Mrs Brant or DC Kelly had noticed the unusual pattern of Shipman's prescribing and had decided that it warranted a report or investigation? To a very large extent, any consideration of this question is speculative. I shall be unable to reach any firm conclusions. However, it is necessary to consider what might have happened.

11.99   One possibility is that, if Mrs Brant had appreciated the unusual nature of Shipman's requests for 30mg ampoules, she might have asked him why he wanted them and suggested that, if it was for emergency use or for the relief of acute pain, she could supply smaller ampoules. She might well have had such a conversation on Friday, 26th February 1993. Shipman had asked for four 30mg ampoules in one week. If she had queried his actions at any stage during this course of conduct, I am sure he would have offered her a plausible explanation for his requests. However, I also think it quite likely that he would have stopped using this method of obtaining supplies. He would not have wished to give rise to any suspicion of unusual practice. Without supplies, he could not have killed. He probably did not have another cancer patient from whom he could steal supplies until November 1993. He might have considered using another pharmacy but that might have appeared strange in view of the proximity of the pharmacy at 23 Market Street to his own surgery. The lives of some of his 1993 victims would probably have been saved. I have no doubt that Shipman would have resumed killing when he had another source of supply.

11.100 Had DC Kelly and Mrs Brant discussed the appearance of the CDR during the inspection on 12th July, I have said that it is likely that Mrs Brant would have sought to reassure DC Kelly that Shipman was a thoroughly reliable doctor. DC Kelly would have had no expertise to bring to their discussion. Only if he had mentioned the discussion to his colleague, DC Peers, would there have been any chance that concern would have been raised such as to cause a report to be made to the HODI. Even DC Peers might have taken the view that, if the pharmacist was not worried, there was no need for a report; the amounts of drug were not so large as to give rise to a real suspicion of addiction or dealing. But it is possible that there might have been a report to the HODI. It is also possible that a conversation with DC Kelly might have caused Mrs Brant to reflect more deeply on the matter. She might then have either spoken to Shipman (with the result mentioned above) or possibly decided to speak to Mr Rothman or to contact the RPSGB inspector, Mr Young. In this way too, it is possible that Shipman's prescribing might have come to the attention of the HODI.

11.101 If a report had been made to the HODI, history might possibly have been different. Mr Graham Calder, one of the HODI inspectors, said that the patterns of Shipman's prescribing would have alerted them to the possibility that he was diverting the drugs. Tucked away in the HODI files was the information about Shipman's previous convictions in relation to pethidine in 1976. I am satisfied that the files would have been retrieved. The inspectors' natural reaction, on learning that Shipman had been prescribing another opiate drug in an unorthodox way and collecting it from the pharmacy himself, would have been to suspect him of self-administration. I think the HODI would have launched an investigation.

11.102 What would it have found? First, it would have found that he was not obtaining supplies from any other pharmacy in the Hyde area. I cannot say with certainty that Shipman was not obtaining supplies from outside the area of Greater Manchester, but I consider that it would have been virtually impossible for the HODI to find out whether or not he was. NHS prescriptions would show up in prescribing analysis and cost (PACT) data, but private prescriptions and requisitions would not. The HODI would have been left to investigate the reasons why he had obtained the 12 or 14 ampoules he had obtained at the time its enquiries took place. I have no doubt that the HODI inspectors would have interviewed him.

11.103 What would Shipman have said? I think he would have been unlikely to say that he was using the drugs himself. I think he would have feared that an apparent return to addiction would result in referral to the GMC and possible action on his registration. I think it likely that he would have claimed that he had needed the drugs for patients who were suffering from heart attacks. He would have been able to refer to various patients in whose records he had noted that he had given morphine. Whether their records would still have been available to him to show to the inspectors, I cannot say; they might have been returned to the Tameside FHSA following the patients' deaths. The inspectors might well have asked why Shipman always took a 30mg ampoule, whereas other doctors usually kept 5mg or 10mg ampoules for emergency use. Shipman might well have advanced the same explanation that he used at his trial in 1999, namely that he had got into a 'bad habit' of prescribing more than he needed; he would use what was necessary and throw away the rest.

11.104 It is impossible for me to say whether the HODI inspectors would have been content with his explanation. I would not criticise them if they had been. This strange prescribing would not seem to be very sinister; the individual amounts were not large and the supplies were not obtained with anything like the frequency with which Shipman had obtained pethidine in the 1970s. They might have just warned him to change his 'bad habit' and, if so, I think it likely that he would have done so.

11.105 On the other hand, it is possible that the HODI inspectors would not have been satisfied with his explanation. If they had remained suspicious and decided to contact the patients for whom the drugs had been prescribed, they would have discovered, first, that all but two of the patients had died and they might have found out that six of them had died before Shipman prescribed the drug (although it is far from certain that their enquiries would have extended so far as to establish the dates of death). To explain that, Shipman would have had to suggest that he was 'replenishing his stocks' by prescribing in the name of a patient to whom he had given the drug on an earlier occasion. The two patients who were still alive would have said that they had not received any diamorphine and had had no need for it. This would have confirmed the inspectors' suspicion that Shipman was keeping the drugs, or most of them, for himself. They might have felt it worthwhile to bring in the police with a view to prosecution for unlawful possession of the drugs and, possibly, obtaining them by deception, although I think it unlikely that a prosecution would have proceeded. The amounts of the drug involved were not great. It would have been necessary to involve patients and relatives as witnesses. There would have been a real possibility that Shipman's explanations would have been accepted by a court, had he been prepared to run the risk of a trial.

11.106 Even if the inspectors had uncovered evidence strongly suggesting that Shipman had been keeping the diamorphine for himself, it is unlikely, in my view, that they would have come to suspect him of using it to kill his patients. That possibility would have been almost unimaginable. I think it unlikely that the quality of his care of his patients would have been investigated. Only if the relatives of the deceased patients had been interviewed and if one or more of them had expressed extreme surprise at the suddenness of the death would this possibility have occurred to anyone. Most of Shipman's victims at this period were in poor health, although their deaths did come as a shock and a surprise to their relatives. Had the inspectors or police decided to obtain the medical records of Shipman's deceased patients, they would have found that, in three cases (those of Miss Andrew, Mrs Llewellyn and Mrs Whitehead), Shipman had recorded that he had administered 10mg morphine or morphine sulphate to the patient shortly before death. He would have said that he had done it to relieve pain and that would have appeared to be a reasonable explanation. However, he would not have been able to explain where the morphine had come from. Also, the inspectors would have found that in no case had Shipman recorded that he gave diamorphine. In five of the deceased patients' records (those of Mrs Ashworth, Mrs Heginbotham, Mrs Mullen, Mrs Nichols and Mrs Parker), there was no reference to the administration of any drug before death. If Shipman had said that he had given diamorphine to these patients, it would have appeared that his record keeping was very slack but it might not have occurred to anyone that he had given an overdose and caused the patient's death deliberately. All the patients were quite old. It is just possible that the combined effect of a diligent police officer and a concerned relative might have given rise to the suspicion of deliberate harm. However, in my judgement, this is unlikely.

11.107 There is little doubt in my view that, if the HODI had embarked on an investigation, it would have had a salutary effect on Shipman's conduct. The more thorough the investigation, the more alarmed Shipman would have been and the longer the period for which he would have desisted from killing.

CHAPTER TWELVE

Shipman's Methods of Obtaining Diamorphine in the Years from 1993 to 1998

Introduction

12.1   I have said that, after August 1993, Shipman ceased to obtain diamorphine supplies by prescribing and collecting single 30mg ampoules. From late 1993, he was able to resume what I believe had been his preferred method of obtaining supplies throughout his period in Hyde and was a method he had also used in Todmorden. He would take for himself supplies of the diamorphine that he had prescribed in the names of patients who had some form of cancer, even though some might not be in need of the drug. In this Chapter, I shall describe the circumstances in which he obtained the large quantities of diamorphine which he used to kill a great number of patients between late 1993 and his arrest in 1998. I shall do so by reference to the patients whom he used as a means of obtaining his illicit supplies.

1993

Mr Raymond Jones

12.2   In October 1993, Mr Raymond Jones was found to be suffering from terminal cancer. By November, he was in need of diamorphine for pain relief and he had been given a syringe driver. Shipman visited him quite frequently and the district nurse attended regularly to replenish the syringe. On Monday, 15th November 1993, three 30mg ampoules were dispensed for him at the pharmacy at 23 Market Street and, on 16th and 20th November, twenty 100mg ampoules were dispensed. Finally, on 26th November, fifteen 100mg ampoules were dispensed. These supplies were almost certainly collected from the pharmacy by members of Mr Jones' family and not by Shipman, although I cannot rule out the possibility that Shipman collected the supply on 26th November. As I said in Chapter Seven, the controlled drugs register (CDR) does not record the identity of the person who collects the medicine. Mrs Ghislaine Brant, the pharmacist manager, dispensed all supplies except for the last.

12.3   Mr Jones' patient drug record card (PDRC) is no longer available and so it is not possible to see what record was made of the administration of the drugs, or indeed what the residue was when Mr Jones died on 27th November. Shipman collected whatever had been left over. Fifteen hundred milligrams had been obtained on the day before the death, and it is likely that more than 1000mg was left over. This would be consistent with the recollection of Mr Jones' widow who told the police that Shipman removed two or three boxes of diamorphine ampoules from the sideboard. She said that she was grateful that he did so because it saved her the inconvenience of returning them to the pharmacy. He left behind various other medicines. At Shipman's trial, it was suggested to Mr Jones' widow by Shipman's counsel that Shipman had destroyed the drugs at the premises but she denied that this was the case. At present, there is no requirement that the destruction of a patient's unused controlled drugs should be witnessed by a second person or that any record should be made of the destruction of such drugs. I shall have to consider whether such requirements should be introduced.

1994

Mrs Mary Smith

12.4   The CDR from 23 Market Street shows that, on 17th May 1994, a supply of ten 100mg ampoules of diamorphine was dispensed in the name of Mrs Mary Smith. Mrs Smith had been diagnosed as having lung cancer in 1993. Her condition deteriorated during 1994 and she was prescribed morphine sulphate tablets for pain relief. On 17th May, Shipman made a note in her medical records that he had prescribed diamorphine by syringe driver. In fact, Mrs Smith did not need diamorphine and was never issued with a syringe driver. I have no doubt that the drugs prescribed on 17th May in Mrs Smith's name were, in fact, collected by Shipman and never reached the patient. Later, Shipman killed Mrs Smith, possibly using some of the diamorphine he had obtained in her name.

12.5   Shipman's conduct in prescribing in Mrs Smith's name, presenting the prescription and collecting the drugs for himself, was criminal. He committed the offences of obtaining by deception and unlawful possession of the controlled drugs. These were the same offences of which he had been convicted in 1976 in relation to pethidine. However, whereas in 1975 suspicion fell on Shipman largely because of the quantities he was obtaining for the practice on requisition, a prescription for a modest amount such as this, prescribed in the name of an elderly patient, would never be noticed. Shipman's name appeared in the CDR only as prescriber. A requirement that the collector of drugs should be identified in the CDR would help to alert a pharmacist or a chemist inspection officer (CIO) to the fact, if it were the case, that a particular health professional was making a habit of collecting controlled drugs, ostensibly on behalf of patients. If CIOs were alert to cases where a health professional collected drugs, it would be possible to carry out a cross-check with other health professionals involved with the patient or with other records relating to the patient, to find out whether the patient was in fact receiving the drugs. I shall consider later whether and how this might be done.

Mr Eric Davies

12.6   Mr Eric Davies, a patient of Shipman, died a natural death at Hyde Nursing Home on 8th September 1994. On 23rd July 1994, five 100mg ampoules of diamorphine were dispensed at 23 Market Street, by a colleague of Mrs Brant, in accordance with a prescription issued by Shipman in Mr Davies' name. In fact, Mr Davies did not need diamorphine and did not receive it. His medical notes record that Shipman visited him on 22nd July but do not record that diamorphine was prescribed. At his trial, Shipman said that he had prescribed diamorphine on account of Mr Davies' brain tumour. However, on being shown a letter from Mr Davies' consultant, he agreed that Mr Davies had not needed diamorphine. Shipman then claimed that he had prescribed the drug for Mr Davies' future use. He also claimed that he had told the staff at the nursing home where Mr Davies was resident to collect the drugs. I am sure that Shipman presented the prescription himself and kept the drugs.

12.7   As in the case of Mrs Smith, described above, Shipman's conduct in respect of Mr Davies was criminal but was very unlikely to be detected, as there was nothing about it that would arouse suspicion, at least unless the pharmacist came to be sceptical of his reasons for collecting the drugs. I shall consider later how the legal controls might be changed so as to improve the chances that such illegal conduct could be detected.

1995

Mr Frank Crompton

12.8   Mr Frank Crompton was a patient of Shipman. On 28th February 1995, ten 100mg ampoules of diamorphine were dispensed by Mrs Brant on prescriptions issued by Shipman in Mr Crompton's name. On 18th March 1995, ten 10mg ampoules of diamorphine were dispensed. There is no note in his medical records that Mr Crompton was prescribed opiates and his treatment never involved a syringe driver. The diamorphine dispensed was never, apparently, administered. Shipman killed Mr Crompton at his home on Friday, 24th March 1995. Two days later, he certified that the death was due to a coronary thrombosis.

12.9   At his trial, Shipman was asked about the supply of diamorphine to Mr Crompton. He gave a most implausible reply. He said that Mr Crompton had prostate cancer, which had been successfully treated, albeit with the possibility of secondary cancer. This might have been true. Shipman claimed that he had given Mr Crompton the first prescription for diamorphine on about 28th February, although the drug was not needed at the time. Shipman expressed the opinion that it was good practice to make provision for the time when the drug would be needed. This account was plainly nonsense. The amount prescribed was very large, appropriate for use with a syringe driver. If it were proper to supply a controlled drug 'just in case', it would be appropriate to supply only a small amount. But, in any event, Mr Crompton never suffered severe pain and never needed any diamorphine.

12.10   When asked where the ten 100mg ampoules had gone to, Shipman said that Mr Crompton had destroyed them. Shipman claimed that Mr Crompton had said that he had decided to get rid of the drug and that he had crushed the ampoules with his foot. According to Shipman, Mr Crompton admitted that his actions in destroying his first supply had been 'a little hasty' and he promised that, if Shipman were to give him another supply of drugs, he would keep them safe in his house, in case he needed them. Shipman had therefore given him another prescription. There can be no doubt that Shipman presented both prescriptions, collected the drugs and kept them for himself. This case is yet another example of the method Shipman had used in respect of Mrs Smith and Mr Davies. The implausibility of his explanation demonstrates that it would be difficult for a dishonest doctor to get away with obtaining a large quantity such as was involved in this case if his/her conduct came to the attention of anyone in authority. However, Shipman's conduct in this case would never have come to light had it not been for the investigation into the death of Mrs Kathleen Grundy in 1998.

Mrs Clara Hackney

12.11   On 13th April 1995, ten 100mg ampoules of diamorphine were dispensed at the pharmacy at 23 Market Street against a prescription issued by Shipman in the name of Mrs Clara Hackney. Mrs Hackney was suffering from terminal cancer. However, until very shortly before her death, she was not in severe pain. Her medical records do not suggest that she needed diamorphine. Certainly, there was no question of her needing a syringe driver for which the 100mg ampoules would have been appropriate. On 14th April, Shipman visited Mrs Hackney and hastened her death by the administration of a lethal dose of diamorphine. Exactly how much he gave her I am not sure. It was probably about 30mg.

12.12   At his trial, Shipman was asked about Mrs Hackney and said that he had given her 10mg diamorphine for pain on the day of her death. He agreed that he had not made a note of this in her medical records. When asked what had happened to the rest of the diamorphine, he claimed that Mrs Hackney's sister had destroyed it by crushing the ampoules. I am quite satisfied that Shipman presented the prescription and obtained all ten ampoules himself. He might have used one of them, or part of one of them, to kill Mrs Hackney. This case illustrates the same problems of detection as I described above.

Mr James Arrandale

12.13   In July 1995, Shipman obtained some diamorphine prescribed in the name of Mr James Arrandale, who died from non-Hodgkin's lymphoma on 28th July 1995. For about a week before his death, Mr Arrandale was in need of diamorphine from a syringe driver. The district nurses set it up. Shipman prescribed the drugs, a member of the family collected them from the pharmacy and the district nurses attended each day to recharge the syringe driver. They recorded each administration on the PDRC. This card provides something of an audit trail although, as I have explained in Chapter Eight, the process of recording starts only at the house and the opening balance is not reconciled with the quantity of drug that leaves the pharmacy. In this case, the PDRC shows that Mr Arrandale was being given 40mg diamorphine each day until the day of his death, when the dosage was increased to 60mg. According to the PDRC, all supplies coming into the house were in 10mg ampoules. In the course of the week, forty 10mg ampoules were entered onto the card and a total of 300mg was administered. That would leave ten 10mg ampoules unused after the death. However, examination of the CDR at the pharmacy shows that, in addition to the forty 10mg ampoules that were entered into the PDRC, two prescriptions for five 100mg ampoules were also dispensed, one on 27th July and the other on 28th July. These supplies were not entered onto the PDRC. It is clear that Shipman must have presented those prescriptions and kept the drugs for himself.

12.14   Shortly after Mr Arrandale's death on 28th July, Shipman attended the house and confirmed the fact of death. He removed the syringe driver. He signed the PDRC, saying that he had destroyed the remaining drugs. That implied that he had destroyed them at the house. In fact, he did not; he took them away, telling Mr Arrandale's widow that he would dispose of them. It is now known that he did not do so, but kept them for himself. Four 10mg ampoules of diamorphine found at Shipman's house after his arrest were traced, by their batch number, to Mr Arrandale's supply. When asked about this, Shipman claimed that he had destroyed six ampoules but had kept the rest. He had no rational explanation as to why he had done that.

12.15   In this case, Shipman used two different methods to obtain an illicit supply. First, he issued extra prescriptions in the name of a patient with a genuine need; he presented them at the pharmacy and collected the drugs, keeping them for himself. This type of conduct is difficult to detect. Collecting drugs for a patient who is terminally ill will usually be seen as an act of kindness. It might be seen as insensitive for a pharmacist to query the actions of a doctor who appeared to be considerate of the needs of a patient and his/her family. Second, Shipman took possession of unused diamorphine, as he had done in the case of Mr Jones.

Mr Peter Neal

12.16   In late September 1995, Shipman obtained a supply of diamorphine in the name of Mr Peter Neal, who died of cancer on 23rd September 1995. From 18th September until his death, Mr Neal needed diamorphine from a syringe driver. The district nurse was visiting to recharge the syringe driver and was keeping a PDRC.

12.17   The 23 Market Street CDR shows that, on Monday, 18th September, ten 30mg ampoules of diamorphine were dispensed against a prescription issued by Shipman in the name of Mr Neal. On Friday, 22nd September, ten more 30mg ampoules were dispensed and the PDRC shows that, on that day, 150mg was administered to Mr Neal, on Shipman's instructions. According to the PDRC, that left a stock of six 30mg ampoules. From the CDR it is seen that a second supply of diamorphine (this time three 100mg ampoules) was dispensed for Mr Neal on 22nd September, but this supply was never entered into the PDRC and it is very likely that Shipman collected it and kept it for himself.

12.18   The events of 23rd September are not clear. Mrs Neal asked Shipman to attend, as her husband was in pain. Shipman put the available diamorphine in the syringe and, when this proved insufficient, he left the house saying that he would fetch more. He returned some time later, and put more diamorphine in the syringe. Within a short time, Mr Neal became comfortable; he died later that day. It is not possible to say how much diamorphine Shipman administered to Mr Neal that day. From the rather informal and confusing entry Shipman made on the PDRC, it appears that he might have given 400mg, or possibly even 600mg, although this might well have been a deliberate over-estimate. After the death, Shipman returned and wrote on the PDRC that he had destroyed 'all the drugs'. The amount destroyed was not specified. The pharmacy CDR shows that, on 23rd September, two separate supplies of diamorphine were dispensed for Mr Neal. The first comprised three 100mg ampoules and the second was for seven 100mg ampoules. The time when the drugs were dispensed is not recorded so it is quite possible that the second supply was made after Shipman knew of Mr Neal's death. Whatever the amount of diamorphine Shipman gave Mr Neal that day, it is clear that far more was obtained from the pharmacy than was given to Mr Neal. I estimate that there was an excess of 1000mg, which Shipman must have retained for himself.

12.19   This case illustrates the present lack of control over controlled drugs when they have left the pharmacy. It underlines the need for a formal record to be kept of the movement and usage of diamorphine.

Mr Kenneth Woodhead

12.20   Mr Kenneth Woodhead died at his home on 14th December 1995. He had advanced lung cancer. On the morning of the day of his death, his pain was such that he needed diamorphine from a syringe driver. Shipman prescribed ten 100mg ampoules, which were brought to the house in two boxes, each containing five ampoules. A district nurse set up a syringe driver using, on Shipman's instructions, 200mg diamorphine. That would last for 24 hours. Later in the day, Shipman attended, gave Mr Woodhead an injection and left. Mr Woodhead died very shortly afterwards. I have found that Shipman probably hastened his death by a short period.

12.21   Soon after the death, Shipman returned to the house, dismantled the syringe driver and told Mr Woodhead's sister-in-law that he would take the remaining drugs for destruction. He wrote on the PDRC that he had taken all the drugs for disposal. The following day, the district nurses attending to remove property found that there were three 100mg ampoules of diamorphine at the house. They destroyed them and recorded the destruction. They saw Shipman's note on the PDRC and must have assumed that he had taken away the full box of five ampoules for disposal but had mistakenly left the box of three. They had no reason to be suspicious about his conduct.

12.22   At his trial, Shipman claimed that he had destroyed the five ampoules in Mr Woodhead's kitchen, although that is not consistent with what he wrote on the PDRC. In the absence of a requirement that this destruction be witnessed, there could be no strong evidence to refute this. With the benefit of hindsight, I am sure that Shipman used one of the ampoules in the box of five to hasten Mr Woodhead's death and kept the rest of the box for himself. This case too illustrates the need for a proper record of the administration and destruction of controlled drugs after they have left the pharmacy.

1996

Mr Keith Harrison

12.23   Mr Keith Harrison, who died of lung cancer on Thursday, 6th June 1996, had been using diamorphine in a syringe driver for just over ten weeks by the time of his death. He was in significant pain and his tolerance of the drug had become very high. In the middle of April, he was receiving 600mg daily and this increased to 900mg one month later. In the few days before his death, he was receiving 2400mg daily. Because of the large quantities he needed, the supplies came as 500mg and 100mg ampoules. The district nurses filled the syringe twice daily. Mr Harrison received his morning dose of 1200mg at 8.30am on the day of his death when the remaining stock was recorded on the PDRC as one 500mg and ten 100mg ampoules. There would be sufficient for the evening but more would be needed for the next morning. As a general rule, Mr Harrison's family collected his drugs from the pharmacy but, on occasions, a family friend who worked at the pharmacy delivered them. Before the day of the death, there had been only one occasion when Shipman had delivered them himself. The PDRC tallied with the amounts dispensed for Mr Harrison until the day of his death.

12.24   Mr Harrison died in the early afternoon. His widow telephoned Shipman, who attended. He made an entry on the PDRC, saying:

> **'Patient Died 14.30**
>
> **All Drugs Destroyed.'**

This was countersigned by the district nurse in attendance, Mrs Barbara Sunderland. She recalls destroying the remaining drugs by swilling them down the sink. To her, the expression **'All Drugs Destroyed'** meant that the stock balance recorded on the PDRC had been disposed of. However, alongside the entry to which I have referred, Shipman also wrote:

> **'returned to Chemist for destruction'**.

These two statements are mutually inconsistent.

12.25   Examination of the 23 Market Street pharmacy CDR shows that, on the day of Mr Harrison's death, 12,000mg diamorphine was dispensed on a prescription in Mr Harrison's name. Mrs Brant accepted that Shipman must have collected it. As the CDR does not record the time of a transaction, only the date, it is not clear whether Shipman collected the drugs before he knew of Mr Harrison's death or afterwards. I suspect that, when Shipman attended the house after the death, he was in possession of the extra 12,000mg and deliberately made a confusing and internally inconsistent note in the PDRC which he could later use to substantiate an explanation if questions were asked about the collection of 12,000mg diamorphine for Mr Harrison that day. In the event, no questions were asked about this enormous quantity until Shipman came under suspicion two years later for other reasons. I say that not as a matter of criticism of anyone. But it is alarming that so large a quantity of diamorphine, enough to kill about 360 opioid-naïve people, could be dispensed and handed over with so little control over its future movement. I am sure that Shipman obtained 12,000mg diamorphine on that occasion. At his trial, Shipman said that he had brought the new supply of diamorphine to Mr Harrison's house and that it had all been destroyed there. The lack of any requirement to have destruction witnessed and recorded meant that it was difficult to challenge this assertion. Mr Harrison's widow and the district nurse did not accept that the new consignment had been destroyed but it should not be necessary for such important matters to turn upon the recollection of the individuals present. A formal record should be mandatory.

1997

Mrs Maureen Jackson

12.26   In early July 1997, Shipman acquired more diamorphine, probably 800mg, from Mrs Maureen Jackson. Mrs Jackson was suffering from cancer and, for about two weeks before her death on 7th July 1997, had been in need of diamorphine administered through a syringe driver. The district nurses were attending daily and kept a PDRC. The amounts of diamorphine entered into the PDRC tallied with the amounts entered in the 'drugs supplied' side of the CDR at the 23 Market Street pharmacy until 3rd July. On that day, 2300mg was dispensed on a prescription issued by Shipman in Mrs Jackson's name.

Shipman's entry in the PDRC suggests that he brought only 1500mg into the house that day.

12.27   Now that Shipman's propensity for stealing diamorphine is known, it is reasonable to infer that he had diverted part of Mrs Jackson's supply to his own use. However, this case illustrates the way in which unwarranted suspicion could fall upon either the pharmacist or the district nurse involved. If it had been discovered that 2300mg had been prescribed, but that Mrs Jackson had only benefited from 1500mg, several people could have been suspected of dishonesty. The pharmacist could have diverted part of the supply, putting only 1500mg into the package to be handed over. Second, the person collecting and delivering the drugs could have stolen part of the consignment. In this case, it was Shipman, but any person, a relative, friend or neighbour, could have diverted part of the consignment. Last, the district nurse who received the package of drugs could have taken some of them and entered the balance into the PDRC. It seems to me that a better system of record keeping is required, not only to deter and detect dishonest conduct but also to protect innocent participants in the process.

1998

Mr Lionel Hutchinson

12.28   In about 1996, Mr Lionel Hutchinson, a patient of Shipman, developed prostate cancer. He was successfully treated with hormone therapy and lived for some time after the events I am about to describe. On 1st November 1997, 1000mg diamorphine was dispensed from the 23 Market Street pharmacy against a prescription issued by Shipman in Mr Hutchinson's name. On 7th January 1998, another supply of diamorphine was dispensed on a prescription issued by Shipman in Mr Hutchinson's name. The overwhelming probability is that Shipman presented both these prescriptions, collected the drugs and kept them for himself. It is very unlikely that Mr Hutchinson knew anything about them. This illegal obtaining by Shipman would not have come to light unless he had been investigated in respect of Mrs Grundy's death.

12.29   At his trial, Shipman admitted that, at the time when he wrote these prescriptions, Mr Hutchinson had had no need for diamorphine. He claimed, as he had claimed in the cases of Mr Davies and Mr Crompton, that he was prescribing in anticipation of some possible future need. He said that he had given the first prescription to Mr Hutchinson and believed that the drugs had been dispensed; he did not know what Mr Hutchinson had done with them. He denied therefore that he had collected the drugs himself. In respect of the second prescription, Shipman claimed that he had issued it because Mr Hutchinson had told him that he had left his first supply of drugs in his holiday caravan in Blackpool and needed an additional supply while at home in Hyde. Mr Hutchinson had died by the time of the trial and could not be asked about this highly implausible explanation. If Shipman's name had appeared in the CDR as collector, there could have been no doubt who collected. However, the recording of the collector's name in the CDR will only help in the detection of offences if the record is inspected by someone with the necessary combination of diligence, knowledge and scepticism.

Mr John Henshall

12.30   In Chapter Eight, I described how, on 6th July 1998, Shipman stole five 10mg ampoules of diamorphine from the stock prescribed for and kept at the home of Mr John Henshall, who was suffering from cancer. Shipman simply took the drugs and made an incorrect entry on the PDRC. Mrs Marion Gilchrist, the district nurse, noticed the discrepancy and asked Shipman about the stock shortage. After some prevarication, he told her that he had taken the ampoules to repay a colleague from whom he had previously borrowed a similar amount. She thought this was poor practice but did not suspect him of dishonesty and did not report him.

12.31   By this time, Shipman had killed his last victim, Mrs Grundy, and had aroused the suspicions of her daughter, Mrs Angela Woodruff, by forging a will in which Mrs Grundy left all her property to him instead of to her family. The fact that Shipman obtained diamorphine illicitly on 6th July suggests that he intended to kill again. However, on 19th July, Mrs Woodruff visited Mrs Claire Hutchinson, one of the patients whom Shipman had involved as a witness in his plot to forge Mrs Grundy's will. Soon afterwards, Mrs Hutchinson told Shipman that Mrs Woodruff had visited her and he must have realised that Mrs Woodruff was likely to report her concerns to the police. He had not killed again by the time of his arrest on 7th September 1998.

Conclusion

12.32   That Shipman was able to obtain large amounts of diamorphine in the ways I have described and to avoid detection for so long demonstrates the need for improved record keeping of controlled drugs at and after the time of dispensing. Four measures come to mind. First, the recording in the CDR of the identity of a person collecting controlled drugs from the pharmacy would draw attention to anyone who made a practice of this. Second, the opening of a PDRC (or some similar document) at the pharmacy, on which the amount of controlled drug prescribed and dispensed could be recorded, would or should deter, or allow the detection of, the doctor who wishes to divert part of the supply before delivery of the rest to the patient's home. Third, the keeping of a running record by the district nurses would be more likely to result in the detection of malpractice if someone inspected the completed PDRCs. The PDRCs would also be available, for linkage with the pharmacy and medical records, in the event of an investigation. Fourth, if the destruction of unused controlled drugs had to be witnessed and recorded, the opportunity for theft would be much reduced. I shall consider each of these possible measures in Chapter Fourteen.

CHAPTER THIRTEEN

Controlled Drugs Regulation in British Columbia and Northern Ireland

Introduction

13.1   The Inquiry team considered the systems of controlled drugs regulation in several different jurisdictions and, on the basis of the information gathered, I decided that it would be helpful to hear presentations explaining the systems in operation in the Canadian province of British Columbia and in Northern Ireland. The system in British Columbia was chosen primarily because of its advanced computerised system of review and monitoring of the use of controlled drugs. Northern Ireland was chosen because of the distinctive inspection arrangements that operate there. The presentations were made, at a seminar held by the Inquiry on 12th January 2004, by Dr Brian Taylor, Deputy Registrar of the College of Physicians and Surgeons of British Columbia (CPSBC) and Dr Michael Mawhinney, Misuse of Drugs Inspector for the Department of Health, Social Services and Public Safety, Northern Ireland (the Department). I am grateful to both of them for their contributions.

British Columbia

13.2   British Columbia has approximately 9000 physicians and approximately 800 pharmacies, serving a population of 4.5 million. The CPSBC is responsible for licensing and regulating all physicians practising in British Columbia. It also has a mandate to oversee the quality of medical care provided in the province. Among its responsibilities are the review and monitoring of the use of 'narcotics' or 'narcotic drugs', the Canadian terms equivalent to 'controlled drugs'. In this Chapter, I shall describe only those aspects of Dr Taylor's presentation relating to narcotic drugs, which are of particular interest to the Inquiry.

The Triplicate Prescription Program

13.3   In 1990, the CPSBC introduced the 'Triplicate Prescription Program', for use by physicians when prescribing certain narcotic drugs (described by Dr Taylor as 'heavy duty opioids'). The programme was intended to assist in the prevention and detection of the diversion of such narcotics. It has recently been renamed the 'Control Prescription Program'.

13.4   Under the programme, a physician wishing to prescribe narcotics, other than in a hospital setting, may do so only on a special triplicate prescription pad issued for the purpose. This pad must be used whether the drug is to be paid for by the patient or where its cost is to be reimbursed to the patient under the Canadian system of state subsidised health insurance. Issue of the pads is controlled by the CPSBC. Any physician applying for the issue of a pad may be required to justify his/her application, if it appears that s/he practises in a field of medicine (e.g. radiology) in which it would not be usual to prescribe narcotics. The prescriptions in the pad may be used only by the physician in whose name the pad was issued.

13.5 The prescriptions are printed on special paper, similar to that used for banknotes, which is very difficult to reproduce. A separate prescription must be issued for each drug prescribed. This contrasts with the present position in the UK. The quantity of the drug prescribed must be written both in numbers and in words (as in the UK). The issuing physician must endorse the prescription with his/her unique CPSBC identifying number. The prescription also identifies the patient by name and by his/her unique patient identifying number.

13.6 When the programme was first introduced, each prescription was created in triplicate. The physician would retain one copy of the prescription for his/her own records and would provide two copies of the prescription to the patient for presentation at the pharmacy. After dispensing, the pharmacist would keep one copy and the other would be sent to the office of the Provincial Government, where the data would be manually entered into a central database. According to Dr Taylor, this method of data collection was not entirely satisfactory and about 20% of data was lost. In 1995, a computerised system for the central recording of all prescriptions issued in British Columbia, known as PharmaNet, was introduced. Since that time, the third copy of the prescription has been redundant, as the prescription information is automatically recorded in the central database. The collection of data is complete and the information it yields on analysis more reliable.

13.7 According to Dr Taylor, the programme has produced several benefits. First, the use of the special paper on which prescriptions are printed and the handwriting requirements have reduced the incidence of forgery. Second, each prescription specifically identifies both the prescribing doctor and the patient by their unique identifying numbers. This facilitates any monitoring or investigatory process. Third, according to Dr Taylor, the special prescribing requirements and the use of the distinctive pads cause the physician to pause and think before writing the prescription.

13.8 Under the programme, a prescription is valid for only five days. As I will explain in Chapter Fourteen, many in the UK would not welcome such a brief period of validity. However, according to Dr Taylor, this has not caused any difficulty in British Columbia, where experience has shown that, when narcotics for pain relief are prescribed, the patient normally wishes them to be dispensed immediately.

13.9 The central collection of prescribing data enabled the CPSBC to review the narcotics prescribing profiles of all physicians, so as to identify outliers and those with unusual prescribing practices. These could then be investigated individually. It was also possible to analyse the data by reference to individual patients, so as to reveal, for example, those who were receiving narcotics on prescription from more than one physician at the same time (a practice described in the UK as 'double scripting'). Since the inception of PharmaNet, the CPSBC has used software that enables it to carry out a far wider range of analyses than was possible before 1995.

PharmaNet

13.10 The benefits stemming from the Triplicate Prescription Program were significantly enhanced with the introduction of PharmaNet. PharmaNet is funded by the Provincial Government and was developed with advice and assistance from the CPSBC. A part of the initial impetus for its development was a wish to understand more about the cost of state subsidised prescribing and, to that extent, its genesis can be likened to that of prescribing analysis and cost (PACT) data in England and Wales. There was also a desire to reduce the incidence of prescription fraud and inappropriate prescribing. According to Dr Taylor, PharmaNet also rapidly became a useful therapeutic tool.

13.11　PharmaNet contains the complete known history of drugs prescribed for every resident of British Columbia and, if a visitor to the province requires medication, a record will be created for him/her. At the time of dispensing any drug (not only narcotic drugs), the pharmacist enters the details of the prescription into the PharmaNet database. The previous 14 months' prescribing history for the patient is immediately shown on the pharmacist's computer screen, as is any history of, for example, allergy or adverse drug reaction. The pharmacist is under a professional obligation to consider this information and may, if s/he wishes, seek further details of the patient's prescribing history. It is possible to record on PharmaNet the condition for which medication has been prescribed, although I formed the impression that only limited use is made of that facility.

13.12　The system also provides a summary of information about the drug being prescribed; this is in a form suitable for giving to the patient at the time of dispensing. A 24 hour help desk is available to give further information to the pharmacist, if required, about the profile of the drug being dispensed.

13.13　An 'alert' can be attached to the name of a particular prescriber or patient. This warns the pharmacist not to dispense any prescriptions, which may be subsequently presented, issued by the named prescriber or in the name of the named patient.

13.14　Every community pharmacy in British Columbia has on-line access to PharmaNet. Access is also now mandatory for every hospital pharmacy and accident and emergency department in the province and it is used in the prison system. On payment of a licence fee, PharmaNet is also accessible to physicians. At the time of the seminar in January 2004, about 150 physicians had access but the cost of the licence was proving a disincentive for many.

13.15　Although prescriptions for all drugs, not only narcotics, are entered into PharmaNet, the system makes special provision for the monitoring of narcotics. Each time a prescription for a narcotic drug is entered, an automatic entry is also made in the electronic narcotics log kept by the CPSBC. If a physician receives a supply of a narcotic drug for practice use (or office use, as it is called), the supply will be entered into PharmaNet.

13.16　The CPSBC has a software program that allows it to analyse PharmaNet data by reference to patients, communities, physicians, groups of physicians or drug types. This flexibility enables the CPSBC to focus on particular prescribing issues. For example, it can keep a watch on individual physicians known to have a history of inappropriate narcotic prescribing. It can isolate high prescribers of a particular drug with a view to identifying outliers and problem prescribers. However, it does not monitor physicians by setting 'flags' at certain levels of prescribing. Given the wide scope of possible patient prescribing needs and the numbers of prescriptions involved, it was found that the setting of such flags would be unmanageable. The CPSBC can monitor the overall usage (and the usage in a particular area) of specific drugs that are known to have a high value 'on the street'. It can monitor the prescriptions issued to patients known to be addicted to a narcotic. It can identify double scripting patients. It can look out for addicts who might trade one narcotic drug for another. Dr Taylor said that, without the facilities afforded by PharmaNet, the CPSBC would be 'groping in the dark' in its attempts to monitor the use of narcotic drugs.

13.17   Dr Taylor said that, since PharmaNet was introduced, it is not possible for a physician to prescribe for a patient who has died, because access to the patient's record is quickly stopped following the death. However, he agreed that access would remain open for a few hours after the death, during which time a dishonest physician, such as Shipman, might be able to prescribe in the patient's name and divert the drugs to his/her own use. It seems to me that the existence of an electronic record, in which transactions would be timed, would greatly improve the chances of detecting such dishonest practice if it occurred. Dr Taylor told the seminars that he thought that such prescribing would be likely to be picked up after the event.

13.18   Patients are allowed access to their PharmaNet record. They may also opt into a system whereby a key word (or password) has to be supplied by them before the pharmacist may access their record. Apparently, only about 1% of patients take up this option. In addition to any key word required, a pharmacist or physician wishing to access the system must use his/her user identification number. He or she and all members of his/her staff must sign a confidentiality undertaking before a user number will be issued. An electronic log is created every time the PharmaNet database is accessed so that browsing of the system can easily be detected.

13.19   The College of Pharmacists of British Columbia has prime responsibility for the security of the information in PharmaNet. Only that College and the CPSBC have unfettered access. The system contains information that is of great value to researchers and also to the Government. If the Government or a university research body seeks access, the permission of the College of Pharmacists must be obtained. The College has a committee which handles such applications. It has a duty to safeguard patient confidentiality. Information provided for research or Government purposes is anonymised before release.

Pharmacy Records and Inspection

13.20   Until the introduction of PharmaNet, community pharmacists in British Columbia had to keep a handwritten hard copy record of all transactions relating to narcotic drugs. This was known as the narcotic log and it appears to have been very similar to the controlled drugs register (CDR) still used in the UK. The arrangements for the safe keeping of narcotics and the narcotics log were inspected periodically by federal inspectors based in Ottawa. Since the introduction of PharmaNet, pharmacists can keep an electronic narcotics log and, in fact, the information required is automatically entered into the narcotics log as soon as the prescribing information is entered into the PharmaNet database. The pharmacist must be able to produce a hard copy of the log on request. Inspection of the arrangements for the safe keeping of narcotics and narcotic logs has now been transferred to the provincial Colleges of Pharmacists. In British Columbia, the

College of Pharmacists inspects pharmacy premises, safe keeping arrangements and narcotic logs.

Comment

13.21   I was very impressed by Dr Taylor's account of the systems in British Columbia. The need to keep strict control of narcotic drugs is given a high priority. The use of a special prescribing pad, issued only to doctors who can justify its use, seems to me to be a good idea. The requirement that this pad be used for all prescriptions for the relevant narcotic drugs, not only those to be paid for by the state, is very sensible and allows the monitoring of all usage, including the supplies obtained by a doctor for practice or personal stock. The use of individual prescriber numbers and an individual patient number greatly facilitates monitoring and analysis. The advantages of an integrated computerised system, such as PharmaNet, are obvious.

13.22   As Dr Taylor acknowledged, the demographic differences between the UK and British Columbia mean that some aspects of the British Columbia system could not be directly applied in the UK. I see the force of his suggestion that a UK body charged with the duty of monitoring the use of controlled drugs would have to be regionally based.

13.23   In Chapter Fourteen, I shall consider further the extent to which elements of the British Columbia system might be incorporated into the system in the UK.

Northern Ireland

13.24   Dr Mawhinney was accompanied at the seminar on 12th January by Dr Norman Morrow, the Chief Pharmaceutical Officer (CPO) for the Department. Dr Mawhinney gave a presentation outlining the system of monitoring and inspection of controlled drugs arrangements in Northern Ireland and both he and Dr Morrow answered questions raised by participants to the seminars.

13.25   Northern Ireland has a population of about 1.6 million and is served by approximately 1100 general practitioners (GPs), working in about 370 GP practices. The administration of primary care services is carried out by four health and social service boards and 15 local health and social care groups. The Misuse of Drugs Act 1971 and the Misuse of Drugs (Northern Ireland) Regulations 2001 (the Regulations), which are the same as the mainland Misuse of Drugs Regulations 2001, apply in the province.

The Inspectorate within the Department

13.26   The CPO is responsible for the development and implementation of an inspection and enforcement programme under the legislation covering medicines and pharmacies, including controlled drugs. An Inspectorate has been set up within the Department, comprising the CPO and a small professional group of staff, including a Medicines Inspector, a Misuse of Drugs Inspector (Dr Mawhinney), a Pharmacy Inspector and a Senior Enforcement Officer (with a police background) who can provide investigative support to all members of the team. The Inspectorate has close links with the police, who investigate suspected criminal offences, and with the Crown Prosecution Service (CPS), which offers legal advice and prosecutes on the Department's behalf. It receives administrative support through the Health Protection Branch and professional assistance from the Medical College within the Department.

13.27 The Inspectorate is responsible for inspection and enforcement across a wide range of controlled drug regulation, not just in relation to community pharmacies. Dr Mawhinney explained that, in his capacity as Misuse of Drugs Inspector, he is responsible for the control of the manufacture and distribution of controlled drugs within the province. There is an overlap between his role and that of the Pharmacy Inspector. Dr Mawhinney meets the Pharmacy Inspector on a regular basis to discuss and decide upon strategy.

13.28 Inspectors participate in department-led training and inter-agency training. This covers such topics as the provisions of the Police and Criminal Evidence Act 1984, freedom of information and data protection. Inspectors also undergo continuing professional development. Recently, there has been an opportunity for inspectors to refresh their clinical knowledge. The provision of such training was under discussion at the time of the seminars.

13.29 The inspectors are also involved in the provision of education, which they regard as a key role. At undergraduate level, Dr Mawhinney assists in the design of the law and ethics element of the pharmacy degree at Queen's University, Belfast. The CPO and other members of the team are involved in postgraduate education. Members of the team provide advice and assistance to pharmacists and some undertake to talk to GPs about their responsibilities in connection with controlled drugs. Recently, GPs have been issued with CDRs, readily identifiable by a unique serial number, and have been 'bombarded' with advice about their responsibilities. Dr Mawhinney says that this appears to have resulted in improved compliance with the Regulations.

Inspection of Community Pharmacies

13.30 There are about 500 community pharmacists, who process in the region of 25 million prescriptions each year. This system of inspection is quite different from that operating in other parts of the UK. The Pharmaceutical Society of Northern Ireland, the province's equivalent of the Royal Pharmaceutical Society of Great Britain (RPSGB), does not carry out pharmacy inspections. The police have powers of entry to the business premises of producers and suppliers of controlled drugs, including community pharmacies, and can demand the production of records. They can search premises and seize property. However, they do not carry out routine inspections. For some time, in the 1980s, there was a police chemist inspection officer (CIO). It was found that this officer could not travel safely throughout the province without protection. The post was abandoned and the Police Service of Northern Ireland is not pressing for its reinstatement. It appears that there is no significant loss of useful intelligence about illicit drug use. This may be because, as Dr Mawhinney said, the problems of illicit drug usage are much less serious in Northern Ireland than in other parts of the UK. Although cannabis and 'Ecstasy' are quite widely used, there is far less illicit use of heroin, cocaine and methadone than elsewhere in the UK.

13.31   Legislation requires that all inspectors within the Inspectorate should be qualified pharmacists. Dr Mawhinney thinks this has significant advantages, particularly because the profession has a strong ethical core. He said, however, that he thought that a multidisciplinary team could perform the inspection function equally well.

13.32   Dr Mawhinney stressed that intelligence is vital to a successful system of inspection. The inspectors in Northern Ireland have access to intelligence from a wide range of sources, relating to such matters as, for example, the illicit use of controlled drugs, disciplinary proceedings taken by the General Medical Council and pharmacists suspected of fraud. An addicts register is still maintained in Northern Ireland. Perhaps the most important of these sources of intelligence is the Central Services Agency (CSA), the body performing the functions of the Prescription Pricing Authority (PPA) in the province. This body shares controlled drugs data with the Inspectorate.

13.33   Pharmacy inspections in the province combine the purposes and functions of those of CIOs and RPSGB inspectors on the mainland. They are unannounced. During the course of a routine inspection, the inspector will look at the whole operation of the pharmacy. He or she will also examine the CDR and will reconcile the entries with data obtained by the Department from controlled drug suppliers. This permits a check on the accuracy of entries in the 'drugs obtained' side of the CDR.

13.34   The inspector will also ask the pharmacist to produce the prescription forms for the latest prescriptions entered into the CDR. Such prescription forms are, as on the mainland, kept on the premises until they are sent for processing to the CSA. These prescription forms are checked for compliance with the Regulations and also against the entries in the CDR. The inspector will also examine the physical security of the controlled drugs cabinet. He or she might also gather intelligence.

13.35   The inspector also fulfils an educational role, comparable to that of the RPSGB inspectors on the mainland. He or she imparts news and information about recent developments in pharmacy and gives advice about good practice. Dr Mawhinney said that the combined educational and inspecting roles do not usually clash, provided that the inspectors 'tread carefully'.

13.36   There is only one Pharmacy Inspector for the whole province. He inspects about three pharmacies a day. He has good administrative support and spends only one day a week in the office. He manages to visit each pharmacy about once every 15 months. As he is also responsible for witnessing the destruction of 'out of date' or damaged controlled drugs, the infrequency of his visits can cause problems. These problems are not great, however, because the quantities accumulated are not excessive.

Inspection of Doctors' Surgeries

13.37   The Department has not the resources to carry out routine inspection of the controlled drugs arrangements in GPs' surgeries. However, the Department has arranged with the medical advisers of the health boards that, during their regular visits, known as 'probity visits', they will examine the CDRs held. Dr Mawhinney accepted that such examination is likely to be cursory but thinks that it serves a useful purpose, certainly as a 'stop-gap'. The medical advisers report back any obvious cause for concern and Dr Mawhinney will then arrange a more formal inspection.

Inspection of Other Premises

13.38   The Inspectorate also inspects the premises of manufacturers and wholesalers, on behalf of the Home Office. It aims to inspect such premises at least once each year in the case of major wholesalers and at least once every two years in the case of minor wholesalers. It is also responsible for the inspection of the premises and arrangements made by veterinary practitioners and dentists, although these are not the subject of routine inspection.

13.39   The Inspectorate is also involved in the inspection of the arrangements made by secondary care providers. There are currently 21 hospital trusts in the province and the controlled drugs arrangements at their premises are inspected at least once every three years. The Inspectorate also has responsibility for a range of miscellaneous licensed authority holders including private hospitals, hospices, mountain rescue teams and forensic laboratories.

Monitoring of Prescriptions

13.40   The CSA is a public service body providing wide-ranging support to service deliverers. That support includes the provision of services analogous to those provided by the PPA on the mainland. By agreement with the Director of Pharmaceutical Services of the CSA, the Department's Inspectorate can, as I mentioned earlier, be provided with prescribing information.

13.41   The CSA and the Inspectorate jointly undertake both random and targeted analyses of controlled drug prescriptions. For its random analyses, every month, the CSA will select 12 pharmacies and will extract every Schedule 2 controlled drug prescription dispensed during a particular chosen month. The prescription forms are sent to the Inspectorate where they are examined to ensure that the prescriptions comply with the Regulations. The inspectors also look for trends that might reveal problems, either with particular practitioners or with particular types of drug. Just over 25% of pharmacies are examined annually in this way. Targeted analyses take place when the Department asks the CSA for the prescriptions relating to a particular pharmacy or prescriber or drug.

Private Prescriptions

13.42   Dr Mawhinney explained that far fewer private prescriptions are issued in Northern Ireland than on the mainland. The Department has an unofficial arrangement with community pharmacists whereby, if a private prescription is presented for a controlled drug, the Department will immediately be notified. This arrangement works well.

Enforcement

13.43   The Inspectorate has a flexible approach to enforcement, depending on the circumstances and, in particular, on the gravity of the breach discovered. Where it is found that a doctor or pharmacist has been in technical breach of the Regulations, the initial approach is likely to be to give advice about future conduct, coupled with follow-up to ensure that the advice has been heeded. If the Inspectorate discovered that a GP was addicted to a controlled drug, the circumstances would be investigated by Dr Mawhinney and by the Department's Medical Officer. The relevant health board's medical adviser would also be involved. If it appeared that breaches of the criminal law had occurred, the doctor would be interviewed formally, and the advice of the CPS would be sought as to whether there should be a prosecution. Often, the decision is that the matter should be dealt with as a health problem. Where an investigation revealed more serious breaches of controlled drugs regulations, possibly including fraud, the circumstances would be fully examined by the Inspectorate and then referred to the CPS for prosecution on behalf of the Department.

Discussion at the Seminars

13.44   Dr Mawhinney said that he thought that the framework for inspection in Northern Ireland was very good, although the Inspectorate was under-resourced. He felt that the topic of controlled drugs was not given a great deal of prominence until something went wrong. The Inspectorate would be able to do a better job with only a modest increase in manpower.

13.45   Mr Alan Macfarlane, Chief Inspector of the Home Office Drugs Inspectorate (HODI), said that the Home Office found that co-operation between his department and the Northern Ireland Inspectorate worked well.

13.46   Dr Clare Gerada, Director and Chair of the Royal College of General Practitioners National Advisory Group for Drug Misuse, observed that those responsible for controlled drugs in Northern Ireland were fortunate in that there was very little private prescribing in the province. She said that in England, prescribing on the NHS could be closely monitored but there was no central monitoring or audit of private prescribing of controlled drugs. Private prescriptions were far more likely to be for amounts that fall outside national guidelines. She was of the view that private prescribing consequently gave rise to far greater risks of abuses, such as diversion, than did NHS prescribing. She felt that this was a 'big problem'.

13.47   Dr John Grenville, on behalf of the British Medical Association, said that it appeared to him that the size and location of the inspection operation in Northern Ireland was 'exactly right'. Its value, he accepted, is that it is 'small enough to know what is going on but big enough to have the expertise necessary'. Dr Morrow agreed that the size of the organisation in Northern Ireland did confer certain advantages but also emphasised that what is important is 'to allow the facility to have structures which suit a particular context' so that there is 'some freedom of operation'. He said that, in his view, it should be possible to transfer this situation into England. Dr Grenville suggested that, if this were to happen, then the best size would be something that covered an area equivalent to that covered by a strategic health authority. Dr Morrow agreed and added that a primary care trust (PCT) covers too small an area to allow for the operation of an effective controlled drugs inspectorate.

Comment

13.48   I was very impressed with the way in which the system of inspection of arrangements for controlled drugs operates in Northern Ireland. The centralised nature of the Inspectorate, and its integration with the Department, confer undoubted benefits. I agree with Dr Grenville that the size of the province makes it suitable for a centralised Inspectorate, whereas England would require a regional Inspectorate.

13.49   It seems to me that the main advantage of the system in Northern Ireland is that the Inspectorate covers all aspects of the use and abuse of controlled drugs. On the mainland, the arrangements for inspection are fragmented. Although the HODI has overarching responsibility for controlled drugs, its efforts are focussed mainly on import and export control, the inspection of manufacturers and large-scale suppliers and the issue of licences. With its present resources, it cannot be closely involved with the issues that arise in connection with pharmacies, doctors and poor prescribing practice. In any event, the HODI has no medical or pharmaceutical expertise; it is an investigative organisation with law enforcement functions. Pharmacy inspections are carried out by police CIOs who, individually, may be very interested in and focussed on controlled drugs but are part of an organisation that is not particularly interested in such matters. They too have no real medical or pharmaceutical expertise. There is no proper arrangement for the inspection of GPs' surgeries or dispensaries or for the provision of advice to GPs. PCTs have a great number of other responsibilties and cannot be expected to focus on controlled drugs. The PPA does an excellent job but has no clearly defined links with inspection systems. It seems to me that there is much to be said for an inspectorate, like that in Northern Ireland, which is focussed solely on its responsibility for the inspection and monitoring of all aspects of controlled drug use.

CHAPTER FOURTEEN

The Discussion Paper and the Seminars: Conclusions

Introduction

14.1   In July 2003, the Inquiry issued a Discussion Paper, entitled 'The Use and Monitoring of Controlled Drugs in the Community'. Its purpose was to provide a focus and stimulus for written responses and for discussion at a series of seminars held by the Inquiry over three days in January 2004. Issues arising under the following general topics were discussed:

(a)   prescribing controlled drugs and prescriptions for controlled drugs

(b)   arrangements for security and record keeping for controlled drugs in doctors' surgeries

(c)   arrangements for security and record keeping for controlled drugs in community pharmacies

(d)   computerised record keeping

(e)   inspection and monitoring of community pharmacies and surgeries

(f)   collection and delivery of controlled drugs in the community

(g)   controlled drugs in the community and record keeping

(h)   administration, return and destruction of controlled drugs in the community.

14.2   The Inquiry received written responses to the Discussion Paper from 126 individuals and organisations. A list of respondents appears at Appendix E to this Report.

14.3   The first day of the seminars comprised two presentations, which explained the arrangements for the prescribing and monitoring of the use of controlled drugs in British Columbia and the inspection and monitoring arrangements in Northern Ireland. This seminar has been summarised in the previous Chapter. The second and third days of the seminars were taken up by a discussion of the various topics raised in the Discussion Paper.

14.4   Each of the organisations and individuals taking part in the seminars had an interest in, or involvement with, controlled drugs. The organisations were the Department of Health (DoH), the Prescription Pricing Authority (PPA), the Royal Pharmaceutical Society of Great Britain (RPSGB), the National Pharmaceutical Association (NPA), Macmillan Cancer Relief, the British Medical Association (BMA), the Royal College of General Practitioners (RCGP), the Association of Chief Police Officers (ACPO) and the National Association of Chemist Inspection Officers (NACIO). Those who attended in an individual capacity included Mr Alan Macfarlane, Chief Inspector of the Home Office Drugs Inspectorate (HODI), Professor Richard Baker, Director of the Clinical Governance Research and Development Unit, University of Leicester, and Mrs Kay Roberts, Lead Pharmacist for the RCGP National Drug Misuse Training Programme and pharmacist member of the Advisory Council on the Misuse of Drugs (ACMD). A complete list of participants appears at Appendix F to this Report.

14.5   Participants submitted written responses to the Discussion Paper in advance of the seminars and expanded on those responses in the course of discussions, which were led by Senior Counsel to the Inquiry. Others attending the seminars as observers were able to raise points with members of the Inquiry team and their contributions were passed on to Counsel. The seminars followed the same outline as the Discussion Paper and I shall adopt a similar framework in this Chapter.

14.6   I found the seminars extremely valuable. Participants were familiar with the background to Shipman's misuse of controlled drugs and were very well informed about the issues under discussion. They recognised the potential for the abuse of controlled drugs by healthcare professionals. All participants brought to the discussion their own particular knowledge and expertise and, where applicable, the concerns of those whom they represented. All recognised the need to improve the existing systems of control, while safeguarding the interests of patients. None was over-protective of his/her sectional interest. There were bound to be differences of view on some issues but the argument was always constructive. On occasions, some participants were prepared to express a change of view after hearing the debate.

14.7   In this Chapter, I shall summarise the views expressed by respondents and participants. I shall then express my own views, which will form the basis of my recommendations. However, I stress that my views have been informed not only by the responses to the Discussion Paper and the discussion at the seminars but also by all the evidence I have received, both oral and written. In Chapter Three, I mentioned the principle behind the recommendations in the Duthie Report in 1988. This was that the regulation of the use of controlled drugs should be based upon the **'three Rs'**: reconciliation, record keeping and responsibility. I too have sought to base my recommendations on those requirements.

Should the Freedom to Prescribe Controlled Drugs Extend only to Practitioners in Actual Clinical Practice in a Relevant Field?

14.8   At present, every registered medical practitioner is entitled to prescribe prescription only drugs, including controlled drugs, unless s/he is subject to some specific restriction. It had come to the Inquiry's attention that some doctors prescribe controlled drugs on an occasional basis although they have no list of patients. They may be employed in, or even retired from, a purely administrative post. Such doctors have no professional need to prescribe controlled drugs. They are unlikely to have a good up to date knowledge of the properties and effects of controlled drugs and are therefore at increased risk of making prescribing errors or poor prescribing decisions. Such doctors will not have the benefit of the framework of clinical governance that now exists for all those practising doctors working in the NHS. Any errors of judgement they might make will be unlikely to be noticed. Moreover, if such a doctor were to abuse the privilege of prescribing by feeding his/her own addiction or that of the occasional 'unofficial' patient, the conduct might go undetected. There is much to be said for limiting the right to prescribe controlled drugs to those who need to do so in the course of their professional practice. As I explained in Chapter Three, the value of restricting the freedom to prescribe controlled drugs to those doctors **'in actual practice'** was recognised by the Home Office in the 1920s, but the attempt to enact such a restriction was abandoned.

14.9   Among respondents to the Discussion Paper, there was general support for the idea that some restriction should be imposed on the general freedom of all doctors to prescribe controlled drugs. Dr John Grenville, for the BMA, Professor Baker, and Mr Alaster Rutherford, Head of Medicines Management, Bristol North Primary Care Trust (PCT), all supported the idea in principle. They saw the prescribing of controlled drugs as an integral part of a doctor's practice. They expressed the view that, if a doctor wishes to practise as such, s/he must be able to do so competently and with an awareness of current thinking in his/her chosen field. For them, the fundamental issue was whether a doctor was clinically competent to practise in his/her field; if s/he was, then it would be wrong to curb his/her freedom to prescribe controlled drugs. If s/he was not, then s/he should enjoy none of the privileges of the status of doctor, including the freedom to prescribe controlled drugs.

14.10   Dr Clare Gerada, representing the RCGP, said that it would be necessary to provide a clear definition of what was meant by a term such as 'actual clinical practice'. She thought there were some situations in which it might not be clear whether the doctor was in 'actual clinical practice'. She cited the example of a retired general practitioner (GP) who kept on a few private patients, seeing them only occasionally. Such a doctor has genuine patients and might be said to be in 'actual clinical practice'; even if the prescribing of controlled drugs were restricted to those in 'actual clinical practice', such a doctor would not fall foul of the restriction. Dr Gerada felt that this was not acceptable and she questioned from where such a doctor would obtain his/her clinical support and clinical governance structure. I recognise the force of that point, which, as Professor Baker and Dr Grenville said, is not limited to the prescribing of controlled drugs.

14.11   A second point was raised in the Discussion Paper, as an alternative issue to that of whether the right to prescribe controlled drugs should be limited to those doctors in 'actual clinical practice'. The Inquiry also asked whether, in future, when licensing is brought in, only licensed doctors should be permitted to prescribe controlled drugs. What the Inquiry had in mind was whether the requirement for revalidation, to be imposed by the General Medical Council (GMC) in the near future, would provide a sufficient safeguard for patients and the public. If only those doctors who were in 'actual clinical practice' were to be revalidated, there would be no need to impose the kind of restriction that the Inquiry was considering. Unfortunately, the question was misunderstood by some respondents, who thought that the Inquiry had in mind a special licence for the prescribing of controlled drugs. For example, the Royal College of Nursing (RCN) and Macmillan Cancer Relief expressed a concern that limiting the right to prescribe controlled drugs to doctors holding a licence might compromise patient care if licensed doctors were to fall into the minority. I had never envisaged the need for a special licence, such as exists now for doctors prescribing certain drugs for the treatment of addiction. I think the misunderstanding arose from the Inquiry's use of the word 'licence' instead of 'revalidation'. In any event, now that the Inquiry has a greater understanding of the GMC's revalidation proposals (which I shall discuss in detail in the Fifth Report), it is clear that doctors who are not in 'actual clinical practice', such as those in administrative positions, will be eligible to apply for revalidation. They might well be revalidated and yet not be competent to prescribe controlled drugs, particularly without clinical support and outside a structure of clinical governance. The introduction of revalidation might, however, resolve the problem, envisaged by Dr Gerada, of the doctor who sees a few private patients in retirement. Such a doctor may well decide not to apply for revalidation and would then be obliged to give up his/her vestigial practice.

14.12   The Association of the British Pharmaceutical Industry made the point that pharmaceutical physicians employed in industry, who will have to undergo revalidation in order to remain in post, would probably not be in 'actual clinical practice'. It seems to me that the position of such doctors is a good example of the problem under discussion. I think it is inappropriate for pharmaceutical physicians employed in industry to have the power to prescribe controlled drugs for a patient or indeed for themselves or any member of their families.

14.13   A small number of respondents made the point that doctors might be reluctant to take up administrative posts if re-entry into clinical practice were difficult to achieve. The answer to that point must surely be that, provided they have kept up their relevant skills and knowledge, they should be allowed to re-enter clinical practice; if they have not kept up their skills, then it would hardly be reasonable for them to acquire full prescribing powers and to be 'let loose' on patients without further training and assessment of their competency.

Conclusion

14.14   In my view, it is not right that a doctor should retain the privilege of prescribing controlled drugs from the time s/he is registered as a doctor until death, even when s/he spends a lifetime in administrative posts and never sees a 'real' patient. Doctors not engaged in 'actual clinical practice' are, in my view, far more likely to fall into poor prescribing practice than their actively engaged colleagues. A doctor should be entitled to prescribe or administer controlled drugs (and possibly any drugs) only if s/he needs to do so for the purposes of the 'actual clinical practice' in which s/he is engaged. I think that the concept of 'actual clinical practice' must connote the existence of a direct professional relationship between the doctor and his/her patients. This would mean that a doctor working solely in the area of public health or as an officer of a PCT, for example, should not prescribe or administer controlled drugs. Nor should a GP who has completely retired from practice. A GP who has retired from full-time practice but still undertakes locum work should be entitled to prescribe controlled drugs while s/he remains on the list of a PCT and undergoes whatever requirements are imposed for continuing education, clinical governance and revalidation.

14.15   Within the NHS, I do not think that the imposition of such a restriction should cause practical difficulties. Usually, it will be obvious from the nature of the post held or from the contractual relationship with a PCT whether there will be a legitimate need to prescribe controlled drugs. For a doctor operating wholly in the private sector, the position may be more difficult and it may be necessary for such a doctor to apply for authorisation to an appropriate body, explaining the nature of his/her practice and justifying the need to prescribe controlled drugs. This system operates satisfactorily in British Columbia, where physicians have to apply to the College of Physicians and Surgeons of British Columbia before they are issued with the special prescription forms that are used there for controlled drugs. In this country, the Commission for Healthcare Audit and Inspection (known as the Healthcare Commission) might be an appropriate body to make such decisions. The Healthcare Commission is the body now responsible for the inspection and monitoring of private medicine. Alternatively, if a controlled drugs inspectorate were to be set up, that body would be well placed to fulfil this function.

14.16   A prohibition against the prescribing of controlled drugs by those doctors not required to do so in the course of 'actual clinical practice' should not compromise patient care. It should have the opposite effect. I recognise that such a prohibition would mean that some doctors would not be able to provide appropriate treatment to a patient *in extremis* whom they might encounter in an emergency situation. However, such situations, which would have to involve a retired GP (for example) happening upon the emergency, close to a pharmacy which had no suitable 'non-controlled' alternatives to the controlled drug required, would occur very rarely indeed. Moreover, the Medical Adviser to the Inquiry, Dr Aneez Esmail, has advised me that few lives are saved by emergency treatment such as this and a doctor who is not in 'actual clinical practice' may inadvertently harm or even kill a patient by ill-informed or careless administration of controlled drugs. Shipman, it will be remembered, more than once, diverted diamorphine obtained on this 'emergency' pretext.

14.17   I also recognise that Government policy is moving towards extending, rather than restricting, the categories of healthcare professionals who are allowed to prescribe and administer controlled drugs. What I propose is not inconsistent with this extension. It is envisaged that only properly qualified nurse prescribers, acting in the course of their duties in a specified post, should be allowed to prescribe controlled drugs. It cannot be envisaged that, once having gained their qualification, such nurses should retain their prescribing powers until death.

Should There Be Some Control on Doctors' Prescribing of Controlled Drugs for Themselves, Their Families or Friends?

14.18   There is currently no prohibition against, or restriction on, doctors prescribing controlled drugs for themselves, their families or friends although, broadly speaking, it is regarded as poor practice. There are two main reasons why it is so regarded. First, a doctor who prescribes outside a true professional relationship may lack the objectivity needed for the proper care of the patient. Second, it is by no means unknown for doctors to prescribe for themselves or their families or friends to feed a concealed addiction.

14.19   The Discussion Paper raised the question whether such practice ought to be prohibited and, if not, whether there might be a way of ensuring that such prescribing is more readily detectable. It queried whether a doctor issuing a controlled drug prescription should be required to state on the prescription whether s/he is the patient and whether s/he is in other than an 'arm's length' relationship with the patient. It queried whether a requirement should be introduced that such prescriptions be approved and countersigned by an 'uninvolved' prescriber.

14.20　Among the responses from pharmacists, healthcare professionals other than doctors, and primary care organisations, there was strong support for an absolute prohibition against such prescribing. The Council of the Independent Doctors Forum supported an absolute prohibition.

14.21　Perhaps not surprisingly, the idea received less support from the medical profession generally. The main reason given was that such prescribing might be unavoidable in certain circumstances. The geographical isolation of some practices was felt to be a key factor. In its response to the Discussion Paper, Macmillan Cancer Relief said that, in rural communities, GPs might be called upon to prescribe for terminally ill 'friends'. Restrictions on prescribing controlled drugs in these situations could be medically and ethically unacceptable. The RCGP made the same point. The GMC, which generally regards such prescribing as poor practice and advises that doctors should not have family members on their lists, said that, while a total prohibition against the self-prescribing of controlled drugs might be unobjectionable, a prohibition against prescribing for family and friends might cause significant problems in small communities, where doctors necessarily have social lives, and sometimes extended families, in the communities they serve. These responses highlight the difficulty of defining what is meant by 'family' and 'friends', which would be necessary if any legal restriction were to be applied. The real mischief at which this suggestion was aimed is prescribing outside a professional doctor/patient relationship. It was never intended to suggest that a doctor could never have a friend or relative on his/her list of patients. Most doctors recognise that it is inadvisable to give professional services to those with whom they are closely connected but, in small communities, this will sometimes be unavoidable.

14.22　In its written response, the NPA supported the idea of an absolute prohibition but, at the seminars, its Chief Executive, Mr John D'Arcy, said that the Association had not really taken account of the situation in which a doctor might be called upon to prescribe for a relative in an emergency, which he thought should be permitted.

14.23　The initial view of the BMA was that such prescribing should not be limited, because it is rarely abused (in fact, the extent of the abuse is unknown) and, in rural and remote areas, there will be no alternative. I should point out that such cases of prescribing for family members of which the Inquiry has heard did not occur either in an emergency or in a remote area. At the seminars, Dr Grenville, speaking on behalf of the BMA, explained that attitudes among members of the medical profession to such prescribing were changing and it was increasingly being regarded as a serious matter. Instead of an absolute prohibition, the BMA favoured an approach that placed greater emphasis on the correct and open recording of such prescribing.

14.24　Miss Mandie Lavin, representing the RPSGB, advocated the idea of a special endorsement on a prescription to the effect that the patient was known to the doctor other than in a professional capacity. Mr D'Arcy felt that the NPA would support the idea of a special endorsement on the prescription stating that it had been issued in an emergency. Dr Grenville thought that the idea of a special endorsement might be attractive but had concerns about how such a requirement would be phrased.

14.25 There was broad support for the suggestion that there should be some safeguards to ensure that the prescribing of controlled drugs by doctors for themselves or their families and friends should be monitored. Miss Lavin advocated a requirement whereby a doctor would report to his/her PCT in the event that such a prescription was issued, although she acknowledged that this would leave a *lacuna* with regard to non-NHS prescriptions.

Conclusion

14.26 In my view, it should be a criminal offence for a doctor to prescribe a controlled drug for him/herself, subject to a statutory defence available where the doctor acted in an emergency. Such circumstances would be most exceptional and would arise if, for example, a doctor were in severe acute pain and needed analgesia to provide relief until s/he could receive independent professional medical care. It is, in my view, quite wrong for a doctor to prescribe a controlled drug for him/herself for any non-acute condition. Many doctors who have become addicted to a controlled drug say that the abuse began with unwise self-prescribing for chronic pain, depression, insomnia or anxiety. That may be true. The rule that I propose should greatly reduce the risk of such addiction. In my view, the same rule should apply to the self-administration of a controlled drug taken from a doctor's own or practice stock; it should be unlawful, subject to the statutory defence. The practical effect of this rule would be that a doctor would be able to self-prescribe only a very limited number of controlled drugs, namely the Schedule 2 analgesics, and then only in exceptional circumstances. He or she would, of course, be able to self-administer any drug prescribed by another doctor.

14.27 In my view, it is also highly undesirable for a doctor to prescribe controlled drugs for a member of his/her immediate family or to administer to such a person a controlled drug from personal or practice stock. There are particular risks to the patient when controlled drugs are prescribed by a doctor who cannot exercise full professional objectivity. The prescribing of controlled drugs is but one aspect of the treatment a GP provides. It is generally accepted that everyone should have a GP with whom they have a professional – rather than a personal – relationship. The need for this professional independence is well illustrated by consideration of the example of the woman whose GP husband advises that her back pain or depression should be treated with a controlled drug. He may or may not be right but his objectivity must be questionable. In my view, GPs should not normally treat members of their immediate families and should ensure that they are on the list of another GP. I do accept, however, that, in exceptional circumstances, for example in very remote areas, it may be necessary for a GP to have members of his/her immediate family on his/her list. This is not ideal but, where it is unavoidable, at least there should be the potential for supervision through clinical governance, in particular by the monitoring of controlled drugs prescribing. To facilitate such supervision, I think PCTs should require a doctor who has a member of his/her immediate family on his/her list to inform the PCT of the position. The need for such an arrangement to continue might well be questioned, for example, by a medical adviser or at appraisal. Leaving aside the very limited circumstances where it is unavoidable that a GP has immediate family members on his/her list, it should be regarded as unacceptable for any doctor to prescribe a controlled drug for an immediate family member, save in the type of emergency I mentioned above.

I accept that such emergencies might arise more often for those living in remote areas than for those living within easy reach of a hospital or health centre. The GMC and PCTs should make the position clear.

14.28 Thus, I do not favour an absolute prohibition against the prescribing of controlled drugs for immediate family members. However, I regard it as essential that, when a doctor prescribes a controlled drug for him/herself or for a member of his/her immediate family, the position is clearly acknowledged. I would define the immediate family as comprising a spouse, family partner, children, grandchildren, stepchildren (including the children of family partners), parents and grandparents. A doctor issuing a prescription (whether on the NHS or privately) for a controlled drug within Schedules 2–4 to the Misuse of Drugs Regulations 2001 (MDR 2001) should be required to declare on the prescription, if it be the case, that s/he is prescribing for him/herself or for a member of his/her immediate family. He or she should also be required to state, if it be the case, that s/he is prescribing in an emergency. Administration to anyone, including a family member, of a Schedule 2 drug from personal or practice stock should always, in any event, be recorded in the doctor's controlled drugs register (CDR) as well as in that person's medical records.

14.29 If prescriptions containing such a declaration were likely to come to the attention of someone in authority, a doctor in two minds about prescribing benzodiazepines for his/her spouse or partner, or Ritalin for his/her child, might, I think, decide not to do so. A false declaration or the failure to make a declaration where one was called for would, at the least, be professional misconduct, which in my view the GMC should regard as a serious matter. The presence or absence of such a declaration would also be of relevance in the context of a criminal trial such as that in the case of R v Dunbar[1], to which I referred in Chapter Four, if an issue arose as to whether the doctor was genuinely prescribing in his/her capacity as such.

14.30 I shall recommend that all controlled drug prescriptions, both NHS and private, should be sent to the PPA for processing. Prescriptions with a declaration such as I have described above should be readily identifiable. They could be analysed and monitored by the relevant PCT or the Healthcare Commission or the controlled drugs inspectorate, if one were to be created.

14.31 Although I recognise that it will usually be unwise for a doctor to prescribe controlled drugs for a friend and that such prescribing might conceal diversion of the drug for improper purposes, I do not think it would be practicable to institute any rules designed to curb such a practice. It is almost impossible to draw the line between who is a 'friend' and who is not. In my view, the GMC should make plain that it is bad practice for a doctor to prescribe a controlled drug for anyone with whom s/he does not have a genuine professional relationship. Although it would be difficult to define where the line should be drawn, it will usually be quite easy to recognise cases in which a doctor has crossed the line and prescribed outside a professional relationship. In my view, such cases should be regarded as professional misconduct.

---

[1] [1982] 1 All ER 188

14.32　I do not regard the countersigning of a prescription by a second doctor to be viable or worthwhile. A doctor who is in a position to countersign would be able to prescribe in his/her own name.

Should the Freedom to Prescribe Controlled Drugs for a Patient in the Community Extend only to a Patient's 'Nominated' General Practitioner?

14.33　It is recognised that some patients (almost always addicts) will try to obtain supplies of controlled drugs from more than one prescriber concurrently, a practice known as 'double scripting'. This practice might be carried out with or without the knowledge and connivance of the prescribers. One or both prescriptions might be private prescriptions. The evidence to the Inquiry suggests that double scripting is a significant problem. To counter this problem, the suggestion was made that a patient should be issued with controlled drug prescriptions only by his/her nominated general practitioner.

14.34　There was a general recognition of the advantages that accrue where one doctor has special responsibility for the prescribing of controlled drugs to a patient, whether in the context of palliative care or in that of the treatment of addiction. Dr Gerada, whose special interest is the treatment of addiction, explained that, as a means of reducing diversion of controlled drugs, DoH guidelines require that there should be a named GP for the care of all patients receiving treatment for addiction. She supported this principle even though the requirement can give rise to practical problems.

14.35　Notwithstanding the recognition of these advantages, the concept of such a restriction received very little support from those who responded to the Discussion Paper. The main objection was that its introduction would lead to practical problems. Under the new General Medical Services Contract, which came into effect in April 2004, patients are registered with a practice rather than with individual doctors. It would create real difficulties if only one member of the practice could prescribe any controlled drug for the therapeutic care of a patient. Attention was also drawn to the difficulties such a restriction would create for patients needing palliative care out of hours or while visiting relatives or friends away from their home area. It was also pointed out that a restriction would cause problems for GPs working in collaboration with other doctors in substance misuse clinics.

Conclusion

14.36　I recognise that the nomination of one GP to be responsible for the care of a patient receiving controlled drugs would assist in the prevention and detection of double scripting. However, the imposition of a rule to that effect could have a direct adverse impact upon patient care. There are other ways in which double scripting might be better policed. One would be a system whereby all controlled drugs prescriptions carry a unique patient identifier (as they do in British Columbia) so that patient-specific information can be processed by the PPA and will come to the attention of the monitoring organisation. Another would be the introduction of electronic patient care records, available to all doctors and pharmacists at the time of prescribing and dispensing, about which I shall say more later in this Chapter.

Should Section 12 of the Misuse of Drugs Act 1971 Be Repealed?

14.37   As I have explained in earlier Chapters, the power conferred by section 12 of the Misuse of Drugs Act 1971 (MDA 1971) has fallen into disuse. It has not been used to curtail the freedom of an individual doctor to prescribe, possess, supply or administer controlled drugs since 1986.

14.38   There was a general consensus that some power to restrict the prescribing rights of doctors convicted of controlled drugs offences should exist. Most respondents to the Discussion Paper thought that the power under section 12 should be retained. However, it appeared to me that many of those expressing that view were under the mistaken impression that it was still being actively used.

14.39   Mr Macfarlane was of the view that the power to restrict a doctor's right to prescribe controlled drugs is more appropriately exercised by the GMC or by the doctor's employer or contracting authority, usually a NHS body, rather than by the Home Office. At the present time, the HODI has neither the resources nor the expertise to deal satisfactorily with the issues to be taken into consideration when deciding whether to recommend exercise of such a power.

14.40   Mrs Roberts was concerned that, if section 12 were to be repealed, it should be replaced with something else that would be robust and could be implemented quickly, for the protection of patients. Many respondents echoed these sentiments. Mrs Roberts was not happy with the way in which the GMC dealt with such cases. She referred to one case, of which she knew, in which it took six years for the GMC to remove from the register a practitioner found to have been prescribing irresponsibly. On the other hand, Dr Grenville described a case that illustrated prompt and effective action taken by the medical authorities.

14.41   PCTs and the GMC have the power to take prompt action. The GMC can refer a case to its Interim Orders Committee, which can impose conditions on the right of a doctor to continue in practice pending the full hearing of the case against him/her. Those conditions can include a restriction on prescribing rights. Miss Lavin thought that a doctor's prescribing rights should be automatically suspended following a conviction or caution for controlled drugs offences. Mr Rutherford agreed. He said that, although PCTs can now suspend a doctor from the medical list, thereby preventing him/her from practising in the area of that PCT, the doctor was still free to prescribe in a non-NHS setting. Dr Gerada did not disagree fundamentally with the idea of an automatic suspension following conviction but expressed concern that the immediate withdrawal of a young doctor's right to prescribe controlled drugs, perhaps following weekend recreational drug abuse outside the work setting, might be inappropriate and disproportionate.

14.42   Miss Lavin stressed that, once a restriction has been imposed, there must be a satisfactory method of informing pharmacists of the restriction and of enabling them to confirm the status of a prescriber at any time of the day or night.

Conclusion

14.43 I accept that the Home Office has never been well placed to make decisions about the withdrawal of prescribing rights. It lacks the necessary medical expertise. The GMC and PCTs have the power to restrict the rights of GPs to prescribe controlled drugs, and have ready access to the necessary expertise. I have no means of knowing whether they always use those powers satisfactorily so as to protect the interests of patients and the public. In my view, it would be wrong for Government to remove section 12 from the statute book unless and until satisfied, after an independent review and audit of recent cases, that the GMC and PCTs were taking prompt, sufficient and effective measures in such cases. The Inquiry has examined a number of cases in which the GMC has dealt with doctors convicted of controlled drugs offences. These will be described in the Fifth Report. However, I cannot claim to have carried out a thorough audit. Many of these cases involve a doctor who has become addicted to a controlled drug. My impression is that the GMC focusses mainly upon the treatment of the doctor's addiction. Dishonest conduct is treated as being 'part of the illness' and the assumption is made that, once the illness is treated and under control, prescribing rights should be restored, subject to a period of monitoring. There is limited, if any, investigation into the effect which the doctor's addiction has had or is likely to have on the quality of care given to patients. On the basis of the necessarily limited exercise carried out by the Inquiry, I could not say that I was satisfied that the GMC always strikes the right balance between the rehabilitation of the doctor and the need to protect patients and the public. I have little information about how PCTs deal with such cases. If, on conducting a more complete audit of all the recent cases, the view is formed that the current position is not satisfactory, I think that the Government should retain section 12 and ensure that it can be effectively operated.

14.44 At present, doctors on a PCT list are required to inform the PCT whenever they accept a police caution, are bound over or are convicted of a criminal offence. They are also under a duty to tell the PCT when they become the subject of any criminal proceedings. For the present, my view is that, as soon as a GP is cautioned or convicted in connection with a controlled drugs offence, it should be incumbent upon him/her and on the police to report the caution or conviction to the GMC, which should promptly decide whether, and if so what, action is necessary. In my view, the GMC should also inform the doctor's employer or PCT of the action it intends to take, if any.

14.45 Whenever a curb is placed on a doctor's prescribing powers, the information must promptly be made available, at all times of day, to those who need to know of it, namely the doctor's employer or PCT and, above all, the pharmacists who will give it practical effect. This should not be too difficult to achieve in this electronic age.

14.46 For the sake of completeness, I add that I can well understand why the Government has no intention of using section 13 of the MDA 1971 again. The use of a tribunal to make findings of fact and to advise the Home Secretary in respect of irresponsible prescribing proved unsatisfactory. Such matters must be dealt with by the GMC and/or, in the case of a doctor working in the NHS, by the relevant NHS body. In future, it may be thought appropriate for the Healthcare Commission to exercise similar powers over doctors practising in the private sector.

Should There Be a Policy Shift towards Encouraging the Provision of Community Pharmacies in Rural Areas so as to Reduce the Need for Doctors to Provide Dispensing Services?

14.47   In Chapter Five, I referred to the position of GPs practising in rural areas who provide dispensing services to NHS patients in addition to the usual range of medical services. In the UK, there is a well-established differentiation between the prescribing and dispensing functions; usually, doctors prescribe and pharmacists dispense. The Inquiry raised the issue of whether the present arrangements for determining when and where doctors, rather than pharmacists, provide pharmaceutical services operate in the best interests of patients.

14.48   It is generally accepted that the involvement of a pharmacist in the process of providing medication to a patient acts as a safety check against error. Many respondents to the Discussion Paper, including Dr Jim Smith, Chief Pharmaceutical Officer for England at the DoH, emphasised the importance of the check inherent in the differentiation of functions. Second, it is obvious that, where both prescribing and dispensing functions are carried out by the same person or within the same commercial or professional entity, there is a potential for the loss of professional objectivity or even abuse. Moreover, at present, the arrangements for the inspection of the dispensaries of dispensing doctors appear to be virtually non-existent.

14.49   Several respondents pointed to the benefits of the dispensing doctors' service. The DoH reported that many patients find the arrangement very convenient. That will often be the case as, by definition, the service should be offered only in an area in which pharmacy services are not readily accessible. Dr Smith said that the Office of Fair Trading had recently produced a report on the competition issues raised by the existing legislation and had recommended that any person who met the professional requirements of the RPSGB should be free to set up a pharmacy anywhere. The Government had not accepted that recommendation but was shortly to produce a position paper setting out its proposals for the future.

14.50   Turning to the more practical concerns that arise from the lack of pharmacy expertise available when dispensing doctors dispense as well as prescribe, Dr Malcolm Ward, Chairman of the Dispensing Doctors' Association (DDA), pointed out that a dispensing doctor frequently has a dispenser working in his/her practice. He argued that a trained dispenser can provide an independent safety check. That I accept, although I find it hard to believe that a dispenser who has undergone a brief practical course can do so as well as a pharmacist with five years' professional training. But, in any event, there is no obligation on the dispensing doctor to employ a trained dispenser and my understanding is that many do not. In a post-seminar response, Dr Ward said that the DDA was fully aware of the need to improve the availability and accessibility of dispenser training. He described the provision of such training as a **'huge logistic exercise'**.

14.51   It was pointed out by Dr Grenville that any doctor can supply drugs by personal administration and that this amounts, in effect, to prescribing and dispensing as one process. That is also true, although personal administration of the medication by a doctor occurs relatively rarely when compared with the usual procedure of the prescribing of the medication by a doctor, dispensing by a pharmacist and self-administration by the patient.

14.52   As I mentioned in Chapter Nine, chemist inspection officers (CIOs) do not have the power to inspect the premises of dispensing doctors and their visits to such premises are rare. Detective Constable (DC) Duncan White, Secretary of the NACIO, told the Inquiry that visits to dispensing doctors' premises usually take place only when the doctor invites the CIO to attend because s/he wishes to dispose of 'out of date' controlled drugs. The CIO may then be permitted to look at the records kept and the safe custody arrangements. However, the CIO has no power to require any shortcomings to be remedied. He also said that his colleagues reported to him that, in general, record keeping by dispensing doctors was less than satisfactory, although there were some whose standards of record keeping were 'superb'. In the absence of any system of routine inspection, such evidence is bound to be anecdotal. Mr Macfarlane said that the HODI (whose inspectors do have the power to inspect such premises) does not routinely inspect dispensing surgeries. However, on occasions when its inspectors have viewed the records kept in such establishments, they too have found evidence of poor record keeping.

14.53   Mr D'Arcy spoke of the disparity that exists, in terms of inspections, between pharmacists and dispensing doctors and advocated parity in those arrangements. His views were echoed by Dr Grenville, speaking on behalf of the BMA, who said that all doctors' premises should be inspected as regularly and as rigorously as pharmacies are. This would, he said, be beneficial for doctors and for public confidence in them. Both dispensing doctors and prescribing doctors should be subject to the same rules and regulations as their pharmacist colleagues.

Conclusion

14.54   It is not part of my remit to explore the merits of the 'competition' issues that divide the dispensing doctors and pharmacists. Nor am I inclined to recommend that there should be a policy shift towards encouraging the provision of community pharmacies in rural areas. I cannot fail to observe, however, that, when a doctor both prescribes and dispenses controlled drugs, not only is the opportunity for independent professional scrutiny of the prescription lost but the opportunity for diversion and abuse is far greater.

14.55   Proper inspection of dispensing doctors' arrangements for controlled drugs is, in my view, an imperative. CIOs should have the power and the resources to inspect dispensing doctors' surgeries in the same way that they currently inspect pharmacies. If, in the future, there were to be a controlled drugs inspectorate such powers of inspection should be exercised by that body.

Prescriptions

Should It Be Permissible and/or Encouraged for Controlled Drug Prescriptions to Be Generated by Computer?

14.56   In Chapter Six, I described the special handwriting requirement imposed by the MDR 2001 for the issue of prescriptions for all controlled drugs in Schedule 2 and some in

Schedule 3. I discussed some of the advantages and disadvantages of the current requirement. When the question was raised in the Discussion Paper as to whether this requirement should be removed, there was widespread support for the suggestion that it should be permissible for prescriptions for all controlled drugs to be computer generated.

14.57   It is now Home Office policy that such a change should be introduced. At the seminars, Mr Macfarlane outlined, with some enthusiasm, the many advantages which he believes will accrue from computer generated prescriptions, integrated with computerised systems of record keeping for producers, wholesalers and pharmacists. The HODI has encouraged the experimental development of computerised systems alongside the paper-based records that are currently required. Mr Macfarlane sees real advantages in such an arrangement and believes that any security problems can be resolved, if not perfectly, at least to an acceptable degree.

14.58   Dr Grenville and Professor Baker strongly supported the suggestion for change to computer generated controlled drug prescriptions. In common with many others, they felt that the ability of software systems to alert prescribers to clinical or technical prescribing errors would lead to fewer errors being made. Dr Smith agreed. He said that handwriting problems are responsible for a very large proportion of medication errors, including fatal errors. Moreover, the electronic creation of prescriptions would allow much more efficient transfer and analysis of prescribing data.

14.59   Despite the general support for the proposal, a number of respondents sounded a note of caution. The substance misuse steering group of Kensington & Chelsea and Westminster PCTs said in its written response that writing a prescription by hand acts as a mechanism for doctors to double check the strength and the dose of the drug. Mr Ian Rudd, Macmillan Cancer Relief Principal Pharmacist at the Raigmore Hospital, Inverness, agreed that handwriting brought some advantages. He said that his team runs an electronic prescribing system for patients receiving cytotoxic chemotherapy. He added that, under the new system, prescribing had improved, in that fewer technical errors were being made, but it had been found that prescribers could become careless when using the computer. So, although the system had eliminated technical errors (e.g. a failure to write the word 'tablets'), it had not eliminated clinical errors.

14.60   A number of other respondents did not support computer generation. The ACPO Drugs Sub-Committee was worried that computer generated prescriptions would be easier to forge. The Kensington & Chelsea and Westminster PCTs steering group and others shared this concern. Conversely, some contributors felt that computer generated prescriptions offered greater security against forgery and theft, particularly if allied (as they could be in future) with electronic transmission and some centralised 'real time' system of authentication. Mr Macfarlane said that the Government hopes to introduce provisions for electronic signatures. Manual systems had not, he said, provided 'a perfect insurance against fraud'. The Inquiry received some post-seminar responses suggesting a number of novel and sophisticated methods of ensuring that computer entries are made only by those who are supposed to make them. I am unable to comment on the feasibility of these suggestions.

Conclusion

14.61   The introduction of computer generated prescriptions for all controlled drugs would bring significant advantages by reducing errors and facilitating monitoring. I do, however, think that the change might bring security problems. I am concerned that a dishonest member of staff or a computer hacker might be able to create a controlled drug prescription which cannot be challenged by the pharmacist, when presented, because it appears in all respects to be correct and legitimate. Computer generation of prescriptions for non-controlled drugs, and for controlled drugs in Schedule 4, has been commonplace for some years and I have not been told that these have given rise to any security problems. However, there is probably less incentive to forge such prescriptions than to do so for drugs in Schedule 2. The extent of the security problem which would arise from the computer generation of all controlled drug prescriptions is unknown. Although it appears to be Home Office policy to make this change, it seems to me that the security implications should first be tested in a pilot scheme. As the DoH is currently involved in the development of other computerised systems, including the electronic transmission of prescriptions, to which I shall shortly come, it might be sensible to test the security arrangements of the whole package rather than doing it piecemeal. This would necessarily take some time.

14.62   In the meantime, I shall recommend that the solution, mentioned in Chapter Six, of printing the prescribing information onto the prescription form and then writing it again in the space between the lines, should be adopted more widely, not as a legal requirement but as a matter of good practice. The practice complies with the existing legislative requirement for handwriting. Yet it also provides the advantage of the use of software to provide prompts and alerts and the use of a printer to ensure legibility. The prescription would not take any longer to prepare than at present because the doctor has to enter the prescribing information into the surgery computer in any event, for entry into the patient's medical records.

The Electronic Transmission of Prescriptions and the NHS Care Record

14.63   At the seminars, Dr Smith said that it is now Government policy that, in the future, all prescriptions should be electronically transmitted from the doctor's surgery to the community pharmacy. He said that this is an important aspect of the Government's IT strategy and that there is a firm commitment to it. Successful pilot projects have been carried out, although, because of the current handwriting requirement, these have not included controlled drug prescriptions. The target is for half of all prescriptions to be transferred electronically by the end of 2005 and for all to be so transferred by the end of 2007.

14.64   The electronic transmission of prescriptions is closely related to the Government's plans to introduce a system of electronic healthcare records. Dr Smith explained that the DoH intends that, by the end of 2004, there will exist the beginnings of a national electronic patient record system (the NHS Care Record). Every person in England will have a personal health record on what is described as a 'common spine'. The common spine will contain a record of the patient's significant health events, including prescriptions, arising from both GP and hospital treatment. This record will be accessible to any healthcare professional with the necessary authorisation. Accordingly, once a GP has written a prescription electronically, the prescription will rest on the common spine of the electronic record. The patient will then be able to collect the medication from any pharmacy in the country. Some means of allowing the chosen pharmacist to access the patient's prescription from the common spine is envisaged, although the precise mechanics of this have not yet been decided. The pharmacist would then be able to access a summary of the patient's medical records and would know for what condition the prescription had been issued. It is envisaged that the system will eventually be 'paper free'. Dr Smith said that this system would have all the advantages of the PharmaNet system currently operating in British Columbia, and more besides. However, he stressed that the system was designed not to facilitate the monitoring of prescribing but to improve health care. He said that the DoH was aware that the proposal gave rise to difficult issues of patient confidentiality and consent. He added that, if I was minded to recommend that information from the NHS Care Record should be made available for the purpose of monitoring the use of controlled drugs, I should say so sooner rather than later, because the system specifications and contractual arrangements are already well advanced.

14.65   There was some support from respondents to the Discussion Paper for the electronic transmission of controlled drug prescriptions. Many respondents could see the advantages but some expressed reservations about the security aspects of the proposal. Some felt that it would be a very long time before such systems could be put into practice, either because the funding would not be available to install the equipment or because the systems would not, in the foreseeable future, be sufficiently secure.

Conclusion

14.66   It seems to me that there are a number of potential advantages to be derived from the Government's current proposals, provided the system can be made sufficiently secure. For one thing, as I have said, pharmacists would be able to access information from patients' medical records. Provided that adequate means of identification were required before a patient file was started (so that one patient could not have two files in different names) and provided that all prescriptions, both private and NHS, were recorded on the common spine, there could be greatly improved regulation of controlled drugs. For example, the system would allow the detection of double scripting. A doctor who was asked to prescribe a controlled drug would quickly be able to see when the patient had last received a supply of the drug and in what quantity. He or she would be able to judge whether or not a new prescription was justified and would have 'ammunition' to support his/her refusal if it was not. If a doctor chose to prescribe notwithstanding the fact that the patient had recently received a supply from another source, the pharmacist who was asked to dispense the second prescription should notice the anomaly. Apart from the detection of double scripting, other benefits would accrue. A dishonest doctor would be unable to prescribe for a wholly fictitious patient; there would be no NHS Care Record for the patient. A prescription could not be stolen or lost. Prescribing and dispensing information could be sent automatically to the PPA, saving a great deal of time and money. It would be possible to place an alert on the system so as to prevent a doctor whose right to prescribe controlled drugs had been withdrawn from creating or transmitting a prescription for that type of drug.

14.67 These are real advantages. However, I understand and share the concerns expressed about the security of the computer networks to be used. Not only must secure systems be put in place, but doctors and their staff must be persuaded to use them properly. Shipman's computer system at the Market Street Surgery was password protected. However, all members of staff used the same password and had full access to the patients' records. If access to a GP's computer system were to include the ability to create and transmit prescriptions electronically, and if security were slack, the risk of diversion of controlled drugs would be grave. However, if an 'extra' security measure were introduced into the system for use when a doctor wished to prescribe a controlled drug and this could be accessed only by him/her personally, using a confidential code, then I would have thought that the system would be reasonably secure. Of course, a dishonest or foolish doctor could undermine such a system by deliberately or carelessly sharing his/her code with others. However, if all prescriptions and requisitions for controlled drugs, including those issued privately, could be analysed by the PPA and scrutinised by an appropriate monitoring organisation, then I think that the advantages of the proposed system would outweigh any security problems.

14.68 In any event, it will be some time before the NHS Care Record system with electronic transmission of prescriptions is in general use. In the meantime, it is necessary to consider how a paper-based system should operate for the prescription of controlled drugs. When I speak of a paper-based system, I am referring to prescriptions that are either handwritten on paper or computer generated, printed on paper and signed by the doctor.

NHS and Private Prescriptions

14.69 I explained in Chapter Six that a NHS prescription form is printed in a standard format on special paper. There is no standard format or special paper for private prescriptions. A controlled drug prescription, whether NHS or private, must comply with the requirements of the MDA 1971 and MDR 2001. Under the Dangerous Drugs Regulations 1921, the Home Secretary was granted the power to issue an **'official form'** for the writing of controlled drug prescriptions but this power was never exercised. The Inquiry invited responses to the question whether a special form should now be introduced for all prescriptions for controlled drugs.

14.70 There was a good deal of support for the suggestion that private prescriptions should have the same degree of formality as NHS prescriptions. For example, in its written submission, the Boots Pharmacists' Association suggested that a special controlled drug prescription form, carrying a unique identification number, should be introduced and should be in such a format as could be used for both NHS and private prescriptions.

14.71 Respondents and contributors mentioned a number of potential advantages which would accrue from the use of a special form for controlled drug prescriptions. I note that the Council of the Independent Doctors Forum supported the auditing of controlled drugs prescriptions. The use of a special form would make it possible to put out an alert if a prescription pad were stolen. It would also make forgery of private prescriptions more difficult. If the form were different from the existing FP10, it would be possible to ensure that a doctor who was not entitled to prescribe controlled drugs was not in possession of a pad of forms. It would also be possible to analyse and monitor the prescribing practice of all doctors, both on the NHS and privately, and a much more complete and reliable picture would be obtained. As Dr Smith pointed out, it makes sense for private prescribing information, indeed for private healthcare information generally, to be included on the NHS Care Record; if the object is to improve patient safety, it is desirable that the complete picture, rather than a partial one, be available.

14.72   In Chapter Thirteen, I described the system of prescription forms used for narcotic drugs in British Columbia. Until the introduction of the PharmaNet computer system in 1995, a triplicate form, printed on special paper, was used. One copy was kept at the prescribing doctor's surgery, and two were given to the patient for presentation at the pharmacy. After dispensing, one of those two copies was sent to the Provincial Government's office for entry onto a database. Since the introduction of PharmaNet, the third copy is redundant as the prescribing information is recorded in the computer system. Prescribers have to use a prescription pad which carries their own identification number. Also, the patient is identified by a code number. This means that the data entered into the PharmaNet system can be analysed by reference to individual patients as well as to individual physicians and to particular drugs or groups of drugs.

14.73   Some seminar participants advocated adopting this system in England. Mr Macfarlane was strongly in favour of the idea of the triplicate form system, at least for private (non-NHS) controlled drug prescriptions. He foresees that it will not be possible to ensure that all doctors who prescribe controlled drugs for non-NHS purposes will use a computer. He would think it most helpful if the HODI were to receive a copy of every non-NHS controlled drug prescription.

Conclusion

14.74   I am sure that it would be desirable to introduce a special form for the private prescribing of controlled drugs. The precise practical details would require consideration. It would be possible to adapt the existing FP10 so as to be suitable for private as well as NHS use; tick boxes could be used to indicate whether or not the form was being used for a controlled drug and whether the prescription was being issued under the NHS or privately. Another possibility would be that there should be a special controlled drug prescription form for both NHS and private prescribing, printed on paper of a distinctive colour, with a layout similar to the existing FP10 and with a tick box to indicate whether the form is being used for NHS or private purposes. A further option would be to keep the FP10 for all NHS prescriptions and to introduce a different form for private controlled drug prescriptions. Any of these options would allow for monitoring and analysis of all controlled drug prescribing, not just NHS prescribing. Each prescription would have its own unique identification number. The choice between the various options I have outlined would depend upon several matters. One issue for consideration would be whether to devise a system that would readily be capable of adaptation to the computerised system discussed in the previous section. Another issue is whether the authorities consider that it would be beneficial to have all private prescriptions, not only those for controlled drugs, written on a special form. That is an issue which goes beyond the Inquiry's Terms of Reference and I express no view upon it.

14.75 My preference would be for there to be a special form to be used for all controlled drug prescriptions whether NHS or private. This should be similar to the FP10 but should be printed on paper of a different colour. It should have a tick box to show whether the drugs are being prescribed on the NHS or privately. It should also have space for the declarations I have recommended in paragraphs 14.27–14.29 above. I shall deal with the related question of requisitions in paragraphs 14.127 and 14.133.

14.76 I mentioned in paragraph 14.36 that the inclusion of a patient-specific number on the prescription form, as happens in British Columbia, would assist in the detection of double scripting. The Inquiry has not consulted about the inclusion of such information. Plainly it has potential for monitoring purposes but the proposal raises issues of privacy which would require careful consideration. I shall recommend that the inclusion of a patient-specific number, such as the patient's NHS number, should be considered in the light of the Government's proposals for introduction of the NHS Care Record.

14.77 If a special form capable of being scanned into the PPA system is to be used for all controlled drug prescriptions, I do not think it would be necessary to introduce a triplicate, or even a duplicate, prescription pad such as is used in British Columbia. There, one copy of the prescription is retained at the doctor's surgery. I can see that such an arrangement might help in the monitoring of the doctor's prescribing practice and in the investigation of individual prescriptions if the need arose. However, if a record of the prescription exists at the PPA, the need for this is limited. In British Columbia, the third copy was sent for entry into a central monitoring database. That would not be necessary in the UK if all controlled drug prescriptions, both NHS and private, were sent to the PPA. However, if the HODI were of the view that it would be of real benefit for it to receive a copy of every prescription or requisition for a controlled drug, a duplicate pad would be appropriate.

14.78 Whichever form is chosen, some arrangement will have to be made for the distribution of the stationery. At present, this is done by PCTs but, if prescription pads also have to be issued to doctors practising solely in the private sector, some other means of distribution will have to be found. The DoH or the Healthcare Commission are possibilities. If, in the future, there were to be a controlled drugs inspectorate, that would be the appropriate body to issue the forms. Only doctors who need to prescribe controlled drugs for clinical practice would be entitled to receive such pads. A controlled drugs inspectorate would be best placed to ensure that that occurred. I will recommend that the information on private prescriptions for controlled drugs should be received by the PPA so that it can be processed by them and thereafter monitored locally by PCTs, regionally by the controlled drugs inspectorate, and/or nationally by the Healthcare Commission.

14.79 Recognising that systems will allow for all information recorded on a prescription to be read and analysed, the question then arises as to what extra information, not already mentioned above, should appear on a controlled drug prescription form and does not currently appear.

Should a Prescription for a Controlled Drug Bear the Time as well as the Date of Issue?

14.80　The idea that a controlled drug prescription should bear the time of issue as well as the date arose because Shipman was able to prescribe controlled drugs in the names of certain patients after those patients had died. If the time of issue of the prescription had been recorded, it would have been relatively easy to establish that he knew that the patient was already dead at the time he issued or presented the prescription. Such information would aid the detection of dishonest practice and might also act as a deterrent.

14.81　While many respondents were unsure as to what such a requirement would achieve, the written response of Boots the Chemists (Boots) recognised the potential benefit of such a requirement, stating that it would assist in any investigation of what was thought to be suspicious practice. Boots did, however, also point out that, for handwritten prescriptions, such a requirement might prove detrimental if accidental omission at the time of issue delayed the pharmacist in dispensing the prescription. Boots suggested that a solution might be to permit dispensing if a prescription was clinically correct and to make it the responsibility of the PCT to deal with any administrative errors.

Conclusion

14.82　I do not think it necessary to require the time of prescribing to be entered on handwritten prescriptions. This would add to the doctor's burden without producing any great benefit save in a tiny minority of cases. However, since computer systems have an in-built clock, I think it would be sensible if, when generation by computer is permitted, the time of issue were to be printed on all computer generated controlled drug prescriptions. In a fully computerised system, it would also be possible to record the time at which a prescription for a controlled drug was dispensed at the pharmacy. The computerised recording of information such as this would not add to the burden on the doctor or pharmacist and would serve as a useful investigative tool for the police and HODI inspectors in investigating cases of illicit obtaining of controlled drugs. It would, for example, have been invaluable in the investigation of Shipman's offences.

What Information about the Prescriber Should Appear on the Prescription Form?

14.83　At present, a prescription has to contain the full name and address (within the UK) of the prescriber. As I mentioned in Chapter Six, a NHS prescription also carries the individual prescriber code of the doctor to whom the pad of prescriptions has been issued, as well as details of the PCT within whose area the doctor practises. The individual prescriber code is an identifying number, which allows the PPA's computer system to allocate the prescription to a particular prescriber. It is not the prescriber's GMC registration number. A private prescription does not require a prescribing number and need not contain the doctor's GMC registration number. The question asked in the Discussion Paper was whether all private and NHS prescriptions for controlled drugs should contain the professional registration number of the prescriber.

14.84　There was very strong support for this suggestion among the respondents to the Discussion Paper. Many felt that there should be parity between the requirements for prescribing within the NHS and privately.

14.85   During the seminars, I was reminded that the doctor who signs a NHS prescription is not necessarily the doctor whose details, which include the individual prescriber code, are printed on the prescription. Sometimes, doctors working within the same practice will use each other's prescription pads. Some doctors working in general practice do not have a pad of their own. For example, a GP registrar (trainee) does not have his/her own pad and uses the pad of one of the principals in the practice. Similarly, a locum or salaried GP assistant does not have a personal pad. Prescriptions issued by deputising doctors bear the individual prescriber code of the doctor with whom the patient is registered. There are three significant consequences of these arrangements, which, I understand, may soon change. A doctor with a portfolio practice, who works as a locum and possibly for a deputising service, cannot audit his/her own personal prescribing; nor can s/he produce his/her personal data for the purposes of appraisal. Of greater importance perhaps is that, if such a doctor were a 'rogue' prescriber of a certain drug, this could not be identified by prescribing analysis and cost (PACT) data. Third, the prescribing data of the GP principal whose pad is used by a locum or registrar does not accurately reflect his/her prescribing practice; the data is 'blurred' by the inclusion of prescriptions issued by other doctors. This latter point is of some importance as the scrutiny of prescribing data is now an important aspect of the clinical governance of GPs, a topic I shall discuss in greater detail in the Fifth Report.

14.86   Dr Gerada mentioned that, when she issues a prescription for a patient registered with another doctor, it comes out of the printer, not in her name but in the name of the doctor with whom the patient is registered. The result is that her personal PACT data and those of her partners are inaccurate. Later in the discussion, she was told that it would be possible to adjust the computer to correct this situation. However, if this is happening in Dr Gerada's practice, it may well be happening in others. Dr Gerada and Dr James Robertson, a GP and a member of the ACMD, both stressed that the real usefulness of PACT data was to focus on the prescribing of the group of doctors in a practice rather than of individuals. Once the group saw its collective figures, its members would examine the position internally and correct any anomalies. That is all very well and I am sure that this happens in many practices. However, there are two reasons why it is not satisfactory to rely on internal control. First, abnormal prescribing practice by one member of a group of, say, six doctors may well be concealed within the global figures; if only one member of the group is prescribing abnormal amounts of diamorphine and the rest are prescribing slightly less than average, the collective data may appear quite normal. Second, collective data may have been perfectly adequate to monitor the spending habits of a practice but it cannot be of value where one of the main objectives is to monitor an individual doctor's clinical practice.

14.87   During the discussion, I pointed out that, if prescribing data were to be used for the purposes of clinical governance and/or revalidation, it would have to be prepared on an individual basis to be of any use at all. Everyone seemed to recognise that, at present, the individual data is not at all accurate. Apart from the reasons I have already mentioned, there is another. In many practices, the doctors will take turns to be the 'duty' doctor for the signing of large numbers of repeat prescriptions. He or she will sign these possibly on his/her own pad or possibly on the pad of another doctor and, often, without having any real clinical input into the choice of medication. He or she will check to make sure the prescription seems reasonable but that is all. Such an arrangement means that the individual prescribing data of the doctors concerned are inaccurate. The data shows only the collective picture.

14.88 The participants recognised the potential importance of accurate personal prescribing data for the purposes of clinical governance, including the monitoring of the use of controlled drugs. I have learned of two ways in which the problems of inaccurate data might be tackled. At the seminars, Dr Smith explained that a new system of dealing with repeat prescriptions had been successfully piloted in several areas and would soon be put into general operation. Under this system, a doctor who wishes to prescribe medication on a long-term basis will write a prescription to provide for periodic consignments over a period of up to a year. The patient will leave the prescription at the pharmacy of his/her choice, will collect the drugs every few weeks and need not return to the surgery until the expiry of the prescription. The pharmacist will be responsible for reviewing the appropriateness of the continuing supplies dispensed under the prescription during its currency. Not only will this system save a great deal of time for GPs, it will, as Dr Smith pointed out, allow greater accuracy of the prescribing data because the whole quantity supplied under the prescription will be attributed to the doctor who made the original decision. Dr Esmail has told me that, in his practice, the doctors have adopted a system whereby a doctor who wishes to prescribe a drug for a substantial period will issue a prescription for, say, a month's supply and will, at the same time, authorise the issue of repeat prescriptions for a further period of up to six months. Any repeat prescriptions issued under that authority will be assigned to the doctor who issued the initial prescription. When the authority expires, if the patient seeks further supplies, a doctor ought to give full consideration to the appropriateness and dosage of the drug s/he is to prescribe, which may cover the next six months. If this is done, the accuracy of the prescribing data is ensured.

14.89 After listening to the discussion about the inaccuracy of individual prescribing data, Professor Baker expressed the view that the best solution might be to ensure that all prescribers had their own prescription pads and that they contained their unique GMC (or other professional registration) number. The professional registration number could also be applied to private prescriptions.

14.90 Ms Christine Dalton, Director of Pharmaceutical Policy and Services at the PPA, supported the idea that, for the sake of accuracy, prescribers should not use each other's pads or each other's individual prescriber code. Initially, she said that the PPA would not welcome the use of a GMC registration number. There are more digits in a GMC number than in an individual prescriber code. As all data has to be keyed in by hand, any increase in the number of keystrokes to be made has a significant financial impact. However, this will not matter for long, as the PPA is installing a system whereby prescription forms will be scanned into the computer. When that comes about, as it is intended to do between 2005 and 2007, the additional digits will present no problem. Evidence received earlier from the PPA was to the effect that it would be quite practicable for the PPA to process private prescriptions provided they were on a form that was similar in size, weight and layout to the existing FP10.

Conclusion

14.91 The discussion I have just described related to prescriptions for all prescription only medicines, not just controlled drugs. From the point of view of the Inquiry, whose interest is at present focussed mainly on the latter, it seems to me to be vital that all controlled drug prescriptions, whether NHS or private, should be accurately attributable to the prescriber who made the decision to issue. Without that, any attempt at monitoring for abnormal prescribing is likely to have limited success. In my view, the best means of achieving this is by ensuring that all prescribers use their own prescription pad, marked with their professional registration number.

14.92 For the wider issues of clinical governance, it is also, in my view, important to collect accurate individual prescribing data relating to all prescription only drugs. I shall recommend that all prescribers should use only their own pads marked with their own professional registration numbers. Once long-term prescriptions have taken the place of frequent repeat prescriptions, individual prescribing data should then be much more accurate. When electronic prescribing becomes a reality, as I am sure it eventually will, some means must be found of applying an electronic signature, associated with the prescriber's registration number. I do not think that will be difficult.

Should the Number of Days' Treatment or the Amount of Controlled Drugs Covered by a Single Prescription Be Limited?

14.93 The possibility of introducing a limitation on the amount of a controlled drug that may be prescribed on a single prescription was raised as a potential mechanism for reducing the risk of diversion. The Prescribing Support Unit report entitled 'Audit of Controlled Drugs Prescribing in England for the Financial Year 2002/03' identified the routine prescribing of abnormally high quantities of controlled drugs on individual prescription forms.

14.94 There was broad consensus among respondents to the Discussion Paper that it would be appropriate to limit the period of time covered by a single prescription for controlled drugs to a supply sufficient to last for 28 days.

14.95 At the seminars, Dr Grenville, for the BMA, said that he would be very loath to prescribe amounts of a controlled drug intended for a long period. He recognised that they might be traded. Dr Gerada and Dr Grenville drew attention to the fact that many patients holiday abroad for long periods and some even go abroad to die. They felt that flexibility was required. However, Mr Macfarlane pointed out that to take a substantial quantity of controlled drugs abroad would breach UK export controls, unless a licence was obtained; it might also breach the law of the receiving country. It would be acceptable to take, say, two weeks' personal supply abroad without a licence but to take three months' supply would be unlawful.

14.96 Dr Smith said that, subject to the problem of patients going overseas, the DoH would support the idea of a 28 day limit. To restrict supplies to any greater extent might impinge on patient care and cause unacceptable inconvenience. In the view of the DoH, however, it was also very important to distinguish between the drugs listed in the various Schedules; so, for example, while 28 days should be the norm for Schedule 2 drugs, the DoH would not want to see the period restricted to 28 days in the case of Schedule 5 products. Dr Smith said that, although some people question the utility of a lot of Schedule 5 products, there is no doubt that many people find them beneficial for chronic mild to moderate pain. To limit the period of time covered by prescriptions for such products would put unwarranted burdens on patients, prescribers and pharmacists.

14.97 Some respondents involved in palliative care were opposed to the proposal that a limit should be placed on the amount of a drug, such as diamorphine, that can be prescribed on one prescription. However, Mr Rudd, from Macmillan Cancer Relief, who had consulted quite widely on the issue, said that the consensus among those to whom he had spoken was that a limit of 28 days' supply was a reasonable compromise between the competing interests of convenience and security.

Conclusion

14.98 I see the force of Dr Smith's observation about Schedule 5 products and do not think that there is any reason why the amounts to be supplied on a single prescription need be limited. These are, by definition, products which are relatively unlikely to be abused or diverted. With controlled drugs from Schedules 2–4, I think that it would be appropriate to limit the period of time to be covered by a single prescription to 28 days. The evidence suggests that there is a substantial leakage of drugs such as the benzodiazepines onto the illicit market from patients for whom the drugs have been prescribed, presumably in greater quantities than they actually needed. Although doctors are urged to prescribe modest amounts and not to allow patients to take such drugs on a long-term basis, it appears that many doctors continue to prescribe quite large amounts.

14.99 As for patients who wish to spend the winter abroad and take a personal supply of controlled drugs in any of Schedules 2–4 with them, it would appear that it would be unlawful for them to do so without obtaining a licence. If such patients are granted a licence, they can obtain the appropriate quantity under the terms of the licence and export it lawfully. Presumably, the supply would have to be purchased from a wholesaler and paid for; it would not be available under the NHS. Alternatively, the patient might have to make arrangements to receive a supply on prescription in the country in which s/he wished to stay.

Should the Period of Validity of a Controlled Drug Prescription Be Further Limited?

14.100 At present, a pharmacist may not supply a controlled drug in Schedule 2 or 3 to the MDR 2001 on a prescription later than 13 weeks after the date specified in the prescription. The Discussion Paper asked whether this period should be reduced.

14.101 There was broad agreement among respondents and participants at the seminars that 13 weeks is far too long for a controlled drug prescription to be held by the patient before presentation. There is a risk that the prescription will fall into the wrong hands. If a patient really needs a controlled drug, s/he will present the prescription long before 13 weeks have passed. In British Columbia, the period has been reduced to five days and Dr Brian Taylor said that this has not given rise to any problems. Many respondents and some participants were in favour of reducing the period to 7 or 14 days but the majority favoured a period of 28 days, as a compromise between the interests of security on the one hand and convenience to patients on the other.

Conclusion

14.102 I agree with the general view that 13 weeks is far too long for a controlled drug prescription to remain valid before presentation. Although I see the advantage of reducing the period of validity to 7 days, I have come, in the end, to see 28 days as a reasonable compromise.

Relaxation of the Rule Prohibiting Pharmacists from Dispensing other than in Direct Accordance with the Prescription

14.103 At present, the effect of the rules for the form and content of many controlled drug prescriptions is that a pharmacist is not permitted to dispense other than in strict accordance with the prescription. Any alteration must be effected by the prescriber in his/her own handwriting. The Discussion Paper asked whether this rule should be relaxed in the case of handwritten prescriptions and, if so, to what extent and with what alternative safeguards in place.

14.104 The question was raised because of concern expressed by pharmacists. Miss Lavin said that community pharmacists often receive prescriptions which are technically defective but where the intention of the prescriber is clear. In such circumstances, the pharmacist will usually try to speak to the doctor to arrange for an amended prescription to be provided. However, it is not always possible to make contact and, even when it is, doctors are sometimes unwilling to co-operate in the correction of a technical error. The RPSGB advises pharmacists that they should act in the best interests of the patient. In such circumstances, they should adopt a pragmatic approach. If the patient needs the medication without delay and if the pharmacist is not in doubt about the prescriber's intention, the RPSGB advises that s/he should dispense the prescription and ask the prescriber to amend it retrospectively. Miss Lavin acknowledged that the RPSGB may thereby be advising pharmacists to break the law. The Society would like to see some official relaxation of the rule so that pharmacists could amend a defective prescription themselves, where they were certain of the prescriber's intent, possibly without the need to ask the prescriber to ratify the amendment afterwards. Mrs Roberts would also welcome such a relaxation of the existing rule.

14.105 Mr D'Arcy, for the NPA, supported the position of the RPSGB. He emphasised that pharmacists face a real, not just a theoretical, risk of prosecution if they dispense prescriptions that do not comply with the MDR 2001.

14.106 Mrs Roberts described another kind of situation in which a pharmacist may have a genuine need to disobey the instructions given on a prescription. A drug dependent patient might arrive at a pharmacy to take an instalment dose of methadone which has been validly prescribed. The pharmacist might realise that the patient is not in a fit state to take the drug. He or she is then in a dilemma. If s/he gives the drug, s/he might harm the patient; if s/he refuses, arguably s/he is in breach of his/her duty to dispense the drug.

Similarly, a drug dependent patient, receiving a certain quantity of methadone every day, might fail to attend for several days. If s/he then turns up, demanding the usual dose, the pharmacist might be concerned that the amount prescribed is too great, given the break in treatment. Mrs Roberts said that, in such cases, the pharmacist should be able to make a clinical judgement as to what to do and should not be bound to dispense in accordance with the terms of the prescription.

Conclusion

14.107 In my view, there should be some relaxation of the law so as to allow a pharmacist to exercise his/her discretion whether to dispense a defective prescription for controlled drugs, where the intention of the prescriber is clear. In such a case, the pharmacist should be able to amend the prescription so that it complies with the MDR 2001. I do not see why there should be any need for the pharmacist to send the prescription back to the prescriber for ratification. Miss Lavin said that some doctors are unwilling to co-operate with pharmacists by correcting errors; certainly, to do so increases their workload. In my view, provided that the pharmacist is satisfied that the intention of the prescriber is clear, that the defect is only technical and that the pharmacist is content to make the correction and take professional responsibility for dispensing the drug, that should be sufficient. The exercise of such discretion is appropriate, given the professional status of pharmacists. I envisage that the increased use of computer generated prescriptions would reduce the incidence of technical prescribing errors.

14.108 Mrs Roberts raised the more general issue of whether a pharmacist should be able to exercise his/her discretion to refuse to dispense a prescription either in strict accordance with the terms of the prescription or at all. I am not sure that the legal position is entirely clear, where a pharmacist refuses to dispense a prescription or declines to administer an instalment dose. It seems to me that it should be a usual part of a pharmacist's professional duty to refuse to dispense or administer any controlled drug if, in the pharmacist's professional judgement, refusal to do so would be in the patient's best interests.

Should the Prescription Record the Condition for Which a Drug is Prescribed? To What Information about the Patient Should a Pharmacist Have Access?

14.109 At the moment, there is no requirement for a prescription to carry an indication of the medical condition for which the medication is prescribed. The only place where that is recorded is in the patient's GP records. Pharmacists do not have access to those records at present. In Chapter Seven, I explained why pharmacists are of the view that they ought to know the nature of the condition for which a drug has been prescribed. Only then can they apply their expertise to the issues of whether the prescribed drug and its dosage are appropriate.

14.110 The question was raised for discussion at the seminars. Mr D'Arcy, for the NPA, favoured the suggestion that pharmacists should know for what condition a drug has been prescribed. He emphasised that pharmacists are increasingly assuming an enhanced role in patient care. They try to ensure that patients get the best from the medicines they take. Mr D'Arcy said that understanding why a patient is taking a medicine (not just a controlled drug) can help in that process. Understanding the purpose of the drug would help the pharmacist to decide whether the drug and dosage prescribed were appropriate and would operate as a check against the inappropriate use of controlled drugs. Mr D'Arcy acknowledged that a requirement to state the nature of the patient's condition on the prescription would give rise to issues of patient confidentiality but said that the NPA was, nonetheless, supportive of such a requirement. Issues of confidentiality also arise in the context of the NHS Care Record at present proposed by the DoH. Mr D'Arcy said that, when such electronic records are brought into use, pharmacists should have access to them for the purpose of finding out for what condition medication has been prescribed.

14.111 For similar reasons to those given by Mr D'Arcy, Mr Rutherford, Head of Medicines Management at Bristol North PCT, was also in favour of the idea that the patient's condition should appear on a prescription. He considered that pharmacists need to know the nature of the patient's condition in all cases, and particularly when the prescription is issued privately.

14.112 Miss Lavin, for the RPSGB, supported the idea but raised a practical concern. She said the Society would not wish pharmacists to be compelled to require such information before a prescription could be dispensed. In other words, the Society would not want another requirement to be introduced if it was unlikely to be met by doctors, resulting in yet more prescriptions that might have to be queried or returned by pharmacists.

14.113 There was a good deal of opposition to the proposal, mainly because of perceived problems of patient confidentiality. Dr Smith said that there had been a spread of views within the DoH team, but they had come down against the proposal because, while paper prescriptions remain in use, there would be a danger that the patient's medical condition would become known to anyone who saw a prescription. However, Dr Smith pointed out that, when the NHS Care Record is introduced, the patient's diagnosis will be available to pharmacists who have access to the record. He did not doubt the value of the information to the pharmacist and the contribution that could be made to patient safety by providing it.

14.114 Mr Rudd, for Macmillan Cancer Relief, had canvassed the views of a number of patients and frontline carers to discover their reaction to the suggestion. One patient who suffered from ovarian cancer did not want her condition to be known to the young part-time assistant in the pharmacy in the village in which she lived, because the assistant was in the same class at school as the patient's daughter. However, she would have been quite happy for the information to be passed direct to the pharmacist via a computer connection.

14.115 Dr Grenville, for the BMA, supported the idea that the pharmacist should know the nature of the patient's condition, but he said that this should happen only if the patient had been told what the diagnosis was and had consented to the disclosure of that information to the pharmacist. He thought that many patients would consent if the reason was explained to them. Dr Taylor told me that, although the facility to provide this information is available in British Columbia, it is rarely used by doctors there.

Conclusion

14.116 The potential benefit that could accrue to a patient if a community pharmacist had access to information about the patient's condition is well recognised. The main objection arises on the ground of patient confidentiality. I discussed some of the issues in Chapter Seven. I noted that a patient's GP records are seen by the staff at his/her GP's surgery and the patient's consent is not sought for that disclosure. GPs could not operate effectively unless their staff were allowed to see patient records. Similarly, hospital records are seen by all members of the clinical team, including nurses and pharmacists (and inevitably some administrative staff), without reference to the patient. These groups of people who have access to the records are under a duty not to disclose confidential matters but they are allowed to exchange information within the group for the purpose of providing clinical care. I cannot see any reason why a community pharmacist should be in any less favourable a position to advise the patient than a hospital pharmacist. However, I can understand why some patients might feel unhappy about a particular member of staff in a community pharmacy seeing a prescription that described the nature of their condition. I understand that it might be difficult for some patients to use a different pharmacy where they are not known.

14.117 In my view, if it were explained to patients why it was for their benefit that the pharmacist should know for what condition their medication had been prescribed, most would consent to the pharmacist being given the information on the prescription. I see no reason why there should not be a space on the prescription form for a brief description of the patient's condition which should be completed if the patient consents. In other words, I agree with Dr Grenville. I would add that, because completion of the box would not be compulsory, a pharmacist would not be prevented from dispensing the medication just because it had not been completed. When the NHS Care Record is introduced, I hope that pharmacists will be given access to the common spine so that they will be able to find out the nature of the condition for which any medication has been prescribed.

14.118 I mention in passing that, if the patient's condition had appeared on prescriptions in the past, it would have been much more difficult for Shipman to obtain 30mg ampoules of diamorphine, as he did in 1993. He repeatedly prescribed 30mg diamorphine as a single dose for patients who were apparently opioid-naïve and for whom such a dose would have been fatal. He would have been discouraged from obtaining the drug in this way had he been required to record a diagnosis that was either inconsistent with what he had written in the patient's medical records, inconsistent with the patient's true condition or inappropriate for the administration of diamorphine. However, I would not have made any recommendation for change for that reason alone. I make it because I believe that information which helps a pharmacist to assess the correctness of a prescription is of benefit to patients.

General Practitioners' Controlled Drugs Registers

Should General Practitioners Have to Keep a Controlled Drugs Register? If So, What Should the Requirements Be?

14.119 In Chapter Five, I explained that the MDR 2001 require a GP who keeps a stock of Schedule 2 controlled drugs to maintain a CDR. At present, the CDR must comply with the requirements of Schedule 6; it must be in paper form and must record all transactions by which controlled drugs are obtained or supplied. I also explained that, nowadays, many GPs have a poor understanding of their duties with regard to the CDR and regret the lack of any advice on the subject. Police CIOs do not inspect GPs' CDRs. Until 1991, regional medical officers (RMOs) used to inspect GPs' CDRs but many GPs have not had their CDRs examined since then. As there has been virtually no inspection of GPs' arrangements for the keeping of controlled drugs and their CDRs for some years now, the Discussion Paper questioned whether it was necessary or appropriate for GPs to be under a continuing obligation to keep a CDR. At paragraph 5.31, I mentioned that the requirement to keep a CDR would not deter a dishonest doctor from keeping an illicit supply of a controlled drug; nor would inspection of the CDR of a dishonest doctor necessarily reveal the existence of illicit supplies.

14.120 Respondents to the Discussion Paper were almost universally of the view that GPs should be required to keep a CDR if they kept a stock of controlled drugs. No one doubted its usefulness. The view was that there should be a common format for paper CDRs and it should be permissible for a GP to keep an electronic CDR. Some GP respondents mentioned the lack of inspection of their CDRs. The Council of the Independent Doctors Forum reported that, at a meeting of members, all members present said that they had maintained a CDR for many years but not one had ever had his/her CDR inspected.

14.121 Among respondents, there was also strong support for the suggestion that GPs within the same practice who shared the use of an emergency bag should be allowed to keep one CDR which identified who administered or otherwise disposed of the drugs.

14.122 At the seminars, there was universal acceptance that a CDR must be kept. Again, no one doubted its usefulness. Some participants felt that the requirements as to how the CDR should be kept should be flexible, so as to meet the needs of individual practices. Dr Grenville suggested that each GP practice should propose a standard operating procedure (SOP) for the use of controlled drugs, which would be adopted subject to the approval of the PCT or other body responsible for clinical governance. In some practices, doctors might wish to keep their own stocks, in which case they would have to keep their own CDRs; other practices might prefer to have a common stock and to share the use of an emergency bag. In such cases, a common CDR would be appropriate.

14.123 Mr Macfarlane said that, although in a group practice it seemed logical to keep a common stock of controlled drugs, he felt it was of paramount importance that each doctor in the practice should be personally accountable for the controlled drugs administered by him/her. The RPSGB agreed.

14.124 Dr Gerada, who has made a study of the use of controlled drugs in general practice, considered that, if a group practice were to maintain a central stock of controlled drugs, there should be a CDR for the central stock and each individual doctor's bag should have its own CDR. When a doctor took a drug from the central stock, that should be entered, presumably as a 'drug supplied' in the central CDR and as a 'drug obtained' in the CDR for the individual doctor's bag. Dr Grenville said that the practice where he had worked for much of his professional life had had such a system for over 20 years. Dr Gerada said that someone had to be responsible for physically checking the contents of the central stock periodically. This should be done weekly if controlled drugs were not often used but daily in the case of a busy out of hours service, where usage would be very frequent.

14.125 Professor Baker expressed the hope that an electronic system could be developed whereby a record would be made at each stage when a doctor removed a controlled drug from the surgery cabinet, placed it into his bag and administered it to a patient. Professor Baker acknowledged that there had to be a human element to such a system in that the drug stock had to be regularly checked against the electronic record.

14.126 Mr Macfarlane explained that, at present, commercial organisations providing out of hours services were licensed to hold controlled drugs and could supply them to the doctors employed by them. Proper records have to be kept and should be inspected by the HODI. Mr Macfarlane said that, in future, it was likely that the distinction between deputising services and co-operatives might become blurred. I think he must have had in mind the change by which, as from January 2005, PCTs will become responsible for the provision of out of hours services in their area and may choose to provide these services in a variety of different ways. Dr Grenville was asked to explain what happened at present, where GPs banded together into a co-operative to provide out of hours services. He said that the position was variable. In the co-operative for which he sometimes works, each doctor is expected to bring with him/her any Schedule 2 drugs that might be required and to be responsible for maintaining the necessary CDR.

14.127 On a slightly different but related topic, Dr Grenville suggested that a doctor should be required to obtain his/her stocks of controlled drugs from a nominated pharmacist or wholesaler. He was concerned that a doctor who intended to abuse controlled drugs could present requisitions at any number of pharmacies and this might well not be noticed by a CIO. Mrs Roberts and Dr Robertson explained that, in Scotland, there is a special form, a GP10A, on which GPs order controlled drugs for their bags for use within the NHS. This makes it possible for such requisitions to be monitored.

Conclusion

14.128 Despite the fact that the duty to keep a CDR will not deter a dishonest doctor from secreting an illicit supply of controlled drugs as Shipman did, it seems to me that the duty should be retained. Given the different practical arrangements that doctors may wish to make with regard to their individual and collective use of controlled drugs, I do not think it is sensible to suggest a 'one size fits all' procedure for the keeping of CDRs. Instead, a number of suitable SOPs should be drawn up from which an individual practice should be able to select the model most appropriate for its arrangements. Adherence to such SOPs should be mandatory and should be inspected on a regular basis.

14.129 I agree with Dr Gerada's view that, if a practice chooses to keep a joint stock of controlled drugs and to allow members of the practice to withdraw drugs for their personal bags, there must be a central CDR and a 'satellite' CDR for each bag. Any doctor working as a locum for a practice should be expected either to comply with the practice SOP or to make his/her personal arrangements to provide Schedule 2 drugs and to accept responsibility for keeping the necessary CDR. Whichever arrangement is adopted, all parties should be clear about where responsibility lies.

14.130 In my view, a doctor or practice should be able to choose whether to keep CDRs in paper or electronic form. In either event, the CDR should contain a running balance. All SOPs should specify the frequency with which the actual stock must be checked against the balance. In my view, it is desirable that responsibility for making such a physical check should be shared between all members of a practice, the practice manager and any registered nurses. It should certainly not be a duty assigned to any one person.

14.131 Advice as to compliance and best practice should be issued nationally and should also be available from PCT officers in the course of the annual clinical governance visit or review or at other times.

14.132 It is essential that, when new arrangements for the provision of out of hours services are made, there is complete clarity as to who is responsible for the provision of Schedule 2 drugs and for the keeping of the appropriate CDR. Here again, there should be an approved SOP and the capacity to monitor and enforce its provisions. I suggest that the Healthcare Commission (or, if it comes into being, the controlled drugs inspectorate) should be responsible for approving SOPs for GPs in private practice and for ensuring compliance.

14.133 I agree with the suggestion that the obtaining of controlled drugs on requisition should be better regulated. I think that requisitions should be written on the special form that I have suggested should be used for controlled drug prescriptions. The doctor could write on the prescription form that the drugs were required 'for practice use'. The requisition would be sent to the PPA and entered onto the database. The acquisition of the drugs would then show up in PACT data. Some doctors apparently buy their supplies direct from a wholesaler rather than a retail pharmacy. If that practice were to continue, wholesalers would have to be required to send the requisition forms to the PPA. Dr Grenville suggested that GPs or practices should purchase all controlled drugs stocks from a nominated pharmacist or wholesaler. Although, in itself, that is a sensible suggestion, I do not think such a restriction is necessary provided that all requisitions go to the PPA for analysis and that the doctors' complete controlled drugs data will be available for monitoring. Those monitoring the usage of controlled drugs will have to take account of the fact that some GPs order supplies for the use of all members of the practice.

Should the Dispensing of Controlled Drugs Be Confined to Specialist Pharmacies?

14.134 The question of whether the dispensing of controlled drugs should be confined to specialist pharmacies arose because there was some evidence before the Inquiry that many pharmacies were only rarely required to dispense controlled drugs in Schedule 2 and kept very few in stock. Accordingly, their staff had little experience of such drugs. There was a clear preponderance of opinion from respondents that all pharmacies should continue to be allowed to dispense all controlled drugs. The view of Macmillan Cancer Relief, expressed at the seminars by Mr Rudd, was that any reduction in the number of pharmacies allowed to supply controlled drugs would restrict patient choice. However, his organisation recognised the advantage to patients of the service of pharmacists with particular expertise in palliative care or the treatment of chronic degenerative diseases.

14.135 Dr Gerada said that she could see advantages in pharmacists developing special expertise in particular areas of work, such as the use of controlled drugs in the treatment of addiction or chronic pain. However, she was not suggesting that pharmacies or pharmacists without such special expertise should be prevented from dispensing controlled drugs. She thought it would cause problems for patients if there were to be any such restriction.

14.136 Mr Rutherford expressed a similar view, pointing out that, although the number of pharmacies specialising in palliative care was likely to grow, there would be a continuing need for patients to access controlled drugs from all NHS pharmacies. Dr Smith said that, although the DoH envisaged that pharmacies would become increasingly specialised, this would not be directed from the centre through regulation but would arise as the result of contractual arrangements made at local level.

14.137 Mr D'Arcy said that the NPA did not see the benefit of restricting the number of pharmacies able to dispense controlled drugs. He also envisaged problems if specialist pharmacies were created. He referred to the example of a pharmacy in north London which specialised in providing services for patients addicted to drugs. Mr D'Arcy commented that this had created substantial disruption to the pharmacy concerned and also to the local neighbourhood. Mr D'Arcy also highlighted the security issues that can arise if a pharmacy is known to be dealing with large quantities of controlled drugs.

Conclusion

14.138 It is clear, in my view, that the development of specialist expertise in the use of controlled drugs by some pharmacies will bring benefits to patients. However, the existence of pharmacies where specialist expertise is available is quite consistent with the continuing freedom of all pharmacies to dispense controlled drugs when called upon to do so. I accept that to restrict the right to dispense controlled drugs to a limited number of pharmacies would have an undesirable effect on patients' access to the drugs they need.

Pharmacy Controlled Drugs Registers

What Record Should Be Kept of the Identity of the Person Collecting Controlled Drugs from the Pharmacy?

14.139 Examination of the CDRs in which Shipman's prescriptions for diamorphine were recorded reveals no clue as to who had collected the drugs or as to whether that person was the patient, a relative or friend of the patient, a district nurse or Shipman himself. Under the present law, a person who collects certain poisons from a pharmacy has to sign the poisons book. A person who collects a controlled drug on requisition from a pharmacy on behalf of the doctor who has ordered it has to produce the signed authority of that doctor. My experience of trying to collect a parcel from a Royal Mail delivery office is that it will not be handed over without the production of some form of identification and the provision of a signature. By contrast, a person who collects a controlled drug which has been prescribed for a patient need produce no authority from the patient and no identification; nor is s/he required to sign any record.

14.140 The Discussion Paper posed the question whether a pharmacist should be required to obtain some proof of the identity of a person collecting a controlled drug dispensed on a prescription and/or to record the name of that person. If so, what type of identification would be appropriate? Where should the information be recorded?

14.141 A majority of respondents favoured a requirement that the pharmacist should obtain some proof of the identity of the person collecting controlled drugs and record the details. However, some concerns were expressed, mainly by pharmacists. Very few suggested that it would be unreasonable to expect the pharmacist to record the name of the collector or that it would be unreasonable to expect the collector to provide his/her name and address.

14.142 The main concern expressed by pharmacists was that many patients and their representatives do not carry any form of identification. It would be undesirable if a pharmacist were unable to supply a controlled drug urgently needed just because identification was not available. The Pharmaceutical Advisers Group said that it would not like to see pharmacists being held legally responsible for verifying a collector's identity. The RCN drew attention to the problem of 'rough sleepers' who may have no identification papers and whose signature or mark acknowledging receipt may have no practical value. A number of respondents said that a strict rule would be impracticable but that a requirement that pharmacists should use their discretion would be desirable.

14.143 Many respondents and participants took the view that doctors and other healthcare professionals collecting a controlled drug on behalf of a patient should be required, unless personally known to the pharmacist (as they often would be), to provide some form of photographic identification.

14.144 At the seminars, Mr Rutherford emphasised the need for some form of identification to be provided before a controlled drug was handed over. He stressed that the need for this was increasing because so many pharmacies were now being run by locums who could not be expected to have personal knowledge of their clientele, not even the doctors practising in the area. He thought that nowadays most people carried a driving licence with a photograph. He recognised that there would be some patients who could not provide any identification. In their case, he advocated the keeping of a photographic record of the patient in the pharmacy computer.

14.145 Mr Rudd supported the suggestion that some form of identification should be provided and that a record should be made of the name of the person who collected the drug and the nature of the identification provided. Mr D'Arcy agreed that identification was desirable but expressed concern that a pharmacist might not be able to dispense the drugs if no identification was forthcoming. Miss Lavin agreed with that but thought that, if the pharmacist could exercise discretion to dispense the drugs even though no identification had been produced, that concern would be allayed. It was generally accepted that, in many cases, the person collecting would be known to the pharmacist and the pharmacist would not need to see identification but would record in the CDR that the collector was 'known to me'.

Conclusion

14.146 In my view, it is wholly unsatisfactory that a person who is not known to a pharmacist should be able to collect a controlled drug without providing, at least, his/her name and address. Possession of a controlled drug without proper authority is a criminal offence. A requirement that a person collecting such a drug should produce some form of identification seems to me to be a valuable deterrent to wrongful collection. The recording of the name and address of a collector would be a valuable investigative tool if and when it appeared that a controlled drug had been diverted.

14.147 In the case of a controlled drug supply that has to be recorded in the CDR (i.e. the supply of a drug within Schedule 2), the pharmacist should be required, before agreeing to supply the drug, to ask the name and address of the person seeking to collect it. If the patient is collecting the drug him/herself, the pharmacist should record that fact in the CDR. If the collector is not the patient, the pharmacist should record his/her name and address in the CDR. The pharmacist should also be required to ask to see some form of identification, unless the person attending is personally known to him/her. The pharmacist should record the form of identification provided or should note that the person attending is personally known to him/her. If no identification is forthcoming, the pharmacist should have discretion to supply or withhold the drugs but, if the drugs are supplied, the pharmacist should record that no identification has been produced. Pharmacists should be very cautious about supplying a controlled drug to a person who is not known to them and has not produced identification. I recognise the possibility that a pharmacist who refuses to supply a controlled drug to a person who does not or cannot produce evidence of identity might be subjected to a threat of violence. In such circumstances, the pharmacist should not risk injury but should report the circumstances to the police.

14.148 Any person presenting a prescription or requisition for a controlled drug who claims to be a doctor or other healthcare professional, acting in his/her professional capacity and seeking to collect controlled drugs, should, if not known to the pharmacist, be required to produce identification, preferably his/her professional registration card. This might arise when a healthcare professional collects drugs for practice use purchased on requisition and also drugs prescribed for patients. The relevant information should be recorded in the CDR.

14.149 The discussion at the seminars related to drugs the supply of which has to be recorded in the CDR. However, there is a danger of diversion of other controlled drugs, particularly benzodiazepines. I think it would be too onerous to expect a pharmacist to demand identification in every case where drugs in Schedules 3 and 4 are dispensed. However, I see no reason why a collector should not be required to write and sign his/her name on the back of a FP10 or the new official form which I hope will soon be provided for controlled drug prescriptions. I do not think this would be too much to ask. At present, pharmacists have to ask persons presenting a NHS prescription to provide information about the patient's prescription charge exemption. If, as is usual, the same person presents the prescription and collects the drugs, only one signature will be needed. If a different person attends to collect the drugs, a further signature would be required but this would not take long.

Electronic Controlled Drugs Registers

14.150 In Chapter Seven, I explained some of the disadvantages arising from the CDR currently used in most pharmacies. One of these is that the CDR must be kept in hard copy form. The process of entering data is time consuming. To a large extent, the time is wasted because much of the same information is keyed into the computerised patient medication records (PMRs). If it were permissible to keep an electronic CDR, the CDR could be connected to the PMR. Time and effort would be saved.

14.151 In the Discussion Paper, the Inquiry asked whether pharmacists should be permitted to keep an electronic CDR in preference to one in hard copy. There was very wide support for that idea.

14.152 The question also arose whether an electronic pharmacy CDR might usefully be linked to a wholesaler's records so as to ensure that all controlled drugs which appear in the wholesaler's records as being delivered to the pharmacy were automatically entered into the 'drugs obtained' side of the pharmacy CDR. At present, a dishonest pharmacist can order and receive drugs and avoid entering them into the CDR. Mr Macfarlane expressed the hope that this linkage could be made. Several respondents to the Discussion Paper, however, including the RPSGB, expressed concern about the possible confidentiality implications a system such as this system might entail. At the seminars, Miss Lavin said that the RPSGB could support such a system provided that adequate safeguards were inserted to ensure that patients' details were not being shared with wholesalers. I do not see that that will present a problem, as the linkage would be between the wholesaler's records and the 'drugs obtained' section of the CDR.

14.153 The Discussion Paper also raised a number of other issues related to more sophisticated methods of connected electronic record keeping. I have mentioned earlier the DoH's proposals for a NHS Care Record and for the electronic transmission of prescriptions between surgeries and pharmacies. At the seminars, great enthusiasm was expressed about these proposals. I have already said that it seems to me that many benefits would accrue from such a system. Mr Macfarlane also described the benefits of electronic linkage of controlled drugs prescribing information held by doctors with that held by pharmacies, wholesalers and producers. I observe only that I can see real benefits in a system which, at a stroke, allows the simultaneous sending of dispensing information back to the prescriber's surgery, to the PPA, into the CDR and to the pharmacy's stock ordering system.

Conclusion

14.154 I think that the use of electronic CDRs should be permitted. Their use would save much time and would facilitate inspection and monitoring. I also think it would be useful if pharmacy CDRs were linked to the electronic systems of wholesale suppliers of controlled drugs in order to minimise the risk of diversion.

Should the Controlled Drugs Register Contain Details of Drugs other than Those in Schedule 2?

14.155 At present, only transactions involving drugs in Schedule 2 are required to be recorded in the CDR. The Discussion Paper invited views as to whether, if and when electronic CDRs were in general use, this requirement could usefully be extended to controlled drugs in other Schedules. The Inquiry had recognised that it would be far too onerous to expect a pharmacist to record in handwriting the very large number of supplies of drugs within Schedules 3 and 4.

14.156 Responses to these questions were very mixed. Several respondents questioned the value of such a requirement. Others acknowledged that many controlled drugs within Schedules 3 and 4, such as the benzodiazepines, are commonly abused and thought that improved auditing of the use of such drugs would be of benefit.

14.157 At the seminar, Mr D'Arcy explained that the issue was one of balancing the importance of improved audit of the drugs in Schedules 3 and 4 against the increased work the requirement would impose on pharmacists and those charged with auditing the information collected. However, he accepted that, if, in future, there were to be a fully integrated electronic network, which included a CDR, there would be no additional work for the pharmacist if transactions in drugs within Schedules 3 and 4 had to be entered in the CDR. I think he also accepted that, even before the fully integrated network is in place, if a pharmacy had a computerised CDR linked to its PMRs, there would not be much additional work if the CDR requirements were extended to drugs in Schedules 3 and 4. Underlying his contribution was the point that the information is worth collecting only if it is going to be used.

14.158 Mr Macfarlane supported the idea with enthusiasm. He looks forward to the introduction of a fully integrated computerised system, including a CDR, because this will allow greatly improved audit and control; it will also make it easier to detect theft or diversion of controlled drugs by pharmacy staff. Mr Macfarlane also explained that the Home Office hopes to be able to simplify the categorisation of controlled drugs into Schedules and thereby to streamline the application of the Regulations. In a post-seminar response, Miss Lavin said that the RPSGB would welcome reorganisation of the Schedules so as to reflect more accurately the degree of risk associated with each controlled drug and to group each drug logically with its prescription, recording and storage requirements.

Conclusion

14.159 For the time being, it would not be feasible to extend the CDR requirements beyond their present scope. However, if and when electronic CDRs come into general use, it plainly would be feasible for all controlled drugs transactions to be subject to recording requirements. Whether it would be worthwhile collecting and analysing this data is, as Mr D'Arcy said, a balancing exercise. Plainly the cost of analysis would be considerable. I cannot express a view. However, it can be worth collecting data even if it is not analysed because the information can be useful in an investigation if the need arises. I can understand why Mr Macfarlane considers that the process would be worthwhile.

14.160 It is beyond the scope of this Inquiry to make recommendations relating to the rationalisation of the categorisation of controlled drugs into Schedules. However, I confess that I was delighted to hear from Mr Macfarlane that there exists a proposal to simplify the categorisation and to streamline the regulatory framework. I have personally found it difficult to grasp the intricacies of the Regulations. I recognise that pharmacists, who deal with them on a daily basis, do have a full understanding. But I am sure there must be many people, such as doctors and police officers, who need some knowledge of the Regulations, who find them very complicated to digest and difficult to remember. I think there is scope for simplification and, in a post-seminar response, the RPSGB has indicated that it would welcome a more logical grouping of controlled drugs. In my view, the essential criterion should be, 'How great a social evil is the misuse of this drug?' If great, strong regulatory measures are needed. If modest, less regulation is required.

Should the Controlled Drugs Register Contain a Running Balance?

14.161 During the oral evidence, I had been told that some pharmacists took the view that, under the existing Regulations, it was not permissible to include a running balance in the CDR. Others, such as those in charge of pharmacies in the ASDA stores, consider themselves free to use a form of register that includes the provision of a running balance. Among respondents to the Discussion Paper, there was strong support for the proposal that a running balance should be included in a pharmacy CDR. For example, CIOs supported the proposal; such a record would make the task of inspection easier and more effective.

14.162 There was, however, some resistance to the suggestion, particularly from the NPA. In its written response, the NPA said that a requirement to record a running balance would be of only limited value. Moreover, if the keeping of a running balance of controlled drug stocks were a legal or professional requirement on pharmacy owners and pharmacists, this would impose a disproportionate burden. The balance would have to be adjusted for every receipt and every supply, doubling the number of entries to be made.

14.163 Concern was also expressed by some respondents about the possibility that minor inaccuracies in the recording of stock might lead to prosecution of the pharmacist involved for technical breaches of the Regulations where the pharmacist was not at fault. Others raised concerns about the difficulty of keeping an accurate record of the stock of viscous fluids, which are not easily measured with accuracy. It appears that it is usual practice for manufacturers or wholesale suppliers to supply slightly more of a liquid preparation than the bottle officially contains. This is described as 'overage'. It was suggested that a pharmacist might find him/herself in difficulty if left with 'overage'.

14.164 At the seminars, Mr Macfarlane expressed strong support for the proposal that a running balance should be kept. He recognised some practical problems, particularly those to be encountered when the balance was first introduced, but felt that these could be overcome. He felt that the benefits would far outweigh any difficulties. It was clear, however, that he envisaged that a running balance would be a feature of an electronic CDR, rather than one kept on hard copy.

14.165 Miss Lavin said that the RPSGB fully supported the inclusion of a running balance in all CDRs, whether kept on paper or electronically. She spoke of the advantages to the audit process. She had personal experience of working in a hospital and said that running balances are always kept in hospital pharmacies. She had been amazed to discover that this was not so in community pharmacies. She said that the practical problems relating to overage and the measuring of viscous fluids were very minor and pragmatic solutions could be found. For example, in hospital pharmacies, any overage was written off and the register countersigned.

14.166 Mr D'Arcy raised another concern of the NPA, that, for registers kept in paper form, the keeping of a running balance would be extremely complicated because pharmacists would have to have a separate page for every form or size of ampoule of every controlled drug. So, for example, a pharmacist might have to keep as many as 36 separate sections for morphine sulphate products alone. However, Miss Lavin made the point that this problem was more theoretical than real. Most pharmacists stocked only the drugs that the local doctors regularly prescribed and she did not think that the number of separate sections to be used would present a problem. Mr D'Arcy accepted that his example had been extreme but he remained concerned about the practicalities of keeping a running balance in a paper CDR. He was more sanguine about its introduction onto an electronic register.

14.167 Mrs Roberts, who has had some years' experience of keeping a running balance in a hard copy CDR, and is enthusiastic about the usefulness of such a balance, gave a number of examples of the ways in which minor practical difficulties can be overcome.

14.168 Mr Macfarlane concluded by saying that it would be a simple matter to amend the existing legislation to make it clear that it would be permissible to keep a running balance in the CDR. Then, as an interim measure, it could be made plain that it would be regarded as good practice to keep such a balance. When electronic CDRs are in general use, it could then become a requirement to keep a running balance.

14.169 In a post-seminar response, the NPA raised another objection to the introduction of running balances and reiterated several of the points already discussed. The new point related to the burdensome nature of the procedures that would have to be gone through every time there was a change in the pharmacist on duty. It was said that there would have to be a full audit of all controlled drugs. Following receipt of that response, the Inquiry invited ASDA to comment on the experience of its pharmacies operating a CDR with a running balance. ASDA said that the current version of its CDR, which has been in use for about a year, has caused very few problems. It provides a running balance and a column to record the name of the person collecting the drugs. ASDA pharmacies do not carry out an audit every time there is a change of pharmacist but check the running balance every week. In that way, any discrepancy is discovered and corrected quickly. ASDA reported that the keeping of a running balance has resulted in the detection of a locum pharmacist who was manipulating the records and had stolen a large number of amphetamine tablets from a number of different ASDA pharmacies.

14.170 In a post-seminar response, Miss Lavin answered some of the objections raised by the NPA. She said that the keeping of a running balance is not found to be unduly onerous by the many pharmacies who do this on a voluntary basis. These include all hospital pharmacies and many 'multiples'. She said that, in New Zealand, the keeping of a running balance is standard practice. She expressed the view that the keeping of a running balance should be a statutory requirement, and not just a professional obligation on doctors and pharmacists. She also said that, in her view, it was not unduly onerous to conduct an audit each time there was a change of pharmacist on duty. Such an audit should be regarded as best practice.

Conclusion

14.171 There is general agreement that the maintenance of a running balance is a valuable tool in the audit of controlled drugs. The experience of those who have kept a running balance suggests that the practical difficulties that some respondents foresee are not as great as is feared. I do not think that the introduction of a requirement to keep running balances for Schedule 2 controlled drugs would be unduly burdensome, even while paper CDRs are still being used. However, it would seem to me that a sensible way to proceed would be for the Home Office to make it plain that, far from there being any official objection to the keeping of a running balance, such a procedure should be regarded as good practice. The RPSGB should publicise the new position. When electronic CDRs have come into general use, the keeping of such a balance should become compulsory. By then, as Mr Macfarlane observed, pharmacists would be prepared for the change.

Should the Controlled Drugs Register Contain the Professional Registration Number of the Prescriber?

14.172 At present, the name of the person prescribing a controlled drug is recorded in the CDR. If the prescriber is a local doctor and if the pharmacist's writing is clear, it will usually be easy to identify the prescriber. However, if the doctor is not a local practitioner or if his/her name is a common one or if the pharmacist's writing is not easy to decipher, it might not be possible subsequently to identify the prescriber of a controlled drug from the entry in the CDR. It is important for inspection and investigation purposes that prescribers should be readily identifiable. The Discussion Paper raised the question whether the prescriber's professional registration number should be recorded in the CDR.

14.173 From respondents, there was almost unanimous support for the suggestion. Although the NPA initially questioned whether recording this information would be of any benefit, at the seminar, Mr D'Arcy accepted that it would be. Mr Macfarlane and Dr Smith both supported the idea. DC White, of the NACIO, said that such a requirement would be of value to CIOs.

Conclusion

14.174 In my view, the recording of a prescriber's professional registration number in the CDR would be a valuable tool in the monitoring of controlled drug prescribing and in the investigation of cases of suspected diversion or irresponsible prescribing. This requirement would be more practicable if all controlled drug prescriptions carried the prescriber's registration number, as I think they should. I recognise that, while CDRs are manually kept, the recording of this number would be an additional burden upon the pharmacist. However, it may be that this burden could be reduced by the compilation of a list of names and professional registration numbers of the doctors whose names frequently appear in the CDR. Then it would be necessary only for the pharmacist to write the registration number of any prescriber who was not on the list. The introduction of an integrated electronic system could result in the automatic recording of the registration number.

Should the Controlled Drugs Register Identify the Pharmacist Responsible for Dispensing the Drug?

14.175   At the present time, there is no requirement that a pharmacist should identify him/herself when making an entry in the CDR. In a pharmacy where only regular staff are employed, the pharmacists all recognise each other's handwriting and there is little difficulty in identifying who was responsible for which transactions. However, where locum pharmacists are used, difficulty might arise. When electronic CDRs are introduced, there will be no handwriting to recognise. The Discussion Paper raised the question whether the pharmacist responsible for the transaction should be identified in the CDR.

14.176   Among respondents, there was strong support for this proposal. It was suggested that the pharmacist's RPSGB number should be provided. The RPSGB raised the question of whose name or number should be recorded if two pharmacists were responsible for the transaction.

14.177   At the seminar, Miss Lavin explained that sometimes one pharmacist will be responsible for approving the prescription and allowing it to be assembled and labelled. By the time the drugs are collected, that pharmacist may have gone off duty and another pharmacist might be responsible for handing over the drugs. After some discussion, she agreed that the pharmacist who handed the drugs over took responsibility for the supply and for the making of an entry in the CDR; accordingly it was that pharmacist's number that should be recorded.

Conclusion

14.178   In my view, it is imperative that the pharmacist responsible for a supply of controlled drugs should be positively identifiable from the CDR. This should not depend on the recognition of handwriting. I have no doubt that, when computerised registers are in use, a simple means of automatic identification of the pharmacist will be possible.

Should the Current Two-Year Time Limit for the Retention of a Controlled Drugs Register Be Extended? If So, to What Period?

14.179   At present, a CDR must be kept for two years from the date of the last recorded transaction. The inadequacy of this arrangement can be demonstrated by the Shipman case. Fortunately, the CDR at 23 Market Street went back to 1991. It was possible to examine Shipman's prescribing of diamorphine between 1991 and 1998. It would have been useful to the Inquiry if a register covering the 1980s had been available. However, if the register had become full in, say, 1996, and had been destroyed in 1998, it would have been impossible to trace his prescribing of the drug or to find out when he had appropriated it, and in what quantity. There must be many investigations of diversion of drugs or irresponsible prescribing where the period under investigation is longer than two years.

14.180 The DoH and some other respondents to the Discussion Paper felt that it would be appropriate for the CDR to be retained for a period of seven years after the date of the last entry, and all the participants at the seminars thought that this requirement would be satisfactory. Miss Lavin pointed out, however, that some controlled drugs have a very long shelf life. She would not wish a CDR to be destroyed if it contained a record of the purchase of a drug that remained in stock. She said that this would be only an occasional problem.

Conclusion

14.181 In my view, retention of a CDR for two years after the date of the last entry is not long enough. I would think that retention for seven years would be reasonable for the purposes of investigation of past practices. If it is thought that the problem mentioned by Miss Lavin could be resolved by extending the period to, say, ten years, I would be in favour of a general rule to that effect. I do not think it desirable that a pharmacy should have to examine the date of purchase and remaining shelf life of its stock before deciding whether it is entitled to destroy a CDR. When electronic records are used, it should be possible for them to be kept almost indefinitely.

Inspection Arrangements

14.182 In Chapter Five, I explained that at present the controlled drugs arrangements in GPs' surgeries are not routinely inspected and that there is an unfortunate paucity of advice available to them on such topics. In Chapter Nine, I outlined the current practice for the inspection of the arrangements for controlled drugs in community pharmacies. The HODI has an overarching responsibility for the enforcement of the legislation but, in most areas, the function of routine inspection is carried out by police CIOs. In a few areas, there is no routine CIO inspection. I also explained that the present arrangements are not ideal and that some chief constables do not regard the function as an appropriate use of police resources.

14.183 The Discussion Paper raised the question whether CIOs should continue to inspect CDRs and the safe custody arrangements for controlled drugs in pharmacies. It also asked whether CIOs should continue to be under a duty to look out for signs of irresponsible prescribing of controlled drugs. If not, should this duty be assigned to others and, if so, to whom? The question was also raised as to who should inspect the controlled drugs arrangements in GPs' surgeries and provide any necessary advice. How should dispensing doctors be treated? A wide variety of views was expressed by respondents and the issues were discussed at some length at the seminars. In the event, a remarkable degree of consensus was eventually reached.

14.184 Before describing the discussion, it may be helpful to recapitulate the main functions of CIO inspection. Pharmacy inspection is designed to ensure compliance with the MDR 2001 by the pharmacy staff. The CIO should look out for signs of illegal or improper practice by the pharmacy staff. Inspection should give the police access to valuable intelligence about the possible misuse of controlled drugs in the area. Finally, the CIO is expected to look out for signs of irresponsible prescribing by doctors and for signs of diversion, particularly by healthcare professionals. If it existed, a system of routine inspection of GPs' CDRs, SOPs and safe custody arrangements might be expected to improve compliance with the relevant regulations.

14.185 DC White, of the NACIO, has six years' practical experience as a CIO. He first sought to impress upon me the need for pharmacy inspections to take place. No one dissented from that proposition and I accept it without reserve. DC White confirmed that, despite attempts to improve the coverage and quality of police inspections, they remain unsatisfactory in some places and non-existent in others. However, he had no doubt that the inspection of registers and safe custody arrangements is properly a police function and that a background in general police work is of great value to a CIO. He accepted that a police background was not essential and that, given appropriate training and experience, persons from other backgrounds could do the work well. It was necessary for whoever did the job to spend a considerable time in the post to gain the experience necessary to be effective. He pointed out that, at present, civilian personnel do not have the legal powers to enter pharmacies, inspect arrangements and demand the production of records; special authorisation has to be obtained from the Home Secretary when a civilian is appointed as an inspector.

14.186 Mr Macfarlane expressed the view that, if adequate resources were dedicated to the CIO service, it would operate well. In particular, he saw positive advantages in the deterrent effect of a police officer performing the task. He thought that the involvement of the police strengthened the hand of a pharmacist who might otherwise have difficulty in dealing with addicts. Police expertise in investigation was also invaluable. He was not opposed to the idea that civilian police personnel might carry out inspections and thought that it would be useful if the process of authorising them to do this were simplified.

14.187 Assistant Chief Constable (ACC) David Francis, representing ACPO, said that his organisation accepted that CIOs must continue to carry out inspection duties for the present. However, the ACPO view was that, in the longer term, the police should be relieved of their responsibility for routine inspections but should retain involvement in intelligence work and in the investigation of offences that came to light.

14.188 Mrs Roberts pointed out that there are two forms of inspection of pharmacies, one by the police and one by the RPSGB, and that the two types of inspector have quite different forms of expertise. The police have knowledge of the law, and the RPSGB inspectors have clinical knowledge and experience. The job of pharmacy inspection requires both forms of expertise. This function, she suggested, should be carried out by an independent inspectorate which should employ personnel with both forms of expertise.

14.189 A particular concern lay behind Mrs Roberts' suggestion. She said that prescribers, social workers and patients, particularly drug misusers, had voiced concern to her about the use made by the police of the information contained in CDRs. They felt that it was wrong for the police to have access to confidential medical information. For that reason, she would prefer to see inspections carried out by an independent body. Later in the discussion, DC White explained how he resolves the difficulty mentioned by Mrs Roberts; he is scrupulously careful to ensure that any intelligence passed on to colleagues does not identify patients by name unless such disclosure is justified on public interest grounds by reason, for example, of the very serious nature of a criminal offence under investigation. He said that the NACIO is trying to ensure the adoption of a similar approach by all forces.

14.190 Dr Robertson said that he shared Mrs Roberts' concerns about the fragmentation of the current inspection arrangements. He, like Mrs Roberts, saw the solution in the formation of an integrated team. He considered that the role of inspection required significant medical expertise. Inspection of pharmacies and GPs' surgeries should be a local health function, according to Dr Robertson. Those carrying it out should have an advisory role but should also have access to police expertise, in case of need. He envisaged inspection being carried out at PCT level, to nationally set standards. The inspectors would report back to a central agency.

14.191 ACC Francis very much liked the idea of a national model for inspection. However, he did not think it appropriate that the inspection function should operate at a local (PCT) level. He thought a regional level would be more appropriate. Nor did he agree with Dr Robertson's emphasis on the medical and advisory aspects of inspection. He said that what was needed was more robust inspection and improved investigation; the motivation should be better law enforcement.

14.192 The discussion then moved on to the detection of irresponsible prescribing and whether police CIOs were best placed to carry out this task. Dr Grenville immediately picked up the idea of an integrated team. What was needed, he said, was a multidisciplinary team comprising people with the necessary skills and expertise to spot and investigate fairly any signs of abnormal prescribing. He said that the approach should be partly by analysis of statistical information and partly through investigation of apparent abnormalities. Local knowledge would also be necessary. He thought that, if the team had the necessary expertise, it would command the support and respect of the medical profession. Dr Gerada agreed with Dr Grenville. She felt that, if the right expertise were brought to bear on the PACT data, most prescribing abuses would be rapidly uncovered. She stressed that the processes of monitoring and investigation must cover private as well as NHS prescribing.

14.193 The discussion then turned to the question of how an inspectorate employing multidisciplinary teams might be organised. Dr Smith, for the DoH, strongly supported the general aim of improving and integrating the inspection and monitoring of controlled drugs by means of such teams. However, he said that it would not be appropriate for such an inspectorate to be driven from the centre by the DoH. The DoH's policy, he said, is to retrench from operational functions and to concentrate on policy issues. He suggested that, if a regional structure were sought, the inspectorate might be operated at strategic health authority (SHA) level or possibly by groups of SHAs. Alternatively, he suggested that the inspectorate might be located in regional Government offices, where there was already a Home Office and DoH presence. He said that there were eight such regional offices in the country, which he thought was about the right number for a regional inspectorate, and he thought that these organisations were accustomed to multi-agency work. A further possibility would be the Healthcare Commission, which is expected to have a regional presence in future. He also expressed the view that, if there were to be an inspectorate, the RPSGB's inspectorate should be part of the new framework. Miss Lavin was enthusiastic about the idea of a multidisciplinary inspectorate. She thought that the RPSGB would be anxious to share its experience and expertise with a new controlled drugs inspectorate but would not wish an inspectorate to be seated within its organisation.

14.194 Mr Macfarlane said that, if there were to be a new inspectorate, it would have to take on responsibility not only for pharmacies but also for doctors, dentists and veterinary surgeons. He agreed that it should fulfil the whole range of responsibility for monitoring and inspection in connection with controlled drugs. However, he said that, in recent years, the HODI had been moving away from involvement with the medical profession. It has focussed on its licensing and investigative functions. If the HODI were to take responsibility for a new inspectorate with a wider remit, this would be a 'new ball game'. He agreed that an inspectorate with a wide remit would require a multidisciplinary team.

14.195 Dr Grenville found the idea of a regional structure attractive. He said that he thought many doctors would welcome the kind of inspection visits that used to be made by the RMOs. Although many doctors found any inspection to be an intrusion, they recognised that it had to be done. He thought that there should be no artificial distinction between the way in which prescribing and dispensing GPs were treated, although there might need to be a difference of emphasis.

14.196 Dr Grenville then went on to expand upon the view, expressed earlier by Dr Robertson, that a multidisciplinary inspectorate should be firmly based within an organisation that was primarily concerned with health, as opposed to law enforcement. He favoured an emphasis on medical expertise and the advisory aspects of inspection. He said that it would be a mistake to base an inspectorate on the foundation that people who misused drugs were criminals. He said that criminal activity connected with controlled drugs was driven by addiction, which is an illness. He said that, if a controlled drugs inspectorate were based within a 'health' organisation, the approach would be one of 'learning and improving and preventing', whereas if it were based in the Home Office or with the police, the approach would be one of 'blaming and shaming'. ACC Francis and DC White emphasised the need for an inspectorate to tackle the criminality aspect and the leakage of controlled drugs into the criminal world. I expressed the view, with which ACC Francis agreed, that there must be an element of both approaches and, for that reason, the organisation should, if possible, be based on neutral ground. Dr Robertson thought that the work to be done by the inspectorate would be 'largely medical' and that the criminal justice element would be 'pretty minimal', although essential. His view was that local knowledge was necessary, so the organisation should be run at PCT level. Dr Gerada thought that a 'bigger picture' was needed and that a regional organisation would be preferable to one located at PCT level. Mr Rutherford agreed with Dr Gerada and reminded the Inquiry that primary care organisations had changed a great deal in recent years and that it might be dangerous to set up an organisation that would depend on the continuance of the PCTs. He thought that a regionally based organisation could have links with PCTs so that local knowledge would be available.

14.197 Professor Baker spoke in favour of a regional organisation which could make use of medical and law enforcement expertise. He would like to see such a body taking responsibility for services other than GPs and pharmacies, including hospices and nursing homes. He thought that PCTs might have a role to play in that they might undertake the analysis of PACT data, possibly in accordance with instructions given by the regional body.

14.198 Dr Michael Mawhinney, Misuse of Drugs Inspector for the Department of Health, Social Services and Public Safety, Northern Ireland, thought that a local structure would be inappropriate for England, with its large population, and said that his organisation, which covers the whole of the province, has good relations with local NHS bodies.

14.199 ACC Francis did not think that the creation of multidisciplinary inspection teams would adversely affect the enforcement of the law relating to controlled drugs provided that the new organisation had clearly defined objectives and accountability. DC White expressed concern about the view held by some of the 'health agencies' that their own people could investigate their own members; he did not think this was 'safe'. I think his concern was that there might be a lack of independence if doctors were allowed to investigate doctors. He also stressed the usefulness of the intelligence gathered from pharmacy inspections, particularly in the detection of double scripting and leakage of controlled drugs onto the illicit market.

Conclusion

14.200 I found this part of the seminars most helpful. A general consensus emerged that there must be a proper system of inspection of the controlled drugs arrangements and of CDRs kept by pharmacists, GPs and dispensing doctors. Inspections should be co-ordinated with the monitoring of prescribing practice. There must be the facility to investigate expertly any concerns discovered.

14.201 It seems to me that the ideal solution would be the creation of an inspectorate comprising small multidisciplinary teams, operating regionally but co-ordinated nationally. For this purpose, I think that England could sensibly be divided into about six to eight regions. As I indicated earlier, I think that the inspectorate should be based 'on neutral ground' so that it cannot be dominated by either the medical or the law enforcement ethos. As it happens, neither the DoH nor the Home Office would be willing to provide a base for such an inspectorate, but I see no reason why both Departments should not co-operate closely with it, as the Home Office does with the Inspectorate in Northern Ireland. The Home Office would be free to concentrate on licensing, importation and exportation and the inspection of businesses licensed to manufacture controlled drugs.

14.202 Each regional team would include pharmacists, doctors, inspectors and investigators, at least some of whom would have a law enforcement background. The team would be responsible for inspecting the arrangements in pharmacies, dispensaries and surgeries, as to both the safe keeping of stocks and the maintenance of CDRs and other records. In principle, prescribing and dispensing doctors should be inspected, just as pharmacies are at present. It might sometimes be thought necessary for an inspection to be carried out by a doctor or pharmacist and an investigator with a law enforcement background. The need for independence and an arm's length approach is one reason why a regional structure would be preferable to a local one. The inspectorate could also be responsible for the supervised destruction of controlled drugs.

14.203 It should also be responsible for the monitoring of the prescribing of controlled drugs by means of analysis of PACT data. At present, monitoring of all prescribing is carried out at PCT level and there is no reason why that should not continue. However, in my view, the monitoring of controlled drugs should also be done by the inspectorate. First, the inspectors will have or will soon acquire considerable expertise in controlled drugs. Second, they will develop a broader view of trends and practices than would be possible for an individual PCT. Third, they will be better placed to detect diversion of controlled drugs by peripatetic healthcare professionals. It is, in my view, imperative that the inspectorate should have access to all prescribing information, whether the prescriptions were issued on the NHS or privately. Inspectors and investigators would require access to background information about the doctor or pharmacist under scrutiny and, in some cases, might even require access to patient records. Potentially, this might give rise to problems of patient confidentiality. However, it appears that computer technology might provide a solution to such problems by allowing access to anonymised information from healthcare records. If that is not possible or sufficient, the investigators would have to seek the consent of patients as the HODI and the police do at present.

14.204 I share the view of ACC Francis that the inspectorate should have clearly defined objectives. I would wish the inspectorate to provide advice and assistance to those who are trying to comply with the law, even though not always fully successfully. However, I would expect it to be rigorous in the investigation of anyone suspected of acting unprofessionally and of anyone thought to be breaking the law deliberately. Investigations could be assigned to suitable members of the team. If it appeared that a criminal offence had been committed, the case could be passed to the police or the Crown Prosecution Service for further process. If less serious matters were discovered, the inspectorate might administer informal warnings or refer a complaint to the GMC, the RPSGB or the RCN.

14.205 The police would cease to carry out routine inspections of pharmacy CDRs. They would be able to undertake such work as they wished for the purpose of intelligence gathering and would probably wish to maintain close links with the inspectorate and, in some cases, with pharmacists.

Collecting Controlled Drugs from the Pharmacy

Should Healthcare Professionals Continue to Collect Controlled Drugs from Pharmacies?

14.206 In earlier Chapters, I have described how Shipman collected controlled drugs from the pharmacy, ostensibly on behalf of patients but keeping them for his own purposes. The Discussion Paper raised the question of whether such a practice should be prohibited. The vast majority of respondents to the Discussion Paper and all seminar participants were in favour of allowing healthcare professionals to continue to collect drugs from pharmacies, provided that the identity of the collector of controlled drugs was recorded in the CDR.

Conclusion

14.207 I do not think that healthcare professionals should be prohibited from collecting controlled drugs on behalf of patients. I have already said that the collector of any Schedule 2 controlled drug should be identified in the CDR and the collector of drugs in Schedules 3 and 4 should be asked to sign the prescription. Any collector not known to the pharmacist should be asked to produce identification. Any collector unknown to the pharmacist who claims to be a healthcare professional should be required to produce identification and his/her professional registration number.

14.208 Individual NHS trusts providing district nursing services may wish to impose additional requirements, for example, requiring district nurses to notify their managers when they intend to collect controlled drugs on behalf of patients. That is a matter for them.

Information about Controlled Drugs Provided by the Pharmacist for the Patient

14.209 There is a sharp contrast between the strict regulations governing the arrangements for controlled drugs before they are handed over the pharmacist's counter and the virtual absence of any such regulation thereafter. When a controlled drug is handed to the patient or his/her representative, it is quite usual for no greater warning to be given (about safe custody or the risk of diversion) than is given in respect of any medicines. Often, the patient will be unaware of the existence of any special legal rules relating to the drug, for example, that possession of the drug without the authority of the patient would be a criminal offence.

14.210 The Discussion Paper, therefore, raised the question whether an explanatory leaflet should be handed out by the pharmacist with each controlled drug prescription (or possibly only with each new prescription), explaining the key issues relating to controlled drugs and emphasising the need for safe storage and disposal. It raised the connected question whether the pharmacist should be under a professional duty to explain to whoever collects the controlled drugs the potential for abuse of the drugs and the need to keep them safe.

14.211 There was strong support for the idea of an explanatory leaflet among the respondents to the Discussion Paper. However, several respondents, among them Boots and Lloyds Pharmacy Limited, were concerned that such a leaflet might frighten patients into not taking their medication, thereby compromising their treatment. One respondent said that a GP should explain the function of all drugs and should advise the patient (or the patient's representative if appropriate) of the special need for caution with regard to controlled drugs.

14.212 At the seminars, Mrs Roberts said that leaflets on the safe storage of medicines should refer to all medicines and not specifically to controlled drugs. She felt that special reference to controlled drugs might deter patients from taking their medication. Mr D'Arcy, for the NPA, confirmed that the labelling of drugs as 'controlled drugs' has a propensity to alarm. Mrs Roberts also highlighted the fact that some cytotoxic drugs which are not controlled drugs are more toxic than controlled drugs. Mrs Roberts' view was shared by the RPSGB which, in its written response, stated that it would not support any recommendation that singled out controlled drugs from other prescription only medicines, because by definition all prescription only medicines are potent medicines and capable of misuse.

14.213 Mr Rutherford said that he thought that the public should be educated about all dangerous medicines, not only controlled drugs. He mentioned that, every year, children in England die from taking iron tablets and tricyclic antidepressants. He said that patients have to be given information about the medicines they are taking if they are to understand their medical conditions. This educational process causes some problems. Patients can be worried by the information they receive and some even feel stigmatised when they go to pharmacies to collect controlled drugs because they fear that the counter staff will think they are drug addicts. Issues such as this must be resolved, he said.

14.214 In principle, the DoH supported the idea of a patient leaflet to accompany controlled drugs. Dr Smith said that the DoH had recently commissioned the National Prescribing Centre to draft an appropriate leaflet. The result was, however, to use Dr Smith's language, 'quite scary' and he thought that trying to find the right language to make the essential points is very difficult. He accepted the view, expressed by ACC Francis, that it is wrong for a patient or a patient's representative to be unaware of the legal implications of being in possession of a controlled drug.

14.215 Mr Rudd had informally discussed the issue of patient information with members of a small reference group. A minority expressed concern about causing alarm to patients but the majority view was that many people are more worried by their ignorance about what they have in their possession. Macmillan Cancer Relief was, therefore, supportive of improved patient information.

14.216 Dr Gerada said that the RCGP supported the idea of a patient leaflet and wanted it to contain information about storage of drugs and their disposal and return to the pharmacy. Although she understood it was important that patients should not be frightened into not taking their medicine, she thought that, in fact, patients are better informed than they are given credit for. She said that some computers allowed doctors to print off extracts from the British National Formulary and it was quite common practice to give this detailed information to patients.

Conclusion

14.217 As I understand it, the modern approach to medical treatment is that the patient should be helped to understand the nature of his/her condition and the treatment to be provided. When a drug is prescribed by a GP, the doctor will usually explain its nature and purpose. However, I think it is not always possible for a patient to take in everything that s/he is told and that many patients would benefit from having the oral information provided confirmed in written form. When a doctor is prescribing a controlled drug, s/he will wish to explain the purpose of the drug and the way in which it is to be taken, rather than having to deal with practical issues such as safe keeping. In my view, those practical issues would be more appropriately dealt with by a pharmacist than by a GP. But, again, I think it would be helpful if the messages were to be reinforced in writing. As I observed during the seminars, more could be done, by posting notices in pharmacies, to educate the public about the need to keep drugs safe and to return leftovers for destruction.

14.218 Dealing specifically with controlled drugs, I am very sceptical of the suggestion that patients will be afraid to take their medication if they are told about its properties and the risk of diversion. I sense that Dr Gerada is right when she says that patients know and understand more than they are given credit for. I think that the attitude that patients in general cannot be told about their controlled drugs is patronising. I can accept that some very elderly people might be confused by too much information and might also be alarmed if told that the drugs they are taking would be attractive to a drug addict. However, I think that it should be a general rule that pharmacists should give to patients or their representatives a proper and accurate description of the controlled drugs prescribed, warn them of the particular need to keep the drugs safe because of the risk of diversion and advise them that arrangements must be made for the safe disposal of any drugs left over. This advice should be given orally and should also be available in leaflet form. I can see that some care must be taken in the preparation of the leaflet and that pharmacists will need some guidance about how best to convey the advice to patients. I would accept that pharmacists should have discretion to give only limited information to those patients who they believe would be alarmed to receive the usual advice. The RPSGB should formulate guidance for pharmacists as to what should be said and could provide a helpful lead in the preparation of the information leaflets.

The Audit of Controlled Drugs in the Community

Creating an Audit Trail by the Use of Bar Coding

14.219 At paragraph 7.67, I discussed the possibility of creating an audit trail by recording the batch numbers of controlled drugs in the pharmacy CDR. I concluded that the idea was not practicable. However, the possibility of identifying the drugs dispensed using bar coding also arose for consideration. Everyone is now familiar with bar coded products. Supermarkets use this technology, both to charge customers at the checkout and as a means of stock control. The Discussion Paper asked whether bar coding might be used as a means of providing an audit trail of controlled drugs.

14.220 A substantial number of respondents considered that bar coding would be a useful innovation. At the seminars, the RPSGB fully supported its introduction, saying that it would provide several advantages. Dr Smith explained that, at present, the DoH had no firm commitment to bar coding. However, it recognised its potential usefulness for audit purposes, by permitting the tracking of products through the supply chain. He also said that bar coding is now quite old technology and mentioned that a newer technology, radio frequency tagging, might provide even greater benefits. Mr Macfarlane said that development work was in progress on a radio frequency tracking system for all medications. Although the purpose behind these developments was not improved compliance with Home Office controls, he was confident that it could be used to that end. Moreover, the system could be applied to individual ampoules of a controlled drug. The system would comprise a database which recorded every single pack of medication at the point of manufacture and could track it through every stage of the distribution process. It is beyond the scope of the Inquiry to consider such developments in detail. It is not clear to me whether the use of modern technology will allow there to be an audit trail of controlled drugs beyond the pharmacist and into the hands of an individual patient. If so, the opportunity for the police or a controlled drugs inspectorate to detect improper diversion of controlled drugs would be much improved.

Should a Continuing Record Be Kept of the Transfer, Administration and Disposal of Controlled Drugs Once They Have Been Dispensed by the Pharmacist?

14.221 I have mentioned that, once controlled drugs leave the pharmacy, there are no legal requirements as to the conditions in which they are stored; nor is there any requirement that a record should be kept of their administration or destruction. Above any other single factor, it was this absence of control after dispensing that enabled Shipman to obtain diamorphine illicitly and to avoid notice. It would be highly desirable to tighten the MDR 2001 in this respect. The problem is how to do it.

14.222 In Chapter Eight, I described the system by which district nurses keep a patient drug record card (PDRC) to record the administration of diamorphine in syringe drivers. They do so, not because there is any legal requirement to do so but as a matter of good professional practice. Such records provide a valuable measure of audit and control. Desirable as it might be to require a record of consumption of all controlled drugs, it is obvious that it would be impractical to expect patients who take controlled drugs at home to keep such a record. However, where a healthcare professional is involved in the administration of the drug, as is usual with opiate drugs in injectable form, it plainly is practicable for records to be maintained. If the keeping of such a record were a legal requirement rather than a professional one, it would be possible to require doctors as well as nurses to comply.

14.223 At present, the district nurse creates the record when the controlled drug (usually diamorphine) arrives at the patient's home. The district nurse would not necessarily know how much of the drug had been prescribed by the doctor or dispensed by the pharmacist. Shipman was able to divert supplies of diamorphine to his own use by presenting a prescription he had issued, collecting the drugs and removing part of the consignment before delivering it to the patient's home. Also, because there is no legal requirement for the return or destruction of unused drugs to be recorded, Shipman was able to claim that he had taken leftover diamorphine for destruction when, in fact, he had taken it for himself.

14.224 The Discussion Paper raised the question whether, in the case of controlled drugs to be administered by a healthcare professional, a continuing record should be kept of the transfer, administration and disposal of the drugs after dispensing. This would take the form of a PDRC, which would be opened by the pharmacist and sent to the patient's home with the drugs. As the drugs were administered, the card would be completed by the district nurse or other administering healthcare professional. When the drugs had all been used, the card could be returned to the GP to become part of the patient's medical record. If any drugs remained unused, their destruction could be recorded on the card, which could then be returned to the GP.

14.225 The idea of such a continuous record card received support from the majority of respondents to the Discussion Paper. It was recognised to have the potential at least to extend, and possibly to complete, the audit trail. However, some pharmacists expressed concern about the practicalities of such a scheme.

14.226 At the seminars, there was general agreement that a record should be kept of controlled drugs which were to be administered by healthcare professionals. It was agreed that it would not be unduly onerous to ask pharmacists to issue the card. It was suggested that the card should record, not only the amount dispensed, but also the dosage ordered on the prescription.

14.227 Concerns were expressed about what should happen to the card when it was complete. At present, the PDRCs kept by district nurses are kept with the patient records maintained by the nurses' employers and are not married up with the patients' GP records. Nor, in most areas, are the cards audited; in Tameside, samples of completed PDRCs are now 'reviewed'.

14.228 Mr D'Arcy said that there would be difficulties if the cards had to be returned to the pharmacy when the drugs had been used. He thought that cards would be lost and that healthcare professionals would not always make entries on the right card. He thought the system sounded 'convoluted'.

14.229 Dr Grenville supported the idea in principle but thought that 'closing the audit loop' would be very resource intensive. He wondered whether the task of audit could be assigned to the new controlled drugs inspectorate that had been discussed earlier and said that it was for society to decide what resources should be spent on audit. He recognised that there would be some value in marrying the PDRCs with the patients' medical records, although he said that good practice already required that a doctor should keep a detailed record of the dosages ordered.

14.230 Professor Baker thought it would be of benefit if the information from the PDRC were kept with or entered into the patient medical records. Even if all records were not audited, they would be available for examination if an investigation had to be undertaken. Random reviews might be useful. Dr Gerada and Dr Robertson agreed. Mr Rutherford made a practical suggestion, which, he thought, would make the task of record keeping easier. He said that, if manufacturers had to apply 'peel-off' labels to controlled drugs containers, the person administering the drug would be able to stick the label onto the PDRC instead of writing an entry. Then if any drugs were unused, the labels could be removed from the container at the time of destruction (whether in the home or in the pharmacy) and a record kept of exactly what had been destroyed. In its response to the Discussion Paper, the RCGP suggested that small bung-topped bottles could be used for the supply of controlled drugs, instead of (as at present) closed ampoules which have to be broken in order to open them. Also, the bottles could be supplied in a divided box. When a bottle of drugs had been used, it could be replaced in the box, without its bung. When all the drugs had been used, the box of empty bottles could accompany the completed PDRC to its destination, to demonstrate that all the drugs had, in fact, been used or, if it were the case, destroyed.

Conclusion

14.231 The evidence about Shipman suggests that a PDRC, if properly completed, would provide a valuable audit trail for the controlled drugs for which it could be used. In my view, there should be a statutory requirement on healthcare professionals to maintain such a record.

There may be several ways in which the practical arrangements could be made. One is that, when a Schedule 2 injectable drug left the pharmacy, for administration in the community, it would be accompanied by a PDRC which would record the form and amount prescribed, the form and amount dispensed and the dosage as ordered on the prescription. That would become the 'master' PDRC. The healthcare professionals would be required to record all administrations of the drugs on the master PDRC. The record would include a running balance. Every new supply would have its own PDRC. When a new supply (with its PDRC) was brought to the patient's home, the healthcare professional would enter the new stock onto the master PDRC, so that a running record would be maintained. All cards issued by a pharmacy would have to be kept with the master PDRC, to provide a means of checking that the entries in the 'drugs obtained' side of the card accurately reflected the amounts that had left the pharmacy. When the treatment was completed, or after the patient's death, all the PDRCs would be sent to the PCT, which would carry out a review and, possibly, check the PDRCs against the pharmacy records. If no cause for concern arose, the PCT would send the completed records to the patient's GP, to be married up with the other records. If and when there is a controlled drugs inspectorate, it might wish to carry out an occasional audit of PDRCs.

14.232 Another possibility would be for the pharmacy to issue, with the drugs, a peel-off label on which the amount prescribed, the amount dispensed and the dosage would all appear. The healthcare professionals involved would provide a blank PDRC, as they do now. They would apply the label to the PDRC as an opening entry and the labels from any subsequent supplies could be applied so as to provide the running record. In other respects, the system would work as described above.

14.233 The destruction of any unused drugs would be recorded on the card, wherever it took place, in the manner set out in paragraph 14.251 below. The card would then be sent to the PCT (or kept by the PCT if it had carried out the destruction) or controlled drugs inspectorate and from there, after audit or review, it would be sent to the patient's GP. If the patient had died in the meantime, it is likely that, by the time audit was complete, the GP records would have been sent to the PCT. The master PDRC would then be kept with those GP records, in case an investigation had to take place.

14.234 If implemented, these proposals would do much to deter and/or detect the obtaining of drugs by the methods deployed by Shipman. However, they would not detect a doctor who issued a prescription for a controlled drug, presented it at a different pharmacy from the one usually used by the patient's family, collected the drugs and kept the whole consignment for him/herself. That deficiency is not, in my view, a reason to reject the proposal. If a doctor collects drugs from the pharmacy, his/her name will (if another of my proposals is implemented) be recorded in the CDR and should come to the attention of the CIO or, if there is one, the controlled drugs inspectorate. The inspectorate could then cross check the CDR with the PDRC and would soon discover if a supply had not been delivered to the patient's home and entered on the PDRC.

Should Two Healthcare Professionals Witness Every Administration of Injectable Controlled Drugs in the Community?

14.235 The Inquiry heard evidence that, since the discovery of Shipman's crimes, a special rule has been introduced in Tameside, whereby controlled drugs are administered by two district nurses or healthcare professionals rather than one. This practice was introduced in order to protect the nurses from unfounded allegations of diversion or other impropriety. The Discussion Paper raised the question of whether it should be introduced as a general requirement.

14.236 There was strong opposition to the idea from all groups responding to the Discussion Paper. The objections were that it would be administratively difficult to achieve and far too resource intensive. It would be impracticable to apply to doctors visiting patients out of hours. I was told that it would result in terminally and chronically ill patients being left in pain. The same concerns were voiced in the seminars.

14.237 The Inquiry had been interested in whether a requirement that controlled drugs be administered by two healthcare professionals would benefit patient safety. Dr Smith said that the DoH had researched the issue of double-checking and confirmed that there was no statistical evidence to prove that double-checking leads to error reduction. I can understand how the knowledge that a procedure will be checked may, in some instances, cause the person performing that procedure to become lax.

Conclusion

14.238 I shall not recommend that controlled drugs should be administered by two healthcare professionals rather than one. The adverse resource implications would far outweigh any possible advantage in reducing the risk of diversion of the drugs. However, if any employer of district nurses considers that such a measure is practicable and useful, for the protection of its staff or the reduction of the risk of diversion, it should remain free to impose it, as happens at present in Tameside.

The Disposal of Unused Controlled Drugs in the Community

14.239 In paragraph 7.71, I explained that out of date or contaminated Schedule 2 controlled drugs can be lawfully destroyed only in the presence of a person authorised by the Home Secretary. At paragraph 7.75, I explained that Schedule 2 'patient returns' can be supplied to a doctor or pharmacist for the purpose of destruction; the destruction can take place without formality. As I have said, Shipman was able to divert diamorphine by taking for himself amounts left over after the deaths of his terminally ill patients. It would have been lawful for him to take possession of the drugs to destroy them provided that the personal representative of the deceased patient consented. It was not, of course, lawful for him to keep the drugs for himself. As I explained in paragraphs 8.31 to 8.33, the legal position relating to controlled drugs left over after a patient's death is unsatisfactory; they are the property of the deceased's personal representative and only s/he can give authority for them to be destroyed.

14.240 The Discussion Paper raised a number of questions about the destruction of unused controlled drugs. Who should be empowered to dispose of unused controlled drugs? Should two healthcare professionals be required to witness every destruction of unused controlled drugs in the community? After a patient's death, is it desirable that controlled drugs, that were the patient's property, should pass to the patient's estate? What arrangements should be introduced so as to enable unused drugs to be returned to safe custody after the patient's death? Should a PCT be empowered or required to take possession of leftover controlled drugs in such circumstances? Should there be a duty imposed on a 'responsible person' to ensure the safe return or disposal of those drugs?

Ownership after Death

14.241 At present, controlled drugs dispensed at a community pharmacy belong to the patient for whom they are prescribed, even if s/he has been exempt from any prescription charge. Often, in cases where the patient has been nursed in the community, district nurses destroy Schedule 2 controlled drugs following a patient's death, relying on the consent of a relative in attendance. However, there must be many occasions when this practice is not strictly lawful, because the relative may not be the deceased's personal representative. I make this point, not because I wish to discourage district nurses from their present practice, which seems to me to be eminently sensible, but to underline the need for a change in the law.

14.242 The Inquiry heard evidence that the present legal position can sometimes give rise to problems. Mrs Roberts had heard of an occasion when the family of a deceased patient had refused to allow the removal of leftover controlled drugs. This type of problem could apply to all controlled drugs in Schedules 2–4. Of those who expressed a view, the overwhelming majority of respondents to the Discussion Paper and all participants in the seminar thought that ownership of controlled drugs should not pass to the patient's estate on death.

14.243 The Department of Constitutional Affairs (DCA) suggested that it would be far simpler if controlled drugs never became the property of the patient in the first place. They should remain the property of those who supplied them, usually a pharmacy. After the death, the deceased's personal representatives should be under a specific duty to account for any controlled drugs or to return them to the supplier.

Conclusion

14.244 It is undesirable that any controlled drugs in Schedules 2–4, unused at the time of death, should pass to the patient's estate. The DCA has suggested one possible solution. Another, which I think would be more practicable, is that all controlled drugs should become the property of the Crown on the death of the owner. There may be other solutions. Whatever solution is adopted, no person should be able to assert a right to the ownership or possession of controlled drugs prescribed for a deceased patient when requested by an appropriately authorised person to allow their destruction in, or removal from, the patient's home.

Witnessing and Recording Destruction

14.245 At present, a patient may lawfully destroy or authorise another person to destroy any controlled drugs lawfully in his/her possession. A patient may also supply or authorise another person to supply any controlled drugs to a pharmacist or doctor for the purpose of destruction. Doctors and pharmacists, receiving such controlled drugs, are authorised by regulation 27 of the MDR 2001 to destroy them without formality; there is no legal requirement that the destruction should be witnessed by another person or recorded. As a matter of good practice, many pharmacists do make a record and ask a witness to sign it.

14.246 There was almost universal support for the proposal that the destruction of unused Schedule 2 controlled drugs should be accompanied by a degree of formality. Many thought that two professional persons (such as pharmacists or doctors) should be present to undertake and observe the destruction and to sign an appropriate record. A number suggested that pharmacy staff and coroners' officers could be included in the category of those authorised to observe and sign the record of destruction. Some respondents thought that a lay person should be able to observe and sign the record where destruction was undertaken by a healthcare professional. Others said that this would not provide a sufficient safeguard, as the lay person might not understand the significance of what was taking place and could easily be hoodwinked into approving a false record. Some expressed the view that it would be inappropriate to ask a relative to witness the destruction of drugs of a deceased patient soon after the death. In my view, it is not appropriate to involve a lay person as a witness to the destruction of unused drugs.

14.247 The discussion then turned to where the destruction of controlled drugs should take place. It was recognised that it is desirable that it should occur as soon as possible. Concern was expressed about the danger to relatives or district nurses if they were required to return drugs to a pharmacy or other place for destruction. It was said to be preferable for the drugs to be destroyed at the patient's home, even if that did mean that they had to be put into the sewage system. I feel bound to observe that there have been several campaigns to persuade patients to return all unwanted drugs to a pharmacy for destruction and no one seems to have been worried about the risks in connection with controlled drugs. Also, no one seems to be greatly concerned about the safety of relatives or healthcare professionals who collect controlled drugs from a pharmacy and take them to a patient's home. At that stage, the risks must be just as great as, if not greater than, when leftovers have to be dealt with. However, that is not a reason to ignore the risks of transporting controlled drugs. Mr Ian Hargreaves, on behalf of the RCN, opposed the idea that district nurses should have to transport such drugs as diamorphine in their vehicles.

14.248 Professor Baker thought that, if two healthcare professionals were present at the home, the best course was to destroy any unwanted drugs immediately. A record should be made. Dr Gerada said that the RCGP recommended that there should be a tamper-proof bin in the patient's home into which the unused drugs should be put. The bin could then be collected and the drugs incinerated.

14.249 Dr Smith said that the DoH had given much thought to the issue of disposal of controlled drugs and to the possibility of setting up return schemes within PCTs in England. One possibility might be for the DoH to impose a formal requirement on PCTs to implement schemes for the collection, return and safe disposal of all medicines in accordance with waste disposal regulations. Insofar as community pharmacists currently undertake the informal destruction of controlled drugs returned to them, Dr Smith said that the DoH was considering whether to impose contractual requirements of record keeping and safe handling. However, it was not expected that the pharmacists would be obliged to provide a collection service from patients' homes. Mr D'Arcy said that the NPA would resist 'tooth and nail' any suggestion that pharmacists should be required to retrieve medicines from patients' homes.

Conclusion

14.250 It seems to me that it would be desirable if PCTs were to provide a service whereby all controlled drugs in Schedules 2–4 were collected from the homes of deceased patients and taken away in safe conditions and disposed of appropriately. However, I recognise that this might be thought to be too resource intensive. In the absence of such an arrangement, I shall focus upon the issues of greatest concern. These seem to me to be, first, the safe, prompt and recorded destruction of Schedule 2 injectable drugs and, second, ensuring that healthcare professionals are aware of their obligations and the options available to them. In my view, PCTs should be under an obligation to ensure that suitable arrangements are in place for the disposal of controlled drugs and that the healthcare professionals in the area are aware of them.

14.251 In my view, it would be beneficial to formalise the arrangements for the destruction of all Schedule 2 controlled drugs at the home of a deceased patient. However, I think that it will be practicable to impose formal statutory requirements only in relation to injectable controlled drugs in Schedule 2 (for which a statutory PDRC will exist). I shall recommend that the destruction of such drugs takes place in the following approved manner. It should be undertaken by one person and witnessed by another. Full details should be recorded on the PDRC. These details should include the form and quantity of the drugs destroyed and the date, time, place and mode of destruction. Both persons present should enter their names and signatures on the PDRC. The classes of persons who I suggest should be entitled to undertake or witness such destruction would be doctors, pharmacists, registered nurses and suitably trained law enforcement officers (such as CIOs and coroner's officers), inspectors of any new controlled drugs inspectorate and officers of the local PCT. However, in practice, such destruction would almost always fall to district nurses and GPs. As I have made clear, destruction would normally be expected to take place in the patient's home but that might, exceptionally, not be possible or desirable. In such cases, the removal of such drugs from the home should be subject to the same recording and witnessing requirements as destruction. Transport, most commonly to a pharmacy, could be effected by one person, provided that a record had been made by two. Members of the public, including the patient's family, would not be allowed to remove or destroy the drugs.

14.252 Frequently, district nurses (and very occasionally GPs) will be asked to remove or destroy non-injectable Schedule 2 drugs when attending the home of a deceased patient. In order to minimise the risk of diversion of such drugs, I suggest that rules of professional conduct and/or an employer's protocol should require that the same degree of formality should apply to their removal or destruction by nurses or GPs as applies to injectable Schedule 2 drugs, albeit not on the same statutory footing. The PDRC could be used for making the relevant record, although the information could be recorded on some other suitable form if, for example, the patient's treatment had not involved the creation of a PDRC. Such requirements, applicable to all Schedule 2 controlled drugs, would render it far more difficult for healthcare professionals to divert such drugs. The same degree of formality would not apply to removal by the families of deceased patients, who should be allowed and encouraged to return such non-injectable unused controlled drugs to the pharmacy.

14.253 When any unused Schedule 2 controlled drugs are returned to the pharmacy or doctor's surgery for destruction, their destruction should be carried out and witnessed in the approved manner as described in paragraph 14.251 above. When destruction takes place in the pharmacy or surgery, it should be recorded on the PDRC, if there is one, or otherwise in the pharmacy or surgery records, possibly in the CDR.

14.254 I do not think it appropriate that I should make any recommendations as to the precise means by which controlled drugs should be destroyed. I was shown one proprietary method by which the drugs were rendered unusable by being mixed with a liquid which later solidified. I have no doubt that there are many different ways of dealing with this problem, all perfectly effective.

Summary

14.255 In this Chapter, I have considered a large number of possible changes to the regime for the regulation of controlled drugs. My conclusions, which form the basis of my recommendations for change, have been formulated as a result of the evidence I have received and the views expressed in the responses to the Discussion Paper and at the seminars. Some of the ideas discussed I have found to be useful and feasible; others I have rejected as ineffective or because they seem likely to place a disproportionate onus on those professionals who would be responsible for implementing them. Some of my recommendations are particularly designed to deter or detect unlawful conduct of the kind perpetrated by Shipman. Others are not directly related to him but are designed to improve the safety of patients in using controlled drugs and to deter and facilitate the detection of any kind of unlawful conduct. I have listed my recommendations in a section that appears immediately after the Summary at the beginning of this Report.

14.256 The implementation of many of my recommendations would require primary legislation and some would involve the reallocation of, and possibly an increase in, existing resources. For example, I have recommended the formation of a controlled drugs inspectorate to take over the role of the CIO in the inspection of pharmacies. It would also provide for the inspection of both the dispensaries of dispensing GPs and the arrangements made by GPs (including those operating in the private sector) for the safe custody of controlled drugs and for their CDRs. The inspectorate would also be responsible for monitoring the use of controlled drugs by means of data provided by the PPA. It could, in addition, provide advice to doctors and pharmacists on controlled drugs issues and, as happens in Northern Ireland, its members could be involved in education and training. I make this recommendation because, at present, the monitoring of the use of controlled drugs and the inspection of the records kept and the safe custody arrangements in place are patchy and fragmented. They are carried out by police officers who do not have the necessary pharmaceutical or medical expertise or by medical advisers for whom controlled drugs are but one of many responsibilities. An inspectorate should provide expertise and cohesion.

14.257 One of the threads running through my recommendations is the need to apply the same degree of regulation and monitoring to the use of controlled drugs in the private sector as is applied within the NHS. My recommendations include the use of a special prescription pad (possibly in duplicate) for controlled drugs prescribed (or obtained on requisition) by doctors in the private sector as well as under the NHS. The controlled drugs inspectorate could be responsible for the issue of the special prescription pads or a special access code for use if and when electronic generation and transmission of prescriptions is introduced. The inspectorate could ensure that only those doctors with a clinical need to prescribe such drugs would be authorised to do so. The inspectorate would also be aware of the identity and professional address of all doctors authorised to keep controlled drugs, and could arrange appropriate inspections. No doubt, the inspectorate would maintain a list of those authorised. All controlled drug prescriptions should be sent to the PPA for entry into its database and subsequent analysis and monitoring by the inspectorate.

14.258 My recommendations have focussed mainly on devising provisions that will make it more difficult for healthcare professionals to obtain controlled drugs by illicit means and will help to detect their activities if they occur. However, these recommendations should be considered against the general background of the legislation relating to controlled drugs. The framework of controlled drugs legislation has remained virtually unchanged for more than 30 years. The requirements in relation to prescriptions and record keeping are out of date and require modernisation. The Schedules to the MDR have been amended in a piecemeal fashion so that they are now an almost incomprehensible maze of provisions. I earnestly hope that the recommendations in this Report will provide an opportunity for the framework to be looked at afresh. A simplified and principled structure for the regulation of controlled drugs should be developed. The Home Office is aware of the need for improvements in many areas. However, it seems that the impetus for modernisation is coming largely from the DoH through its development of IT systems which are designed primarily to improve patient care rather than to facilitate the regulation of controlled drugs or the monitoring of their use. It seems to me that a joint approach between the two departments is needed so that the legislative framework can be changed to allow for the use of computer technology with an eye on improved regulation and monitoring of controlled drugs as well as on improved patient care.

APPENDIX A

Selected Pages from 23 Market Street

Controlled Drugs Register

MISUSE OF DRUGS ACT

REGISTER

OF

DIAMORPHINE
(Heroin or Diacetylmorphine)

And its Salts, also of any preparation, admixture, extract or other substance containing any proportion of DIAMORPHINE (Heroin), &c.

OBTAINED or SUPPLIED

Published by

THE NATIONAL PHARMACEUTICAL ASSOCIATION

MALLINSON HOUSE,

38-42 ST. PETER'S STREET, ST. ALBANS, HERTS AL1 3NP

This Register contains
7 pages for purchases
24 pages for sales.

Record of DIAMORPHINE, &c., supplied

Date on which the transaction was effected	NAME	ADDRESS	Particulars as to licence or authority of person or firm supplied to be in possession	Amount supplied	Form in which supplied
1.10.91	Q		Dr A	20	Diamorpheaing 30 y HCl
13.11.91	Dr J		Dr B	500 ml 2500 mg	Diamorphine Hcl 5mg/5ml
3/12.91	By 3/12.91 Destroyed in my presence — 4 Apps Diamorph ('0 mg inj) @ 0.5 Dom Ofor 4 due git				
18.2.92	Dr A		For Practice use	1 × 5	Dianorph inj 5mg/amp.
6.3.92	$		Dr C	5 × 5	Dimorph inj 30 y/ml
10.3.92	8		Dr D	5 × 5	Dianorph inj 30 mg/ml
11.3.92	Richard Ranch	3 Pottinger St Ashton u Lyne	Wholesaler	2 × 5	Diacetph inj 100 mg/ml
16.3.92	Mr P		Dr B	200 ml	Dianorph HCl 1mg/1ml.
16.3.92	W.		D. Shipnan (FIVE)	2 br	Dianorph HCl 30 y/ill inj
19.3.92	Destroyed 1box out of date 5 AMPS Diamorphine INT.. 10mg Dawid Your CRISO 19/3/92		Signed order	1 × 5	Diamorphine HCl 10mg inj
15.5.92	14/7.92		Dr F	100 mg Diamorph HCl	Diamorphine HCl 10mg inj
21.10.92					

SALES

M.D.A.
Register of DIAMOR-
PHINE, &c.

Page Eight

Record of DIAMORPHINE, &c., supplied

Date on which the transaction was effected	NAME	ADDRESS of person or firm supplied	Particulars as to licence or authority of person or firm supplied to be in possession	Amount supplied	Form in which supplied
15.12.92	Dr G [signature] 26/11 cr		Signed Order	1 r 5	Diamorphine 5mg inj
22/4/93	Laura Readfearn		Dr Shipman	1	Dianorph 30mg inj HCl
22.2.93	Hardu Freeman		Dr Shipman	1	Dianorph 30mg inj HCl
25.2.93	C. Hyslelwthn		Dr Shipman	1	Dianorph 30mg inj HCl
26.2.93	Lilian Ibbotson		Dr Shipman	1	Dianorph 30mg inj HCl
22.3.93	A. Whitehead		Dr Shipman	1	Dianorph 30mg inj HCl
17.4.93	H Andrew		Dr Shipman	1	Dianorph 30mg inj
17.4.93	Sarah Ashworth		Dr Shipman	1	Diamorphine HCl 30mg inj
27.4.93	Fanny Nichol		Dr Shipman	1	Diamorphine HCl 30mg inj
27.4.93	M Parker		Dr Shipman	1	Diamorphine HCl 30mg inj
5.5.93	Edna Llewellyn		Dr Shipman	1	Diamorphine HCl 30mg inj
5.5.93	2 Fullo		Dr Shipman	1	Diamorphine HCl 30mg inj
26.5.93	Dr Ralph		Dr Shipman	1	Diamorph HCl inj 30g
30.6.93			Dr H	10	Dianorph HCl inj 30mg

SALES

Record of DIAMORPHINE, &c., supplied

Date on which the transaction was effected	NAME of person or firm supplied	ADDRESS	Particulars as to licence or authority of person or firm supplied to be in possession	Amount supplied	Form in which supplied
	12/7/93				
27/7/93			Dr C	15 x 30mg	Amps Diamorph HCl.
28/7/93			Dr C	10 x 30mg	Amps Diamorph HCl.
28/7/93			Dr C	10 x 30mg	Amps Diamorph HCl.
14.8.93	E. Ralphs		Dr Shipman	once	Inj Diamorph HCl 30mg.
27.8.93	L Fallows		Dr Shipman	1x	Inj Diamorph HCl 30mg
25.9.93				1x5	Inj Diamorph HCl 10mg
25.9.93				1x5	Inj Diamorph HCl 30mg.
15.11.93	Dr Jones		Dr Shipman	3.	Inj Diamorph HCl 30mg
16.11.93	Dr Jones		Dr Shipman	20	Inj Diamorph HCl 100mg.
20.11.93	Dr Jones		Dr Shipman	20	Inj Diamorph HCl 100mg
26.11.93	Mr Jones		Dr Shipman	15 x	Inj Diamorph HCl 100mg.
11.1.94			Dr C	6	Inj Diamorph HCl 30mg
11.1.94			Dr C	5	Inj Diamorph HCl 15mg
11.1.94				28	Inj Diamorph HCl 30mg

M.D.A. Register of DIAMORPHINE, &c.

SALES

B

Page Ten

Participants in Phase Two, Stage Three of the Inquiry and Their Representatives

Counsel to the Inquiry

Miss Caroline Swift QC

Mr Christopher Melton QC

Mr Anthony Mazzag

Mr Michael Jones

instructed by Mr Henry Palin, Solicitor to the Inquiry

Participants	Representatives
Co-op Health Care Limited Mayfair Chemists (Hyde) Limited Mrs Ghislaine Brant Mr Peter Rothman Mrs Janice Beesley	Mr John Hand QC and Mr Julian Field, instructed by Mr Mark Field, Branton Edwards Solicitors, Manchester
Department of Health	Miss Emily Formby, instructed by Mr Barrie McKay, Treasury Solicitor's Office
General Medical Council	Miss Beverley Lang QC, instructed by Mr Matthew Lohn, Field Fisher Waterhouse Solicitors, London
Greater Manchester Police and Mr Patrick Kelly, former Chemist Inspection Officer	Mr Michael Shorrock QC and Miss Kate Blackwell, instructed by Mrs Sandra Pope, Greater Manchester Police Force Solicitor
Home Office	Mr James Maxwell-Scott and Mr Andrew O'Connor, instructed by Mr Barrie McKay, Treasury Solicitor's Office
Tameside Families Support Group	Mr Richard Lissack QC, Mr Andrew Spink QC, Mr Paul Gilroy and Miss Harriet Jerram, instructed by Ms Ann Alexander, Alexander Harris Solicitors, Altrincham, Cheshire
Tameside and Glossop Primary Care Trust West Pennine Health Authority	Mr Gerard McDermott QC and Mr David Eccles, instructed by Mr Charles Howorth, George Davies Solicitors, Manchester
Mr David Young, Inspector, Royal Pharmaceutical Society of Great Britain	Ms Kristina Stern, instructed by Ms Katrina Wingfield, Penningtons Solicitors, London

Summary of the Main Legal Requirements

Governing the Possession and Supply of

Controlled Drugs as They Apply to Pharmacists

and General Practitioners

	Schedule 2	Schedule 3	Schedule 4 Part I	Schedule 4 Part II	Schedule 5
Examples of drugs listed in each schedule	Mainly opiates and major stimulants including amphetamine, cocaine, codeine, diamorphine (heroin), dipipanone, fentanyl, methadone, dextromoramide (Palfium), pethidine, quinalbarbitone and methylphenidate hydrochloride	Includes most of the barbiturates and a few minor stimulants. Examples include amylobarbitone, meprobamate, pentazocine, phenobarbitone and temazepam.	Comprises mainly the benzodiazepines including diazepam, lorazepam, nitrazepam and oxazepam	Comprises mainly anabolic and androgenic steroids such as nandrolone and testosterone	Includes certain preparations for which there is negligible risk of abuse. Many of the drugs listed in Schedule 5 are also listed in Schedule 2, but when they are restricted by strength, they become Schedule 5. For example, dihydrocodeine injection is Schedule 2, but certain dihydrocodeine tablets are Schedule 5.
Does the prescription have to include the dose, form, strength (where appropriate) and total quantity of the drug in both words and figures?	Yes	Yes, except temazepam	No	No	No
Does the prescription have to be written in the prescriber's own handwriting?	Yes	Yes, except phenobarbitone and temazepam	No	No	No
In the absence of a prescription, must a requisition in writing be obtained by a supplier (not being a general practitioner) before delivering a drug?	Yes	Yes	No	No	No
Must a record of the transaction be kept in a controlled drugs register?	Yes	No	No	No	No
Do the safe custody requirements (as set out in the Misuse of Drugs (Safe Custody) Regulations 1973) apply?	Yes, except quinalbarbitone and certain oral liquid preparations, none of which are likely to be found in community pharmacy	No, except temazepam, diethylpropion, flunitrazepam and buprenorphine (Subutex)	No	No	No
Must the date of supply be endorsed on the prescription?	Yes	Yes	No	No	No
Must the address of the prescriber be within the UK?	Yes	Yes	No	No	No
Must the destruction of 'out of date' stock be witnessed?	Yes	No	No	No	No
For how long is the prescription valid?	13 weeks	13 weeks	6 months	6 months	6 months (if prescription only medicine)
Must invoices be kept for a minimum of two years?	No	Yes	No	No	Yes

Pages from the Standard

National Pharmaceutical Association

Controlled Drugs Register

MISUSE OF DRUGS ACT

REGISTER

OF

DIAMORPHINE
(Heroin or Diacetylmorphine),

its salts and any preparation, admixture, extract or other substance containing

any proportion of Diamorphine

OBTAINED or SUPPLIED.

This Register contains
13 pages for purchases
18 pages for sales.

Re-order Code: CDR 024

REV 0299

Published by

THE NATIONAL PHARMACEUTICAL ASSOCIATION

MALLINSON HOUSE, 38-42 ST PETER'S STREET, ST ALBANS, HERTS AL1 3NP

Working for
Community
Pharmacy

THE NATIONAL
PHARMACEUTICAL
ASSOCIATION

Record of DIAMORPHINE obtained

Date on which supply received	NAME	ADDRESS of person or firm from whom obtained	Amount obtained	Form in which obtained

PURCHASES

Page One

Record of DIAMORPHINE supplied

Date on which the transaction was effected	NAME	ADDRESS		Particulars as to licence or authority of person or firm supplied to be in possession	Amount supplied	Form in which supplied
		of person or firm supplied				

SALES

M.D.A.
Register of DIAMOR-PHINE

Page Fourteen

APPENDIX E

Respondents to the Inquiry's Stage Three Discussion Paper

Organisations	Author (if named)
Association of Chief Police Officers	Drugs Sub-Committee
Associated Chemists (Wicker) Limited	Mr Martin Bennett, Managing Director
Association of British Pharmaceutical Industry	Dr Richard Tiner, Medical Director
Association of Chief Police Officers in Scotland	Chief Constable William Rae, Honorary Secretary
Barry Shooter Pharmacies	Mr Barry Shooter
Boots Pharmacists' Association	Mr Stan Wheatley, Vice Chairman
Boots the Chemists	Mr Digby Emson, Pharmacy Superintendent
Bristol North Primary Care Trust	Mr Alaster Rutherford, Head of Medicines Management
British Medical Association	Ms Sally Watson, Director of Political & Representational Activities
British Veterinary Association	Ms Clare Lynch, Executive Assistant, Policy
Canterbury and Coastal Primary Care Trust	Primary Care Sub-Group
Central Cornwall Primary Care Trust	Mr Graham Brack, Pharmaceutical Adviser
Cherwell Vale Primary Care Trust	
City and Hackney Teaching Primary Care Trust	Mr Jonathan Mason, Head of Prescribing and Pharmacy
Commission for Health Improvement	Dr Linda Patterson OBE, Medical Director
Community Practitioners' Health Visitors' Association	Ms Obi Amadi, Lead Professional Officer
Company Chemists' Association	Mr Colin Baldwin, Chief Executive Officer
Co-operative Pharmacy Technical Panel	Mr Duncan Bowdler, Secretary
Co-ordinated Addictions Network of NHS Argyll and Clyde and the Clinical Services Group (Addictions) of the Renfrewshire and Inverclyde locality of NHS Argyll and Clyde	Ms Sarah Harris, Specialist Pharmacist in Substance Misuse
Department for Constitutional Affairs	Mr Chris Morter, Civil Law Development Division
Department of Environment, Food and Rural Affairs	Mr Jim Scudamore, Chief Veterinary Officer and Director General for Animal Health and Welfare

Organisations	Author (if named)
Department of Health	Mrs Janet Walden, Branch Head Investigations and Inquiries Unit
Department of Health, Social Services & Public Safety, Northern Ireland	Dr Norman Morrow, Chief Pharmaceutical Officer
Department of Pharmaceutical Sciences, University of Strathclyde	Professor Howard McNulty Mrs Felice Groundland, Teacher Practitioner Ms Karen Billmore, Teacher Practitioner
Devon Local Pharmaceutical Committees	Mrs Sue Taylor, Chief Officer
Dispensing Doctors' Association	Dr Malcolm Ward, Chairman
Forensic Science Society	Professor A R W Forrest, Honorary Editor of the Forensic Science Society and Professor of Forensic Toxicology, Sheffield University
General Medical Council	Mr Paul Buckley, Head of Fitness to Practise and Registration Policy
Greater Glasgow Primary Care Trust	Mr David Thomson, Director of Pharmacy
Greater Manchester Strategic Health Authority	Ms Melanie Ogden, Associate Director, Clinical Governance
Hertsmere Primary Care Trust	Mr Brian Miller, Chief Pharmacist
Highland Primary Care Trust	Ms Jackie Agnew, Trust Chief Pharmacist Ms Sharon Pfleger, Consultant in Pharmaceutical Public Health
Hounslow Primary Care Trust	Ms Janet Cree, Chief Pharmacist, Medicines Management and Prescribing Group
Independent Doctors Forum	Dr Martin Scurr, Chairman
Ipswich, Suffolk Coastal, Suffolk Central and Suffolk West Primary Care Trusts	Ms Esther Johnston, Prescribing Adviser, Ipswich PCT
Kensington & Chelsea and Westminster Primary Care Trusts	Substance Misuse Management in Community Pharmacy Scheme Steering Group
Leeds North West Primary Care Trust	Ms Carolyn Nelson, Prescribing Adviser, Prescribing Sub-Group
Lloyds Pharmacy Limited	Mr Nick Mortimer, Deputy Superintendent Pharmacist
Local Government Association	Mr Noel Towe, Senior Programme Officer

Organisations	Author (if named)
Luton Primary Care Trust	Ms Emma Tomlinson, Quality in Medicines Management Facilitator
Macmillan Cancer Relief	Dame Gill Oliver DBE, Director of Service Development
Marie Curie Cancer Care	Dr Teresa Tate, Medical Adviser & Consultant in Palliative Medicine
Medical Protection Society	Dr Gerald Panting, Communications & Policy Director
Medicines Commission	Professor Parveen Kumar, Chairman
National Association of Chemist Inspection Officers	Detective Constable Duncan White, West Mercia Police, Secretary
NHS Confederation	Dr Gill Morgan, Chief Executive
National Patient Safety Agency	Ms Susan Williams/Ms Sue Osborn, Joint Chief Executive
National Pharmaceutical Association	
National Treatment Agency for Substance Misuse	Dr Nat Wright, GP Adviser Ms Annette Dale-Perera, Director of Quality
Newham Primary Care Trust	Ms Jan Tomes, Assistant Director, Pharmacy & Prescribing
North and East Cornwall Primary Care Trust	Ms Helen Grist, Pharmaceutical Adviser
North Cheshire Hospitals NHS Trust	Eleven Consultant Nurses in Palliative Care
Northern Ireland General Practitioners' Committee	Dr Brian Dunn, Chairman
Nursing & Midwifery Council	Ms Sarah Thewlis, Chief Executive/Registrar
Oldham, Tameside & Glossop Local Pharmaceutical Committee	Mr Ian Short, Secretary
Oxford Pain Research Unit	Mr Philip Wiffen, Pharmacist and Co-ordinating Editor, Cochrane Pain and Palliative Care Group
Pain Society – the British Chapter for the International Association of the Study of Pain	Dr Cathy Stannard, Chair, Pain Society Clinical Governance Committee
Patients Association	Mr Michael Summers, Chairman
Pharmaceutical Advisers Group	Ms Janet Corbett, Secretary
Pharmaceutical Contractors Committee (Northern Ireland)	Mr Terry Hannawin, Chief Executive

Organisations	Author (if named)
Pharmaceutical Services Negotiating Committee	Ms Barbara Parsons Mr Alastair R L Buxton, Head of NHS Services
Prescription Pricing Authority	Mr Michael Siswick, Director of Human Resources
Registered Nursing Home Association	Ms Rosemary Strange, Chair
Royal College of General Practitioners	Dr Maureen Baker CBE, Honorary Secretary of Council
Royal College of General Practitioners – Wales	Dr M G Jeffries, Chairman
Royal College of Nursing	Ms Lynn Young, Nurse Adviser Mr Matt Griffiths, Lead on Nurse Prescribing
Royal College of Nursing – Scotland	Ms Susan Watt, Education & Clinical Effectiveness Advisor
Royal College of Paediatrics and Child Health	Dr Sheila Shribman, Registrar
Royal College of Physicians	Professor Ian Gilmore, Registrar
Royal College of Physicians of Edinburgh	Dr R H Smith, Fellow and Secretary
Royal College of Veterinary Surgeons	Miss Jane Hern, Registrar
Royal Pharmaceutical Society of Great Britain	Miss Mandie Lavin, Director of Fitness to Practise and Legal Affairs
Royal Society of Chemistry	Dr D J Giachardi, Secretary General and Chief Executive
Royston, Buntingford and Bishop's Stortford Primary Care Trust	Ms Christine Tarling, Prescribing Adviser
Scottish Executive (Health Department)	Mr John Davidson, General Medical Services
Scottish Palliative Care Pharmacists' Association	Ms Janet Trundle, Macmillan Specialist Pharmacist in Palliative Care
Scottish Partnership for Palliative Care	Ms Patricia Wallace, Director
Scottish Pharmaceutical General Council	
St Christopher's Hospice, Sydenham	Dr Nigel Sykes, Consultant Palliative Medicine and Medical Director Dr Victor Pace, Consultant Palliative Medicine Ms Penny Hansford, Director of Nursing Ms Margaret Gibbs, Senior Pharmacist
St Lukes Kenton Grange Hospice	Dr Charles Daniels, Medical Director

Organisations	Author (if named)
St Oswald's Hospice	Dr Claud Regnard, Consultant in Palliative Care Medicine
Suffolk Local Medical Committee	Dr R E Mercer, Secretary
Surelines Pharmaceutical Services	Mr Nigel Morley, Managing Director
Surrey & Sussex Strategic Health Authority	Mr Robert Lea, Prescribing Adviser
Swale Primary Care Trust	
Tameside Families Support Group	
Tameside and Glossop Primary Care Trust	Mr David Eccles
Tendring Primary Care Trust	Mr Paul Breame, Head of Medicines Management
Tower Hamlets Primary Care Trust	Ms Heather Walker, Shared Care Substance Misuse Manager for East London & City Drugs Action Team
Walton Centre for Neurology and Neurosurgery NHS Trust and Pain Relief Foundation, Liverpool	Dr T P Nash, Consultant in Pain Medicine
Westminster Primary Care Trust	Medicines Management Group

Individuals	Position Held/Reason for Interest in the Inquiry
Mr Barend Anthon	Principal Pharmacist (Community Liaison), Leigh Infirmary, Wrightington, Wigan and Leigh NHS Trust
Dr Ian Back	Consultant in Palliative Medicine
Professor Richard Baker OBE	Director Clinical Governance, Research and Development Unit, University of Leicester
Mr Nigel Ballantine	Specialist Clinical Pharmacist, Haematology Oncology
Ms Sheilah Blackwell and Mr Andrew Riley	Nurse Consultant Palliative Care, North Staffordshire Combined Healthcare Trust Pharmacy Adviser South Western Staffs Primary Care Trust

Individuals	Position Held/Reason for Interest in the Inquiry
Br Francis	Clinical Nurse Specialist in Paediatric Oncology
Ms Sue Fuller	Pharmacist Inspector for the National Care Standards Commission
Dr John Grenville	General Practitioner, Derbyshire
Dr Karen Groves	Consultant in Palliative Medicine, West Lancashire, Southport & Formby Palliative Care Services
Ms Irene Gummerson	Community Pharmacist, Wakefield
Mrs Leslie Hall	Community Pharmacist
Mr John Hexter	Former Chemist Inspection Officer, Thames Valley Police
Ms Beryl Hill	Community Specialist Palliative Care Nurse
Mr Peter Hopley	Pharmacy Practice Development and Clinical Governance Lead, West Northumberland locality
Mrs Carole Hunter	Area Pharmacy Specialist – Drug Misuse, Gartnavel Royal Hospital, Glasgow
Ms Maureen Kelly	On behalf of a team of Clinical Nurse Specialists, Community Palliative Care, Harrow Primary Care Trust
Dr J D Khan	
Dr Mary Kiely	Consultant in Palliative Medicine, Lead Clinician for Palliative Care, Calderdale and Huddersfield
Ms Louise Lee	Macmillan Nurse Specialist
Mr Alan Macfarlane	Chief Inspector, Home Office Drugs Inspectorate
Dr H J L Morris	General Practitioner, Fordingbridge Surgery
Ms Caroline Peet	Prescribing Adviser, Cambridge City Primary Care Trust
Dr Trevor Rimmer	Macmillan Consultant in Palliative Medicine, Macclesfield District General Hospital

Individuals	Position Held/Reason for Interest in the Inquiry
Mrs Kay Roberts	Co-ordinator, Greater Glasgow Pharmacy Needle Exchange Scheme; Lead Pharmacist for the Royal College of General Practitioners National Drug Misuse Training Programme
Dr James Robertson MBE	Advisory Council on the Misuse of Drugs; General Practitioner and Senior Lecturer, Muirhouse Medical Group and Department of Community Health Sciences, Edinburgh University
Dr Carol Scholes	Macmillan Consultant in Palliative Medicine, Dacorum Primary Care Trust
Ms Lorna Senior	Macmillan Nurse in Outer Hebrides
Mr Alan Stears	Senior Inspector, Home Office Drugs Inspectorate (retired)
Mrs Marion Stevenson-Rouse	Hospital Pharmacist
Dr Pat Strubbe	Palliative Care Doctor, St Elizabeth Hospice, Ipswich
Dr Brian Taylor	Deputy Registrar, College of Physicians & Surgeons of British Columbia
Dr David R Tooth	Kiveton Park Medical Practice
Mr R G Waters	Freelance Superintendent Pharmacist
Ms Julie Whitehead	Macmillan Pharmacist, Macclesfield District General Hospital

APPENDIX F

Participants in the Inquiry Seminars: 12th–16th January 2004

Organisations	Representative(s)
Advisory Council on the Misuse of Drugs	Dr James Robertson, MBE, Member of the ACMD; Principal in General Practice, Muirhouse Medical Group, Edinburgh
Association of Chief Police Officers (ACPO)	Assistant Chief Constable David Francis, South Wales Police, Member of ACPO Drugs Sub-Committee
Bristol North Primary Care Trust	Mr Alaster Rutherford, Head of Medicines Management
British Medical Association	Dr John Grenville, General Practitioner, Derbyshire
Department of Health	Dr Jim Smith, Chief Pharmaceutical Officer for England
Department of Health, Social Services & Public Safety, Northern Ireland	Dr Michael Mawhinney, Misuse of Drugs Inspector
Home Office	Mr Alan Macfarlane, Chief Inspector, Home Office Drugs Inspectorate
Macmillan Cancer Relief	Mr Ian Rudd, Principal Pharmacist (Oncology and Production), Inverness
National Association of Chemist Inspection Officers	Detective Constable Duncan White, West Mercia Police, Secretary
National Pharmaceutical Association	Mr John D'Arcy, Chief Executive
Prescription Pricing Authority	Ms Christine Dalton, Director of Pharmaceutical Policy and Services
Royal College of General Practitioners	Dr Clare Gerada, Director and Chair of the Royal College of General Practitioners National Advisory Group for Drug Misuse; Principal, General Practice, Lambeth
Royal Pharmaceutical Society of Great Britain	Miss Mandie Lavin, Director of Fitness to Practise and Legal Affairs

Individual Participants	Positions Held
Professor Richard Baker OBE	Director Clinical Governance, Research and Development Unit, University of Leicester
Mrs Kay Roberts	Co-ordinator, Glasgow Pharmacy Needle Exchange Scheme; Lead Pharmacist for the Royal College of General Practitioners National Drug Misuse Training Programme
Dr Brian Taylor	Deputy Registrar, College of Physicians & Surgeons of British Columbia, Vancouver

Printed in the UK by The Stationery Office Limited
on behalf of the Controller of Her Majesty's Stationery Office
19320   07/04   969921   19585